NONGOVERNMENTAL POLITICS

HANDBOOK OF POLITICAL SCIENCE
Volume 4

NONGOVERNMENTAL POLITICS

Edited by
FRED I. GREENSTEIN Princeton University
NELSON W. POLSBY University of California, Berkeley

ADDISON-WESLEY PUBLISHING COMPANY

Reading, Massachusetts
Menlo Park, California • London • Amsterdam • Don Mills, Ontario • Sydney

This book is in the
ADDISON-WESLEY SERIES IN POLITICAL SCIENCE

ISBN 0-201-02604-X
ABCDEFGHIJ-HA-798765

PREFACE

Early in his career, the fledgling political scientist learns that his discipline is ill-defined, amorphous, and heterogeneous. This perception will in no way be rebutted by the appearance of a presumably encyclopedic eight-volume work entitled *The Handbook of Political Science.* Indeed, the persistent amorphousness of our discipline has constituted a central challenge to the editors of the *Handbook* and has brought to its creation both hazards and opportunities. The opportunities were apparent enough to us when we took on the editorial duties of the *Handbook;* the hazards became clearer later on.

At the outset, it seemed to us a rare occasion when a publisher opens quite so large a canvas and invites a pair of editors to paint on it as they will—or can. We immediately saw that in order to do the job at all we would have to cajole a goodly number of our colleagues into the belief that our canvas was in reality Tom Sawyer's fence. We did not set out at the beginning, however, with a precise vision of the final product—i.e., a work that would be composed of these particular eight volumes, dealing with the present array and number of contributions and enlisting all the present contributors. Rather, the *Handbook* is the product of a long and in some ways accidental process. An account of this process is in order if only because, by describing the necessarily adventitious character of the "decisions" that produced this work, we can help the reader to see that the *Handbook* is not an attempt to make a collective pronouncement of Truth chiseled in stone, but rather an assembly of contributions, each an individual scholarly effort, whose overall purpose is to give a warts-and-all portrait of a discipline that is still in a process of becoming.

We first became involved in discussions about the project in 1965. Addison-Wesley had already discussed the possibility of a handbook with a number of other political scientists, encouraged by their happy experience with a two-volume compendium of highly respected review essays in social psychology (Lindzey, 1954), which has since been revised and expanded into a five-volume work (Lindzey and Aronson, 1968–69).

Of the various people to whom Addison-Wesley aired the handbook idea, we evidently were among the most persistent in encouraging such a project. No doubt the reason was that we were still close to our own graduate work in a department where a careful reading of many of the chapters in *The Handbook of Social Psychology* was in some ways more fundamental to learning our trade than a comparable exposure to many of the more conspicuous intellectual edifices of the political science of the time. Gardner Lindzey, in writing his introductory statement to the first edition of *The Handbook of Social Psychology* (reprinted in the second edition), described *our* needs as well as those of budding social psychologists in saying that

> the accelerating expansion of social psychology in the past two decades has led to an acute need for a source book more advanced than the ordinary textbook in the field but yet more focused than scattered periodical literature. . . . It was this state of affairs that led us to assemble a book that would represent the major areas of social psychology at a level of difficulty appropriate for graduate students. In addition to serving the needs of graduate instruction, we anticipate that the volumes will be useful in advanced undergraduate courses and as a reference book for professional psychologists.

With the substitution of "political science" in the appropriate places, Lindzey's description of his own purposes and audiences reflects precisely what we thought Addison-Wesley might most usefully seek to accomplish with a political science handbook.

In choosing a pair of editors, the publisher might well have followed a balancing strategy, looking for two political scientists who were poles apart in their background, training, and views of the discipline. The publisher might then have sought divine intervention, praying for the miracle that would bring the editors into sufficient agreement to make the planning of the *Handbook*—or *any* handbook—possible at all. Instead they found a pair of editors with complementary but basically similar and congenial perspectives. We were then both teaching at Wesleyan University and had been to graduate school together at Yale, at a time when the political science department there was making its widely recognized contribution to the modernization of the discipline. Each had recently spent a year in the interdisciplinary ambience of the Center for Advanced Study in the Behavioral Sciences. Moreover, we were both specialists in American politics, the "field" which in 1973 still accounted for three-quarters of the contributions to *The American Political Science Review*. There were also complementary divergencies. Within political science, Polsby's work and interests had been in national politics and policy-making, whereas Greenstein's were more in mass, extragovernmental aspects of political behavior. Outside political science, Polsby's interests were directed more toward sociology and law, and Greenstein's tended toward psychiatry and clinical and social psychology.

To begin with, neither we nor the publisher could be sure without first gathering evidence that the discipline of political science was "ready" for a handbook comparable to the Lindzey work. We were sure that, if it was at all possible for us to bring such a handbook into being, we would have to employ the Aristotelian tack of working within and building upon existing categories of endeavor, rather than the Platonic (or Procrustean) mode of inventing a coherent set of master categories and persuading contributors to use them. First, at our request the publisher inquired of a number of distinguished political scientists whether they felt a need would be served by a handbook of political science similar to *The Handbook of Social Psychology*. This inquiry went to political scientists who had themselves been involved in extensive editorial activities or who were especially known for their attention to political science as a discipline. The responses were quite uniform in favoring such a handbook. The particular suggestions about how such a handbook might be *organized,* however, were exceptionally varied. But fortunately we had asked one further question: What half-dozen or so individuals were so authoritative or original in their contributions on some topic as to make them prime candidates for inclusion in any political science handbook, no matter what its final overall shape? Here agreement reemerged; the consultants were remarkably unanimous in the individuals named.

Seizing the advantage provided by that consensus, we reached the following agreement with the publisher. We would write the individuals who constituted what we now saw as a prime list of candidates for inclusion as authors and ask whether they would be willing to contribute to a handbook of political science, given a long lead time and freedom to choose the topic of their essay. (We did suggest possible topics to each.) It was agreed that unless we were able to enlist most of those with whom we were corresponding as a core group of contributors, we would not proceed with a handbook. Since all but one of that group indicated willingness to contribute, we signed a publishing agreement (in September 1967) and proceeded to expand our core group to a full set of contributors to what we then envisaged as a three-volume handbook, drawing on our core contributors for advice. Our queries to the core contributors were a search not so much for structural and organizational suggestions as for concrete topics and specific contributors to add to the initial list.

The well-worn term "incremental" suggests itself as a summary of how the table of contents of *The Handbook of Political Science* then took shape. As the number of contributors increased, and as contributors themselves continued to make suggestions about possible rearrangements in the division of labor and to remark on gaps, the planned three volumes expanded to eight, most of which, however, were shorter than the originally intended three. Throughout, Addison-Wesley left it to us and the contributors, within the very broadest of boundaries, to define the overall length of the project and of the individual contributions. And throughout, we urged the contributors not to seek intellectual anonymity in the guise of being "merely" summarizers—or embalmers—of their fields but rather to endeavor to place a distinctive intellectual stamp on their contributions.

A necessary condition of enlisting the initial group of contributors was a production deadline so far in the future as to dissolve the concern of rational individuals about adding to their intellectual encumbrances. As it turned out, our "safely remote" initial deadline (1970) was in fact a drastic underestimation of the number of postponements and delays.* Along with delays there have been occasional withdrawals, as individual contributors recognized that even with a long fuse the task of preparing a handbook article would be a major one and would inevitably preempt time from other projects and interests. Departing contributors were often helpful in suggesting alternatives. Both through the late enlistment of such substitutes and through the addition of collaborators taken on by invited contributors, we feel we have been spared a table of contents that anachronistically represents only the cohort of those individuals who were responsible for the shape of political science circa 1967.

Whether one builds a handbook table of contents a priori or ex post facto, *some* basis of organization emerges. We might have organized a handbook around:

1. *"political things"* (e.g., the French bureaucracy, the U.S. Constitution, political parties);

2. *nodes or clusters in the literature* (community power, group theory, issue voting);

3. *subdisciplines* (public administration, public law, comparative government, political theory, international relations);

4. *functions* (planning, law-making, adjudication);

5. *geography* (the American Congress, the British Cabinet, the politicoeconomic institutions of the U.S.S.R.);

6. or any combination of the above and further possibilities.

Any of our colleagues who have tried to construct a curriculum in political science will sympathize with our dilemma. There is, quite simply, no

---

* For the comparable experience of *Handbook of Social Psychology* editors with delays, see Lindzey, 1954, p. vii, Lindzey and Aronson, 1968–69, p. ix.

sovereign way to organize our discipline. Although much of our knowledge is cumulative, there is no set beginning or end to political science. Apart from certain quite restricted subdisciplinary areas (notably the mathematical and statistical), political scientists do not have to learn a particular bit of information or master a particular technique at a particular stage as a prerequisite to further study. And the discipline lacks a single widely accepted frame of reference or principle of organization. Consequently, we evolved a table of contents that to some extent adopted nearly *all* the approaches above. (None of our chapter titles contains a geographical reference, but many of the chapters employ one or more explicitly specified political systems as data sources.)

The protean classifications of subspecialization within political science and the ups and downs in subspecialty interests over the years are extensively reviewed by Dwight Waldo in his essay in Volume 1 on political science as discipline and profession. A further way to recognize the diversity and change in our discipline—as well as the persisting elements—is to note the divisions of disciplinary interests used by the directories of the American Political Science Association, the membership of which constitutes the great bulk of all political scientists. A glance at the three successive directories which have been current during our editorial activities is instructive.

The 1961 *Biographical Directory of the American Political Science Association* (APSA, 1961) represents a last glimpse at a parsimonious, staid set of subdisciplinary categories that would have been readily recognizable at the 1930 Annual Meeting of the Association.

1. American National Government

2. Comparative Government

3. International Law and Relations

4. Political Parties

5. Political Theory

6. Public Administration

7. Public Law

8. State and Local Government

In the next *Biographical Directory* (APSA, 1968), there appeared a categorization that was at once pared down and much expanded from the 1961 classification. A mere three "general fields" were listed. The first was "Contemporary Political Systems." Members electing this general field were asked to specify the country or countries in which they were interested, and those countries were listed parenthetically after the members' names in the subdisciplinary listing, presumably out of a desire to play down the importance of "area studies" as an intellectual focus and to accentuate the importance of functional or analytic bases of intellectual endeavor. "International Law, Organization, and Politics" was the second general field, and "Political Theory and Philosophy" was the third. But the 26 categories in Table 1 were provided for the listing of "specialized fields." They included some venerable subdivisions, perhaps in slightly more fashionable phrasing, and other distinctly nonvenerable subdivisions, at least one of which (political socialization) did not even exist in the general vocabulary of political scientists ten years earlier. In this *Handbook*, the 1968 categories have many parallels, including the general principle of organization that excludes geography as a specialized field criterion while at the same time recognizing that political scientists can and should study and compare diverse political settings. Diplomatically avoiding the presentation of a structured classification, the editors of the 1968 *Directory* relied on the alphabet for their sequence of specialized fields.

TABLE 1 Subdisciplinary categories used in *Biographical Directory* of the American Political Science Association, 1968

1. Administrative law
2. Administration: organization, processes, behavior
3. Budget and fiscal management
4. Constitutional law
5. Executive: organization, processes, behavior
6. Foreign policy
7. Government regulation of business
8. International law
9. International organization and administration
10. International politics
11. Judiciary: organization, processes, behavior
12. Legislature: organization, processes, behavior
13. Methodology
14. Metropolitan and urban government and politics
15. National security policy
16. Personnel administration
17. Political and constitutional history
18. Political parties and elections: organizations and processes
19. Political psychology
20. Political socialization
21. Political theory and philosophy (empirical)
22. Political theory and philosophy (historical)
23. Political theory and philosophy (normative)
24. Public opinion
25. Revolutions and political violence
26. State and local government and politics
27. Voting behavior

Even with this burgeoning of options, many members of the discipline evidently felt that their interests were not adequately covered. Goodly numbers took advantage of an opportunity provided in the questionnaire to the APSA membership to list "other" specialties, referring, for example, to "political sociology," "political behavior," "political development," "policy studies," "communication," "federalism," and "interest groups."

The 1973 *Biographical Directory* (APSA, 1973) attempted still another basis of classification, a revised version of the classification used in the 1970 *National Science Foundation Register of Scientific and Technical Personnel.* Braving a structured rather than alphabetic classification, the authors of this taxonomy divided the discipline into nine major classes and a total of 60 specialized classifications, with a return to the antique dichotomy of foreign versus U.S. politics. The specifics of the 1973 listing are given in Table 2.

TABLE 2 Subdisciplinary categories used in *Biographical Directory* of the American Political Science Association, 1973

I	Foreign and Cross-National Political Institutions and Behavior
1.	Analyses of particular systems or subsystems
2.	Decision-making processes
3.	Elites and their oppositions
4.	Mass participation and communications
5.	Parties, mass movements, secondary associations
6.	Political development and modernization
7.	Politics of planning
8.	Values, ideologies, belief systems, political culture
II	International Law, Organization, and Politics
9.	International law
10.	International organization and administration
11.	International politics
III	Methodology
12.	Computer techniques
13.	Content analysis
14.	Epistemology and philosophy of science
15.	Experimental design
16.	Field data collection
17.	Measurement and index construction
18.	Model building
19.	Statistical analysis
20.	Survey design and analysis
IV	Political Stability, Instability, and Change
21.	Cultural modification and diffusion
22.	Personality and motivation
23.	Political leadership and recruitment
24.	Political socialization
25.	Revolution and violence
26.	Schools and political education
27.	Social and economic stratification

(continued)

V   Political Theory

28. Systems of political ideas in history
29. Ideology systems
30. Political philosophy (general)
31. Methodological and analytical systems

VI   Public Policy: Formation and Content

32. Policy theory
33. Policy measurement
34. Economic policy and regulation
35. Science and technology
36. Natural resources and environment
37. Education
38. Poverty and welfare
39. Foreign and military policy

VII   Public Administration

40. Bureaucracy
41. Comparative administration
42. Organization and management analysis
43. Organization theory and behavior
44. Personnel administration
45. Planning, programing, budgeting
46. Politics and administration
47. Systems analysis

VIII   U.S. Political Institutions, Processes, and Behavior

48. Courts and judicial behavior
49. Elections and voting behavior
50. Ethnic politics
51. Executives
52. Interest groups
53. Intergovernmental relations
54. Legislatures
55. Political and constitutional history
56. Political parties
57. Public law
58. Public opinion
59. State, local, and metropolitan government
60. Urban politics

As will be evident, the present *Handbook* contains articles on topics that appear on neither of the two recent differentiated lists and omits topics on each. Some "omissions" were inadvertent. Others were deliberate, resulting from our conclusion either that the work on a particular topic did not appear ripe for review at this time or that the topic overlapped sufficiently with others already commissioned so that we might leave it out in the interests of preventing our rapidly expanding project from becoming hopelessly large. There also were instances in which we failed to find (or keep) authors on topics that we might otherwise have included. Hence readers should be forewarned about a feature of the *Handbook* that they should know without forewarning is bound to exist: incompleteness. Each reviewer will note "strange omissions." For us it is more extraordinary that so many able people were willing to invest so much effort in this enterprise.

It should be evident from our history of the project that we consider the rubrics under which scholarly work is classified to be less important than the caliber of the scholarship and that we recognize the incorrigible tendency of inquiry to overflow the pigeonholes to which it has been assigned, as well as the desirability that scholars rather than editors (or other administrators) define the boundaries of their endeavors. Therefore we have used rather simple principles for aggregating essays into their respective volumes and given them straightforward titles.

The essays in Volume 1 on the nature of political theory which follow Waldo's extensive discussion of the scope of political science are far from innocent of reference to empirical matters. This comports with the common observation that matters of theoretical interest are by no means removed from the concerns of the real world. And although we have used the titles *Micropolitical Theory* and *Macropolitical Theory* for Volumes 2 and 3, we have meant no more thereby than to identify the scale and mode of conceptualization typical of the topics in these volumes. Here again the reader will find selections that extensively review empirical findings.

Similarly, although the titles of Volumes 4, 5, and 6 on extragovernmental, governmental, and policy-output aspects of government and politics may appear to imply mere data compilations, the contents of these volumes are far from atheoretical. This is also emphatically true of Volume 8, which carries the title *International Politics*, a field that in recent decades has continuously raised difficult theoretical issues, including issues about the proper nature of theory. Volume 7 carries the title *Strategies of Inquiry* rather than *Methodology* to call attention to the fact that contributors to that volume have emphasized linking techniques of inquiry to substantive issues. In short, contributions to the eight volumes connect in many ways that can be only imperfectly suggested by the editors' table of contents or even by the comprehensive index at the end of Volume 8.

It can scarcely surprise readers of a multiple-authored work to learn that what is before them is a collective effort. It gives us pleasure to acknowledge obligations to five groups of people who helped to lighten our part of the load. First of all, to our contributors we owe a debt of gratitude for their patience, cooperation, and willingness to find the time in their exceedingly busy schedules to produce the essays that make up this *Handbook*. Second, we thank the many helpful Addison-Wesley staff members with whom we have worked for their good cheer toward us and for their optimism about this project. Third, the senior scholars who initially advised Addison-Wesley to undertake the project, and who may even have pointed the publishers in our direction, know who they are. We believe it would add still another burden to the things they must answer for in our profession if we named them publicly, but we want to record our rueful, belated appreciation to them. Fourth, Kathleen Peters and Barbara Kelly in Berkeley and Lee L. Messina, Catherine Smith, and Frances C. Root in Middletown kept the paper flowing back and forth across the country and helped us immeasurably in getting the job done. Finally, our love and gratitude to Barbara Greenstein and Linda Polsby. And we are happy to report to Michael, Amy, and Jessica Greenstein, and to Lisa, Emily, and Daniel Polsby that at long last their fathers are off the long-distance telephone.

Princeton, New Jersey   F.I.G.
Berkeley, California   N.W.P.

REFERENCES

American Political Science Association (1961). *Biographical Directory of The American Political Science Association,* fourth edition. (Franklin L. Burdette, ed.) Washington, D.C.

American Political Science Association (1968). *Biographical Directory,* fifth edition. Washington, D.C.

American Political Science Association (1973). *Biographical Directory,* sixth edition. Washington, D.C.

Lindzey, Gardner, ed. (1954). *Handbook of Social Psychology,* 2 volumes. Cambridge, Mass.: Addison-Wesley.

Lindzey, Gardner, and Elliot Aronson, eds. (1968–69). *The Handbook of Social Psychology,* second edition, 5 volumes. Reading, Mass.: Addison-Wesley.

CONTENTS

Chapter 1 Political Participation   1
Norman H. Nie, University of Chicago
Sidney Verba, Harvard University

What Is Political Participation?   1
Why Is Participation Important?   4
The Study of Political Participation   5
The Dimensions and Modes of Participation   7
How Active Are Citizens?   22
The Process of Politicization   30
Who Participates?   38
The Consequences of Political Activity   60
The Rationality of Political Activity   68

Chapter 2 Public Opinion and Voting Behavior   75
Philip E. Converse, University of Michigan

The Nature of Public Opinion   77
The Psychology of Public Opinion   78
Variation in the Character of Public Opinion   89
Diagnosis and Prognosis   93
The Nature of Voting Behavior   111
Determinants of Individual Voting Choice   113
Macrocosmic Change in Voting Systems   136
Voting Systems and the Representation of Public Opinion   148
Conclusion   156

Chapter 3 Interest Groups   171
Robert H. Salisbury, Washington University

Introduction   171

Modes of Analysis	177
Typologies	182
Group Origins and Growth	189
Internal Patterns	201
Modes of Interaction	207
The Impact on Society	219

Chapter 4 Political Parties   **229**

Leon D. Epstein, University of Wisconsin

Defining the Subject	229
Approaches to the Study	234
Competitive Patterns	238
Organization	248
Candidate Selection	257
Governing Role	260
Reconsideration	266
Index	**279**

CONTENTS OF OTHER VOLUMES IN THIS SERIES

Volume 1   **POLITICAL SCIENCE: SCOPE AND THEORY**

    1   *Dwight Waldo.* Political Science: Tradition, Discipline, Profession, Science, Enterprise

    2   *J. Donald Moon.* The Logic of Political Inquiry: A Synthesis of Opposed Perspectives

    3   *Dante Germino.* The Contemporary Relevance of the Classics of Political Philosophy

    4   *Felix E. Oppenheim.* The Language of Political Inquiry: Problems of Clarification

    5   *Brian Barry and Douglas W. Rae.* Political Evaluation

Volume 2   **MICROPOLITICAL THEORY**

    1   *Fred I. Greenstein.* Personality and Politics

    2   *David O. Sears.* Political Socialization

    3   *Moshe M. Czudnowski.* Political Recruitment

    4   *J. David Greenstone.* Group Theories

    5   *Dennis J. Palumbo.* Organization Theory and Political Science

Volume 3   **MACROPOLITICAL THEORY**

    1   *Samuel P. Huntington and Jorge I. Domínguez.* Political Development

    2   *Robert A. Dahl.* Governments and Political Oppositions

    3   *Juan J. Linz.* Totalitarian and Authoritarian Regimes

    4   *Michael Taylor.* The Theory of Collective Choice

    5   *Charles Tilly.* Revolutions and Collective Violence

    6   *Arthur L. Stinchcombe.* Social Structure and Politics

Volume 5   **GOVERNMENTAL INSTITUTIONS AND PROCESSES**

1   *Harvey Wheeler.* Constitutionalism

2   *William H. Riker.* Federalism

3   *Anthony King.* Executives

4   *Nelson W. Polsby.* Legislatures

5   *Martin Shapiro.* Courts

6   *Mark Nadel and Francis Rourke.* Bureaucracies

Volume 6   **POLICIES AND POLICYMAKING**

1   *Harold D. Lasswell.* Research in Policy Analysis: The Intelligence and Appraisal Functions

2   *Joseph A. Pechman.* Making Economic Policy: The Role of the Economist

3   *Harvey M. Sapolsky.* Science Policy

4   *Charles E. Gilbert.* Welfare Policy

5   *Duane Lockard.* Race Policy

6   *Robert C. Fried.* Comparative Urban Policy and Performance

7   *Bernard C. Cohen and Scott A. Harris.* Foreign Policy

8   *John G. Grumm.* The Analysis of Policy Impact

Volume 7   **STRATEGIES OF INQUIRY**

1   *Clement E. Vose.* Sources for Political Inquiry: I Library Reference Materials and Manuscripts as Data for Political Science

2   *Jerome M. Clubb.* Sources for Political Inquiry: II Quantitative Data

3   *Harry Eckstein.* Case Study and Theory in Political Science

4   *Hayward R. Alker, Jr.* Polimetrics: Its Descriptive Foundations

5   *Richard A. Brody and Charles N. Brownstein.* Experimentation and Simulation

6   *Richard W. Boyd with Herbert H. Hyman.* Survey Research

7   *Gerald H. Kramer and Joseph Hertzberg.* Formal Theory

8   *Herman Kahn.* On Studying the Future

Volume 8   **INTERNATIONAL POLITICS**

1   *Kenneth N. Waltz.* Theory of International Relations

2   *Dina A. Zinnes.* Research Frontiers in the Study of International Politics

3   *George H. Quester.* The World Political System

4   *Richard Smoke.* National Security Affairs

5   *Robert O. Keohane and Joseph S. Nye, Jr.* International Interdependence and Integration

6   *Leon Lipson.* International Law

1
POLITICAL PARTICIPATION

NORMAN H. NIE AND SIDNEY VERBA

Political participation is one of those terms that can have so many meanings that it ultimately loses its usefulness. The term is applied to the activities of people from all levels of the political system: the voter *participates* by casting his or her vote; the secretary of state *participates* in the making of foreign policy. Sometimes the term is applied to political orientations rather than activities: the citizen *participates* by being interested in politics. And sometimes the term applies to participation outside of politics as we usually think of that term: citizens *participate* in the family, the school, etc.

It is not for us to determine what the term "really" means. But the wide range of meanings suggests that it is best to begin by indicating how we will delimit the term in this essay, for when one uses the more limited notion we shall describe, political participation can represent an interesting and coherent field of study. (For discussion of alternative definitions see Milbrath, 1965; McClosky, 1968; Verba, 1967; Weiner, 1971.)

WHAT IS POLITICAL PARTICIPATION?

By political participation we refer to those legal activities by private citizens which are more or less directly aimed at influencing the selection of governmental personnel and/or the actions they take. The definition is rough but adequate for delimiting our sphere of interest. It indicates that we are basically interested in *political* participation, that is, in acts that aim at influencing *governmental* decisions. Actually, we are interested more abstractly in attempts to influence "the authoritative allocations of values for a society," which may or may not take place through governmental decisions. But like most political scientists who start out with such an abstract concern, we shall concentrate on governmental decisions as a close approximation of this more general process.

Our concept of participation is broader than some, narrower than others. It is a broad conception in that we are interested in a wide variety of ways in which citizens participate in relation to varied issues. In particular we do not limit our concern to citizen participation in the electoral process through voting and campaign activity but will consider various other ways in which citizens can be active. Often, by explicit choice or by default because other data are not available, voting turnout is used as the measure of citizen participation. This is usually the case when one is comparing rates of participation across a large number of units, like the American states (Sharkansky and Hofferbert, 1969), or across nations (Needler, 1968; McCrone and Cnudde, 1967) or over time (Burnham, 1965). But political participation does not take place only at election time, nor is participation at election time necessarily the most effective means of citizen influence. Though elections are a major means of citizen control over government officials, they are rather blunt instruments of control. For the individual or for particular groups of citizens the most important political activities may be those in the between-elections period, when citizens try to influence government decisions in relation to specific problems that concern them.

On the other hand, our conception of political participation is narrower than some. For one thing we focus on the activities of private citizens—those citizens who are not acting in roles in which they are professionally involved in politics. In professional roles we include government officials, party officials, and professional lobbyists.

Furthermore, we focus on acts that aim at influencing the government by affecting either the *choice* of government personnel or the *choices made by* government personnel. We do not deal with what can be called "ceremonial" or "support" participation, in which citizens "take part" by expressing support for the government by marching in parades, working hard in developmental projects, participating in youth groups organized by the government, or voting in ceremonial elections. The distinction is important, especially in an era when so much attention is focussed on the political mobilization of citizens in the "support" sense. This is what is meant by participation in many of the developing societies of the world and often in the developed as well (for discussions see Weiner, 1971; Townsend, 1967; Nettle, 1967). In contrast, the kind of participation in which we are interested—perhaps it should be labelled democratic participation—works the other way: it emphasizes a flow of influence upward from the masses and, above all, it does not involve support for a preexisting unified national interest but is part of a process by which the national interest or interests are created.

Our focus is narrower than some in another way. We are interested in participatory *activities*. We do not include in our definition of participation, as some have, attitudes toward participation—one's sense of efficacy or one's civic norms. (See Almond and Verba, 1963; Alford and Scoble, 1968; Matthews and Prothro, 1962; Berelson, Lazarsfeld, and McPhee, 1954. The latter use interest in politics as the sole means of measuring participation beyond the vote.) These psychological orientations may be important as sources of participation, but we are more interested in the actual behavior of citizens in attempting to influence the government.

Third, we limit our attention largely to participation vis-à-vis the government. The argument has been made that effective participation depends on opportunities to participate in other spheres—family, school, voluntary associations, the work place. A participatory polity may rest on a participatory society (Almond and Verba, 1963; Eckstein, 1961). We do not quarrel with this assumption. But we do not attempt to describe and explain patterns of participation outside of those that are more narrowly *political,* that is, aimed at affecting the government.

One last limitation in our focus: our concern is with activities "within the system"—with legal ways of influencing politics. This eliminates from our span of concern a wide range of acts—riots, assassinations, and all other sorts of civil violence—through which private citizens might try to influence the government. This is not to argue that these are less significant or less worthy of study than are legal activities. They are simply another topic, since legal activities represent a set distinctive enough in origin and impact to be worth special consideration.

This does, however, raise one interesting consideration about political participation in different societies. Under certain circumstances political participation (as we use the term) may simply not exist, or at least may not exist for relatively large segments of the society. Bendix's discussion of medieval society provides such an example (Bendix, 1964, p. 43ff). This means further that what might be considered political participation in one country may be considered conspiracy or sedition in another. Indeed, one of the most interesting topics of study vis-à-vis political participation is the process by which the definition of what participation is legally permissible is extended, and access to those legally permissible acts is expanded to new segments of the population (Marshall, 1965; Rokkan, 1961; Bendix and Rokkan, 1964). Rather than dealing with that complicated topic we confine our analysis to participation in modern democratic societies that have well-established legal opportunities for political activity—in particular the right to vote in meaningful elections, the right to associate with and/or to organize political parties or other politically relevant groups, the right to petition the government, and the crucial auxiliary rights of free speech, free assembly, and free press. The subject of participation remains fascinating even after the legal question is settled, for the legal opportunity to participate leaves open the question of who can and does take advantage of the opportunity (Rokkan, 1961, 1966).

WHY IS PARTICIPATION IMPORTANT?

Participation, when and if effective, has a particularly crucial relationship to all other social and political goals. According to democratic theory, it represents a process by which goals are set and means chosen in relation to all sorts of social issues. It is assumed that through participation the goals of the society are set in such a way as to maximize the allocation of benefits in a society to match the needs and desires of the populace. Participation is not committed to any social goals but is a technique for setting goals, choosing priorities, and deciding what resources to commit to goal attainment.

Participation is important for another reason: it not only communicates the citizen's needs and desires to the government but also has other more direct benefits. It is, some have argued, a prime source of satisfaction per se— satisfaction with the government, satisfaction with one's own role. Furthermore, participation has been viewed as an educational device through which "civic virtues" are learned. As John Stuart Mill, one of the many advocates of this position, put it, "Among the foremost benefits of free government is that education of the intelligence and of the sentiments which is carried down to the very lowest ranks of the people when they are called to take part in acts which directly affect the great interests of the country" (Mill, 1873). Through participation, one learns responsibility.

In this sense participation has more than instrumental value; it is an end in itself. Indeed, one can argue that under conditions of democratic norms one's self-esteem is seriously damaged if one does not participate in the decisions that affect one's own life. From some perspectives, lack of ability to participate can imply lack of full membership within the system.

There is currently a debate among social scientists about the normative implications of research on political participation. In part the issue is: To what extent should the study of political participation be limited to the actual participatory situation in democratic societies (which leaves many observers gloomy) or expanded to consider alternative possibilities: new participatory opportunities, new participatory groups, new participatory techniques? (Walker, 1966; Dahl, 1966; Thompson, 1970).

And even if one focusses on that which can be empirically studied—the current or past situation vis-à-vis participation in democratic societies—there is debate on the adequacy of the democratic participation system for communicating the needs of the citizens and for setting social policy. There are two reasons the system of participation in a democracy might be found inadequate. One has to do with the extent to which the citizenry indeed knows its own interests. Conservative critics of participatory mechanisms argue that citizens do not have the skill to calculate the consequences of their acts. Therefore they may damage their own best (but unrecognized) long-run interests by short-range and ill-conceived demands. (Walter Lippmann, in numerous writings, has stressed this point; see Lippmann, 1965.) More radical critics often agree that citizens do not know their own best interests, but this is because of a "mobilization of bias" whereby citizens are socialized to be unaware of their own interests and political capabilities (Bachrach and Baratz, 1963). This critique of the adequacy of participatory mechanisms is hard to deal with empirically, and as Thompson points out (1970, pp. 15–19) many theorists of participation take it as given that citizens are autonomous and the best judges of their own interests.

The second reason that participatory mechanisms might be considered inadequate is that the interests of citizens might be inadequately or unequally communicated because citizens are on the average not active enough or are unequally active. This topic is more amenable to study. And though what exactly is adequate or inadequate is more normative than empirical, the question of how much participation there is and how equally it is distributed is empirical. And this is a question we consider below.

THE STUDY OF POLITICAL PARTICIPATION

The study of mass participation in politics has benefited greatly from the so-called behavioral revolution in political science. The availability of facilities for analyzing large quantities of data nicely fits the needs of students of participation, and the fact that the individual citizen is usually the unit of analysis provides the large number of cases needed for quantitative analysis. Thus political participation is a field with a wide empirical literature. The data tend to come from sample surveys of populations or voting records, and because these quantitative techniques "travel easily," studies have been conducted in a variety of countries. The result is a growing body of generalizations about participation, which have received at least some confirmation in a variety of settings.

Such a vast body of literature does not lend itself easily to summary, nor is it our intention to attempt such a summary. (A comprehensive summary, up to the mid-1960s, is found in Milbrath, 1965. See also Lane, 1959; McCloskey, 1968.) But a few inadequacies of a rather general sort ought to be noted. For one thing, the ready availability of voting data has led to a concentration on that activity as the indicator of political participation and to an inadequate conceptualization of the variety of other ways in which citizens can participate. As we shall suggest, voting is an inadequate indicator of participation. Second, sample surveys are less useful in dealing with relatively rare but potent modes of political involvement (such as participation in demonstrations) since activists engaged in this type of participation are few and are therefore hard to analyze in sample surveys. And finally, by focussing on the individual citizen as the unit one pays less attention to the consequences of participation: whether or not citizen activity has an impact on governmental decisions and particularly, under what conditions and on what types of issues participation makes a difference in terms of governmental responsiveness.

In the remainder of this essay we will attempt to take a broad overview of the subject of political participation. We are interested in participation as a dependent variable (i.e., in the question of what leads to participation) and as an independent variable (i.e., what are the consequences of participation?). Our overview can be summarized in the following figures.

Certain social processes lead citizens to participate; this citizen activity (which we call the "participation input") in turn affects governmental action. Most studies have focussed on the first problem: How do citizens come to participate? But they have done so without adequately considering the domain of participation itself. Our argument is that there are a variety of ways of participation that are likely to have different consequences. Thus we will focus first in this essay on the middle box of the above diagram—the character of participation. We will consider the ways in which citizens can participate and offer some evidence as to how many citizens participate in the various ways in several different nations. We will follow that by a discussion of the first box— the process of politicization. And we will end with some consideration of the usually untouched question—the consequences of participation.

Our goal is not a comprehensive coverage of all that has been said on participation. Rather we will try to present a coherent statement of what participation is and what its origins and its consequences are, using data to illustrate our points where they are available. A good deal of the data cited will come from an in-progress study of participation in a comparative framework directed by the authors (cf. Verba and Nie, 1972; Verba, Nie, and Kim, 1971). Since the study is still in progress, our examples will not always cover the full range of nations for which data were collected. In addition, we will consider findings from other studies.

THE DIMENSIONS AND MODES OF PARTICIPATION

Most studies of participation have, we believe, paid little attention to the question of the alternative ways in which citizens can participate. There are several reasons for this. Participation has been placed within the context of electoral politics and has thus come to be defined as voting or perhaps as voting plus some additional campaign-related activity. Further, the assumption has often been that participation is a unidimensional phenomenon; participatory acts differ in terms of the amount of activity they index and, aside from that fact, can be thought of as interchangeable. Many scholars believe that what counts is the amount of participation engaged in by a citizen, not the type of act in which the citizen engages. Berelson, Lazarsfeld, and McPhee argue, for instance, that "almost all measures of political involvement and participation are highly correlated with one another and for analytical purposes, interchangeable" (1954). And others such as Lane (1959) and Milbrath (1965) argue for a hierarchy of political acts such that the citizen who engages in more difficult acts is almost certain to also engage in the easier ones.

But participation is more than the vote and more than activity in the electoral system; participation is not a unidimensional phenomenon. Rather, there are alternative ways in which citizens can participate, and these alternative ways differ in terms of the types of citizens who engage in them, the processes by which citizens become active, and the governmental response that the various modes of activity can influence. In short, the citizenry is not divided simply into gladiators and nongladiators. Rather, there are many types of gladiators engaging in different acts with different motives and different consequences.

The Dimensions of Participation

The range of specific activities in which citizens can engage in attempting to influence the government is very wide. We can give some order to the specific acts by considering four general dimensions that vary among political acts.

1. The type of influence exerted. Citizen activities can affect the behavior of governmental leaders in two ways: they can communicate information about the preferences of citizens and/or they can apply pressure on political leaders to conform to these preferences. They do the latter by threatening a leader with some loss or promising some reward, such as a gain or loss of votes. Some political activities communicate a wealth of information about citizen preferences, others less. Some put the government under greater pressure, others less. And, as we shall indicate at the end of this essay, these differences have an effect on the response of leaders to different types of activity.

2. The scope of the outcome. Most political science analysis has focussed on government policies that have a collective impact and that affect the entire society or large segments of it. The outcome of an election affects all citizens, voter and nonvoter alike. A tax reform bill or a governmental decision on foreign policy has a collective impact on all citizens. It has been argued that this is the essence of governmental activity, that the outcome of such activity cannot be decomposed (Olson, 1965; Coleman, 1971). But governments make decisions not only about broad social policies. Often they produce outcomes that will affect only a particular citizen or the citizen's immediate family. The government issues a zoning variance so that an individual may enlarge a home, provides a license, grants an exemption from the army because of a family hardship, removes an unsightly telephone pole, offers agricultural assistance, or agrees to provide a better water supply to a given home. Any particular instance of such an act has little effect on the collectivity, but such day-to-day decisions may have an intense impact on an individual or a family. And the impact may depend on the citizen's knowledge, skill, and activity, that is, on the effectiveness of participation.

Thus, rather than thinking of all governmental activity as having a collective impact, one might distinguish among such activities in terms of their scope, that is, the number of citizens affected. This is clearly a problem of degree and not a simple dichotomy. But though the extreme of a fully collective or fully particularized outcome is never reached, the distinction between governmental actions in terms of the degree to which they have collective or particularized impact is useful if we want to understand the ways in which citizen participation affects those actions.

A full understanding of the ways in which one can participate requires that we consider the citizen as participant in relation to large collective outcomes (as we do when we look at the citizen as a voter). But it is also important to consider participants in relation to narrower governmental actions, as when they attempt to influence some governmental decision specifically relevant to their own lives. Thus an important dimension of participation has to do with whether the participatory act is intended to and can in fact influence a particularized outcome, a collective outcome, or both.

3. The conflict dimension. Political participation inevitably raises questions of the generation and reconciliation of conflict in a society. Insofar as governmental benefits are limited, activity by one group to obtain something for itself may injure the interests of others. But one can make distinctions among participatory activities in terms of the extent to which conflict with others is involved. Some political activities are engaged in against other participants; one set of participants tries to gain some beneficial outcome at the expense of another. In other cases participants seek some beneficial outcome under circumstances in which there are no "counterparticipants"; their gain does not imply clear losses for others. Citizens do not always participate in order to defeat some alternative proposal set forth by an opposed group; rather, they often work to mobilize resources, to bring the apathetic over to active support, to move inert institutions in order to accomplish some goal to which there is little if any opposition.

Again, the distinction is not a clear dichotomy. No benefit for an individual or group is costless for others. But participatory situations clearly differ in the extent to which the situation is a zero-sum conflict, with winners and losers, rather than an attempt by one group to influence a policy to which there is no clear opposition. The conflict dimension is undoubtedly related to the scope of the potential outcome. The wider the impact of the outcome, the more likely is it that there will be opposing groups active in relation to it. If the governmental outcome that the participants seek has a narrow impact, having a noticeable effect on the participants alone and affecting others only indirectly, this increases the likelihood that the participatory situation will not be characterized by intragroup conflict.

4. Initiative required. This dimension is similar to (indeed taps one component of) the "difficulty of the act" criterion, which has been the usual one within the literature. We are interested in the amount of time and effort needed for an act of participation but more so in how much initiative is needed by the individual in choosing when to act and how to act.

The Modes of Participation

These four distinctions among types of political acts, when combined in different ways, produce what one can consider alternative systems by which the citizenry influences the government. Most analyses of politics have involved the study of situations in which large groups of collaborating citizens oppose each other in relation to some outcome affecting the entire collectivity. Party competition for control over governmental offices is the prototype, but this approach also describes other clashes over major governmental policies that affect many citizens. At the other extreme are those citizen-government interactions in which the citizen acts alone, the outcome affects only the individual involved, and there is no direct opposition by any other citizen.

The usefulness of these dimensions can be seen if we consider some of the actual ways in which citizens can be active. The dimensions help distinguish among these ways.

1. Voting. Voting is the most frequent citizen activity. It exerts influence over leaders through pressure: leaders adjust their policies in order to gain votes, since the vote determines who holds elective office. But the vote communicates little information about citizen preferences to leaders. The act itself conveys no explicit information, and the information implicit in the fact that votes go to one candidate rather than another is inadequate to express the specific preferences of the citizen. The scope of the outcome is very broad, affecting all citizens. This combination of low information about citizen preferences and high pressure with broad outcomes for leaders is what gives voting its unique characteristic as a blunt but powerful instrument of control over the government.

With respect to the last two dimensions of participation described above, voting does involve the citizen in conflict, since the electoral situation is by definition a conflictual one, at least if the election is competitive. And voting differs from other political acts in that it requires relatively little initiative, the occasion for voting being presented to the citizen in the form of regular elections.

These characteristics of voting are fairly obvious, but they are useful because they highlight some contrast with other modes of citizen activity.

2. Campaign activity. Like voting, participation in election campaigns is a part of the electoral process. Through this mode of action citizens can increase their influence over the election outcome beyond the one vote allocated to each of them. Like the vote it exerts a great deal of pressure on leaders, and for the same reason. But it can communicate more information about the participants' preferences because campaign activists are a more clearly identifiable group with whom candidates may be in close contact.

Campaign activity, like voting, produces collective outcomes, and it involves the citizen in conflictual situations. But more initiative is required of the citizen than is the case with voting; campaign activity is clearly a more difficult political act than is voting.

3. Citizen-initiated contacts. As we pointed out, much of the study of participation focusses on activities that are part of the electoral process. But between-election activity is significant as well. To find other means of participation we might consider first that kind of activity most different from the electoral situation. Both voting and campaign activity take place in response to elections, whose content and timing are set for the citizen and in which the substantive issues are controlled by candidates and officials. At the other extreme are those instances in which individuals with particular concerns initiate contacts with government officials about these concerns. Here we have the individual vis-à-vis the government or some small segment of the government. He or she acts alone and determines the timing, target, and substance of the act of participation. This type of participation, which we call citizen-initiated contacts, represents a third type of political activity.

Citizen-initiated contacts have one distinctive characteristic when considered in relation to the dimensions of participation, particularly the scope of the outcome. Only this mode of participation can reasonably be expected to result in a particularized benefit. The individual participant takes the initiative in contacting a government official and, most importantly, "chooses the agenda" of the act of participation, that is, decides what to contact about. The "choosing of the agenda" by the citizen-contactor—something that is possible for contacting activity only—is crucial for two reasons. It ensures that the subject matter of the participatory act is salient and important to the individual, and it makes possible particularization of the subject matter to the individual. Under such circumstances, a citizen may still contact about some general social problem, for example, writing a congressional representative about the War in

Vietnam or complaining to a local governmental official about some general failure in performance—but such a citizen may also contact about a particular, purely personal or family problem. Contacting, as our discussion implies, communicates extensive information about the preferences of the citizen, but it probably exerts little pressure, coming as it does from a single citizen.

The potential outcome dimension is most crucial for distinguishing citizen-initiated contacts from other acts. On the conflict dimension we assume that such contacts do not usually involve direct conflict with other citizens. Finally, since the individual chooses the occasion to participate as well as the subject matter and the official to contact, such activity requires quite a bit of initiative on the part of the contactor.

4. Cooperative activity. Finally we can mention another regularly utilized mode of participation outside of the electoral process. This fourth type of activity involves group or organizational activity to deal with social and political problems. In this case the individual does not act alone as in citizen-initiated contacts but rather joins with others to influence the actions of government. However, like citizen-initiated contacts and unlike electoral participation, cooperative group activity is initiated by private citizens and may take place at any time and in relation to any type of issue or problem of concern to the group. It may involve activity within formal organizations as well as informal cooperation among citizens.

Cooperative activity is significant because it can combine information about citizen preferences (since citizens come together to work on a particular issue) with pressure (since leaders are more likely to respond to a number of citizens than to a lone contactor). As for the scope of the outcome, when a citizen cooperates with others, either in informal groups or in formal organizations, the likelihood that the political activity will be aimed at some benefit particularized to the individual is reduced. Thus cooperative activity is more likely to be relevant to outcomes of a somewhat collective nature, though the outcome may affect a particular group in the society rather than the entire collectivity. It is somewhat less clear whether such cooperative activity is likely to take place in a situation of conflict with other groups; the conflictual dimension is probably more apparent in cooperative situations than in citizen-initiated contacts, less apparent than in the electoral situation.

Lastly, cooperative activity probably requires some initiative, though the amount of such initiative depends on whether the individual is a relatively inactive member of a cooperative group, helps to form it, or acts as a leader.

We have explicated at some length the differences among various modes of political activity (for a more extended discussion see Verba and Nie, 1972, chapters 3 and 7). The reason is that a general treatment of a topic such as participation proceeds most fruitfully if one first defines and analyzes the subject matter under study. To consider participation to be an undifferentiated phenomenon would be to misunderstand how it relates the citizen to government. The several modes of participation explicated above differ significantly in how they allow citizens to influence the government (what kind of influence is exerted and over what scope of outcome), in the extent to which they involve the citizen in conflict, and in the amount of initiative they require. The difference among the modes of activity is summarized in Table 1. (Citizen-initiated contacts are separated into two kinds: those aimed at influencing a broad social issue, as when a citizen complains to a government official on some general problem, and those aimed at obtaining some particularized benefit from the government. We do this because these two types of citizen contacting differ significantly in scope of outcome and, as we shall see, differ empirically as well.)

TABLE 1   The dimensions and modes of political activity

Mode of activity	Type of influence	Scope of outcome	Presence of conflict	Initiative required
Campaign activity	High pressure, low to high information	Collective	Conflictual	Some
Cooperative activity	Low to high pressure, high information	Collective	Maybe yes, usually no	Some or a lot
Voting	High pressure, low information	Collective	Conflictual	Little
Contacting officials on social issues	Low pressure, high information	Collective	Usually nonconflictual	A lot
Contacting officials on personal matters	Low pressure, high information	Particular	Nonconflictual	A lot

We consider the differences among the modes of activity important because they are more than *a priori* categorizations. Data about participation indicate that the modes form identifiable clusters of political acts, different kinds of citizens take part in these different modes, the process by which one comes to be active differs from one type of participation to another, and different modes of activity have different consequences.

The Empirical Structure of Participation

One way of validating the distinctiveness of the four modes of participation is to examine the empirical relationships among the various political acts. Each mode of activity can be carried out using a variety of specific acts: one can be active in campaigns by ringing doorbells, contributing money to a party, trying to persuade others how to vote. One can be active in the "contacting mode" by

contacting local officials, national officials, contacting by mail, contacting in person. If political acts are not "interchangeable," if there is, as we argue, a multidimensionality to political participation, then the citizen who engages in one specific act within one of the modes should be more likely to engage in other acts within that mode than he or she is to engage in acts in another mode. If the modes differ in the problems for which they are relevant, in the extent to which they involve citizens in conflict, and in the initiative they require, then citizens with particular kinds of problems, different attitudes toward conflict, or different amounts of initiative should be found concentrating their activity in one rather than the other modes.

Such an assumption is indeed supported by empirical analysis of the interrelationship among specific political acts. A factor analysis of a large number of specific political acts assumed to represent examples of activity within the various modes produced a structure strikingly similar in six different nations. (For an extended discussion of these factor analyses as well as the actual data see Verba, Nie, and Kim, 1971; Verba and Nie, 1972, Chapter 4; and Verba, *et al.*, 1973.) The structure was consistent with expectations as to which political acts would cluster together. The results are summarized in Fig. 1, which reports the results of a four-factor, oblique rotation. In the left column are listed nineteen specific acts about which information was obtained in samples in each of the nations. Not all measures exist in all countries. (In Nigeria we have no measures of campaign activity.)

The similarity of results in all six countries is made more convincing by the fact that the various modes of participation are indexed by a somewhat different set of activities in each country. The campaign activities in all six nations load positively on a campaign factor (with the exception of attendance at political rallies in India, which just misses our criterion by loading positively at .38 on that factor). And only one unexpected variable (number 13 in Austria) loads on that factor. The same is true of the various measures of voting: they all load on a voting factor, and other acts do not load there. The third factor varies somewhat from expectations. It combines on a single factor what we have labelled cooperative activity and citizen-initiated contacts for which the subject matter is a social issue. This factor we have labelled "communal activity," referring to all those nonelectoral activities aimed at dealing with a general social issue. And the last factor contains the items on contacting officials on a personal matter.

If one had made no distinction as to the subject matter of the citizen contact, one would have found a pattern quite close to the four modes predicted (see Verba, Nie, and Kim, 1971). (In Nigeria, where there are no measures of campaign activity, separate factors did exist for social contacts and cooperative activity.) But the result when one distinguishes between two types of contacting provides an even cleaner structure. It clearly suggests that the distinctions we made among the alternative modes of activity have some validity. Electoral

Variable	Campaign activity	Voting	Communal activity	Particularized contacting
Modes of participation				

Campaign acts

#	Variable	Campaign activity	Voting	Communal activity	Particularized contacting
1.	Persuade others how to vote	a u ne			
2.	Actively work for a party	A i J U Ne*			
3.	Attend political meetings	A i j U Ne			
4.	Contribute money to a party	i U Ne			
5.	Membership in political clubs	A I j U Ne			

Voting acts

#	Variable	Campaign activity	Voting	Communal activity	Particularized contacting
6.	Vote regularly in national elections		A I J Ni		
7.	Voted in 1964 presidential election		U		
8.	Voted in 1960 presidential election		U		
9.	Frequency of local vote		A I Ni U Ne		
10.	Vote in provincial elections		A Ne		

Communal acts

#	Variable	Campaign activity	Voting	Communal activity	Particularized contacting
11.	Work with others on local problem			i J Ni U ne	
12.	Form a group to work on local problem			i J Ni U ne	
13.	Active membership in community problem-solving organization			a i J u ne	
14.	Contact local official with others			A ni	
15.	Contact extralocal official with others			a	
16.	Contact local official on social matter			A I j ni** u Ne	
17.	Contact extralocal official on social matter			A I j ni** u Ne	

Particularized contacts

#	Variable	Campaign activity	Voting	Communal activity	Particularized contacting
18.	Contact local official on particularized problem				A I J Ni U Ne
19.	Contact extralocal official on a social matter				A I J Ni U Ne

Note:

The letters refer to the six nations for which data are reported: Austria, India, Japan, Nigeria, the United States, and Netherlands.

Capital letter means loading of .65 or greater on expected factor.
Small letter means loading of .40–.65 on expected factor.

*In the Netherlands the activity involves displaying or distributing campaign leaflets or posters.
**In Nigeria these two items formed a separate factor, there having been no campaign activity measures.

Fig. 1. Binorinanian Rotated Pattern Matrix of Participation Variables in Six Countries

modes differ from nonelectoral, and within the electoral mode voting is clearly distinct from campaign activity in terms of the difficulty of the act. And when one considers nonelectoral activity it becomes clear that the scope of the outcome of the act, whether the citizen is seeking a particularized benefit or a more general social goal, plays a major role in distinguishing among such activities.

The factor analyses suggest a similar structure of participation in each of the nations. We can learn more about that structure by considering the relations among the participation factors. What we are interested in is the extent to which the various modes of political activity are related to some common underlying dimension of "activism" and, if such an underlying dimension can be discerned, which modes of activity are most clearly related to it. The relation among the four modes of activity emerges in a higher-order factor solution for the modes of participation. In Table 2 we present for each country the first higher-order factor, which can be taken as the best measure of what is common among the four participatory modes.

TABLE 2   Higher-order factor solution for six countries

Lower-level oblique factor	Austria factor loadings	India factor loadings	Japan factor loadings	Netherlands factor loadings	Nigeria factor loadings	United States factor loadings
Campaign activity	.56	.58	.65	.78	.39 *	.81
Communal activity	.45	.57	.66	.73	.59 **	.66
Voting	.14	.23	.30	.52	.28	.41
Particularized contacting	.23	.40	.16	.25	.14	.09

* This figure is for contacts with a social referent in Nigeria.

** This figure is for cooperative activity and does not include contacts with a social referent as in the other countries.

The data in Table 2 offer some interesting similarities coupled with some differences across the nations. In all of the nations campaign and communal activity are most closely related to the common dimension underlying the several modes. And in all nations voting and contacting on a particularized problem are less well related to that underlying dimension. This result is especially interesting in light of the fact that though both the campaign and communal modes of activity are closely related to this underlying dimension, campaign activity is within the electoral sphere while communal activity is outside of it. There are, however, two characteristics that these two modes of activity have in common: each is a difficult act requiring some initiative and each is focussed on some general social outcome that transcends the narrow problems of the individual.

Particularized contact, except in India, is quite weakly related to the general participation dimension, while the situation with regard to voting is more mixed. In some cases voting forms part of the general participation dimension, in others it does not. That particularized contacting is only weakly related to the general participation factor is consistent with our argument that it is not a "political" act in the ordinary sense of the term: it deals with no questions of a broad social nature. The mixed situation with regard to voting is a bit more complicated but also fairly consistent with our model. Since voting is an "easy" act requiring little motivation, there can be a good deal of variation across nations in the *processes* by which people come to vote. In some cases people may vote on the basis of their own internalized motivation (in which case the vote does measure some underlying commitment to political activity). In other cases they may vote because they are mobilized to do so (in which case the vote gives no indication of the individual's political commitment). As we shall see later, the process by which citizens come to vote is highly dependent on the kinds of institutions that mobilize citizens to political life in the various nations.

The factor analyses support the view that there is a common structure to participation across a varied set of nations. One finds a similar set of modes of activity in each. Furthermore, in each case the communal and campaign modes are most closely linked to a more general dimension of political activity. Particularized contacting, though an interesting mode of activity, is less likely to be an indicator of general political involvement, while voting varies from nation to nation in the extent to which it is related to the general dimension of political activity. The latter finding ought to serve as a warning for those who would use voting rates as indicators of political participation in a cross-national setting.

A parallel analysis of the modes of political activity was performed on data from a study in Yugoslavia (Verba *et al.,* 1973). The Yugoslav analysis produced a different set of modes, but different in ways that were fully predictable given the theoretical dimensions of political activity and some specific differences between the political process in Yugoslavia and that in the other nations. Yugoslavia differs from the nations just discussed in the absence of competitive partisan elections and in the presence of a variety of innovative participatory modes connected with functional spheres of activity—workers' councils and other functional self-government bodies. In Yugoslavia a factor analysis revealed that activity that could be classified as campaign activity (activity to nominate or support a candidate, etc.) falls into the same mode as activity we would consider communal (community actions, projects, etc.). This is different from the other nations but consistent with the general model, since what differentiates campaign and communal activity in the other nations is the fact that the former involves the participant in conflict with other participants. Where there are no competitive parties the distinction does not exist. In addition, a separate mode emerged in Yugoslavia: acts involving participation in functional self-government institutions form a separate factor. On the other hand, voting (in Yugoslavia, as elsewhere, the easiest activity) and particularized contacting are distinctive modes in Yugoslavia as elsewhere.

In short, the Yugoslav analysis provides a strong validation for the meaningfulness of the dimensions and modes of participation in a cross-national context. The dimensions predict a similar set of modes in all the other nations and a somewhat different set in Yugoslavia. And we find such a difference.

Political Orientations and Political Activity

We can learn more about the various modes of political activity and further validate the distinctions among them by observing the way in which these modes relate to the political orientations of participants. To simplify the analysis we can confine our attention to three basic political orientations: (1) *general psychological involvement,* which refers to the degree to which citizens are interested in and attentive to politics and public affairs; (2) *strength of partisan identification,* which refers to the presence and intensity of psychological attachment to a political party; and (3) *sense of contribution to the community welfare,* which is based on citizens' beliefs about their relative contribution to the general welfare of the communities in which they live. (See Verba, Nie, and Kim, 1971, pp. 44–45 for more details.)

We focus on these three orientations because they relate in several interesting ways to the set of dimensions by which we differentiate participatory acts.

First, consider our distinction between collective outcomes and more particularized outcomes. We would expect general psychological involvement in politics and public affairs to characterize those who are concerned about broad collective issues rather than particularized ones. Thus voting, campaign activity, and communal participation are all modes of participation which are used primarily for influencing outcomes that have a broad social referent. Since particularized contacting relates only to the narrow problems of the individual and his or her family, we do not expect it to be related to this more general political concern.

However, one other distinction we make among participatory acts leads us to modify our expectation of the relation of psychological involvement to those modes of activity—voting, campaign activity, and communal activity—whose potential outcome is collective. This distinction is the amount of initiative needed to engage in the act. Insofar as one can engage in an activity without taking much initiative, one may be able to participate—perhaps in response to the inducements of others or out of habit—without much psychological involvement. Thus we expect that the relationship of psychological involvement to voting—the act that stands out from the other three in terms of the initiative required—will be weak.

While we expect psychological involvement to differentiate on the public/private dimension and secondarily according to the degree of initiative required, strength of partisan identification should cut in somewhat different directions. Not surprisingly we expect to find voting and campaign activity to

be highly correlated with strength of partisan identification. Much more critical to our argument about the distinctive character and function of the four
modes is our expectation that neither communal activity nor particularized
contacting will be related to the strength of partisan identity. Much of what we
have learned about the communalists through our factor analysis leads us to
suspect that they are concerned about community problems around which
there is an absence of partisan conflict and counterparticipants. Further, we expect to find little or no relationship between partisan identity and particularized contacting, simply because such psychological attachments to political
parties would appear to have little relevance to a citizen's propensity to contact
public officials about highly particularized issues and services.

Sense of contribution to the community, the third orientation, should reveal a somewhat different pattern. Particularized contacting should have little
relationship to this orientation, for such participation discharges no public
obligation but rather aims at private reward. On the other hand, we predict
that the modes of participation related to collective outcomes will reveal positive associations with this orientation. And this should be particularly true for
communal activity in comparison with voting and campaign activity if we are
correct in assuming that the former activity is less conflictual and more directed toward a general benefit than are the latter.

The relevant data as to the relation between activity and orientations are
in Fig. 2. That figure presents the results of a multiple regression analysis,
which utilizes the three orientations as predictor variables for the four modes
of participation. A separate regression was performed on each mode of participation in each nation. An additional regression analysis, on the average correlations across five nations, was also performed in order to determine the *average* impact of each orientation. The coefficients are standardized partial betas
displaying the direct explanatory contribution of each orientation. In this way
we can assess the unique relationship of psychological involvement, strength of
partisan identity, and sense of contribution to community welfare to each
mode.

Campaign activity. As predicted, psychological involvement in politics is
closely associated with campaign activity in all the nations. The partial betas
are quite high and fairly uniform from country to country. Strength of identification with political parties is also associated with campaign activity in each
of the nations, though the betas are considerably smaller in this instance. Sense
of contribution to the community is positively related to campaign activity in
the three countries for which we have both measures, but its relationship is
hardly substantial. The findings indicate a similarity in the "meaning" of campaign activity to participants across the several nations. These findings will
become more interesting when they are compared with the patterns of orientations which characterize the other modes of activity.

Campaign activity	U.S.A.	India	Japan	Austria	Nigeria	Five-nation average
Psychological involvement in politics	.42	.37	.34	.51	**	.40
Strength of partisan identity	.13	.11	.16	⸴15	**	.13
Sense of contribution to community welfare	.09	.10	.07	*	**	.09
Multiple r	.44	.46	.45	.55		.48

Voting	U.S.A.	India	Japan	Austria	Nigeria	Five-nation average
Psychological involvement in politics	.28	.05	.15	.04	.18	.14
Strength of partisan identity	.15	.22	.13	.21	.18	.16
Sense of contribution to community welfare	.09	.04	.08	*	.08	.06
Multiple r	.36	.24	.26	.22	.31	.27

Communal activity	U.S.A.	India	Japan	Austria	Nigeria	Five-nation average
Psychological involvement in politics	.39	.44	.36	.30	.37†	.36
Strength of partisan identity	.04	.04	.07	.00	.11†	.03
Sense of contribution to community welfare	.23	.11	.15	*	.10†	.15
Multiple r	.48	.50	.45	.30	.48	.44

Particularized contact	U.S.A.	India	Japan	Austria	Nigeria	Five-nation average
Psychological involvement in politics	.10	.26	.13	.13	.08	.14
Strength of partisan identity	.02	.03	.08	.00	.07	.03
Sense of contribution to community welfare	.01	.07	.02	*	.06	.04
Multiple r	.11	.30	.17	.13	.14	.16

Source: Verba, Nie, and Kim, *The Modes of Democratic Participation*, p. 49.

* Sense of contribution to welfare not asked in Austria.
** Campaign participation not ascertained in Nigeria.
† For simplification, we combined "cooperative acts" and "socialized" contacts into one index of communcal acts.

Legend: If Beta ≤ .09 blank   If Beta = .15–.20

If Beta = .10–.14   If Beta = .21

Fig. 2. Partial Betas of Three Predictor Orientations for the Four Modes of Participation in Five Countries (data not available for Netherlands and Yugoslavia—will be reported in future publications of our cross-national program in political participation and social change)

Voting. The pattern of orientations associated with voting, the other mode of electoral activity, is in some ways similar to and in some ways different from that associated with campaign activity. As predicted, strength of partisan identity is the strongest and most consistent predictor of voting among the three orientations. In India and Austria the relationship is strong and in the other countries it is moderate to strong. Furthermore in three of the four countries for which we have information on both voting and campaign activity, partisanship is more closely associated with voting than it is with campaign activity, a finding that suggests the degree to which voting is dependent on habitual attachments to political parties.

The relationship of psychological involvement to voting is consistently much smaller than is its relationship to campaign activity. The average partial betas of psychological involvement and voting is .14; of psychological involvement and campaign activity, .40. This accords with our expectations: citizens vote on public issues, but because voting requires the lesser amount of initiative it can be engaged in with little psychological involvement.

This is clearer if we look beyond the average coefficient, which is quite misleading because the relationship varies quite a bit from nation to nation. The relationship of psychological involvement and voting is strongest in the United States, moderate in Japan and Nigeria, but almost nonexistent in Austria and India. The pattern of relationship of psychological involvement to voting is, interestingly, parallel to the relationship of voting to the other three modes of activity as revealed in the higher-order factor solution in Table 2. In those countries—the United States and to a lesser extent, Japan and Nigeria—in which voting is part of the general participant syndrome, as evidenced by its strong loading on the overall activity dimension, its relationship to psychological involvement is also strong. On the other hand in those countries—India and Austria—in which voting bears little or no relationship to general propensity for political activity, there is little or no relationship to psychological involvement. In nations in which voting is part of a participant syndrome, it appears to be associated with concern about public life. In other nations it is unrelated to such orientations and is associated more strongly with partisan attachment.

Unlike campaign activity, voting differs in its meaning for the individual elector from nation to nation. Attachment to political parties appears to accompany regular voting in all the nations, while the association of psychological involvement with voting is dependent on whether voting is part of a general participant syndrome. Finally, sense of contribution to community welfare, as expected, has little or no bearing on voting.

Communal participation. The pattern of orientations which characterizes communal participation differs in some very significant ways from the orientation patterns of voting and campaign activity. As expected, psychological involvement in politics is strongly associated with communal activity in all of the nations, and the magnitudes of the relationships are very similar to those for campaign activity. However, the similarity between campaign activity and communal participation ends here. Strength of partisan identification has little relationship to levels of communal participation. In the United States the beta is negative, and only in Nigeria does the coefficient approach our criterion for a substantial relationship. In addition, we see some substantial relationships between sense of contribution to the community and communal activity. In the United States this feeling of contribution is strongly associated with communal participation, and the relationship is moderate to strong in all the other countries. A picture of the type of citizen who becomes a communal activist begins to emerge. Like the campaign activist, he or she appears to be interested and concerned about political and public affairs but, unlike the campaigner, does not tend to have strong partisan attachments. This citizen's involvement in consensual rather than conflictual issues is also evidenced by his or her sense of contribution to the overall welfare of the community. The consistent cross-national difference between campaign and communal activity, despite the fact that the two modes of activity are part of the overall activity syndrome and are associated with psychological involvement in politics, is strong support for our contention that participation is multidimensional.

Particularized contacting. The pattern of orientations for particularized contacting is strikingly uniform across the nations and strikingly different from the other activities. None of the orientations is strongly associated with this mode of participation. The associations for strength of partisanship and sense of contribution to the community welfare are negligible in all the nations. And this is as we anticipated, for there is little reason to expect that this kind of activity should be associated with a strong sense of contribution to the community welfare or a strong identification with political parties.

Furthermore, on the average, the relationship of psychological involvement in politics to particularized contacting is also quite small. Only in India does there appear to be a substantial relationship between this mode of participation and psychological involvement in politics. This corresponds to the fact that there is a close relationship of such contacts to the overall activity dimension in India, while there is no such relationship elsewhere. The higher-order factor analysis in Table 2 indicates that India is the only nation for which particularized contacting demonstrates a strong relationship to the general activity dimension.

An interesting parallel has emerged between the structure of participation and the relation between psychological involvement and the modes of activity, a parallel that may help us understand what holds the modes of activity together. Campaign and communal activities form the core of a participation continuum in each nation; they are also most closely related to a general psychological involvement in political matters. Particularized contacting is unrelated to the other acts except in India, and it is unrelated to psychological involvement except in India. Voting is in general relatively weakly related to the other acts, especially in India and Austria, and it is also generally weakly related to psychological involvement.

What this suggests is that those modes of participation which are closest to a more general participant continuum are held together by the fact that they depend on (or at least are accompanied by) a general psychological concern with political matters. This finding is consistent with the conclusions of Almond and Verba (1963) as well as those of Alex Inkeles (1969) on the existence of a participant syndrome of political activities and civic involvement. But the data also suggest that there are important modes of activity which may fall outside this syndrome and for which there is little accompanying general political motivation.

HOW ACTIVE ARE CITIZENS?

The four modes of political participation provide a framework within which we can present some data on how active citizens are. While these data are descriptively interesting and help us understand the place of participation in politics, the reader ought to be warned about the comparability of such data. The measurement across nations of amounts of political activity is subject to a number of limitations inherent in cross-national comparisons. (See Verba, Nie, and Kim, forthcoming; Verba, 1971.)

To compare the frequency with which citizens in one nation report that they are active in a particular way with the frequency of such reports elsewhere is to assume that one has something equivalent to compare. But the validity of a comparison of such frequencies can be questioned in two ways. In the first place the measurements are quite dependent on the techniques used to elicit the information. Secondly the meaningfulness of comparisons of frequencies of political activities depends on certain assumptions as to the equivalence of these activities within the respective societies. Acts that appear to be similar may differ in their impact on politics. And political acts that appear the same may differ in how difficult they are from nation to nation and may, therefore, indicate different levels of active involvement. Voting is a prime example: the lower turnout rate in the United States compared with some other countries is probably due less to political passivity among Americans than to differences in the methods of voter registration (Kelley, Ayres, and Bowen, 1967). Furthermore, the social circumstances surrounding political participation may differ such that an act in one country represents a greater commitment than a similar act elsewhere. Voting is again an example. In India voting is a much more passive act than in the United States; Indian citizens are mobilized by parties and leaders rather than by their personal involvement in political matters (Verba, Ahmed, and Bhatt, 1971).

The reader should keep all these qualifications in mind in considering the data in Table 3. Despite their limitations they have enough intrinsic interest to be worth consideration. We report the proportions of the population active in the various ways we have been discussing based on data from seven nations. The data reported are the proportions of the sample who indicated that they participated in various activities about which they were questioned. (Citizens were questioned about other activities as well, more specific to each nation, but for our purposes here we have limited ourselves to the set of activities that have the greatest face similarity.) In each case a citizen is considered as active in relation to a particular act if he or she reported having ever engaged in it, except for voting, for which only those who can be considered fairly regular voters are reported as active. (A more precise definition is in the footnotes to Table 3.)

Voting rates do vary widely across the countries, with the European nations and Japan outvoting the others. When it comes to the three campaign activities one finds a fair degree of similarity across the three more industrialized nations—Austria, Japan, and the United States. A very high proportion in Japan reports attendance at a political rally (though the extent to which such an item really measures active involvement in the political process is unclear). Otherwise the figures on activity range from fairly small percentages up to about one-quarter of the sample. The ways in which citizens become involved in partisan activity differ. In Austria and to a lesser extent the Netherlands citizens are more likely to belong to a political organization than actually to work for a candidate or party. In Japan and the United States formal membership is much rarer, but about one-quarter of the sample indicates it has worked for a party. The rates of party membership and campaign activity in India, on the other hand, are somewhat smaller.

The patterns vis-à-vis communal activities offer some interesting contrasts. The first three items of communal activity involve cooperation with one's fellow citizens—the first via a formal organization, the other two in more informal groups. This seems most widespread in Yugoslavia, Nigeria, and the United States, with India, the Netherlands, and Japan having some moderate frequency of informal group activity and Austria the least (though in the latter case the comparison is uncertain due to a substantial difference in the measure used). One finds individual activity—for example, a citizen contacting an official on a civic problem—occurring most frequently in the United States, similarly frequently (with regard to local officials) in Japan and Yugoslavia, but relatively infrequently elsewhere.

Finally, we can consider the proportion of the citizens which reports having brought a personal problem to a government official, either within the community or on a higher level. This takes place most frequently in the Netherlands and Yugoslavia, followed by Austria, India, the United States, Japan, and Nigeria.

A few conclusions do emerge clearly from the table, perhaps the most ob-

TABLE 3   Percentages of citizens active in various ways in seven countries

	Austria	India	Japan	Netherlands	Nigeria	United States	Yugoslavia
Voting							
Regular voters[b]	85	48	93	77	56	63	82
Campaign activity							
Members of a party or							
political organization[c]	28	5	4	13	a	8	15
Worked for a party[d]	10	6	25	10	a	25	45
Attended a political rally[e]	27	14	50	9	a	19	45
Communal activity							
Active members in a community							
action organization[f]	9	7	11	15	34	32	39
Worked with a local group on							
a community problem[g]	3	18	15	16	35	30	22
Helped form a local group on							
a community problem[h]	6	5	5	a	26	14	a
Contacted an official in the							
community on some social problem[i]	5	4	11	6	2	13	11
Contacted an official outside							
the community on a social problem	3	2	5	7	3	11	a

Particularized contacting

Contacted a local official on a personal problem [j]	15	12	7	38	2	6	20
Contacted an official outside the community on a personal problem	10	6	3	10	1	6	[a]
Number of cases	1769	2637	2657	1746	1799	2544	2995

[a] Not asked.

[b] Vote regularly in both local and national elections.

[c] Formal membership in political parties in Austria, India, and the Netherlands; in political clubs in the United States and Japan; in the League of Communists in Yugoslavia. Item not asked in Nigeria.

[d] Worked for a political party in an election. In the Netherlands refers to displaying or distributing posters or leaflets. In Yugoslavia refers to any electoral activity.

[e] Refers to attending an election meeting or rally. In Yugoslavia refers to attending a voters' meeting.

[f] Active member of an organization that is in turn active in community affairs. In Yugoslavia refers to taking part in a formally organized community action.

[g] Refers to working with an informal group on some community matter. In Yugoslavia refers to taking part in an informal community action. In Austria refers to cooperating with others to bring community problems to the attention of officials.

[h] Helped form a group such as mentioned in [g] above.

[i] In Yugoslavia this item contains contacts both in and out of the community.

[j] In Yugoslavia this item contains contacts both in and out of the community.

vious having to do with the diversity of patterns displayed. It is by no means clear how one would rank the nations in terms of frequency of political activity. On voting one finds Japan displaying greatest frequency; on membership in a political organization, Austria; on cooperative activity, Yugoslavia, Nigeria, and the United States; on contacting on a personal matter, the Netherlands.

Nor does the amount of participation vary clearly with level of affluence or economic development. India does tend to have fewer participants than the other countries, but Nigerians report a high frequency of participation of certain kinds. If one expands one's view of participation beyond the electoral process one finds a richer and more variegated pattern of participation than if one sticks to voting and campaign activity.

Voting is the only political act that a large part of the citizenry engages in. No other political act (with the exception of the large proportion that has attended a political meeting in Japan) is engaged in by more than one-half of the citizens in any country. In India no political act other than voting is engaged in by more than 18 percent of the citizenry. In short, only a minority of citizens takes part in any of the specific acts listed on Table 3. Widespread activity—that is, activity engaged in by close to or more than half of the population—is found largely for those acts that are relatively easy. The main characteristic of voting and attendance at a political rally is that the citizen does not have to take the initiative in choosing when and how to be active. The occasion for the activity (the election, the campaign meeting) is provided by others.

The conclusion is simple: citizens in each country have a wide repertory of ways in which they can participate (and, of course, our questions do not exhaust that repertory). In different countries citizens will choose different ways to take part. Such a conclusion hardly contributes to a generalized understanding of political change and development, if by such understanding we mean the formation and testing of general hypotheses about political participation. But it does warn against overly simple generalizations linking political participation to social change without taking into account the wide range of ways in which citizens can and do participate.

Protests and Other Such Activities

The above discussion paid no attention to protest activities—marches, demonstrations, and more direct actions—even though many of these clearly fit into the scope of our concern, being both legal and aimed at influencing the government. It is difficult to obtain accurate figures, but it is likely that relatively few citizens have taken part in such activities. One study, conducted in the United States during the height of the Vietnam War protests, found only eight citizens (out of 1500 interviewed) who had ever taken part in a demonstration about Vietnam—about one-half of one percent (Verba and Brody,

1970). And another study of a city in upstate New York found that about 2 to 3 percent of the white citizens had ever attended a protest demonstration, and 4 percent said that they had attended a protest meeting (Milbrath, unpublished manuscript). And Lipsky's study of rent strikes in New York shows that the participation by renters was not nearly as widespread as one might have been led to believe by the media (Lipsky, 1970, pp. 73–80).

But two points should be made about such activity. Only a small percentage of the citizenry as a whole may take part in demonstrations, but large proportions of particular groups with high visibility may be involved. Thus the same study that found that only 2 to 3 percent of whites had taken part in a street demonstration found that 11 percent of blacks had. And one does not know the proportion of college students that has taken part in antiwar demonstrations, but it is certainly likely to be larger than the minuscule percentage of the population as a whole that has done so. One study of France at the time of the May 1968 crisis found 8 percent had taken part in some demonstration (Converse and Pierce, 1970).

The second point is more important. One goal of political participation is to communicate to political leaders. Protest activities, even when engaged in by a small percentage of the population, speak very loudly indeed. The main point to be made about the New York rent strikes (Lipsky, 1970) is not that so few took part but that such a small number could make such a big splash, in part by appearing to be more in number than they actually were. Furthermore, a small percentage of the population is still a substantial number of people. If one extrapolates from the one-half of one percent estimate of Vietnam War protesters, one gets close to a million protesters. The very fact that the activity goes outside usual channels increases its salience, as does the penchant of the mass media for reporting such activities. (See Skolnik, 1969, for a discussion of the role of violent protest in American politics.)

The Concentration of Participation

The data presented in Table 3 above are consistent with one of the more widely accepted findings of recent research on political activity: only a small minority of the citizenry is active beyond the act of voting. This generalization is usually supplemented by the generalization that political acts form a structured hierarchy such that those who engage in the more difficult acts (i.e., the least frequent acts) are likely to engage in all more frequent ones. (See Lane, 1959, pp. 93–94; Campbell *et al.*, 1960, p. 51; Dahl, 1961, pp. 276–77; Milbrath, 1965, pp. 16–21; and Butler and Stokes, 1969, pp. 24–25.)

However, if, as our factor analysis suggests, political activity is multidimensional, then acts may not form a clear hierarchy and more people may be active —some in one way, others in other ways—than one would expect if acts formed such a hierarchy. Consider the data in Table 3. On the basis of the fact that the proportion engaging in any particular political activity beyond the vote rarely exceeds one-third of the population, one is tempted to conclude that only about a third of the citizenry ever engages in any political activity beyond voting. Such a result is possible given the data in Table 3, but it is by no means necessary. If 28 percent of our Austrian sample belongs to a political organization, and belonging to a political organization is the act (beyond the vote) performed most frequently in Austria, it would be compatible with such data to conclude that the proportion of citizens that participates beyond the vote is no more than 28 percent. But this would be the case only if political activities formed a hierarchy whereby those who performed less frequent acts also performed the more frequent ones.

To put it another way, if political activities formed a perfect Guttman scale, the 28 percent that belongs to political organizations in Austria would contain all those citizens who engaged in less frequent acts; the degree of concentration of participation could be simply inferred from the marginals on a table such as Table 3.

That the participatory acts should form a Guttman scale accords with the general view of participation as an essentially unidimensional phenomenon. Under such circumstances the citizen who performed the relatively difficult (i.e., infrequent) act of contacting an official would be certain to engage in the easier act of attending a rally. But our analysis above indicates that participation is not a unidimensional phenomenon. The alternative modes of activity are useful for different purposes and are engaged in by citizens who have different attitudes toward politics. If this is the case, the citizen who contacts an official may not attend a political rally—even if that act is easier—simply because he or she is not interested in that kind of activity. Some citizens might specialize in partisan, others in nonpartisan, activity. Under such circumstances the more difficult political acts would be more dispersed throughout the population than the assumption of a Guttman-scale hierarchy would imply.

In Fig. 3 we present the proportion of citizens in each of six countries that is active beyond the vote, that is, engages in one or more of the other political activities, aside from voting, listed in Table 3. In Fig. 3 we also indicate the proportions that engage in at least one of the acts beyond the vote, in at least two acts, and so forth up to those who engage in at least six or more acts. Note that we say *at least* one and *at least* two, etc., indicating that the groups partially overlap: the proportions listed as engaging in at least one act contain those who engage in at least two, and so on. And we also compare the *actual proportions* active beyond the vote with the proportions that *one would find*, given the marginal distributions in Table 3, if political activity were maximally concentrated, that is, if the acts formed a perfect Guttman scale, in which those performing the less frequent acts always performed the more frequent acts.

The pattern is essentially the same in each nation. The assumption of maximum concentration of activities predicts fewer citizens active in at least

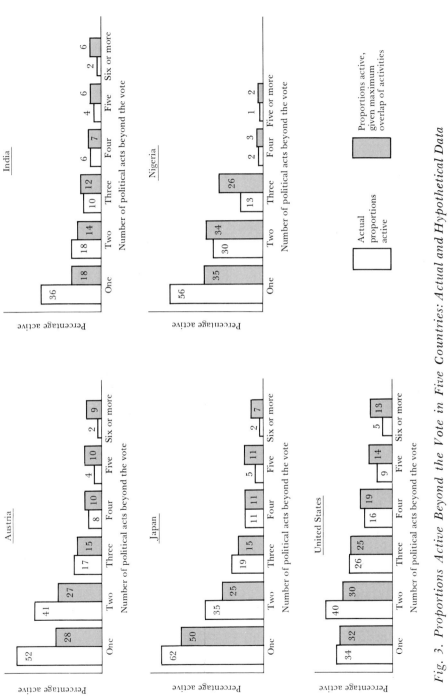

Fig. 3. Proportions Active Beyond the Vote in Five Countries: Actual and Hypothetical Data

one activity beyond the vote than is in fact the case and predicts more citizens in the most active category, performing six or more political acts, than is in fact the case. In Austria, for instance, the most frequent act beyond voting is membership in a political organization and is performed by 28 percent of the sample. Were political activity maximally concentrated, only 28 percent of the citizenry would be active beyond the vote. In fact, 52 percent engages in some activity beyond voting. The point is that many citizens who are not members of political organizations obviously engage in other kinds of activities which are less frequent than such membership; these citizens may contact officials, belong to community organizations, and so forth.

Or consider the other end of the graph for Austria. If participation were maximally concentrated, one would expect to find a much larger group of "superactivists"—people who engage in six or more activities beyond the vote —than one finds in fact. Maximum concentration of political activity predicts that 9 percent of the citizenry will fall in this supercategory; in fact, 2 percent does.

These graphs make a substantive point: participation does not form a fully hierarchical set of activities in which those who engage in one type of activity are certain to engage in other less costly and time consuming activities. If that were the case and participation were maximally concentrated, one would have the situation in each country reflected in the data in the shaded bars: in general, only a minority of the population would be active beyond voting, ranging from 50 percent in Japan down to 18 percent in India and averaging about 33 percent of the population across the five nations. A small but substantial proportion would be superactivists—an average of 7 percent across the nations. In fact, the proportions that are at least moderately active are larger— over 50 percent of the population in each nation. The exception is India, but there the proportion is still twice as large as the 18 percent predicted by maximum concentration. And the proportion that is superactivist averages about 2 percent. Thus, participation is more dispersed than the marginals might lead one to expect: a larger proportion of the populace in each case is at least moderately active and a smaller proportion intensely active.

But one ought not to exaggerate our argument in the other direction. The various political acts do not maximally overlap, but they are, nevertheless, positively correlated. Thus, though one finds fewer superactivists than one would expect if activity were maximally concentrated, one finds more such activists than if there were no underlying participation dimension.

THE PROCESS OF POLITICIZATION

We have thus far discussed participation per se—its nature, its components, how much there is of it. Such a discussion is a necessary preliminary to any analysis of the two most important questions asked about the relationship between political participation and other aspects of politics: What is it that leads to participation? What are the consequences of participation?

The two questions are closely linked. The answer to the question of what leads to participation will tell us who in fact participates: All citizens? Citizens from certain social classes? Citizens with certain attitudes? Depending on the process by which citizens come to participate, participant populations of particular compositions are created. If education plays a major role, the participant population comes heavily from the educated segments of society; if mobilization by parties plays a major role, the participant population comes more heavily from those affiliated with political parties. To the extent that participation induces leaders to respond to the participants, it makes a good deal of difference who participates.

Participation of citizens is, at least in the framework of Western European history, a relatively new idea. As Bendix puts it, "The eighteenth century appears as a major hiatus in Western European history. Prior to that time the masses of the people were entirely barred from the exercise of public rights. Since then they have become citizens and in this sense, participants in the political community" (Bendix, 1964).

The political history of Europe in the late nineteenth and twentieth centuries can be written as the history of the expansion of opportunities to participate in the political process. Bendix and Rokkan (1964) discuss the entry of the lower classes into the national political arena in terms of the extension of two social rights that set the stage for political participation (the right to form combinations and the right to an education), as well as in terms of the spread of political rights (the right to the franchise and to the secret ballot). But the extension of rights, as they point out, is not the same as the use of those rights. This is so for two reasons: (1) participation is a voluntary act—one can choose to participate or not—and (2) participation, especially effective participation (i.e., participation that makes a difference in the behavior of the governmental leaders), depends on the availability of a particular set of resources—time to take part, material resources where needed, information, and other skills. The crucial point is that after participation is made legally available to all, motivation to participate and the resources to make participation possible remain unequally distributed.

In this section of our essay we will focus on the differential participation that remains after rights to participate have been (more or less) universalized. Given legal equality with regard to the availability of opportunities to be politically active—universal suffrage, freedom to support, join, or form political organizations including political parties, freedom to petition the government—what is it that makes some citizens active and others not? The question as phrased is a micropolitical one: What forces lead one individual to be active while another is not? But the question also has implications of a macropolitical nature. The forces that affect the political activity of individuals and the particular distribution of those forces in a society determine the "shape" of the participant population; changes in those forces produce changes in the shape of the participant population.

Modernization, Urbanization, and Participation

Most studies have shown that participation is accompanied by a syndrome of supportive attitudes—a sense of political efficacy, information about politics, a sense of obligation to participate (Almond and Verba, 1963; Inkeles, 1967). In turn these civic attitudes are associated with certain socioeconomic characteristics: higher social status such as advanced education, increased income, higher-status occupations; involvement in voluntary associations; exposure to the mass media; exposure to an urban environment (Almond and Verba, 1963; Nie, Powell, and Prewitt, 1969; McCrone and Cnudde, 1967; Olsen, 1970; Inkeles, 1969). In short, political participation seems to be associated with "development" or "modernization" or whatever other term one wants to use for this general process.

Most studies have attempted to find from among the variables discussed above the combination that best fits the data on the process by which citizens come to participate. Such a method tends to be used—and to be necessary—when one is dealing with aggregate data across a large number of societies. But this approach has weaknesses: in particular, it does not allow sufficient differentiation among the various factors that go into the model. In general, the various factors such as education, urbanization, industrialization, and media exposure are all closely related to each other. A general analysis putting them together on the basis of measurements across a large number of countries makes it difficult to distinguish among them.

Let us consider the role of urbanization in relation to political activity. The study of urbanization illustrates why one must disentangle the various processes associated with "modernization."

The subject is one for which there are conflicting interpretations and conflicting data. On the one hand, various studies indicate that citizens in urban settings are likely to be more politically active. Milbrath provides an apt summary of these studies:

> Persons close to the center occupy an environmental position which naturally links them into the communications network involved in policy decisions for the society. They receive from and send more communications to other persons near the center. They have a higher rate of social interaction, and they are more active in groups than persons on the periphery. This central position increases the likelihood that they will develop personality traits, beliefs and attitudes which facilitate participation in politics. There are many more political stimuli in their environment, and this increases the number of opportunities for them to participate. . . .

One of the most thoroughly substantiated propositions in all of social science is that persons near the center of the society are more likely to participate in politics than persons near the periphery.... Persons near the center receive more stimuli enticing them to participate, and they receive more support from their peers when they do participate. (Milbrath, pp. 113–14; see also pp. 128–30)

And Milbrath cites twenty-eight studies to support this point.

On the other hand, a variety of studies have found little direct association between urbanization and political participation. This is particularly true when other social characteristics are taken into account—communications structure, social class, or organizational structure. The conclusion of Nie, Powell, and Prewitt is typical of these studies: "It appears that living in an urban environment has no significant effect on rates of national participation." (Nie, Powell, and Prewitt, 1969; Neubauer, 1967; McCrone and Cnudde, 1967).

Furthermore, the somewhat contradictory data are bolstered by somewhat contradictory models of what happens to citizens as they move from rural peripheral places to urban centers. One model, which can be called the "mobilization model," predicts an increase in participation. Another, which can be called the "decline-of-community model," predicts a decrease.

The mobilization model. This model predicts increased participation as one of the concomitants of urbanization. The quotation from Milbrath summarizes not only the findings of empirical studies but also the reasons offered for the increase in participation in the urban setting. The key variable appears to be the stimulation that comes from such an environment: exposure to more communications, interaction with others involved in politics, support from peers for such activity, and the development of personality traits compatible with political activity (Deutsch, 1961; Lerner, 1958).

The decline-of-community model. This alternative model predicts the decline of participation as citizens move from the smallness and intimacy of town or village to the massive impersonality of the city. In the small town the community is of a manageable size. Citizens can know the ropes of politics, know whom to contact, and know each other so that they can form political groups. In the larger unit politics is more complicated, impersonal, and distant. In addition, "modernization" shatters political units. What were once relatively independent communities providing the social, economic, political, and cultural services that individuals need become small towns in a mass society. Such communities no longer have clear economic borders as citizens begin to commute to work. They have more permeable social boundaries as recreational and educational facilities move out of the community, and they cease to be well-bounded political units as local services become more dependent on outside governmental authorities.

All these changes, according to the decline-of-community model, should reduce the level of participation within the community. For one thing, the government of the local community loses its importance. Local participation becomes less and less meaningful. Furthermore, the attention of individuals becomes more diffuse. They no longer concentrate on their local community. Rather, they are exposed to a wider political realm where meaningful participation is much more difficult because of its larger size and greater complexity (Cole, 1921, 1920; Dahl, 1967).

That two alternative models can exist side by side is not unexpected, given the fact that the study of this subject is in its early stages. But the conflicting testimony of the data is harder to comprehend. We can suggest three reasons why contradictory findings appear. First, there is failure to distinguish adequately among community types. Many studies focus on the size of the community as the measure of urbanization. But the size of a community does not tell about the degree to which the community provides a stimulating urban environment, nor does it tell the extent to which it is an independent, relatively self-governing entity. The small suburb is quite different from the isolated town of similar size. The second reason for conflicting data is that small towns, suburbs, and big cities are not only different sociopolitical environments, but they also contain people who differ—in their socioeconomic level, ethnicity, and age. If one finds higher activity rates in cities than in the countryside, is that the result of the urban environment or of the fact that urban dwellers are likely to be of higher socioeconomic status than rural people? Unless one separates the effects of individual characteristics from the effects of the environment on participation, one will not understand the impact, if any, of the community. The third reason for conflicting data is implicit in our discussion of the several modes of participation. Different modes of activity should be more or less sensitive to the nature of the community environment.

In an analysis of political activity in a number of American communities we have attempted to take these problems into account. Several conclusions clearly emerge. (See Verba and Nie, 1972, Chapter 13, for a full discussion.)

1. Correcting for the demographic compositions of different types of communities makes a difference. The high rate of political activity found in American suburbs and the low rate in rural areas appear to be a function of the kinds of people who live there, not of the nature of the community. On the average there is more activity in suburbs than in small, isolated towns, but if one controls for the demographic characteristics of the residents the opposite turns out to be the case. That is, if one compares individuals of similar social characteristics—educational levels, occupation, etc.—one finds more activity in relatively smaller and more isolated places.

2. The data tend generally to support the decline-of-community model. In particular it appears that the "boundedness" of the community is closely related to how active citizens are. Table 4 presents some data on political participation rates in two kinds of communities of roughly equal size—small isolated cities and small suburbs. (The figures represent scores on standardized scales measuring various kinds of participation. The scores control for the demographic differences between residents of the two types of communities. See Verba and Nie, 1972, Chapter 13, for details.) The mobilization model would predict more activity in the small suburb since it is close to the more stimulating environment of the large city. The decline-of-community model would predict the opposite since the suburb lacks just those characteristics of "boundedness" that the small isolated city gains from the fact of its isolation. The data clearly support the decline-of-community model. On each measure of participation one finds more participation in the isolated city than in the small suburb. This holds even for participation in national politics, suggesting a possible spillover effect from activity on the local level. In short, the data support an interpretation that the nature of the community does make a difference in participation over and above the effects of the characteristics of the individual citizens who live there. The difference it makes is related to the degree to which the community is isolated enough so that the citizen has a well-defined political unit within which to participate.

TABLE 4   Isolated cities and small suburbs compared *

Mean participation rates (corrected)	Isolated cities	Small suburbs
Overall activity	26	−22
Voting	−10	−22
Campaign activity	23	−24
Communal activity	32	−7
Particularized contact	57	−21
Local activity	8	−61
National activity	15	−16

* Student's *t* indicates all comparisons on this table are significantly different.

Source: Verba and Nie, *Participation in America,* p. 243.

We can look more closely at the factor of boundedness. The decline-of-community model clearly predicts that participation will be lower in places that are not well bounded, for the simple reason that the attention of the potential participant is diffused across a large number of places. The citizen lives in one place, works in another, and may take part in social life elsewhere.

The politics of each place may be equally relevant, as there is no single center on which to focus his or her participation.

In the United States we have tested these expectations directly. In a number of communities we gathered data on a wide range of community characteristics. Several measures tap the degree of boundedness of the community. One such indicator is the degree to which governmental services are located in the community. A second measure is of the density of voluntary associations within the community, that is, the number of such associations adjusted for the size of the community. A third is of the extent to which citizens both live and work in the community, a distinction based on the proportion of residents that lives in the community but commutes to work and the proportion that works in the community but lives outside it. Finally, we have two measures of communication: one of the richness of the internal communication channels (are there newspapers or other media specific to the community?) and one of the richness of external media (how available are external newspapers or radio and TV stations?). The more internal communication there is, the greater the community boundedness. The more external communication there is, the less the community boundedness.

Each of these indicators relates to the degree to which the community can be considered to have a life of its own. In Table 5 we relate these characteristics to the degree of local participation within the community (corrected for the socioeconomic characteristics of the citizenry). It is clear from the table that in all cases communities that are well bounded have more local participation than those that are not. In some cases the difference is quite striking. In relation to the availability of organizations in the community, about one standard deviation on the participtation scale separates the most from the least well bounded communities. The data on the measure of commuting are even more striking. The amount of commuting into and out of the community has a quite skewed distribution, separating off at either end a few sharply different communities—one set in which very few citizens both live and work in the community and another in which there are few commuters either in or out. In places where the population has a high proportion of commuters the rate of local participation is over one standard deviation below the average for places where there are few commuters. And though the availability of internal communication does not raise local participation much, the existence of external media significantly depresses local activity, just as the decline-of-community model would predict. When one remembers that we are dealing with rates of participation corrected for the other social characteristics of citizens, these data offer strong support for that model.

3. The last point documented by our analysis of the difference in rate of political activity across types of community is that different modes of participation are differentially affected by the nature of the community. The decline-of-com-

TABLE 5   "Boundedness" of the community and local activity: corrected scores

	Less well bounded ←			→ More well bounded	Ratio
Availability of services in the community	Few −19 [a] (35) [b]			Many 24 (29)	.23 [c]
Number of available voluntary organiza- tions per capita	Few −38 (16)	Some −19 (16)	Many −4 (6)	Very many 61 (16)	.34 [d]
Amount of work force that commutes in or out to work	Many −62 (5)		Some 2 (48)	Few 60 (7)	.28 [c]
Density of internal communications channels	Low −5 (33)			High 6 (28)	.09
Density of external communication channels	High −26 (32)			Low 3 (28)	.29 [d]

[a] Figures are mean corrected participation scores on a local participation index.
[b] Figures in parentheses are the number of communities in that category.
[c] Significant at the .05 level.
[d] Significant at the .01 level.
Source: Verba and Nie, *Participation in America*, p. 245.

munity model holds best for what we have called communal activity—non-partisan activities, often cooperative and informal in nature, to deal with community problems. These activities are most frequent in relatively small and well-bounded places. On the other hand the situation is more mixed in relation to activity in political campaigns. For this kind of activity there is less difference across community types; if anything, there is some advantage to the less well bounded places.

These analyses have been conducted most fully on data from the United States. Some comparable data are reported for Japan and India in Fig. 4, which displays mean levels of campaign and communal participation for rural and urban communities in the two countries. The participation scores are corrected for the confounding individual effects of socioeconomic status, sex, and other social characteristics. The classification of the communities as rural and urban is crude. What is reported in the table is the mean corrected participation rates for small rural isolated places and for urban centers (participation scores for intermediary types of communities are not presented).

Crude as the analysis is at this stage, the findings closely parallel those encountered in the United States. The decline-of-community model closely fits

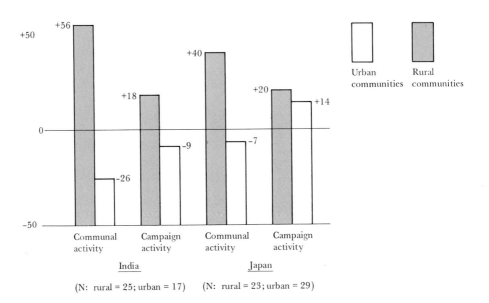

Fig. 4. Mean Activity Rates in Rural and Urban Communities: India and Japan

the data vis-à-vis communal participation. In India and Japan the increased complexity and size of large urban population centers as well as the loss of face-to-face interaction seem to produce a steep decline in the rates in which average citizens come together in attempts to solve community problems. On the other hand, the patterns in regard to campaign activity are more mixed. The data support the mobilization model in India but not in Japan. In Japan both modes of participation occur more frequently in rural communities. However, where the difference in rates of communal participation between rural and urban communities is dramatic, the corresponding disparity in campaign activity is relatively small.

In short, the comparative data are consistent with a generalization to the effect that participation dependent on cooperation among citizens declines rather drastically as communities become larger and lose their distinctiveness.

WHO PARTICIPATES?

In no society is the activist portion of the population a representative sample of the population as a whole. In most societies that have been studied and for most kinds of political activity, a person is more likely to be politically active if he is male, middle-aged (rather than young or old), relatively wealthy, well educated, and, perhaps, from the dominant ethnic, religious, or racial groups. This means that if political leaders pay attention to the preferences of those who are active (which is likely, since it is the activists who are communicating those preferences), they will pay attention to views of particular people with a particular set of problems and they may ignore the preferences of large segments of the population which are inactive.

Consider, for example, some data from the United States. In our study of participation in the United States (Verba and Nie, 1972, Chapter 6) we divided the population into various kinds of activists. We found that about 22 percent of the population could be considered inactives and about 11 percent "complete activists," that is, engaged in all kinds of activity.

Figure 5 presents some data on the extent to which particular social categories—those with higher education, Catholics, blacks, women, etc.—are over

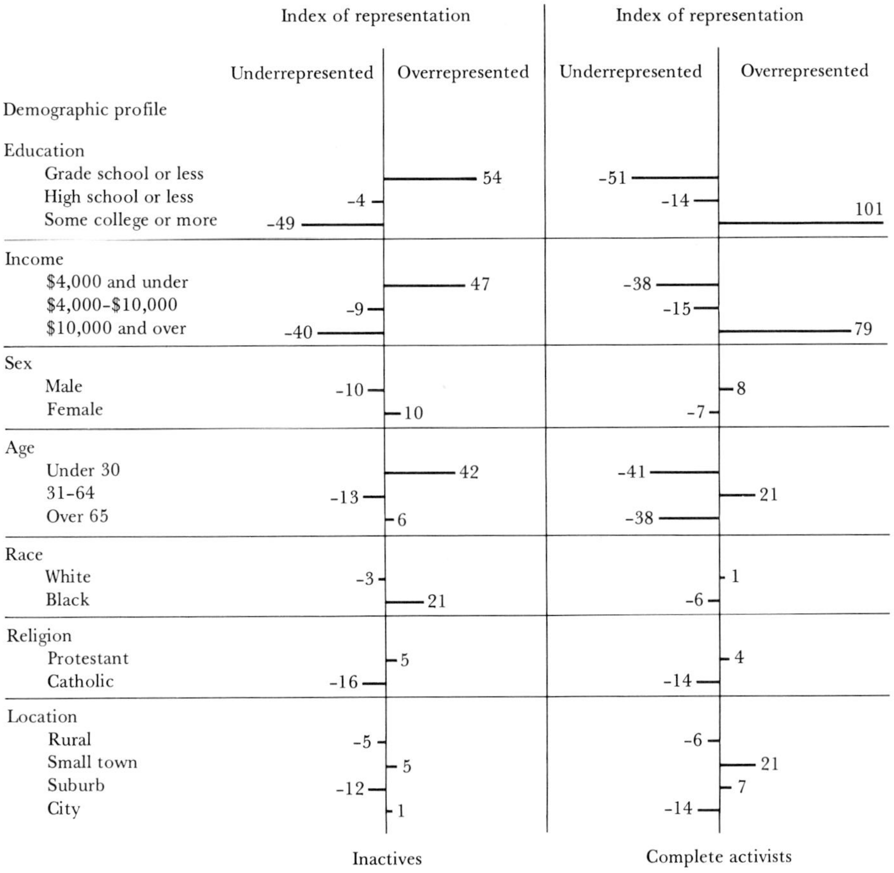

Demographic profile	Inactives (Index of representation)	Complete activists (Index of representation)
Education		
Grade school or less	54	−51
High school or less	−4	−14
Some college or more	−49	101
Income		
$4,000 and under	47	−38
$4,000–$10,000	−9	−15
$10,000 and over	−40	79
Sex		
Male	−10	8
Female	10	−7
Age		
Under 30	42	−41
31–64	−13	21
Over 65	6	−38
Race		
White	−3	1
Black	21	−6
Religion		
Protestant	5	4
Catholic	−16	−14
Location		
Rural	−5	−6
Small town	5	21
Suburb	−12	7
City	1	−14

Source: Verba and Nie, *Participation in America*, pp. 98, 100.

Fig. 5. Demographic Profile of Inactives and Complete Activists in the United States

or underrepresented in each activist type. The measure of over and underrepresentation is simply the ratio of the proportion of a particular social category found among the inactives (or among the complete activists) to the proportion of that social category in the population as a whole.

This figure clearly illustrates a point that is already well documented in the literature. Those citizens with lower social status—low levels of education or income—are greatly overrepresented among those who are politically inactive, while the upper-status groups are underrepresented among the inactives. This is clearly seen in the top two sections of Fig. 5, where the data on education and income are presented. To take a concrete example, consider the data on education. Citizens with no high school education formed 28 percent of our sample, but they are 43 percent of the inactives, leading to an overrepresentation score of +54. Similar results would have been obtained had we used a measure of occupational status.

Additional patterns of over and underrepresentation can be discerned: men are somewhat underrepresented among the inactives, women somewhat overrepresented. Young people are quite a bit more likely to be inactive, as to a lesser extent are those over 65, while those in the middle years are somewhat less likely to be in the inactive group. Blacks are substantially overrepresented among the inactives, whites a bit underrepresented. There is some difference between Protestants and Catholics, with the latter less likely to be inactive. And as far as place of residence goes, the inactives tend slightly to come from small towns.

The passive citizen, thus, comes disproportionately from these groups: those with lower social status, blacks, the young, and, to a lesser extent, women, Protestants, and those who live in small towns. The complete activists are the mirror image of the inactives and come from upper-status groups. In addition, complete activists come disproportionately from those in the middle-age groups and from small towns. Catholics are somewhat less likely to be complete activists and there is a small (but quite small) tendency for Blacks and women to be underrepresented among the complete activists.

Analysis of data from other nations would show patterns of over and underrepresentation of various social categories among the inactives and the complete activists. In most nations the overrepresentation of men among the complete activists and the overrepresentation of women among the inactives is much more apparent than in the United States (Verba, Nie, and Kim, forthcoming).

Socioeconomic Level and Political Activity

We would like to explore more fully one aspect of this problem: the extent to which the activists in a society come disproportionately from the more advantaged members of the society—from the wealthier and better educated citizens. The extent to which this happens, we assume, will have major impact on the kinds of messages communicated to political leaders by political activists and on the kinds of policies that leaders pursue in response to such messages. As the data in Fig. 5 indicate, the activists in the United States come disproportionately from those who are advantaged in socioeconomic terms. Closer analysis of the data indicates that this overrepresentation of the "haves" among the activists derives from two sets of forces. On the one hand, individuals of high socioeconomic status are found to have attitudes that motivate them to be politically active. They are more interested in politics, have a greater sense of political efficacy, and feel a greater sense of obligation to be a participant. In addition they have more well-developed cognitive skills. These attitudes make it likely that all else being equal, the upper status citizen will be more politically active (Verba and Nie, 1972, Chapter 8).

In addition to these motivational forces that act on the individual citizen, we found that a variety of other forces in American society tended to increase the participatory advantage held by the more affluent and better educated citizens. In particular we focussed on the way in which two sets of institutions mobilize citizens to political activity: political parties and voluntary associations. In each case we found that the ways in which these institutions mobilized political activists gave an extra boost to the political activity of the haves in comparison with the have-nots.

Voluntary associations were found to have a significant effect on the political activity rates of their members. Since voluntary association members come disproportionately from the upper-status groups in the United States, this boost in political activity, in turn, goes disproportionately to such groups. The result is that the participation gap between the haves and the have-nots is increased (Verba and Nie, 1972, Chapter 11).

The parties in the United States, on the other hand, do not draw their supporters disproportionately from the upper social strata. While the Republicans do attract their supporters from the more affluent and better educated, this is counterbalanced by the fact that the more numerous supporters of the Democratic party come disproportionately from those who are somewhat lower on the socioeconomic scale. But both of the parties mobilize to political activity those of their supporters who are more affluent and better educated. The result, as with voluntary associations, is that parties give a disproportional boost to the political activity of the haves (Verba and Nie, 1972, Chapter 12).

Socioeconomic Status and Participation in Cross-National Perspective

The analysis of data from the United States indicates that socioeconomic advantage (SEA) and political activity are quite closely related. Comparison with other nations shows some striking cross-national variation in the strength of that relationship. Table 6 reports the correlations between our overall scale of political participation and a scale of socioeconomic advantage in seven countries. The scale of political activity is a composite measure of the various

TABLE 6   Correlations between socioeconomic
level and participation scales in seven countries

	Correlation
Austria	.11
India	.36
Japan	.12
Netherlands	.18
Nigeria	.24
United States	.35
Yugoslavia	.35

modes of participation. The scale of socioeconomic level is a composite of the individual's educational and income levels (plus a measure of the ownership of certain material possessions in those nations in which income measurements are particularly difficult; for details on these scales see Verba, Nie, and Kim, forthcoming). As one can see, the relationship is stronger in the United States, India, and Yugoslavia than it is in Austria and Japan, with Nigeria and the Netherlands falling somewhere in between.

The distinction among the nations is, we believe, an important one. It means that the activist portions of the population in India, the United States, and Yugoslavia are less representative of the population as a whole (in socioeconomic terms) than is the case in Japan and Austria. This fact can be seen in Fig. 6, which illustrates the implications of the correlation coefficients in Table 6 in terms of the composition of the participant stratum of each society.

Figure 6 divides the population in each nation into six equal-sized groups based on their rate of political activity, from the least active sixth of the population to the most active. Within each activity level we show the distribution of citizens from the top, middle, and lower third of the SEA scale. If each activist level were representative of the population as a whole in SEA terms we would find each activity level containing one-third from each of the SEA levels. In fact, we find, as the relationship between SEA and participation led us to expect, that the most active citizens come disproportionately from the haves, the least active from the have-nots. But the variation among nations in the strength of the SEA/participation relationship is also reflected in the data. Consider the top participant stratum in each nation (the far left bar on each respective bar graph). In Austria and Japan that activist stratum comes disproportionately from the "have" portion of the population but only to a minor extent—about 40 percent rather than the 33 percent one would find if the activists were representative of the population as a whole. In the other nations the top activists contain a majority from the upper third of the socioeconomic

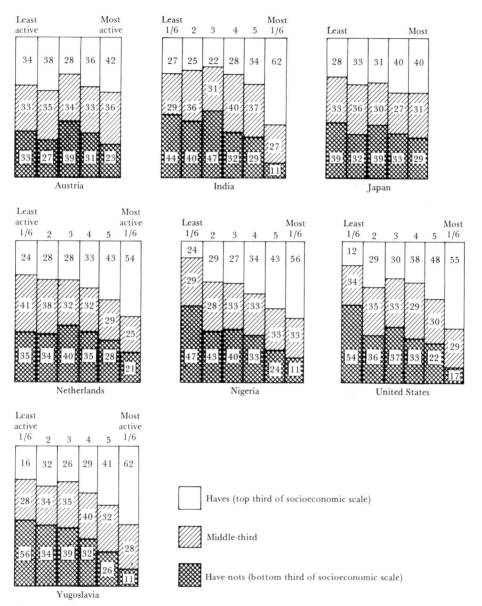

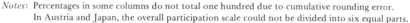

Notes: Percentages in some columns do not total one hundred due to cumulative rounding error.
    In Austria and Japan, the overall participation scale could not be divided into six equal parts.

Fig. 6. Class Composition of Participant Groups for Seven Countries, by Percentage

distribution, and in India and Yugoslavia over 60 percent of the activists come from that SΓ \ stratum.

Figure 6 illustrates a potential consequence of the varying relationships between SEA and participation. In Austria and Japan the activists are more representative of the population than in nations in which there is a closer SEA/participation relationship. Insofar as participation is the mechanism for communicating citizen preferences to political leaders, the activists in Austria and Japan are more likely to communicate the preferences of a wide cross section of the population than is the case in nations in which the activists come more disproportionately from the advantaged members of the population.

Furthermore, evidence that these are "real" differences across the nations, not merely the results of our particular samples, can be found if we turn to an independent data file we have on local political leaders in these same seven nations. These interviews allow us to test whether similar differences exist across nations in the extent to which local leaders come disproportionately from the more advantaged groups. Table 7 presents some data on this.

TABLE 7   Advantage and participation: cross-section and leader samples compared for seven countries

	Cross-section data file		Local leader data file	
	Correlations of socioeco- nomic advan- tage and participation	Percentage of activist citizens who come from top third of socioeconomic advantage scale	Percentage of local leaders who come from top third of socioeconomic advantage scale	Percentage of local *elected* officials who come from top third of socio- economic ad- vantage scale
India	.36	66	99	99
Yugoslavia	.35	62	87	87
United States	.35	55	89	87
Netherlands	.18	54	82	76
Nigeria	.24	56	97	96
Japan	.12	40	69	50
Austria	.11	42	66	64

On this table we repeat some data from Table 6 and Fig. 6: the correla- tions between advantage and participation found in our cross-section inter- views and the proportion of the activists that comes from the top third of our socioeconomic advantage scale. We rank the nations in terms of the strength of the advantage/participation relationship. Next to it we place some data from our leader interviews: the proportions of our sample of local leaders that fall in the top third of our scale of socioeconomic advantage.[1] The latter is a good indication of the extent to which local leaders are "unrepresentative" of the population as a whole in terms of socioeconomic advantage. And we present that information for all the local leaders in our sample as well as for those who are locally elected officials.

As one might expect, local leaders come predominantly from the upper socioeconomic group in all seven nations. If they came proportionately from each advantage level one would find 33 percent of the leaders coming from the top third of the socioeconomic advantage scale. In fact, the proportions are much higher in each nation. But what is most striking is that the ranking of the nations in terms of the extent to which the local leaders come disproportionately from the "haves" is almost identical with the ranking found within the cross-section sample of the extent to which advantage and participation are related. Note in particular the contrast in terms of leader background between the countries in which the advantage/participation relationship found in the cross-section data was strong (India, the United States, Yugoslavia) and those in which that relationship was weak (Japan, Austria), with the Netherlands in between.[2] The data offer some important confirmation that what we find as a pattern in our cross-section interviews is reflected in terms of the social groups from which local leaders are recruited.

The leadership data are interesting from another point of view. They suggest that the cross-national differences found among the mass public in the strength of the relationship between socioeconomic level and political participation have consequences in terms of who is recruited into leadership positions. It is likely that the activist portion of the mass public forms the recruitment pool from which political leaders are drawn. And the more that the activist portion of the public overrepresents the "haves" rather than the "have-nots," the more will this tendency be exaggerated in the leadership ranks.

The Process of Politicization

The cross-national differences in the strength of the relationship between socioeconomic level and participation pose a most interesting puzzle. What are the sources of these differences? The similarity among a set of nations as heterogeneous as India, the United States, and Yugoslavia only heightens the puzzle.

We can only sketch out our attempt to explain the differences among the nations. At the time of this writing a full scale analysis is still in process. But an outline of our explanation will be useful because it will allow us to illustrate more generally the kinds of processes that determine who becomes a political activist in a society. The variation across nations in the strength of the relationship between socioeconomic level and political activity is, we believe, due to the interaction of two processes. One process operates on the individual level and operates uniformly across nations. The other process operates on the institutional level and is more contingent on the variations across nations in institutional pattern.

The individual level process can be summed up in a simple generalization: all else being equal, citizens at higher socioeconomic levels will be more active in politics than those at lower levels. The generalization is consistent with most of the data we have seen from a variety of nations. (For instance, see the studies listed in Milbrath, 1965, pp. 114–28.)

The reason the haves are generally more active than the have-nots appears to be that higher socioeconomic status brings with it a set of motivations which makes it more likely that an individual will become a participant. The more educated or more affluent individual is more likely to be interested in politics, more likely to have a sense of political efficacy, and more likely to have the necessary monetary and other resources that allow him or her to be active politically.

TABLE 8   Correlations between socioeconomic level and political involvement in six countries

Austria	.36	Netherlands	.31
India	.39	Nigeria	.36
Japan	.34	United States	.36

The data in Table 8 support this cross-national generalization. The table reports the relationship between a scale of political interest and socioeconomic level in the various nations we have been considering. Unlike the relationships between socioeconomic level and political activity, the relationship between socioeconomic level and political interest shows relatively little variability across the nations. In each case the relationship is relatively strong, for survey data of this sort. In addition to having the motivations reflected in Table 8, those with higher socioeconomic status are likely to have resources that facilitate their political activity. These include material resources useful for political activity as well as cognitive resources such as information about politics and knowledge of the political ropes.

These generalizations about the motivations and resources of upper-status individuals cannot, of course, explain the *variation* across the nations in the strength of the participation/socioeconomic-level relationship. But the nature of the generalization gives some clues as to where to search for those additional forces that result in the differences among the nations. The generalization about the relationship between socioeconomic level and participation refers to characteristics of individuals which make it more likely that a person of higher socioeconomic level will *volunteer* to participate given the opportunity to do so. The additional forces that modify that likelihood can be thought of as constraints on these propensities; they inhibit the activity of some citizens below what it would ordinarily be if the individual forces associated with socioeconomic status were operating or they stimulate the participation of other citizens above that level.

The constraints can be of several kinds. In our research we have focussed largely on institutional constraints—the activities of particular institutions such as political parties and voluntary associations in mobilizing citizen activity (or inhibiting it). In addition we have considered the impact of political ideologies on citizen activity. These constraints, it should be noted, do not necessarily reduce the participation disparity between the haves and the have-nots. The impact of these constraints on the participation disparity depends on who is constrained and in which direction. If institutions mobilize lower-status citizens to activity levels beyond those that their socioeconomic level would predict or inhibit the activity of upper-status citizens below the levels that their socioeconomic level would predict, the participation disparity between the haves and the have-nots will be reduced. If institutions do the opposite—stimulate upper-status citizens to even higher levels of activity or inhibit the activity of lower-status citizens—the participation disparity between the haves and the have-nots will be increased. In short, such institutions as political parties and voluntary associations can operate to increase or diminish political inequality within a society. They do this by changing the degree of inequality which would exist if only the individual forces that lead to the greater participation of the haves were operating.

Testing for the existence of these two sets of forces and estimating their relative impact poses somewhat of a problem. Ideally one would want to observe citizens unconstrained by institutional forces to see if their activity rates were predictable solely on the basis of their individual socioeconomic characteristics. Obviously we cannot create such a political vacuum by removing, for instance, the Austrian parties to see how participation appears in their absence. But there are several ways in which we can attempt to validate our argument.

In the first place we can compare a variety of modes of political activity and involvement. Certain kinds of political activity ought to be more susceptible to institutional inhibition than others, either because institutional channels are needed to pursue that activity or because institutions might be motivated actively to try to mobilize such activity. Other acts ought to be more immune from institutional constraints. If our model is correct, this means that for the latter kind of political involvement we ought to find a fairly high degree of cross-national uniformity, in that the individual forces (which, we hypothesize, operate uniformly across nations) ought to produce a similarly strong relationship between socioeconomic status and political activity in each case. For activity that is more susceptible to institutional constraint we ought to find greater variability across nations in the strength of that relationship, paralleling differences in the institutional structure of the various nations.

TABLE 9 Correlations between socioeconomic level and various political acts in seven countries

	Overall activity scale	Political participation measures			Political involvement measures	
		Voting	Campaign activity	Communal activity	Political discussion	Political interest
Austria	.11	—.06	.13	.16	.36	.36
India	.36	.05	.31	.26	.42	.39
Japan	.12	.02	.07	.12	.28	.34
Netherlands	.18	.08	.09	.23	.36	.31
Nigeria	.24	.10	*	.28	†	.36
Yugoslavia	.35	.19	**	.21**	†	.45
United States	.35	.24	.30	.29	.36	.37
Range of correlations	.25	.30	.24	.17	.14	.14

* No measure of campaign activity in Nigeria.
** Combination of communal and campaign activity.
† No measure of discussion in Nigeria or Yugoslavia.

The data in Table 9 are generally quite consistent with this expectation. We compare the correlations between socioeconomic level on the one hand and several modes of political activity on the other. In addition, we provide data on the relationship between socioeconomic level and two measures of political involvement—political discussion (based on questions about discussions of politics in various settings) and of political interest (based on questions about the individual's concern for political matters). Compare voting or campaign activity with political discussion and political interest. In the latter case, in which we expect little institutional constraint since one does not need specific institutional channels to discuss politics or to be interested in politics, we find the expected cross-national uniformity with all correlations relatively strong and fairly similar. In the case of voting and campaign activity, in which we would expect institutional channels to be useful for political activity and institutions likely to attempt to mobilize citizens to that activity, we find greater cross-national differences in the strength of the relationship. The relationship of communal activity to socioeconomic level falls in between these two sets of relationships. Since communal activity consists of a combination of individual acts and acts carried out in concert with informal and formal groups, this middle result is not unexpected.

The data are thus consistent with our expectation that individual-level forces would operate in a uniform manner across nations if it were not for the constraining forces of other institutions.

Political Parties and Political Participation

We have not yet considered the role of institutions directly. This will give a better test of our model and also indicate how institutions can modify the relationship between socioeconomic level and political activity. We cannot present the full array of data needed to trace the impact of institutions on political activity (this will be dealt with in Verba, Nie, and Kim, forthcoming), but we can illustrate this process by presenting some data on the role of political parties. We simplify the data by lumping all parties in a nation together (i.e., asking how the party system as a whole affects the participation disparity between the haves and the have-nots) and by concentrating our attention on campaign activity. A fuller exposition would require us to consider different types of parties, alternative modes of activity, and the role of voluntary associations.

How can institutions such as political parties affect the relationship between socioeconomic level and political activity? The *extent* to which the institutional constraint of parties modifies that relationship depends on (1) the degree to which parties *dominate the channels* of political participation and (2) the nature of the *population base* from which they draw citizens into political activity.

1. The greater the extent to which parties dominate the channels of participation, the more effect will they have on modifying the individual-level relationship between socioeconomic level and participation. This is simply to state that the more the voluntary aspect of participation is suppressed, the more the relationship between socioeconomic advantage and participation will change. Parties can dominate the channels to political activity in one of two ways. One, an affiliation with such an organization may be necessary for political activity. If so, the unaffiliated citizen, no matter what his or her level of education or income (or concomitant level of motivation and resources), will be *less* active than if the channels to political activity were "free." Unaffiliated citizens will be "locked out" of politics. Conversely, party affiliation may be *sufficient* to mobilize affiliated citizens to political activity. In this case the affiliated citizen will be more active than his or her level of education and income would predict; he or she will be "pulled into" politics.

2. The extent of the change in the relationship between socioeconomic level and participation also depends on the population base from which the political parties in a society draw their support. Some parties have indistinct population bases; they draw their support from all segments of society. Others have quite distinct bases from which they draw their support; they have particular attachments to a specific population segment identified by occupation, religion, ethnicity, region, or some other characteristic. The greater the extent to which parties and organizations have distinctive population bases, the greater is the potential that they will modify the socioeconomic level/participation relation-

ship. This is because they will stimulate or inhibit the participation of groups that are likely to have distinct locations on the socioeconomic advantage scale. This will have a greater effect on changing the shape of the relationship of status to participation than would be the case if they stimulated or inhibited participation for citizens across all socioeconomic levels.

The extent to which the activities of parties will modify the socioeconomic level/participation relationship depends, thus, on the degree to which they dominate the channels of participation and on the degree to which they draw their support from distinctive population bases. But this does not yet tell us *how* they will change the shape of that relationship. This depends on the location on the socioeconomic scale of the groups stimulated to participate or inhibited from participation. If parties stimulate the participation of social groups low on the socioeconomic scale, the participation disparity between the haves and the have-nots will tend to be reduced. On the other hand a party might have a population base located high on the socioeconomic scale. If the participation of such a group is stimulated, the disparity in participation between the haves and the have-nots will increase.

Figure 7 contains data relevant to these concerns. We graph the relationship between a scale of campaign activity and a scale of socioeconomic level for each of five nations. On each graph we plot the relationship between socioeconomic level and campaign activity for each of three groups of respondents, categorized by the strength of their party affiliation—for those with no affiliation, those with weak party identification, and those who identify strongly with a political party. (Fuller explanation of the measures will be found in Verba, Nie, and Kim, forthcoming.) In addition we place a "minimal activity line" on the graphs. Scale scores below that line reflect at best a most marginal involvement in such activity.

The graphs provide some important information relevant to our concerns. They indicate the effects of both party affiliation and socioeconomic level on political activity. The farther apart the lines reflecting the activity rates of the strong partisans and the independents, the greater the relationship of party to campaign activity. The steeper the slope of the various lines, the greater the relationship of socioeconomic level to campaign activity.

Several points can be noted about the data in Fig. 7. For one thing, in those nations in which there is a weak relationship between socioeconomic level and campaign activity—Austria, Japan, and the Netherlands—the relationship between party affiliation and campaign activity is stronger. The average "distance" in campaign activity scores between the independents and strong partisans is greater in those three nations than in the United States or India. This suggests that the potential exists in those three nations for party affiliation to modify the relationship between socioeconomic level and individual-level political activity.

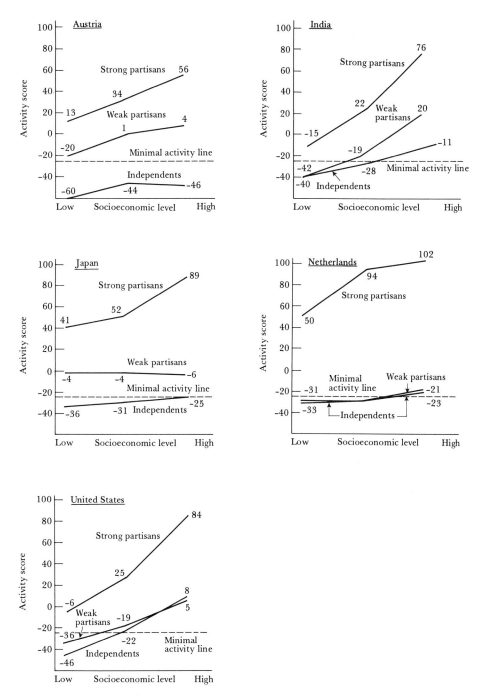

Fig. 7. Socioeconomic Level and Campaign Activity for Strong Partisans, Weak Partisans, and Independents in Five Countries (no measure of campaign activity in Nigeria; in Yugoslavia campaign and communal activity form a combined mode)

How in fact this happens can be seen by considering the graphs for Austria, the Netherlands, and Japan. They all have one characteristic in common: people who have no partisan affiliation (the independents) score very low on the campaign activity scale no matter what their socioeconomic level. In each case, affiliation with a party appears to be a necessary condition for political activity. Of particular importance are those in the upper category of the socioeconomic hierarchy who have no partisan affiliation. In each case their activity level is at or below the minimal activity line. Their high socioeconomic level should make them active, but their lack of partisan ties reduces their activity.

Compare this situation to that in the United States or India. In these two nations there is a difference in the rate of campaign activity between independents who are low on the socioeconomic scale and those who are high on that scale. In this sense, the absence of a partisan affiliation does not erase differences based on socioeconomic level. Partisan affiliation is not a necessary condition for campaign activity. This can be seen by considering those independents who come from the top portion of the socioeconomic scale. In both nations they participate well above the minimal activity line (though in India they score below the population mean and in the United States above that mean).

The difference between the two sets of nations is clearest when one considers the independents. For strong partisans in all five nations there is a positive slope to the relationship between activity and socioeconomic level. Those strong partisans who are from the upper reaches of the socioeconomic scale outparticipate those lower down on that scale. In this sense, partisan affiliation does not eliminate the effects of socioeconomic level among the strong partisans in the way it eliminates those effects among the independents.

Nevertheless, there is a difference between Austria, Japan, and the Netherlands on the one hand and the United States and India on the other. In the former three nations those strong partisans who come from the lower level of the socioeconomic scale participate well above the mean for the population as a whole (particularly in the Netherlands and Japan).

In the United States and India the lower-status strong partisans participate below the mean for the population as a whole. In other words, in the former three nations the fact of strong party affiliation appears to overcome lower socioeconomic status to bring that group into political activity. In India and the United States the fact of lower socioeconomic status seems more important.

The contrast between the two sets of nations helps explain the ways in which parties may affect the participation gap between the haves and the have-nots. In those societies in which the relationship between socioeconomic level and campaign activity is weak, the political parties appear to contribute to the weakness of that relationship by so dominating the channels of political activity that those not affiliated with a party are inactive no matter what their socioeconomic level. In particular, those with high socioeconomic status but no partisan affiliation are reduced to levels of activity below what their socio-economic attributes would predict. Among the strong partisans the participation disparity between the haves and the have-nots is not eliminated. But the data suggest that those strong partisans who come from the lower socioeconomic levels are pulled into higher levels of political activity than they would ordinarily be in.[3]

Though we cannot present data on the other modes of political activity, they offer some interesting contrasts to campaign activity. When it comes to voting, political parties in all countries tend to mobilize the political activity of citizens from across the various socioeconomic levels. Those who have no party affiliation are equally inactive no matter what their socioeconomic status; those who have a strong affiliation are equally active no matter what their socioeconomic level. In this sense, partisanship appears to approximate a necessary and sufficient condition for voting. The one exception to this pattern is found in the United States, where socioeconomic level makes a difference in voting turnout among those who are affiliated with a party as well as among the unaffiliated.

On the other hand, when it comes to communal activity one finds that partisan affiliation does not eliminate the effects of socioeconomic level in any of the nations, either among the independents or among the strong partisans. This is, of course, consistent with our expectation that such activity would be freer of institutional constraint from parties than would campaign activity or voting.

The Social Bases of Party Support

We can take the argument one step further by asking why it is that the parties in Austria, Japan, and the Netherlands act to reduce the participation disparity between the haves and the have-nots. Again, we can only summarize a more involved study. The generalization that appears consistent with our data is that parties mobilize political activists in ways that reduce the participation disparity between haves and have-nots, where (1) there are clear poles of political contestation in a society and (2) the political parties in the society (or at least some of them) have fairly clear connections with one or the other of the contesting groups.

In those nations in which parties reduce the participation disparity between the haves and the have-nots we find that (1) there are particular population groups that have quite close connections with a party; (2) these groups also form one of the main poles of political contestation in the society; (3) these groups overparticipate, that is, they are more active in politics than one would expect given their socioeconomic characteristics; and (4) their participation is closely related to their party affiliation, that is, it is those members of the group who are affiliated with the group's party who are the overparticipators.

The nature of these groups differs from nation to nation, depending on the particular pattern of political contestation in the nation. In Austria one finds the clearest example of the pattern of reduced disparity between the haves and have-nots in the farm segment of the population, with its strong Catholic identification. This group is closely linked to the Austrian Peoples' party (the ÖVP) and is much more active in politics (particularly campaign activity) than one would expect from its relatively low position on the educational and income hierarchies; its party affiliation is particularly closely related to its activity rates. One finds a similar (though less pronounced) pattern in the opposite pole, among the nonreligious blue-collar workers who are closely aligned with the Austrian Socialist party (SPÖ).

The point is that under conditions of clear social cleavage, where parties have a particular relationship to a group clearly on one side or another of the cleavage pattern, the parties appear to be able to mobilize citizens to activity on the basis of their connection with one or the other of the cleavage groups. Thus, such mobilization clearly undercuts somewhat the effect of socioeconomic level. When a group that is mobilized through its party affiliation has a relatively low position on the socioeconomic scale, as with the farm segments in Austria and Japan, the effect is to greatly reduce the relationship between socioeconomic status and participation.

The similarity among Austria, Japan, and the Netherlands in this respect helps explain the puzzling similarity among India, the United States, and Yugoslavia. There is, of course, much cleavage and conflict in each of these latter three nations. But for varied reasons the political parties within the three do not structure that conflict, that is, they are not clearly aligned with one or the other of the conflicting groups. In the United States this derives from the broad base of the two parties and their general looseness of organization, in India from the fact of the dominance of the Congress party (at least at the time we conducted our study) and in Yugoslavia from the absence of a competitive party system. In each case the reason is different but the result is similar: the individual forces associated with socioeconomic status play a freer role in relation to political activity in these countries than they do in countries in which parties play a more significant role in mobilizing particular segments of the society to political activity.

The fact that the parties such as those in Austria mobilize the political activity of those fairly low on the socioeconomic scale (such as the farmers or the nonreligious blue-collar workers) would seem to be inconsistent with our individual-level generalization that the haves are likely to be more active than the have-nots. But we can see our generalization reconfirmed if we look within these social segments. Parties bring into political activity the more affluent and better educated members of those social groups that they mobilize to campaign activity. This is illustrated in Fig. 8. Here we plot the relationship between socioeconomic level and our scale of campaign activity for those groups par-

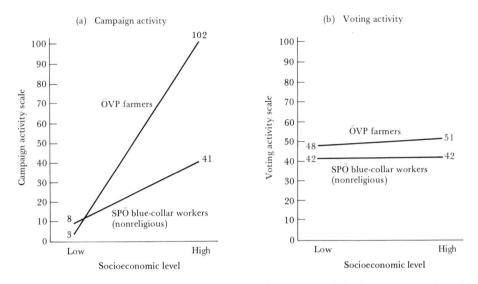

Fig. 8. How Parties Mobilize the More Affluent of Their Supporters: Austria

ticularly attached to and mobilized by the two main Austrian parties—the Catholic farmers, who support the ÖVP, and the nonreligious blue-collar workers, who support the SPÖ.

As one can see, within these groups the relationship between socioeconomic status and campaign activity is striking. This is especially the case among the farmers, but it is true as well for the blue-collar workers. When the ÖVP mobilizes political activists from its particular base in the farm sector of society or when the SPÖ mobilizes its supporters from among the nonreligious blue-collar workers, it mobilizes the more advantaged of its supporters.

Figure 8 presents data on voting as a contrast to the campaign activity data in Fig. 7. When it comes to voting there is little difference between the more and less advantaged members of the two Austrian cleavage groups; the poorer farmers and the poorer blue-collar workers are as active as their better-off counterparts.

The distinction between campaign activity and voting ties into our earlier discussion of the difference between these two modes of activity. Voting is a relatively easy act, less dependent on those motivations and resources that come with higher socioeconomic levels. Thus political parties, working to bring out the vote from their support base, can mobilize their supporters to vote from across the various levels. When it comes to campaign activity, the resources and motivation associated with higher socioeconomic status become important, and the participation disparity between the haves and have-nots reemerges.

Put more generally, it would appear that social conflict, particularly when structured by political parties, enhances political equality.[4]

Political Beliefs and Participation

We have illustrated the ways in which institutional affiliation affects the participation rates of groups and how institutions such as political parties can modify the tendency for those higher on the socioeconomic scale to outparticipate those lower on that scale. Institutional mobilization is not, however, the only way in which this modification can take place. In addition, lower-status citizens can be motivated to political activity through various kinds of belief systems or ideologies, particularly those that make explicit their disadvantaged status. We argue that one of the reasons for the close correlation of socioeconomic status and political activity in the United States is the absence of a sense of class consciousness among lower-status Americans. The absence of a class-based ideology is closely related to the absence of a class-based political party. The consequence is that the "classlessness" of American politics, upon which observers have often commented, has the paradoxical result of making socioeconomic level more important as a determinant of who is politically active.

We did, however, find several examples of belief systems that formed the motivational basis of political activity. The clearest example is the role played by group consciousness among American blacks. American blacks, we found, are less active in politics than American whites. This is clearly a function of their lower average socioeconomic status. If one controls for the difference in socioeconomic levels between blacks and whites, one finds blacks in the United States slightly outparticipating the white population. In addition we found that those blacks who manifested a sense of group consciousness (who mention race in answer to a variety of open-ended questions about the major problem in the nation or community or the major conflicts in the community) participated at or above the activity rate for whites. The data on blacks are consistent with what one would expect from a group brought to politics by a sense of group consciousness. They participate less than whites but more than one would expect given their social and economic conditions. And among those blacks who manifest some consciousness of group identification, the rate of participation is as high as that of whites and higher than one would expect given their other social characteristics.

The relationship between socioeconomic status as an inhibitor of black participation and group consciousness as a means of overcoming that inhibition is seen quite clearly in Fig. 9. The various bars represent the participation rate both of whites and blacks and the participation rates of blacks controlling for group consciousness, social status, and for both simultaneously. In the first place, blacks participate on the average less than whites (bars A and B). The crosshatched horizontal bar is a measure of the gap between the two races in average participation. The gap, we have indicated, derives largely from the difference in education, income, and occupational level between the two groups.

The average black participation rate illustrated in bar B is made up of

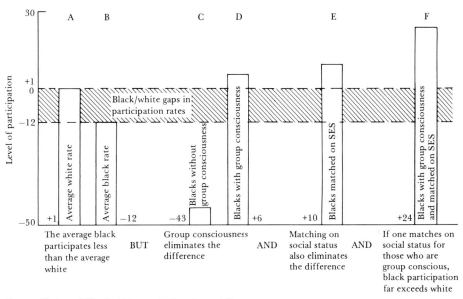

Source: Verba and Nie, *Participation in America*, p. 161.

Fig. 9. Effect of Group Consciousness and Social Status on Black/White Differences in Participation

both those blacks who manifest group consciousness and those who do not. If one considers separately those who do not manifest group consciousness (bar C), one finds that blacks participate substantially less than whites. But if one considers those blacks who are conscious of group identity in relation to politics (bar D), one finds that they participate somewhat more frequently than whites. Despite the somewhat lower socioeconomic status of this group, its group consciousness bridges the gap between the average black rate and the average white rate.

The situation is even clearer if we consider the participation rates of blacks corrected for their lower social status. In bar E we see the corrected level for all blacks. This corrected level moves above that of the average white. And if we correct the participation rate of those blacks who are conscious of group identity (bar F), we find a participation rate far exceeding that of the average white.

In short, there are two ways black participation rates can be brought up to the level of white rates. (1) If blacks were not disadvantaged in social-status terms they would not be disadvantaged in terms of participation (bar E). Given the fact of disadvantage, however, we find that they overcome this through group consciousness (bar D). (2) If blacks were to close the socioeconomic gap that separates them from whites and still maintain a sense of group consciousness, they would far exceed whites in participation (bar F). The situation is of course hypothetical. If the socioeconomic gap were closed perhaps much of the basis for group consciousness would be gone. The most significant fact is that the gap in participation can be so completely closed by the awareness of group identity. (For a fuller account see Verba and Nie, 1972, Chapter 10. Some parallel data on Harijans [untouchables] in India are in Verba, Ahmed, and Bhatt, 1971.)

Longitudinal data from the Survey Research Center of the University of Michigan on the changing rate of black political activity are consistent with this interpretation. In 1952 black participation was well below what one would have predicted given their level of education. At that time they were under-participating vis-à-vis their expected level. From 1952 through 1964 one finds a sharp growth in campaign activity rates well above what would have been projected on the basis of their increasing educational level. From 1960 on, blacks have been participating above what one would have projected based on their socioeconomic level. (See Verba and Nie, 1972, Chapter 14.) The result of the rapid growth in black campaign activity is seen in Fig. 10, in which we

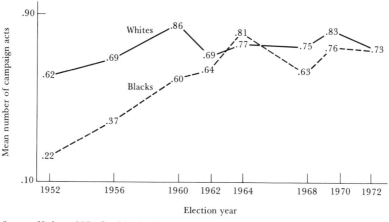

Source: Verba and Nie, *Participation in America*, p. 255.

Fig. 10. Campaign Activity Rates: Whites and Blacks

plot the actual rate of campaign activity over the two decades for blacks and whites. What is most apparent is the rapid narrowing of the participation gap between the two races between 1952 and 1964. In 1964 blacks were slightly more active than whites in the campaign, and though their rate declines some-what from the peak of 1964, the gap between the races remains narrow. The data over time are quite consistent with what one would expect as the result of a process of political mobilization through the development of group consciousness.

In contrast, we can see how participation disparities can survive in the absence of group consciousness. The data in Fig. 11 are in clear contrast to those in Fig. 10. In Fig. 11 we plot the rate of campaign activity over time for three different white educational groups—those who have not completed high school, high school graduates, and those with some college. Unlike the situation vis-a-vis the black-white differences, we see no such tendency for a diminution of the participation gap between the social levels among whites. Rather, the gap remains roughly the same or, if anything, increases throughout the two decades. If our interpretation is correct, the data over time on the participation gap between blacks and whites reflect the way in which a sense of group consciousness (which evolved among blacks in the 1950s and 1960s) can reduce disparities in political activity across socioeconomic levels. The data on upper and lower status whites illustrates the consequences of the absence of such a sense of group (or class) consciousness among lower status whites.[5]

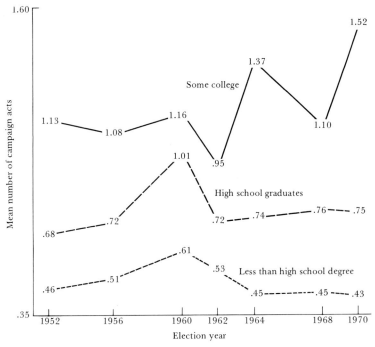

Source: Verba and Nie, *Participation in America*, p. 256.

Fig. 11. *Mean Number of Campaign Activities for Three Educational Levels among Whites*

THE CONSEQUENCES OF POLITICAL ACTIVITY

Does political activity make a difference? The answer depends on what kind of difference one is seeking. Much of the literature on participation has focussed on the difference participation makes for the level of citizen support for the political system (Lipset, 1960; Eckstein, 1961; Almond and Verba, 1963). Our major concern in this essay is with participation as an instrumental act by which citizens communicate their preferences to political leaders and/or pressure those leaders to comply with those preferences. The relevant consequences of participation from this perspective are the responses of government officials to citizen activity. Does citizen activity make a difference in what political leaders do?

We will present some data on this subject from two perspectives. First we will explore the consequences of participation from the point of view of the kinds of preferences that participatory activities are likely to carry to political leaders. Secondly we will consider some data on the responsiveness of political leaders to citizen initiatives.

Participation and the Communication of Preferences

The fact that the participants in a society are but a minority of the population as a whole creates the potential that the participant few will communicate to political leaders a set of preferences that are quite different from those of the populace as a whole. This is more likely to be the case the less representative the activist population is in demographic terms. On the other hand, it is possible that the activists will have preferences like those of the less active members of the population (and in this sense can represent them via their activity).

In a sense we are asking whether it would make a difference if political leaders paid attention to the activists rather than to the populace as a whole. The answer of a variety of studies is that the political activists are a far from representative body in terms of preferences. Studies show that letter writers on public matters are not representative of the preferences of the populace as a whole. Letter writers tend to fall in the more extreme categories of a liberalism-conservativism scale, with a tendency to be on the conservative side (Converse, Clausen, and Miller, 1965). The citizens who wrote letters on the War in Vietnam tended to have a distribution of preferences that was somewhat more polarized (i.e., either hawkish or dovish and less middle of the road) than the populace as a whole, while tilting somewhat in a hawkish direction (Verba and Brody, 1970). In a similar manner Ranney has shown that voters in primary elections are by no means representative of all voters (Ranney, 1972). In addition, the mode of political activity makes a difference in terms of the preferences of those who engage in it. Those who wrote letters on the Vietnam War were somewhat more hawkish than the populace as a whole, while those who took part in demonstrations were quite a bit more dovish (Verba and Brody,

1970). The point is simple: political leaders who read public preferences by observing the views of the activists saw something different from what they would have seen had they conducted a poll of the public as a whole; and what they saw depended on the mode of activity to which they were sensitive.

The same point can be illustrated in relation to our data on the degree of overrepresentation of the more affluent and better educated in the activist population in the United States. Table 10 compares the views of a sample of the American population as a whole with the views of those who are relatively inactive (who fall below the median on our activity scale) and with the views of those who fall in the top 5 percent of our activity scale. The first three items represent the responses of citizens to a question on the most important problem in their community. The political leader attentive to the activists would find an agenda of salient community problems different from that found in the inactive portion of the population. No one among the activists mentioned poverty as a serious community problem, whereas a small but noticeable group of 6 percent among the "silent majority" mentioned such a problem. In contrast the activists were more likely than the inactives to mention community educational needs as well as the need to cut taxes. The last item on Table 10 reports responses to a question as to who has an obligation to help poor people in America: Does the government have such an obligation or must the poor help themselves? The data show that the political leader paying attention to the activists would see a majority saying that the government had no such obligation to the poor. If the leader had observed the preferences of the silent majority he or she would have found only about half as much support for this position.

TABLE 10   Actives and inactives compared: the United States

	Whole sample	"Silent majority" *	Most active**
Percentage saying poverty is most serious community problem	4	6	0
Percentage saying high taxes are most serious community problem	7	3	11
Percentage saying better education is most serious community problem	27	7	36
Percentage saying that the government has no obligation to help the poor	38	28	51

* Those below the median on our activity scale.

** Those in the top 5 percent of our activity scale.

The data illustrate the consequences of the fact that the activists in America come from the more affluent and better educated segments of society and, thereby, communicate preferences different from those in the populace as a whole. We can confirm that this is the case by "correcting" the policy preferences of citizens for the demographic composition of the various active and inactive groups. We do this by removing from our measures of political preferences, through regression analysis, the effects of various sociological characteristics associated with both political preferences and political participation (for details on the technique used see Verba and Nie, 1972, pp. 287–88 and Appendix D). These characteristics are socioeconomic status, sex, race, and age. Do the differences in proportions holding individualistic views on matters of welfare policy in various activist groups exist over and above what one would expect given the sociological composition of these groups? If such differences remain, we may have evidence that preferences have an independent effect on participation. If they disappear, the relation between preference and participation has been explained away by the relation of sociological characteristics to both.

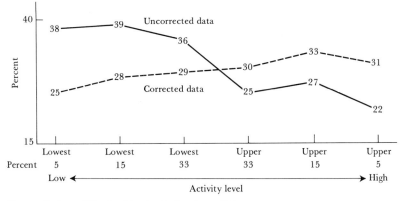

Source: Verba and Nie, *Participation in America*, p. 288.

Fig. 12. Proportion Reporting a Serious Personal Welfare Problem among Activists and Inactives: Uncorrected and Corrected Data

Consider the data in Fig. 12. In that figure we show the proportions of various active and inactive groups which report that they were faced with a serious personal welfare problem. These data are plotted on the solid line. The proportion with such severe welfare problems declines as one moves from the inactive to the active population. But if we correct the attitude measure for the expected frequency of such problems among various sociological groups, we find that the result (the dotted line) presents almost no difference among the groups on various levels of activity. In other words, the underrepresentation in the activist population of citizens with severe welfare problems can largely be explained away by the underrepresentation among the activists of those with lower social status. In fact, if any more direct relationship between the salience of welfare problems and participation remains, it is in the opposite direction of the uncorrected data—those with such problems are slightly more likely to be active.

These data suggest that one ought to find cross-national differences in the degree to which the preferences of the activists are representative of the more affluent and better educated members of the society; these differences should parallel the differences we have documented in the relationship between socioeconomic level and political activity. Some quite preliminary data from three of the nations we are considering support this position. Table 11 repeats some data for the United States found on Fig. 12—the proportions of the activist and inactive portions of the population reporting a serious welfare problem—and presents parallel data for India and Japan. In all three nations the inactives are more likely than the actives to have such problems, but there is variation among the nations as to the extent to which the actives and the inactives differ in this respect. The difference between the two groups is least in Japan, the nation that has the weakest advantage/participation relationship of the three nations reported on the table. In other words, Table 11 is consistent with a conclusion that the varying degree to which participation is linked to socioeconomic advantage does have consequences in terms of the nature of the problems communicated to political leaders through participatory mechanisms. The more the have-nots are underrepresented among the participants, the less likely it is that their particular needs will be communicated.

TABLE 11   Percentages mentioning a family or personal problem of a "subsistence" kind, by rate of political activity, in three nations

Country	Least active citizens	"Middle majority"	Top activists
India	62	59	48
Japan	33	32	27
United States	38	31	22

Participation and Leader Responsiveness

We have thus far dealt with the consequences of participation in a hypothetical manner: How would the actions of political leaders differ if they paid attention to the preferences of the activist portion of the citizenry rather than to the citizenry as a whole? To study the response of political leaders more directly one has to move beyond the cross-section sample of populations and their preferences to the linkage between such preferences and leader activities or governmental programs. Few studies have attempted this. It is relatively easy to come by data on the preferences of the public, but the connection between public preferences and leader responsiveness is more difficult. Several studies have made such connections using interview data on the level of congressional districts (Miller and Stokes, 1966) or aggregate data on the level of states (Fry and Winters, 1970; Booms and Halldorson, 1973).

In our study of participation in the United States we attempted to gauge the impact of citizen activity on leader responsiveness by using data gathered from leaders in the same communities in which we had interviewed samples of the citizenry. Within each community we were able to develop a measure of citizen/leader concurrence, that is, the extent to which local leaders and the local citizenry agree on community priorities. There is evidence that such a measure of citizen/leader concurrence taps the extent to which the local leadership responds to the preferences of the local citizens. (For details see Verba and Nie, 1972, Chapters 17–19.)

What effect does citizen participation have on the extent of citizen/leader concurrence? A few of the more salient results are worth mentioning.

1. For one thing, citizen activity does make a difference. There is a tendency for leaders to be more responsive to the citizenry in communities with high participation rates than in communities with lower participation rates. This is seen in Fig. 13, in which we plot the relationship between the mean rate of citizen activity in the community and the level of leader responsiveness to the local citizenry. Responsiveness is highest in the most active communities and generally lower in less active communities. (The correlation between citizen activity and leader responsiveness is .32 [level of significance = .01].)

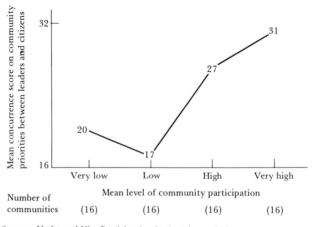

Source: Verba and Nie, *Participation in America*, p. 313.

Fig. 13. Corrected Community Participation Rates and Concurrence between Citizens and Community Leaders on Community Priorities

2. But the relationship between activity and responsiveness is curvilinear. The lowest level of responsiveness is not in the least-active communities but in the next to the lowest category of community in terms of citizen activity. This is to be expected if one remembers that the activists are not a representative sample of the citizenry as a whole. Where there is very little activity, leaders are relatively free to respond or not to respond to the preferences of the citizenry; and they respond at moderately low levels. As one moves to communities with a moderate but limited amount of participation, leaders respond to the preferences of the activist few and pay less attention to the bulk of the population, which is inactive, resulting in lower responsiveness to the citizenry as a whole. As participation becomes more widespread, leader responsiveness to the citizenry as a whole increases.

3. This interpretation is confirmed if one disaggregates the measure of concurrence between local leaders and the citizenry into measures of concurrence between leaders and citizens at various levels of activity. This is plotted in Fig. 14. Figure 14 repeats the relationship presented in Fig. 13 between citizen activity and leader responsiveness, but the measure of responsiveness is reported separately for those who are most active in the community, for the moderately

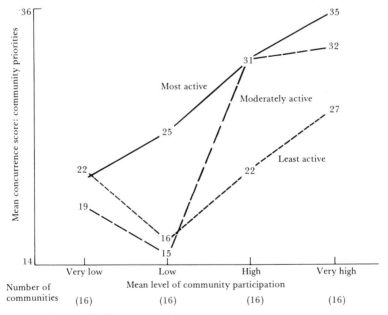

Source: Verba and Nie, *Participation in America*, p. 317.

Fig. 14. Corrected Community Participation Rates and Concurrence between Citizens and Community Leaders on Community Priorities, at Three Levels of Activity

active, and for the least active. As our interpretation would predict, the responsiveness of leaders to the active portion of the population goes up in a linear manner as participation increases; there is no curve in the relationship. On the other hand, the responsiveness of leaders to the less active citizens does decline as one moves from the least active communities to the next category of communities in terms of activity.

4. In general one can distinguish between the *level* and the *equality* of leader responsiveness. Where participation is lowest, the level of leader responsiveness to the public as a whole is low; but active citizens receive no more responsiveness than inactive ones. As participation rates rise in a community, the level of leader responsiveness goes up, but the equality of that responsiveness declines. In more active communities there is a wide gap between leader responsiveness to the active and to the inactive citizens. In the most active communities, however, though inactive citizens receive less responsiveness than active ones, the former receive more responsiveness than do similarly inactive citizens in less active communities. In this sense the inactives appear to reap the benefit of the activity of their fellow citizens.

5. However, participation does not increase inequality if the participants are representative of the population as a whole. This can happen in highly consensual communities, where the participants have the same preferences as the nonparticipants. In such cases all modes of activity lead to higher levels of responsiveness. But where consensus is low—where active and inactive citizens have different preferences—increased participation can result in decreased levels of responsiveness. This is particularly the case where the mode of participation involved conveys a large amount of information about citizen preference. (For data see Verba and Nie, 1972, Chapter 19.)

6. Finally, our data show that voting as a mode of activity has an important effect on leader responsiveness despite the fact that it conveys relatively little information about citizen preferences. Voting appears to be most effective in conjunction with other modes of activity. This is seen in Fig. 15, in which we plot the relationship between the three nonvoting modes of activity and leader responsiveness but do so separately for communities with a high rate of voting turnout and communities with a low rate. The contrast between the two types of community is clear. In communities in which voting rates are high, the other three modes of activity are quite powerful in increasing concurrence. Where voting rates are low, the other modes of activity make little difference.

The data on the interaction between voting and the other modes of activity bring us around full circle to our opening discussion of the various modes of political participation. The reason for our distinction among the modes of activity was that they relate the citizen to the government in differing ways.

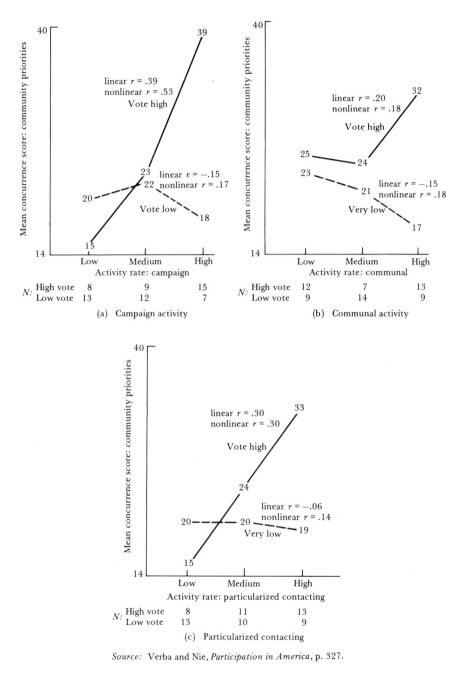

Source: Verba and Nie, *Participation in America*, p. 327.

Fig. 15. *Corrected Community Participation Rates and Concurrence, at Three Levels of Activity, in Communities with High and Low Voting Rates*

One characteristic that distinguishes the various modes of activity is the amount of information a mode communicates to governmental leaders about the preferences of the activists and/or the amount of pressure it places upon governmental leaders to comply with those preferences. Voting differs from other modes in that it is high in pressure (since leaders will want to avoid electoral defeat) but low in information. Other modes of activity communicate more information, though they may exert less pressure. The data in Fig. 15 indicate the extent to which the modes of activity, though different, form an interlocking system. High voting turnout, by itself, does not lead to high levels of responsiveness. This is seen in Fig. 15, in which the high and low voting communities are compared under the condition of low activity in the other modes. Nor does high activity in the other modes lead to responsiveness if voting is low. But when voting is combined with other activity—the former applying pressure for compliance with citizen preferences, the latter supplying information about these preferences—the result is significantly higher levels of responsiveness.

THE RATIONALITY OF POLITICAL ACTIVITY

We will end this essay with some remarks about the rationality of citizen activity. There are two issues usually discussed in relation to the rationality of political participation: Is it rational for citizens to take part in politics? (Given the costs of political activity, are the probable benefits worth the time and effort?) And, secondly, when they take part in politics do they do so rationally? (Do they act in ways that maximize the probability of achieving whatever benefits they would want?)

The discussions of citizen rationality usually take place in relation to the vote: Is it rational to vote? Do citizens vote rationally? The bulk of the literature is on the subject of issue voting: Do citizens vote on the issues or on the basis of less "rational" criteria such as candidate personality or habitual party identification? Such discussion involves a consideration of whether citizens have clear and consistent views on issues and have information about the issue positions of candidates (Converse, 1964; Key, 1966; Nie and Andersen, 1974; Pomper, 1972; Boyd, 1972; Kessell, 1972; Brody and Page, 1972; Shapiro, 1969; Riker and Ordeshook, 1968).

We do not want to get into the intricacies of this debate. This volume of the *Handbook* contains an excellent discussion of the rationality of voting by Philip E. Converse, which clarifies many of the issues involved. But we would like to place the question of the rationality of political participation into the broader perspective one has when one considers political activities beyond the vote. In some sense, to raise the question of citizen rationality in relation to the vote is to raise that question under circumstances in which such rationality is most difficult. The vote, as we have indicated, differs from other activities in that it carries relatively little information about citizen preferences and affects only broad "systemwide" outcomes. The consequence of the latter fact is that the "agenda" of the election is not set by the voter, who does not choose the candidates or the issues that divide the candidates. The result is that the choice in the election is likely to articulate rather poorly with the specific "agenda" of the individual—the problems that concern this individual and the particular solutions that he or she favors for such problems. And, of course, the individual citizen is but one of a large number of participants in the electoral process; the outcome is little affected by one individual's vote.

The circumstance is quite different when one comes to such an activity as particularized contacting. The subject matter of the contact is narrow, it is personally selected (i.e., the citizen decides what "agenda" to bring to the government official), and it tends to be of great importance to the individual (though the outcome of the contact may have little broader social impact). Finally, citizens' own activity makes a big difference in relation to the outcome. In general we find that citizens know what they want in relation to particularized contacting and have a fairly good idea of the appropriate channels. Their activity seems quite rational in this area.

When it comes to other modes of activity, one does not find as close a match between the citizen's personal agenda and the subject of the political activity. But such activity as group-based communal activity (when an informal or formal group takes a position on some community matter) is likely to reflect the specific needs and problems of the individual participant more than does the subject matter of the election. One can still argue (Olson, 1965) that where the participant group is large, it is more rational for the individual to "free-ride" on the activity of others and not to participate. But the size of groups involved in communal activity may be fairly small, and the activities of an individual may make a greater difference.

Our purpose is not to denigrate the vote in favor of more particularized political activities. As our analysis shows, the vote in combination with activities that are richer in information-carrying capacity makes a most potent political force. We simply want to point out that voting is but one of the ways in which citizens can influence the government and that when one considers the full range of citizen activities one finds greater room for rationally instrumental citizen activity.

Indeed, the instrumentality of political activity is best indicated by the data we have presented on leader responsiveness. Political activity does make a difference. Where citizens are active, leaders are responsive. But, above all, leaders are responsive to the activists. If a particular citizen is not active, particularly in those modes of activity that communicate a lot of information about citizen preferences, political leaders will pay attention to the preferences of those others who are active.

We have tried to cover a wide range of topics in relation to citizen participation. We have not presented a comprehensive account, nor have we attempted to cover the literature. Perhaps we can end with a broad, usually vague, but important normative question: Is participation a good thing or a bad thing? Ought one attempt to maximize citizen participation, or are smaller amounts more desirable? (See Walker, 1966; Dahl, 1966.) The question is often posed in terms of the consequences of varying levels of citizen activity for political stability or for democracy. But consider the question from the point of view of leader responsiveness. Our data make clear that political activity can have somewhat ambiguous results from a normative point of view if one's goal is equality. If the haves outparticipate the have-nots (as they tend to do), political activity is likely to result in greater benefits for those who are already better off.

But the moral of the story is not that less participation is better, even though participation can have antiegalitarian consequences. Rather, the moral is not to leave political activity to the other fellow—for it will be his or her preferences that leaders will hear and to which they will respond.

NOTES

1.   That is, we use the same cutting points in terms of education and income that we used to determine the top third in the cross-section sample.

2.   The case that deviates is Nigeria, in which, like India, almost all leaders come from the top third of our socioeconomic advantage scale. But given the shape of that scale in those two countries—a very high proportion of the population is low in terms of education and income—the fact that all leaders fall in the top of the distribution is perhaps to be expected.

3.   That upper-status independents in Austria, Japan, and the Netherlands participate less than they ordinarily would in campaign activity and that lower-status strong partisans participate more than they ordinarily would is supported by a comparison of the rates of political discussion of these groups with their rates of campaign activity. If one creates a scale of political discussion standardized in the same way as for campaign activity, one finds upper-status independents much higher on the discussion scale than on the campaign activity scale, while the lower-status strong partisans score much lower on the scale of political discussion than they do on the scale of campaign activity.

4.   We cannot present data here on the role of voluntary association in this process. But analysis suggests a similar, and in some cases more potent, role played by such institutions.

5.   In our analysis of the United States data we did find a clear example of the mobilizing role of political beliefs among the white population. This was the role of relatively conservative economic beliefs, which appear to play a major role in mobilizing the political activity of upper-status Republicans. The result of this type of mobilization, of course, is to increase the participation disparity between the haves and the have-nots. (See Verba and Nie, 1972, Chapter 12.)

REFERENCES

Alford, Robert A., and Harry M. Scoble (1968). "Community leadership, social status and political behavior." *American Sociological Review* 32:259–72.

Almond, Gabriel A., and Sidney Verba (1963). *The Civic Culture.* Princeton: Princeton University Press.

Bachrach, Peter, and Morton S. Baratz (1963). "Decisions and non-decisions: an analytic framework." *American Political Science Review* 57:632–42.

Bendix, Reinhard, ed. (1964). *Nation Building and Citizenship.* New York: Wiley.

Bendix, Reinhard, and Stein Rokkan (1964). "The extension of citizenship to the lower classes." In Reinhard Bendix (ed.), *Nation Building and Citizenship.* New York: Wiley.

Berelson, Bernard, Paul F. Lazarsfeld, and William N. McPhee (1954). *Voting.* Chicago: University of Chicago Press.

Booms, Bernard H., and James R. Halldorson (1973). "The politics of redistribution: a reformation." *American Political Science Review* 67:924–33.

Boyd, Richard W. (1972). "Popular control of the public policy: a normal vote analysis of the 1968 elections." *American Political Science Review* 66:429–49.

Brody, Richard A., and Benjamin I. Page (1972). "Policy voting and the electoral process: the Vietnam War issue." *American Political Science Review* 66:979–95.

Burnham, Walter Dean (1965). "The changing shape of the American political universe." *American Political Science Review* 61:7–28.

Butler, David, and Donald Stokes (1969). *Political Change in Britain.* New York: St. Martin's Press.

Campbell, Angus, Philip E. Converse, Warren E. Miller, and Donald E. Stokes (1960). *The American Voter.* New York: Wiley.

Cole, G. D. H. (1921). *The Future of Local Government.* London: Cassell.

_____ (1920). *Guild Socialism Restated.* London: L. Parsons.

Coleman, James S. (1971). "Political money." *American Political Science Review* 65:1074–87.

Converse, Philip E. (1964). "The nature of belief systems in mass publics." In Donald E. Apter (ed.), *Ideology and Discontent.* New York: Free Press.

Converse, Philip E., and Roy Pierce (1970). "Basic cleavages in French politics and the disorders of May and June, 1968." Paper prepared for presentation at the 7th World Congress of Sociology held at Varna, Bulgaria, 1970.

Converse, Philip E., P. E. Clausen, and W. E. Miller (1965). "Electoral myth and reality: the 1964 election." *American Political Science Review* 59:321–36.

Dahl, Robert A. (1961). *Who Governs? Democracy and Power in an American City.* New Haven: Yale University Press.

_____ (1966). "Further reflections of 'The elitist theory of democracy.'" *American Political Science Review* 60:296–305.

Dahl, Robert A. (1967). "The city in the future of democracy." *American Political Science Review* 61:958–70.

Deutsch, Karl (1961). "Social mobilization and political development." *American Political Science Review* 60:493–514.

Eckstein, Harry (1961). *A Theory of Stable Democracy*. Princeton University, Center of International Studies.

Fry, Brian, and Richard Winters (1970). "The politics of redistribution." *American Political Science Review* 64:508–22.

Inkeles, Alex (1969). "Participant citizenship in six developing nations." *American Political Science Review* 63:1120–41.

Kelley, Stanley, Jr., Richard E. Ayres, and William G. Bowen (1967). "Registration and voting: putting first things first." *American Political Science Review* 61:359–77.

Kessel, John (1972). "Comment: the issues in issue voting," *American Political Science Review* 66:459–65.

Key, V. O. (1966). *The Responsible Electorate*. Cambridge, Mass.: Harvard University Press.

Lane, Robert A. (1959). *Political Life: Why People Get Involved in Politics*. New York: Free Press.

Lerner, David (1958). *The Passing of Traditional Society*. New York: Free Press.

Lippmann, Walter (1965). *The Essential Lippmann: A Political Philosophy for Liberal Democracy*. Edited by Clinton Rossiter and James Lare. New York: Random House.

Lipset, Seymour Martin (1960). *Political Man*. Garden City, N. Y.: Doubleday.

Lipsky, Michael (1970). *Protest in City Politics: Rent Strikes, Housing and the Power of the Poor*. Chicago: Rand McNally.

McCloskey, Herbert (1968). "Political participation." *International Encyclopedia of the Social Sciences*, vol. 12, pp. 252–65.

McCrone, Donald J., and Charles F. Cnudde (1967). "Towards a communication theory of political development." *American Political Science Review* 61:72–80.

Marshall, T. H. (1965). *Class, Citizenship and Social Development*. Garden City, N. Y.: Doubleday.

Matthews, Donald R., and James W. Prothro (1962). *Negroes and the New Southern Politics*. New York: Harcourt, Brace and World.

Milbrath, Lester W. (1965). *Political Participation*. Chicago: Rand McNally.

─────────── (n.d.). "Study of political participation in Buffalo." Unpublished manuscript.

Mill, J. S. (1873). *Considerations on Representative Government*. New York: Holt.

Miller, Warren E., and Donald E. Stokes (1966). "Constituency influences in Congress." In Angus Campbell, Philip E. Converse, Warren E. Miller, and Donald E. Stokes (eds.), *Elections and the Political Order*. New York: Wiley.

Needler, Martin C. (1968). "Political development and socioeconomic development: the case of Latin America." *American Political Science Review* 62:889–97.

Nettle, John Peter (1967). *Political Mobilization: A Sociological Analysis of Methods and Concepts*. London: Faber.

Neubauer, Dane (1967). "Some conditions of democracy." *American Political Science Review* 61:1002–9.

Nie, Norman H., Bingham G. Powell, and Kenneth Prewitt (1969). "Social structure and political participation: developmental realtionships," parts 1 and 2. *American Political Science Review* 63:361–78, 808–32.

Nie, Norman H., with Kristi Andersen (1974). "Mass belief systems revisited: political change and attitude structure." *Journal of Politics* 36:540–91.

Olsen, Marvin E. (1970). "Social and political participation." *American Sociological Review* 35:682–96.

Olson, Mancur (1965). *The Logic of Collective Action*. Cambridge, Mass.: Harvard University Press.

Pomper, Gerald M. (1972). "From confusion to clarity: issues and American voters, 1956–1968." *American Political Science Review* 66:415–28.

Ranney, Austin (1972). "Turnout and representation in presidential primary elections." *American Political Science Review* 66:21–37.

Riker, William H., and Peter C. Ordeshook (1968). "A theory of the calculus of voting." *American Political Science Review* 62:24–42.

Rokkan, Stein (1961). "Mass suffrage, secret voting and political participation." *European Archives of Sociology* 2:132–52.

——————— (1966). "Electoral mobilization, party competition and national integration." In Joseph LaPalombara and Myron Weiner (eds.), *Political Parties and Political Development*. Princeton: Princeton University Press.

Shapiro, Michael (1969). "Rational political man: a synthesis of economic and social-psychological perspectives." *American Political Science Review* 63:1106–19.

Sharkansky, Ira, and Richard Hofferbert (1969). "Dimensions of state politics: economics and public policy." *American Political Science Review* 63:867–79.

Skolnick, Jerome (1969). *The Politics of Protest*. Staff Report to the National Committee on the Causes and Prevention of Violence. New York: Ballantine.

Thompson, Dennis F. (1970). *The Democratic Citizen: Social Science and Democratic Theory in the 20th Century*. Cambridge, England: Cambridge University Press.

Townsend, James R. (1967). *Political Participation in Communist China*. Berkeley: University of California Press.

Verba, Sidney (1967). "Democratic participation." *Annals of the American Academy of Political and Social Sciences* 373:53–78.

——————— (1971). "Cross-national survey research: the problem of credibility." In Ivan Vallier (ed.), *Comparative Methods in Sociology: Essays in Trends and Applications*. Berkeley: University of California Press.

Verba, Sidney, and Norman H. Nie (1972). *Participation in America: Social Equality and Political Democracy*. New York: Harper & Row.

Verba, Sidney, Bashiruddin Ahmed, and Anil Bhatt (1971). *Race, Caste and Politics: A Comparison of India and the United States.* Beverly Hills, Calif.: Sage.

Verba, Sidney, Norman H. Nie, and Jae-on Kim (1971). *The Modes of Democratic Participation: A Cross-national Analysis.* Sage Professional Papers in Comparative Politics, vol. 2, no. 01-013.

——————— (forthcoming). *Social Stratification and Political Stratification: A Seven Nation Comparison.*

Verba, Sidney, Norman H. Nie, Ana Barbič, Galen Irwin, Henk Molleman, and Goldie Shabad (1973). "The modes of participation: continuities in research." *Comparative Political Studies* 6:235–49.

Verba, Sidney, and Richard Brody (1970). "Participation, preferences and the war in Vietnam." *Public Opinion Quarterly* 34:325–32.

Walker, Jack (1966). "A critique of the elitist theory of democracy." *American Political Science Review* 60:285–95.

Weiner, Myron (1971). "Political participation: crisis of the political process." In Leonard Binder, James S. Coleman, Joseph La Palombara, Lucian Pye, Sidney Verba, and Myron Weiner (eds.), *Crises and Sequences in Political Development.* Princeton: Princeton University Press.

2

PUBLIC OPINION AND VOTING BEHAVIOR

PHILIP E. CONVERSE

The study of public opinion and the study of voting in mass elections go nicely hand in hand. All of the elaborate electoral machinery that is now devoted, in so many countries of the world, to polling a citizenry for its leadership preferences and, at times, its direct policy desires is an investment in the monitoring of public opinion. In large states, unlike smaller decision-making bodies, elections are a social device for forwarding messages concerning governance from the masses to their governors, and the input, or content, for these voting choices is public opinion. Indeed, general interest in the state of "public opinion," at least in its current egalitarian sense, has quickened markedly over the past century, the period in which most nations of democratic bent have been putting systems of mass elections into operation. Both topics are vitally tied to an ethic of democratic control.

Thus our subject, although dual, is perfectly coherent. Nevertheless the literature on public opinion is itself massive, and the literature on voting behavior is probably greater still. Laid end to end, the received wisdom on the double topic achieves monstrous proportions. Moreover, it is a varied literature. Few subjects in political science have attracted the research attentions of scholars from as many disciplines as these. Economists, historians, psychologists of experimental, testing, clinical, and social persuasion, along with more or less applied statisticians, sociologists, demographers, geographers, and

This essay has been greatly improved by the constructive criticisms of numerous colleagues. Special thanks are owed to the volume editors, Fred I. Greenstein and Nelson W. Polsby, whose insights and suggestions were most numerous and thorough. I also have profited from a variety of comments by Hayward R. Alker, Jr., M. Kent Jennings, Hans D. Klingemann, Warren E. Miller, Norman H. Nie, and William E. Wright. As always, of course, any wrongheadedness that remains from this sifting is my own.

journalists have all seized on these topics for systematic work at one time or another. And their purposes have been as varied as their backgrounds—from the sociologist's use of elections as momentary X rays of social cleavages thrust up into politics, to the economist's concern with variants of maximizing behavior in the political marketplace, to the psychologist's interest in attitude formation and choice behavior. I would be hard pressed in any essay of reasonable proportions to encompass all of these diverse perspectives in an orderly way.

I shall not particularly try for this kind of coverage. The intellectual history of inquiry into these topics, fascinating though it is, must at most be compressed into cameo form.[1] I shall also leave unmentioned a myriad of byways that have been explored at one time or another out of an initial interest in the core subject matter. What I shall try to do is to provide a review of the main lines of the current state of the art. And yet even "state" is a poor word, if it calls to mind something as static as the "steady state." For work in these areas, as in most others, is at its healthiest when ideas are in motion and controversy rages; and controversies there are, in some number. I shall organize much of the discussion around the more basic of these disputes, attempting here to synthesize and there to reject, all the while seeking to portray, as honestly as possible, the situation of inquiry at the time of writing.

I can profit from one great point of economy. Treatments of voting behavior in particular are usually obliged to deal with the character of public participation. However, this ground has been covered with admirable scope in the preceding chapter.[2]

Moreover, the view of electoral institutions which will generally inform this essay accords rather nicely with that outlined by Verba and Nie. Taken as a subprocess in the broader political system, elections constitute a mechanism for communication, influence, and control from the grass roots upward. Yet as Verba and Nie argue, elections are also rather blunt instruments of control. Under most conditions they do succeed in dictating which among competing sets of leaders will in fact govern, although this "power" to choose may be limited more or less according to the nature of differences between the alternative leaders. While elections are occasionally used in the referendum mode, allowing more precise if narrow policy messages to be transmitted, most contests among candidates convey no more than an ambiguous policy mandate. As a communication mechanism the election channel is simply not built to carry much detailed information, and the messages flowing through it emerge vague and noisy, leaving the winners with corresponding latitude for discretionary maneuver.

Furthermore, in the American system elections serve to control only after a lag, which may strike some observers as disquieting. If a leadership embarks on a series of adventures which has nefarious consequences to the public eye, it may be months or years, with permanent damage already done, before a relevant election permits the citizenry to "throw the rascals out." Finally, neither the public nor the election mechanism itself is sheltered from influence in reverse. Although elections are designed for some popular control over political leadership, the leaders can wield a great deal of influence over the character of elections by manipulating the course of public discussion, shaping visions of plausible alternatives, and selecting candidates for office. In a longer run, the leaders also have determining control over the rules of the game which dictate how any particular pattern of votes will be aggregated into legislative seats or executive triumph. In sum, then, elections are like a steering mechanism that is partially loose, gets a slow response to its directives, and is susceptible to tampering, to boot.

Despite all of these shortcomings, few publics that have experienced competitive elections care to be deprived of them, and in an ultimate sense, at least, these mechanisms do represent a rather powerful source of popular control over government. Among other things the "anticipated reactions" of politicians to the possibility of public wrath at the polls undoubtedly gives elections a somewhat finer tuning as a control system than either its own structure or what is known of public inputs might lead one to expect. And, as Verba and Nie have shown, in comparison with the other familiar forms of citizen efforts to influence government, elections appear to carry—as indeed they were designed to do—the most broadly representative voice of the community.

Questions as to the ultimate contributions of public opinion and elections to the character of governance in the broader political system are of course the most basic that political scientists working in this area can pose.[3] How much does public opinion matter in the workings of government? How effective are elections as a means of communicating public opinion? We risk losing sight of these overarching concerns as we delve into the finer dynamics of popular opinion and voting. However, I shall make some effort to keep them in view as we proceed and shall return to confront them more directly toward the close of the essay.

THE NATURE OF PUBLIC OPINION

As V. O. Key once observed, "To speak with precision of public opinion is a task not unlike coming to grips with the Holy Ghost." The observation has high meaning for all who have worked with the concept. There is a cast of the impalpable, the amorphous, and the mercurial to most of what is commonly felt in the political atmosphere as "public opinion"; and while a swelling torrent of sample survey studies over the past three or four decades has devoted enormous resources to more exacting assessments of public opinion, this work has not fully dispelled frustrations at the ambiguity of the notion.

In grounds as swampy as these, of course, controversy flourishes. The broadest conclusions from most empirical work on the subject give a very bleak reading as to the character of public opinion, relative to the idealistic assumptions surrounding the more naive versions of democratic theory. Public opinion, even in a country with education levels as advanced as those of the United States, is portrayed as both wretchedly informed and feebly structured. Indeed there is presumed to be some correspondence between such observed characteristics and pervasive impressions concerning the protean nature of public opinion in a total electorate. However, particularly in recent years this dull portrait has come under some counterattack. As we shall see shortly, the grounds vary widely, from contrary demonstrations with empirical data to dissections of apparent inconsistencies within the portrait itself.

My purpose in this first section will be to arrive at a more balanced view of public opinion which has some hope of squaring with all of the evidence at once. I shall argue, for example, that such famous phrases as "the public is ignorant" and "the voter is no fool" are not, in fact, contradictory and that if we throw in some grains of salt to reduce the flatness of the assertions on both sides, each observation is quite likely to be as true in spirit as vernacular expressions of this sort can ever hope to be. Or again, at a more sophisticated level, I shall demonstrate at a later point that there is no necessary discrepancy between limited opinion formation on a policy dimension and rather substantial relationships linking aggregate voting patterns to relevant demographic indicators. Throughout we shall be trying to establish a comfortable synthesis of findings, which remain perplexing only if interpretations are too simplistic.

We must begin, however, with a brief review of the nature of public opinion, in both its psychological and its aggregative, or distributive, aspects.

The Psychology of Public Opinion

The term "public opinion" is a handy household word for what a psychologist might think of as an aggregation of certain types of attitudes across a community or constituency. An attitude, as classically analyzed, involves some kind of affect toward an object of cognition. Where public opinion is concerned, of course, the objects are assumed by definition to be public ones.

In specifying the role of public attitudes in politics it is often useful to break the subject down into several levels. At the "micro" end we can separate aspects of cognition, or "pure" information concerning the object, from the more affective feeling states that it may evoke. At the "macro" level it is important to recognize that what may be measured as discrete single opinions often tends to come from bundles of interrelated feelings or more generalized beliefs about public matters. At the very largest end of this continuum, when we talk of far-ranging constructions of reality, or "world-views," which have strong affective implications in assessing a very large range of public events, we are likely to resort to terms like "ideology." With such psychological distinctions in mind let us review what seems to be known about the character of public opinion at the grass-roots level.

Information and Opinion Formation

Surely the most familiar fact to arise from sample surveys in all countries is that popular levels of information about public affairs are, from the point of view of the informed observer, astonishingly low. It may well be, for example, that in most countries there is rarely more than a handful of active national political leaders which a majority of their electorates can meaningfully recognize at any one point in time; and very many prominent political figures whose names are rather persistently in the news (such as, in this country, the minority leader of the Senate or a Supreme Court justice) tend to be unknown by all save 5 to 10 percent of the public. Similarly, legislative proposals that have been the center of heated "public" debate for periods of many months and sometimes years are not even recognized by one-third or more of the public, and, further, among those who evince recognition there is a large proportion who can say little about what the proposal is.

Accounts of such pure information-level data are legion, and detailed examples can be found in most texts dealing with public opinion or in the widely used summaries by Erskine (1962, 1963a, b, and c). I am less interested here in building catalogues of instances of this kind than in asking about the interplay between gaps in information and the formation of politically important opinions in the mass public. That is, the critic of such information-level findings who points out that most of the ballyhooed survey items come from the "stray fact" department and that all sorts of vigorous and well-grounded opinions about political options can be formed without, for example, accurate recognition of the minority leader of the Senate is surely right. But what such criticisms ignore is the fact that the information base for the formation of more important and relevant public opinions is equally shot through with holes or "missing links" that go unsuspected by the typical reader of public opinion data.

Good examples of this kind are somewhat harder to find because few survey studies pay much attention to the interplay between information and opinion. Many studies assess information levels, leaning inevitably toward rather stray facts as a basis of the "test," and then quite independently attempt to measure pure opinions on meatier dimensions of public debate. What is rarely done is to explore the information base underlying the opinions themselves. But when this is done the results are frequently both amazing and instructive.

Let us take one example. An opinion poll taken in 1961 just after the Berlin wall was constructed to reduce the flow of defections from East to West asked what the nature of response to this action by the United States government should be, with options ranging from relatively passive acquiescence to aggressive military countermeasures. In this instance the pure opinion item was accompanied by probes assessing what information the respondents held concerning the Berlin situation. It was discovered that a proportion of the sample not much under one-half, including a large number of those who felt that vigorous military retaliation was the appropriate response, did not happen to know that Berlin was encircled in depth by hostile military troops. Perhaps if this information had been more prevalent it would not have changed attitudes dramatically; however, it seems likely that the opinion distribution might have had a rather different flavor, and it is almost certain that few informed observers reading the poll results without the information follow-up (the more normal case) would ever have conceived that such an obvious fact was unknown to a very large minority of the opinion-holders.[4]

I emphasize the way in which informed observers, including political leaders, are likely to read public opinion material because such readings are an integral part of the mass-elite communication system. In other words, it is fully as important to understand the message as received and decoded at the elite end of the system as it is to understand the character of the message as originally intended by the "sending" public. The problem with major discrepancies in information held at both ends of this communication system is that well-informed receivers often find it nearly impossible to comprehend that certain vital and perfectly "obvious" pieces of information defining a situation may be only sparsely understood beneath the message as sent.

Sometimes the missing links at the grass-roots end of the communication are rather subtle. In the spring of 1968 Eugene McCarthy entered the first state presidential primary, in New Hampshire, opposing on the Democratic ballot the sitting president, Lyndon Johnson, who was at the time expected to seek another term of office. McCarthy had in preceding months become the nominal leader among prominent national politicians of the movement toward rapid disengagement from Vietnam, and the peace issue was his major motivation in challenging his Democratic colleague at the polls. There was very little expectation that McCarthy could actually outpoll the president, but the New Hampshire outcome was eagerly awaited as a first test in a considerable period of time concerning growth in public strength of peace feelings.

The McCarthy vote in New Hampshire of 42 percent, against 48 percent for the president, rather widely exceeded the expectations of most observers, and the "message-as-received," both in the popular press and undoubtedly in the presidential entourage itself, was that the attack of the peace movement on administration policies in Vietnam had gained surprising resonance in the American public. The New Hampshire message has commonly been perceived as one important element in Lyndon Johnson's decision not to run again, announced some weeks later.

Survey data collected in New Hampshire, however, cast the "message-as-sent" in a somewhat different light. Certain pieces of the intentions underlying the vote were as expected. McCarthy had been generally seen as taking on the president out of severe disaffection with administration policies, and most of his votes came from Democrats who felt a parallel disaffection on any of a gamut of burning issues, including the conduct of the war in Vietnam in rather central position but extending to discontent over urban riots, "crime in the streets," and the like. Among McCarthy voters was indeed found a clear if small contingent of "doves." However, it turned out that the bulk of McCarthy support came from "hawks" disgusted that the Johnson administration was not pursuing the war with greater bellicosity. The missing link, as the data made clear, was that many New Hampshire Democrats were unaware that McCarthy had taken a clearly "dovish" stance on the Vietnam issue, and hawks voted for him eagerly on the glib assumption that his quarrel with the administration lay in the same direction as their own. Indeed, an understanding of these patterns helps to explain the paradox, widely noted later in that election year, that many voters across the country had moved from a "leftist" McCarthy vote in the primaries to a "rightist" Wallace vote in the general election.[5]

It is hard to fault observers for having interpreted the McCarthy vote in New Hampshire as an outpouring of the peace movement, because it simply strained credulity that a significant proportion of the Democratic electorate in that state had failed to absorb the information concerning McCarthy's peace position. After all, that position had become McCarthy's trademark and raison d'être, and his campaigning in the state prior to the primary had been intensive. The absence on such a substantial scale of *that* particular link might never have occurred to even the observer properly skeptical of public information levels. And yet it is exactly that absence that creates a basic discontinuity between the "message-as-sent" and the "message-as-received."

We have stressed the interplay between low information and oddities in opinion formation, rather than low information levels on stray facts alone, for one or two rather simple reasons. First, it is important to understand that missing links of information are absolutely vital in the formation of what is read as "public opinion" on central political issues, and that if unsuspected these missing links gravely flaw the communication process that is the basic subject of this essay. A second reason for this emphasis is to address frequent criticisms of the dim portrait of public opinion which claim it is simply inaccurate, being based on faulty empirical materials. Such criticisms are invariably addressed to problems in opinion measurement and ignore any evidence arising from deficiencies in the information base underlying the measured opinions. Thus it may be argued, for example, that the wrong opinion questions were asked and that if different items or different wordings had been chosen, a more vigorous and coherent structure of public opinion would have been uncovered. Or, again, it is charged that many of the respondents who appear to be haphazard in their responses or who claim they do not know enough about the matter to venture an opinion are in fact both informed and opinionated but disinclined to betray their private position to an unfamiliar visitor.

Opinions are indeed a rather "soft" area for measurement, and while allegations of the type recited above are vastly overdrawn in terms of other evidence of validity which is often available, the problems mentioned are not, at base, spurious ones. However, by the same token, assessments of information escape most of these criticisms and approach the status of "hard" data. Assessing whether or not a person knows some fact is usually a rather straightforward operation and is far less contingent on the details of question wording than the assessment of pure opinion is known to be. Moreover, motivations toward concealment essentially vanish in such a setting: awareness of factual information can be displayed without betrayal of personal attitudes toward the information or related matters. Indeed, all of the respondents' motivations in the interview setting are oriented toward concealing ignorance, if it is present, so that results showing low levels of information are surely not underestimates.

It is probably for these reasons that criticisms focus on the opinion measurement evidence rather than on the assessments of information. Yet what such an approach misses is the vital connection between the information base and opinion formation itself. If there are important missing links in the information base, then contention over the precise choice of items or wordings is at best only a secondary issue. Question wording is an important problem in its own right, to be sure. But if we are trying to restore confidence in the meaningfulness of opinion formation among voters, as is usually the avowed intent of such reviews, then being completely preoccupied with the details of opinion measurement and giving no attention whatever to the less contestable deficiencies of information, which seem almost endemic on the rare occasions when they are explored, does not constitute a very compelling case.

Indeed, there is a good deal of evidence, often more qualitative, based on interviewer accounts, than quantitative, that many respondents are quite painfully aware of their own information gaps when pressed toward choosing an opinion on many matters of public affairs. When care is taken to build a permissive atmosphere in the interviewing, by pointing out that there is nothing wrong with not having an opinion on some items, the proportion of people who are glad to admit they have no opinion builds considerably higher than when the whole flavor of the interview implies that any normal human being naturally has crystallized some attitude on all the matters under discussion. Furthermore, internal analyses from data drawn even in permissive settings suggest that at least in some instances people try to express opinions that are so vaguely grounded that they are about as likely to reverse their positions at the next sitting as they are to give the same ones.[6]

At the level of the single opinion, then, the portrait of the electorate and its "public opinion" has not in the past been a very reassuring one. Informa-

tion levels are invariably lower than all but the most hardened observers in-
tuitively take for granted. Although the information base beneath asserted
opinions is rarely probed, when researchers do subject it to scrutiny they often
uncover unexpected missing links of information which change the manifest
meaning of the opinion response. Similarly, cross-time, or longitudinal, studies
of the same respondents show a rather surprising instability of response to issue
items, confirming intuitive impressions of weak attitude crystallization and a
general amorphousness in much of what registers as "public opinion."

At the same time it is dangerously easy to carry these observations too far.
They are frequently misinterpreted as saying that not much of anybody has
political opinions about much of anything. This is a disastrous misconstruction, for it fits no data at all. On any kind of reasonable item that taps a major
policy debate, a substantial fraction of the electorate suffers no gross deficiencies of information and has highly developed and often vehement positions of
its own. On at least some issues this is probably true of a vast majority of the
public or otherwise the tenor of political life at the grass-roots level would
surely be different than it is. Moreover, although we shall postpone detailed
discussion until we have laid out the initial bleak portrait, there are signs that
public opinion in the United States in the turbulence of the middle and later
1960s came to display a somewhat firmer "muscle tone" than it had shown
in the preceding decade or two; this phenomenon is helpful in understanding
the reasons for the frequent "flabbiness" of public opinion.

If "public opinion," as customarily measured in either sample surveys or
full-scale elections, is a mix, the proportions of which can vary rather strikingly
according to the special case, of well-formed and well-grounded opinions along
with others that are given with extreme casualness and gaping deficiencies in
information, we might ask why we spend so much time "accentuating the negative" in our accounts. We do so not because the negative features necessarily
outweigh the positive in many situations but because the negative side, while
notorious enough, seems to be ignored with great frequency when public opinion is interpreted. Discoveries as to low information levels are extremely old
hat, and virtually no informed observer—journalist, politician, or academic—
has seen less than dozens of them. But when it comes to the practical interpretation of a vote, a referendum, or a set of opinion poll results the assumption
that there exists a fund of basic information shared in common between the
opinion-giver and the observer seems almost irresistible.

Attitude Structure and Ideology

Any treatment of discrete pieces of information or isolated opinions is, however, somewhat inadequate. It is apparent from the most cursory observation
that specific individual opinions on controversies over public affairs are frequently consistent with and probably informed by more overarching political
beliefs and postures. The politician who takes a liberal or leftist stance on one

cluster of issues is rather likely to lean in the same direction with respect to other political controversies. Often such ideological stances are quite explicit: they depend on highly generalized views as to social causation, the nature of justice, the character of an ideal political order, and the like. Thus, if we have knowledge of a person's deeper value premises, we can more or less predict his or her assessments of more discrete and specific issue controversies.

In fact it is often argued that without such broader frames of reference for the ready evaluation of political detail, making sense of politics would become an extremely onerous and time-consuming chore (see, for example, Smith, Bruner, and White, 1956). Surely the enormous shorthand convenience of various common "ideological" yardsticks is self-evident to anyone who follows political life at all closely. If, for example, we read in the newspaper a short sentence to the effect that a political figure "began his career as a liberal, but since the early 1960s has become progressively more conservative," these few words speak volumes: they provide a useful, if approximate, handle as to how this personage must have behaved at hundreds if not thousands of more specific political junctures in the past, who his political comrades have been and are now, and even, presumptively, what is likely to be expected of him as a political actor in the future.

In view of frequent gaps in information even with respect to rather prominent axes of public policy debate, it has been natural to ask what might be said of broader attitudinal structures and ideological thinking in the general public. About a decade ago I produced an article (Converse, 1964) that tried to address this set of problems with data from the Survey Research Center election study series.

In brief, evidence drawn from the 1956–60 period implies that various opinions expressed on major policy controversies of the day showed remarkably low levels of cohesion, or internal integration, failing to fit together as one might expect if these several positions were being informed in common by more generalized liberal or conservative views. Indeed, the minimal signs of internal integration for the mass public stood in rather sharp contrast to data drawn from political elites (in that instance, members of the United States Congress) on comparable issue items in the same period, which showed that internal integration ran at least moderately high. These findings nicely complemented work by McClosky and his associates (1960, 1964) showing clearer lines of position-taking on the part of political leaders (convention delegates) than among their sympathizers in the electorate at large.

Moreover, longitudinal data involving expressions of opinion on exactly the same items from the same voters over a period of years correspondingly showed that voters had a surprising degree of instability in their policy positions. When my 1964 article was written parallel longitudinal data on elite populations were not available to complete the contrast, although some data that have been generated since do show the expected marked differences between mass and elite in attitude stability.[7]

These contrasts seemed to make sense if information, often missing on the mass side, tends to serve as something of a connective tissue linking superficially disparate ideas and if, in particular, such diverse ideas are less likely in the mass public than in the elite to be evaluated in terms of a limited set of more abstract or overarching frames of reference, such as those provided by ideological constructs. Furthermore, the data I used for the article showed that there were enough differences in opinion crystallization and temporal stability from issue area to issue area even within the mass public to hypothesize that basic to the whole set of patterns was the "centrality" of issues to the individual, in a linked cognitive and motivational sense. That is, the weakest issue areas for the mass public were those most remote from its daily concerns, including foreign policy or domestic issues mainly affecting elite actors, such as relations between government and business. The strongest issue areas at the time were those likely to be seen as "doorstep" matters such as racial desegregation.[8]

In the same period I also presented quite direct evidence addressed to the use of ideological yardsticks by members of the mass electorate. Despite the fact that terms like "liberal" and "conservative" are the most frequently used pieces of ideological shorthand in American political discourse, more than a third of the electorate could supply no meaning for these denotations as of 1960 (Converse, 1964). Adding to this third a substantial number of persons who claimed recognition but gave confused or obviously garbled responses as to the meaning of the distinction, it appeared that not much over half of the electorate had even minimal understanding of such a conceptual yardstick.

Of course, mere recognition of these terms does not ensure high familiarity and certainly is no evidence that the person evincing recognition ever actively uses such a concept in his or her own codings of political personalities, issues, or events. Earlier efforts had been made (Campbell *et al.*, 1960) to ascertain how frequently the liberal-conservative yardstick or other broad and abstract conceptual tools were actively used by members of the electorate, by reading their voluntary discussions of the good and bad points of the major political parties and the presidential candidates. These extended evaluations were coded into a hierarchy of "levels of conceptualization." At the top level were placed "ideologues," respondents who at one point or another gave evidence of evaluating the parties or candidates against some abstract conceptual yardstick—usually, although not exclusively, the liberal-conservative continuum. The second major level was made up of persons who made no such remarks but evaluated these prime political objects in terms of benefits or antagonisms toward interest groups in the society. The third level consisted of persons whose judgments were bound up with highly specific but disconnected policy debates or who seemed to be reacting to a vaguer "mood" of the nation: whether times were generally good or bad. The bottom level contained respondents who introduced no issue concerns whatever in their discussion of the parties and candidates. This coding suggested that as of 1956 only a very limited fraction of the electorate—less than one in eight and perhaps less than one in twenty-five, depending partly on stringency of definitions—registered in the top level, displaying active "ideological thought." [9]

Another set of inquiries into the character of ideological thinking on the part of the "common man" in the same historical period, although from a dramatically different angle, involved clinical or in-depth studies on small samples, the most noteworthy example being research conducted by Robert E. Lane (1962). Lane spent many hours in a probing set of "conversations" about politics, society, and the world with each of fifteen men drawn randomly from voter lists in a "middle-income" housing project. In the course of his interviews he pursued understandings of concepts like "freedom," "democracy," "equality," and "power" as well as more detailed perceptions of the American political scene. The ultimate monograph attempts to draw these political perceptions into coherent attitude portraits that can be understood in terms of the temperaments and experiences of the individual respondents.

Some commentators (e.g., Brown, 1970) have taken the Lane study to be rather contradictory to the sample survey evidence of the character of public opinion and ideology. Survey interpretations are thought to imply that political content is sparse in the mind of the common person and ideology is virtually nonexistent. Yet Lane laid bare a great deal of political content over the course of his extended interviews with men who typically lacked much political sophistication or, in some cases, even political interest. And he addresses the way in which their more abstract political perceptions cohere, often in rather idiosyncratic ways, but nonetheless in configurations that he quite reasonably labels "ideologies."

However, a more sensitive comparison of the interview material and the survey data relieves much of the sense of incompatibility. The reasons for some of the apparent discrepancies lie very close to the surface. Thus, for example, the two sources often deal with mildly divergent definitions as to what constitutes an "ideology." Moreover, the Lane treatment evinces no small measure of frustration at the limits and discontinuities in the trains of political perceptions which his respondents generated. Dead ends were encountered in lines of thought just when it seemed that the individual was on the brink of putting together more powerful, generalized conclusions. Indeed, Lane depends on the concept of "morselization" to express the fact that several of his respondents failed to arrive at more overarching organization of their political thoughts, despite having some of the raw ingredients for doing so.

> Now, the very morselizing tendency that prevents these men from discovering the pattern and significance of an event also prevents them from ideologizing. While they do not place events in the context of a pattern of history or policy, neither do they place them in the context of some... forensic ideology. (Lane, 1962, p. 353)

Such an account fits nicely with survey-based descriptions that stress missing links between bodies of similar information, the weakness of "constraints" between idea-elements, and the paucity of more abstract frames of reference helpful in organizing such information.

If the reality being described is the same, however, the differences in method do lead to rather marked discrepancies in emphasis, particularly with respect to the amount of political content the average person tends to have on his or her mind.[10] It will be vital to some of our later arguments in this essay to understand that the differences in method are closely linked to differences in fundamental purposes of the two types of inquiry.

In effect, Lane comes close to asking his respondents, "What, after all, are your views of politics and the world? What perceptions, feelings, expectations, grievances, or aspirations do you have in this general area?" The typical "closed" survey item is instead a highly focused probe: "People are discussing whether the government should do X or not. Are you in favor of X or opposed to it?" The difference is roughly that between fishing with a net and "fishing" with a rifle.

It would be foolish to conclude that either method is in a general way inferior: each is well-suited to its purpose. Lane's interest lies squarely in the domain of political psychology: the central questions have to do with the way in which individuals develop, process, and generalize whatever political perceptions they may have. With such purposes in view, the broad-net approach is both admirable and essential. It also necessarily sweeps in more content than even dozens of more focused probes could and, being interested chiefly in what *is* present, does not address much attention to what is not.

The more directed probes of "closed" survey items are not very well adapted to these general problems of political psychology, although when many such items are available or are posed to the same individuals over time they can yield evidence concerning attitude structures and stability. What the abbreviated survey approach is admirably suited to assess, however, is the character of the interaction between citizen and government, that is, the functioning of public opinion in the kind of communication system that democratic institutions become in practice, if not necessarily in theory.

This is so for the simple reason that most of the functioning of public opinion in interaction with elites involves political options packaged more in the "bullet," or directed-probe, mode than in the broad-net mode. For example, we know of no referendum items on ballots which ask the voter to write out what has been bothering him or her lately or what he or she would like to see the government do next. The typical referendum item on a formal ballot is tightly focused on a particular "yes-no" policy alternative, which differs from the standard survey opinion item, if at all, chiefly in reduced intelligibility. To be sure, candidates for office do enjoy using the broad-net approach from time to time, asking their constituents in informal interaction what is on their minds. There is also no small interest among elites in sample distributions of responses to salience questions of the type, "What is the most important problem facing the country these days?" to which responses are much more open-ended than are responses to specific issue or policy items. Nevertheless, it seems to be in the nature of governance that elites face an endless sequence of decision points, often thrust on them by circumstance, for which specific policy direction must be chosen. And it is the heart of the democratic tradition that public responses to such forced alternatives be sounded. The mode, whether the subject is Vietnam, civil rights, or tax increases, is inevitably that of the survey-style directed probe.

The limitation of the broad-net approach for these specific purposes, apart from its costliness, is simply that much of the content discovered will be irrelevant to specific topics on which elites may be asking instructions, either in an absolute sense of relevance or because the respondents lack the kind of linking information or overarching perspectives that permit them to bring their knowledge and opinions to bear on these topics. The broad-net approach, as Lane demonstrates, can lay bare various organizing abstractions or generalizations, but if it turns out that these are entirely idiosyncratic or at least oblique to the most common shorthands at the upper levels of the communication system and if the respondents do not even understand the conventional shorthand, then the votes they cast risk misinterpretation when received and decoded as messages on the elite side.

More recently Lane (1973) has provided his own view of the contrasts between the two approaches. He argues that by focusing on the apparent integration or constraint among political opinions, as reflected by their static intercorrelations in aggregates of persons, the survey approach as I had used it fails to take into account the idiosyncratic "political reasoning" by which people link superficially discrepant political attitudes into meaningful, if very personalized, structures of thought. I agree in principle with this observation. Indeed, I made the same argument in my 1964 article by way of introducing a further set of tests that, unlike the static correlations, *would* have some bearing on the idiosyncratic possibility (Converse, 1964, pp. 238ff). I assumed that if unusual combinations of opinion positions were in fact bound into systems of ideas highly meaningful to an individual, then these diverse positions taken separately should show a good deal of stability for that individual over time, even though the private rationale for the particular structure might not be obvious to the analyst without more open-ended questioning. Yet, as mentioned above, the expressed positions under discussion showed remarkable instability for individuals over time, particularly among the large fraction of the electorate with no more than a peripheral interest in politics. These findings seemed to cast great doubt on any likelihood that these particular opinions were typically cemented into even idiosyncratic belief systems.

It is difficult to know how to move the discussion much beyond this point, since neither Lane nor other writers raising the idiosyncratic possibility address in any direct way the pages of negative evidence about stability. However, to prevent misconstruction, it should be made very clear what this negative evidence does and does not imply. It does not say, for example, that idiosyncratic belief systems about politics are nonexistent. I have always assumed they exist in some profusion. Nor does it say that *no* political beliefs within the very narrow set of opinions being surveyed at the time were part of other stable attitude structures, either ideological or idiosyncratic, for any significant portion of the electorate. The data show in fact that opinions were part of stable attitude structures for some people. Nonetheless, the same data do seem to say quite plainly that this limited set of opinions was not widely integrated by the electorate into the ideological wholes commonly presumed for them by observers chiefly exposed to elite attitude structures and discourse. And the evidence of high instability of these opinion positions for the same individuals over time rather strongly suggests that the opinions were not even part of firm but idiosyncratic attitude structures for a majority of the electorate. If such a demonstration had been conducted on an equally limited set of haphazardly selected political topics, it might be of quite paltry significance. But the set of options being examined had been carefully selected to cover the major issue debates that swirled around the elections of the period. It was in terms of exactly these particular themes that election returns were most frequently scrutinized for their policy significance, in an effort to know what it was that the public was saying to its leadership. Hence the apparent widespread lack of integration of these particular opinions into even idiosyncratic systems of political meaning seemed worth comment. Again, however, the purpose of the investigation was somewhat different from that represented by Lane's work.

In short, then, I would conclude that the two approaches to the study of attitude structures and ideology have in no sense produced contradictory findings and indeed have their own distinctive utilities. If one wishes to cover the full gamut of political psychology, including the formation of all manner of political perceptions and the functioning of these perceptions as part of individual personality, then it seems likely that the Lane in-depth approach is to be preferred. If, on the other hand, one's interest in public opinion is limited chiefly to its role in the broader functioning of those mass-elite democratic communication mechanisms most obviously, if not exclusively, embodied in popular elections or referenda, as is the task of this essay, then it is probable that the survey approach is more revealing.

Variation in the Character of Public Opinion

This bleak portrait of public opinion and ideology came largely from the United States, in the period surrounding World War II and especially in the

1950s, when the most intensive work was done. It is natural to ask how time- and culture-bound this portrait is—a question that, if well answered, may help us diagnose the problems of weak public opinion and understand conditions under which it tends to be strengthened. More recent work, particularly in the last few years, has been addressed to this kind of question.

Cross-Time Variation in the United States

A fertile field for inquiry into ideological frames of reference and attitude in- tegration was first provided by the 1964 presidential campaign. It was fertile on at least two counts. First, the campaign produced an unusual emphasis on ex- plicit ideological differences, since the Republican candidate, Barry Goldwater, had in prior speeches and writings adopted a stance as a pure conservative who would offer the electorate "a choice, not an echo." Secondly, the ever-growing racial issue, which had been vigorous in public opinion even during the 1950s but had had limited partisan impact because the Republican and Democratic parties had both been variable in their position-taking, was suddenly drawn into focus as the Goldwater camp let the white South know that he would "go slow" on the most gripping issue for that region. The public around the nation picked up this information on a new party differentiation with dramatic speed.

Field and Anderson (1969) and Pierce (1970) produced partial replications of our earlier estimates (Campbell *et al.*, 1960) of the prevalence of ideological frames of reference and have shown that there was a highly significant increase in the proportion of persons using ideological terms to describe the parties and the candidates in the 1964 election. The usage of ideological terms departs in a modest way from our original readings of the raw protocols. For example, the Field-Anderson reconstruction permits some 21 percent to be classified as "ideo- logues" in the baseline year of 1956, as opposed to 12 percent in the original coding. However, that figure had advanced to 35 percent by 1964, a generous gain. As Field and Anderson point out, much of that gain was due to references made to the candidates, and a reading of the raw interviews has impressed us with the number of persons referring to Goldwater as a "radical," a perception the Democrats had stressed with respect to his "trigger-happy" views on the growing Vietnam conflict. Since in the original coding we had not taken popu- lar political epithets like "Commie" as evidence of ideological thinking unless supported by further commentary of a congruent ideological sort, there is rea- sonable doubt that in the 1964 context we would have taken descriptions of Goldwater as a radical to be proof of an ideological mode of thought. However, the prevalence of this description—and its importance in the apparent height- ened salience of ideology for the electorate in 1964—may help to explain one other anomaly that scholars working with these data have failed to notice. De- spite the facile assumption that Goldwater's leading of the Republican party back to a more explicit and unambiguous conservatism had heightened the ideological clarity of debate, which in turn registered in the salience of ideology for the mass public, one finds that the proportion of that public ranking the Democrats as the more *conservative* of the two parties was actually a bit higher in 1964 than it had been in 1960 or would become by 1968! When the information base of this ideological resurgence is more carefully examined we find, as is so often the case, that all that glistens is not gold.

Another fact that is at least mildly troubling about the salience of ideological criteria in 1964 is that the proportion of the electorate indicating no recognition of terms like "conservative" and "liberal" was almost exactly as great in 1964 as it had been in 1960; indeed, the figure indicating lack of recognition remains essentially constant across the 1960, 1964, and 1968 surveys.[11] Perhaps the best way to reconcile these data is to take cognizance of the fact that they have a somewhat different thrust and in fact refer to rather different reaches of the electorate. Presumably voters in the more informed half of the electorate already had some familiarity with the terms, and when the terms came into high use in the campaign these voters reflected that use in their own descriptions, albeit in mildly garbled form. Thus the active usage measure is situationally elastic. But the high rate of public use of these concepts did not appear to contribute to the schooling of the lower half of the electorate.

Undoubtedly the most striking findings to emerge recently concerning the impact of the crises of the 1960s on the character of public opinion up through the 1968 election are those reported by Nie (1974) and Pomper (1972). Both authors, using somewhat different portions of the Survey Research Center election study series, show that marked gains in the integration of public attitudes on partisan political issues were made, almost suddenly, in connection with the 1964 election and that they remained, by standards of the 1950s, at very high levels through 1968 and, in Nie's case, well beyond. Much of this change as well as a variety of others that appear to have been touched off at about the same time (decline in trust of government, decrease in proportions of party identifiers) are best discussed in the context of voting behavior in our next section. However, aspects bearing most closely on the structure of public opinion are worth reviewing briefly here.

Nie focuses on the intercorrelations of essentially the same policy attitude items that I had earlier used for the 1956–60 period in discussing mass belief systems. He shows that the general interrelatedness, or constraint, among these attitudes shifted upward dramatically in 1964, arriving at levels that are surely comparable to those reported for congressional elite respondents as of 1958. Moreover, the fit of positions in different issue areas was far more coherent in liberal-conservative terms in 1964 than it was in the 1950s. The crises of the 1960s appear to have polarized the mass public more nearly into two camps of public opinion than had been true within any prior portion of the historical record covered by sample survey materials, save possibly the 1930s. Such changes are not hard to map into other things we know of the period, including indicators of domestic violence. But the degree of change remains impressive and theoretically instructive.

Pomper's work (1972) is very complementary. He shows that at the same time in which the internal integration of attitudes was gaining in firmness (and divisiveness), the perceptual links between the major parties and various policy alternatives also became dramatically clearer and more widely agreed on by partisans of differing stripe. Once more, as Pomper points out, it is not hard to relate these changes to historical events. Barry Goldwater was determined to accentuate the magnitude of policy differences between the two major parties. Again, however, it seems impressive that so much change could have been achieved so quickly and that it has endured despite some of the narrowing differentiation of policy positions between the two traditional parties which had recurred by the time of the 1968 election.[12]

To summarize, then, it is clear that a major change occurred in some parameters of public opinion in the United States of the 1960s which many scholars feel is rather basic. It is also clear that the change has been rather sudden, having begun about 1964, a time when a number of other kinds of indicators of mass political life in these election studies also began to shift after at least ten or fifteen years of inertia. It is clear furthermore that this change in the public opinion parameters has displayed something of what we call an "across-the-board" quality, i.e., it is not a change that can readily be traced to some narrow segment of the population but rather is one that can be detected in at least some degree in all demographic groups like sex, race, and region which investigators commonly isolate. This kind of sudden, across-the-board change usually calls up images of external events to which all of an electorate has been a witness at the same moment and to which there has been something of a common reaction, although in the case of polarization on issue positions the reaction may run in opposing directions. All of these change properties fit the most obvious, first-glance causal assumptions about the reasons for change, starting with the Goldwater candidacy of 1964 and proceeding into a deeper and deeper tangle of crises on domestic and foreign fronts throughout the rest of the 1960s.

What is not clear, of course, is whether or not the change in public opinion is permanent. Nor is a closely related question clear: Which is a more normal state of affairs, the public opinion portrait from the 1950s or that from the later 1960s? Some authors, on discovering these or related changes, have linked them automatically to high political turbulence of the later period, which was in most eyes a crisis time in an absolute sense. Thus it is implicit that the 1960s portrait is the abnormal one. Other authors have assumed that the 1950s were an abnormal trough of routine politics and hence that the shape of public opinion in the 1960s is more nearly what is to be expected. Of course, both may be true: the first period may have been abnormally lacking in turbulence and the second abnormally laden with it, a judgment that would imply that, sooner or later, the state of opinion might return to something in between. And finally, for a rough and ready completeness of the set of possibilities, the 1950s may have been quite normal for an earlier period, with the 1960s setting a norm for a New Era.

Diagnosis and Prognosis

In this section I hope to sketch something of a diagnosis and a prognosis. The diagnosis must fit both the 1950s and the period since 1964, although I do not see that bridge as terribly difficult to construct. The prognosis is the riskier business, and I shall take pains to avoid flat predictions. We do not have much hope of gaining perspective on the 1950s and 1960s by moving backward in time, as public opinion data thin out rapidly in that direction. Although it has its own pitfalls, perhaps our best source of perspective, short of the ideal but unchallenging one of waiting to find out, is to consider what seems to be most "normal" in the case of other countries whose electorates have some reasonable similarity to that of the United States. I shall in fact follow that tactic below, and the loose impressions we can glean from such reconnaissance will hint that the state of opinion in the late 1960s was indeed abnormally crystallized and hence, presumably, crisis related, although the later 1950s appears as well to be something of a "local minimum" in several of these regards.

Diagnosis

It seems likely that the heart of the political information problem was sketched out in two brilliant essays by the journalist Walter Lippmann (1922, 1925) over fifty years ago. Lippmann developed a number of worthwhile theses bearing on the relationship of the common citizen to his or her governors in the large modern state, but of these perhaps the most central was the observation—unorthodox for its time—that the average citizen had his or her hands full coping with the events of daily life and therefore was unlikely to devote more than casual attention to the broader political affairs of the nation, which were generally rather remote from his or her immediate needs. Being largely inattentive, the average citizen rarely becomes very well informed.

There is a good deal of similarity between Lippmann's homespun descriptions and more recent efforts to formalize the character of the problem. My dependence in the "Belief Systems" paper on a dimension whereby political objects and disputes varied in their centrality from individual to individual was of this sort. In another vocabulary, the average person in a democracy makes an implicit cost-benefit analysis, and the perceived benefits of having political information usually fail to outweigh either the direct costs or the opportunity costs of acquiring it. What such explanatory constructs have in common is a focus on motivational states.

In most theories of action, motivational states represent relatively elastic and situation-bound terms. Personality, values, and habits are almost by definition stable and enduring: motivation, instead, can change dramatically in the short term according to the details of a situation. Hence we must turn to motivational states to understand the considerable variation observed in the nature of public opinion in the past twenty years. One of my favorite vignettes demonstrating in a relatively pure form the elasticity of information intake is that cited by Miller and Stokes (1963) in their consideration of constituency information about congressional candidates in 1958. In that year less than a quarter of the electorate nationwide claimed to have heard or read anything about the two candidates, incumbent and challenger, competing for the congressional seat in their district. This is a standard example of the low general levels of political information. However, one of the major national political events of the preceding year had been the Little Rock school integration crisis, which had culminated in President Eisenhower's dispatch of federal troops to the area, to the extreme bitterness of the local white population. In the Fifth Congressional District of Arkansas the incumbent representative, Brooks Hays, had been seen as too moderate on the segregation issue due to his efforts to mediate the dispute between President Eisenhower and the governor of Arkansas. On these grounds he was opposed in 1958 by an arch-segregationist write-in candidate, Dale Alford. Here we have a crisis of gripping national proportions which was, nonetheless, compressed in its main impact within a tiny geographic area; a doorstep issue of explosive sensitivity; and an electoral contest geared perfectly along all the lines of extreme inflammation. In the sample for this district, 100 percent of the respondents reported having heard or read something about *both* candidates.

This vignette does not illustrate that the American public is well informed: the nationwide statistics are the more relevant data. What it does illustrate is a set of limiting, or boundary, conditions under which virtually all members of the electorate increase their attentiveness and multiply their information intake by a significant factor. But this happens only when the situation is right and the perceived stakes are high enough—apparently an extremely rare event.

What explanation of the nature of the implicit cost-benefit analysis would, on the one hand, account for such extreme variations in the motivation to attend to public politics and yet, on the other hand, explain the fact that the costs of paying attention seem to outweigh the benefits for much of the electorate much of the time? The form of this calculus has been spelled out in several excellent statements, including those of Downs (1957) and Lane (1973). I shall summarize the general view but with special emphasis on the fact that electorates are enormously heterogeneous with respect to both the cost and the benefit sides of the equation.

On the side of perceived benefits, it is clearly inappropriate to talk of an electorate as though it were of one piece. At one extreme there are the political elites for whom the stakes of political competition are enormously high; the competition affects them day to day and with little respite in the most vital parameters of their lives—their careers, prestige, self-esteem, and most cherished values. Such persons are, of course, a minuscule fraction of the electorate and do not intrude notably on national samples. However, national samples do pick up visible numbers of grass-roots activists for whom engagement and participation is an enormously important avocation. The stakes involved in politics are not objectively as great for them as for the top politicians, but their perceived benefits must remain substantial. There is in addition a rather larger proportion of the electorate, next in line on the perceived-benefits scale, which takes a very serious interest in a range of policy directions that the nation is following, including some policies for which the immediate personal stakes, at least in a narrow sense of the term, are rather obscure. Many anti-Vietnam activists, especially those without draftable near-relatives, were clearly in this category. There are also substantial numbers of people who reap the same psychological pleasure from their side winning as they do from a home-team championship.

But these people are in the upper reaches of the perceived-benefit scale, whether the benefits are from vocation, avocation, principle, or taste. They probably do not describe a majority of most electorates most of the time, for whom perceived stakes are a good deal more feeble and, for some, nonexistent. People in the upper reaches have a built-in difficulty in understanding why everybody does not share the same sense of importance of politics, and at times their lack of understanding escalates to exasperation or moral indignation. But if benefits are narrowly enough construed, the stakes of participation even in the coldest objective sense are very weak for much of the population, and perceptually they seem quite negligible. Aside from the heavy hand of government in draft programs and taxes, the impingement of government on the daily lives of much of the population is largely invisible. Indeed, while populations are well indoctrinated in the horrors of life under political systems other than the one under which they live, large segments of normal populations might not be able to tell on the basis of their daily lives what kind of system *they* live under, short of relying on direct information from national news. Of course, for the upper reaches doing the indoctrinating the stakes of a change of system would be enormous.

Moreover, if the going political choices were actually to have a draft or not, to have taxes or cut them in half, to augment a social security system or abolish it, then the objective personal stakes would increase rather dramatically and, presumably, so would the subjective ones. However, such exaggerated differences in options are almost never at issue, and the few points at which government impingement on daily life has some clarity would differ only marginally in outcomes, if at all, whoever wins power.[13] Add to this the mathematical impotence of one vote in many millions and it is scarcely surprising that the perceived benefits fare badly against the costs of attention for substantial portions of the population. From this point of view, voters are no fools to remain ignorant.

Much of the cost side of the equation is equally obvious, although some aspects deserve elucidation. Since following politics avidly occupies significant time per week and surely grass-roots political activity is notoriously time consuming, there are the obvious opportunity costs of which Lippmann wrote. Time is filled with activities seen to have higher stakes. I have always been intrigued at the visible depression in political attentiveness in the busy stage of people's life cycle, after children arrive in a marriage and when the breadwinners are still finding their occupational niches. If caring for a sick child is incompatible with watching dramatic Senate hearings on television, there is not much question how the time allocation will go, even for someone with substantial political interest.

The aspect of cost associated with information acquisition may be considerably more perplexing, at least under current conditions. For an older time, when the only mass media involved the written word and a significant fraction of the electorate, while perhaps technically literate, found reading a slow and tedious process, the notion of information cost has a good deal of intuitive merit. But in modern America, saturated with the spoken media and endowed with significant amounts of leisure time, the concept of information cost may seem to lose much of its bite. Indeed, with the average American spending close to two hours a day, seven days a week watching television, and with the radio on another hour a day, not to mention high newspaper and magazine circulation, it would seem almost more costly to *avoid* political information than it is to seek it out. Five minutes daily of attentive listening to radio news, which can be accomplished while driving to work, might be enough to keep even very busy people within the upper quartile of Americans with respect to general political information. In this context, then, is the notion of information cost even viable, at least where the simpler and more obvious forms of political information are concerned?

Bombardment with political information and low levels of intake can co-occur only if there is, in a very substantial portion of the electorate, a steady and systematic "tuning-out." Again, the details are familiar: for many people politics just does not compete in interest with sports, local gossip, and television dramas. The condition is mainly motivational and can reverse itself quickly when the occasion arises. Political articles in the newspaper are typically skipped; but when Alford challenges Hays after the president sends federal troops into the state, interest rockets.

I am convinced, however, that there is at the same time a cognitive element to information costs which is not inconsequential in the shaping of public opinion. I would propose that the costs of digesting and retaining the load of incoming political information still differ rather widely from person to person

across the electorate, even if interest is held constant. And the general governing principle is of the "them what has, gets" type: the more political information one already has, the lower the cost of acquiring and, perhaps more important, *retaining* new information. For people already well informed, keeping up
with politics is scarcely dull, is almost effortless, and the notion that information costs something seems almost peculiar.

Yet over the past two decades a proportion of the electorate varying between 60 percent and 70 percent has agreed with the proposition that "sometimes politics and government seems so complicated that a person like me can't
really understand what's going on." The adverb "sometimes" is not well suited
to our purposes here. If it were changed to "usually" or "most of the time," the
proportion of agreement would surely drop drastically. Yet we would imagine
that a very substantial sector of the electorate—perhaps one-third—would continue to agree with the proposition even in this more sweeping form.

Why is there a feeling in the less informed reaches of the electorate that
politics is confusing and complicated? I suspect that it is simply because the
old information brought to bear on new, incoming information is too sparse to
lend it much meaning. If an informed observer hears a surprising policy statement in the news by the secretary of defense, he may prick up his ears and pay
close attention. He relates this information to what he knows of recent policy,
what he knows of the secretary's relationship to the president, what he knows
of past positions the secretary may have taken, and the like, since he is intensely interested to detect even small reorientations of national policy. In
short, he automatically imports enormous amounts of prior information that
lends the new statement high interest. The poorly informed person, hearing
the same statement, finds it as dull as the rest of the political news. He only
dimly understands the role of secretary of defense and has no vivid image
grounded in past information as to the inclinations of the current incumbent.
His awareness of current policy is sufficiently gross that he has no expectation
of detecting nuances of change. So the whole statement is confronted with
next to no past information at all, hence is just more political blather: in five
minutes he probably will not remember that he heard such a statement, much
less be able to reconstruct what was said. This means in turn that four months
later, when confronted by another statement by the secretary of defense, he will
bring as little to it as he did before and hence forget it with equal rapidity.
The whole sequence is much like attending a party in foreign terrain, where
all the conversation turns on personalities that are unrecognizable; it is a
downright dull evening, and there surely are more stimulating ways to spend
one's time. In short, with respect to politics the richness and meaning of new
information depends vitally on the amount of past information one brings to
the new message. So does retention of the information over time.

If the general principle that old information helps to store and retain new
information is true, then it is not hard to understand why electorates are so

extremely heterogeneous in political information, with the most informed having an amount of past information to bear on this or that new information
which differs—if we had any way to measure such things—by astronomical
magnitudes from the amount of information brought to bear by the least informed on exactly the same message.

Hence information cost is a serious problem in the less informed reaches
of the electorate and puts a considerable damper on attentiveness, although it
is next to no problem at all in the upper reaches. And when we recognize that
it is in the less informed reaches where people are, for many reasons, less likely
to perceive serious stakes in being informed about politics in the first place,
then we have come full circle. It is then not surprising that there is a dramatic
inversion of the relative weights of costs and benefits of paying attention to
politics somewhere between the upper and lower edges of mass electorates. And
just where that tilt point occurs (as between, say, the first and second quintile
of the electorate, ordered by "informedness," or between the fourth and fifth
quintile) depends mightily on how central or peripheral in a motivational
sense any particular issue or cluster of issues may be for how much of a population. When the issue referents are remote, attentiveness is worth the candle
only at the higher levels. When they are doorstep issues for large sectors of the
population, such as whether one's child or grandchild will be obliged to ride
a bus to a distant school perceived as being less physically safe than the neigh-
borhood one, then a vastly greater proportion of the population falls above the
tilt point where attentiveness is galvanized.

New Lessons from the 1960s

The preceding diagnosis, with its blend of cognitive and motivational elements, does not in any of its main lines contradict various parallel discussions
in Downs (1957), Campbell *et al.* (1960), or other sources from the 1950s. In
order to see what new lessons changes of the 1960s have provided it is necessary to make a number of finer distinctions in the diagnosis as well as to take
a somewhat more differentiated view of public opinion evidence from the
1960s than has been customary in the recent literature.

In principle, any diagnosis containing major motivational elements, as was
typical of earlier statements, rather easily encompasses the kinds of changes in
public opinion that occurred between the 1950s and 1960s. Thus, for example,
one of the two main classes of factors hypothesized in *The American Voter* as
responsible for low levels of public motivation to monitor partisan political
affairs involved the limited policy differences between the parties as perceived
by the public of the 1950s. Indeed it was noted that "policy differences between
the parties in both domestic and foreign affairs were narrower in 1956 than
they had been in some time" (p. 180). The motivational importance of the
changes documented by Pomper (1972) for the 1960s now has become abun-
dantly apparent, although the new trends do less to change the original diag-

nosis than they do to provide more detailed quantitative estimates as to the elasticity of public opinion in response to actual variations in party differences.

However, there are aspects of data from the 1960s which have been seen as contradicting some of the finer details of diagnoses from the 1950s. For example, Nie (1974) writes:

> The argument put forward to explain the low level of issue consistency encountered earlier in the American public is one which emphasizes certain fundamental limitations *inherent* in mass publics. Mass publics, this argument asserts, simply do not have the ideational sophistication or the contextual knowledge required to organize opinions on diverse issues into inclusive ideologies.

The argument to which Nie refers involves discussions in both *The American Voter* and my piece on "Belief Systems" concerning the role of cognitive limitations as part of a diagnosis of the state of public opinion. Actually, the fact of cognitive limitations in itself is less at issue here than the more specific nature of those limitations—in particular, how mutable they are seen to be. Thus, strictly speaking, for example, failure to possess bits of information vital to the formation of an intelligent opinion on an issue is a "cognitive limitation." However, there is nothing innate or immutable about such a deficiency. Given any kind of surge in motivation to attend to politics, all manner of accessible bits of information, such as Eugene McCarthy's peace position in 1968, can be very speedily absorbed and the "limitation" thereby rectified. However, it is not simply the absence of discrete pieces of information that either we or Nie were addressing under this label. What is at issue is the possibility of less rapidly mutable cognitive limitations.

The discussions of cognitive limitations in our earlier work (Campbell *et al.*, 1960; Converse, 1964) occurred in two rather different contexts, one that implied relative mutability and one that did not. The former discussion sprang from observations concerning the links between attitude crystallization, especially a high rating within the hierarchy of "levels of conceptualization," and the background variable of education. The correlations were strong enough to imagine that cognitive limitations embodied in a very restricted education presented something of a barrier to a sophisticated grasp of politics. In the same passages we pointed out that even data from the 1950s made clear that high political interest over long enough periods of time could produce high sophistication even among very poorly educated people. Thus the barriers were not seen as innate and indeed were predicted to fade progressively with the upgrading of education in the electorate, even if aggregate levels of political interest in the electorate remained constant. But they were surely not seen as limitations that could be overcome in any very short period of time by heightened political interest.

The discussion of still less mutable cognitive limitations arose in connection with active use by the electorate of the kinds of organizing abstractions that the coding of the "levels of conceptualization" was designed to measure. The discussion was, moreover, specifically addressed to the least cognitively endowed stratum of the electorate. For this minority it was suggested that in addition to lack of interest and contextual knowledge there might be much more recalcitrant limits on cognitive capacities to organize political perceptions with the use of capping abstractions, such as the conventional conservative-liberal continuum, or for that matter with the use of more idiosyncratic but still efficient abstractions. In general we predicted that the distribution of the electorate across the levels of conceptualization could be expected to shift slowly upward in a more sophisticated direction with advancing aggregate levels of education and that the distribution could show more rapid change, although only quite limited in degree, if public attention to politics were galvanized by crisis, thereby taking up some of the slack in sagging motivations. What would *not* happen, we surmised, was that the distribution of the public across the levels of conceptualization would show "sweeping change" upward in any short term, even with the sudden onset of major crisis (see Campbell *et al.,* 1960, pp. 250–56).

In point of fact, the dramatic changes of the 1960s summarized by Nie, which surely would qualify as "sweeping," are focused on gains in attitude consistency. The levels of conceptualization are not examined, despite the fact that our discussions of the more recalcitrant types of cognitive limitations were addressed specifically to them. Moreover, as I noted earlier, attempts at partial reconstruction of the levels of conceptualization for periods later than 1956 have shown a more mixed picture than their descriptions have made clear. Thus studies such as those of Field and Anderson (1969) and Pierce (1970) have indeed shown significant gains in apparent ideological sophistication within the more sophisticated levels of conceptualization under the kinds of stimulation represented by events like the "ideological campaign" of 1964. At the same time, no gains in recognition of these concepts registered in the lower 40 percent of the electorate over this period. This constancy at lower levels is in many senses more surprising than the gains at higher levels, given what we know of the nature of political stimulation at the time. It suggests a resistance to change which is quite remarkable. And since the possibility of more nearly immutable cognitive limitations was raised only in connection with the bottom fraction even of this less informed 40 percent, these particular data from the 1960s would scarcely disconfirm such a possibility: if anything they would seem to lend added weight to it.

In other words, if we are to uncover new lessons from the later 1960s and beyond, we cannot take too simplistic a view of either the electorate or the ingredients of public opinion. We must keep in mind that the electorate is not a unitary entity, with everyone moving "upward" or "downward" in unison, but rather is enormously heterogeneous with respect to the ingredients of public opinion. And it is equally important to maintain a differentiated view of at least the four crude levels of public opinion we began to distinguish at the beginning of this essay: the information base, the single opinion, structures of related opinions, and guiding frames of reference of capping abstractions, which are in this context usually ideological.

Now most scholars would assume, and I surely agree, that there is a noteworthy tendency for covariation over these four distinct ingredients. That is to say, relatively high masses of information tend to go with relatively crystallized opinions, relatively integrated attitude structures, and the presence of ordering abstractions. However, while this set of interrelations has an actuarial feeling of likelihood about it which is compelling, we are also aware that these four ingredients are far from perfectly correlated. "Bigotry," for example, is a common epithet for the situation in which extremely strong opinions are formed on a scanty base of information. The research on community controversies over fluoridation proposals outlines the social interaction processes whereby attitude structures can polarize into sharp opposition from group to group across a range of issues despite very limited intakes of relevant information. Hence covariation among these four ingredients of public opinion is scarcely guaranteed by natural law, and I suspect that one of the clearer lessons of the 1960s is that such covariation can be quite limited.

The truly stunning evidence of change in the 1960s seems concentrated at the level of attitude structure examined by Nie. It is deplorable that there is not more of a record, comparable across time, of levels of political information. If an ideal instrument of this kind were available, I suspect it would show levels of information inching upward over the period after 1956, and then taking a more sizable quantum jump in the critical years of the later 1960s. At the same time I would guess that the rate of gain would seem rather small by comparison with the Nie evidence concerning the crystallization of attitude structures and that even by the early 1970s these levels would remain astonishingly low in the eyes of observers not acclimated to such data.

Pomper (1972) has shown impressive change in one aspect of the information situation: knowledge of which party takes which position. However, at least some of this change seems due to increased objective differentiation of party positions in certain major issue areas rather than to increased public attention alone. And, as my earlier example concerning perceptions of Eugene McCarthy in the 1968 campaign (now often recalled as a high-information, high-ideology election) may suggest, amazing gaps in information can occur on a sufficiently broad scale to have vital effects on elections as a communication system. Similarly, while Vietnam had become one of the galvanic areas for opinion formation by 1968 and while a gloss of information about the situation had surely gained broad currency by that time, probes of the bases of information underlying opinions on the issue have not been very reassuring. In short, I feel that there remains sobering evidence on information level even in the late 1960s, despite the fact that there can be little doubt but that the situation in the full electorate and improved significantly since 1956.

With respect to change in the "levels of conceptualization," it is now becoming possible to go beyond the partial reconstructions of change by Pierce or Field and Anderson. Their work on ideological awareness was significant in its own right, although they did not fully reconstruct the original levels of conceptualization measure and their surrogate indicators produced quite different results from the original coding, even for 1956. To the best of my knowledge the only scholars who have gone through the same painstaking qualitative reading of raw protocols which produced the original variable, with considerable training on our 1956 distinctions and with careful checks on intercoder reliability, are Hans D. Klingemann and William E. Wright, in work now moving to publication. The new coding was performed on the study of the 1968 presidential election, a point in the heat of the crisis. Klingemann and Wright have kindly supplied the updated distribution for the American electorate in that year (Klingemann, 1973), which Table 1 lays against the distribution that arose from our original coding in 1956.

Changes that have surely been in these figures over the twelve-year period. Apart from some anomalous movements that are undoubtedly situational (e.g., the gain in party responses at the expense of candidate responses, among those

TABLE 1   Levels of political conceptualization in the United States, 1956 versus 1968

	1956 Percentage (Survey Research Center coding)*	1968 Percentage (Klingemann-Wright coding)
A. Ideology		
I. Ideology	3	5.9
II. Near-ideology	10	17.1
B. Group benefits		
I. Perception of conflict	15	9.1
Single-group interest	18	18.6
II. Shallow group benefit responses	11	5.2
C. Nature of the times	25	24.6
D. No issue content		
I. Party orientation	4	7.8
II. Candidate orientation	9	6.8
III. No content	5	4.9
Total	100	100.0

* The distribution has been slightly modified over that originally published in *The American Voter*, with 4.5 percent "not classified" removed from the distribution to fit the Klingemann-Wright data. Apparently a larger figure of 11.7 percent was left unclassified in the latter case.

giving no issue content), the general trend has been toward greater sophistication, consistent with both advancing education and the galvanizing crises of the 1960s. On the other hand the shifts seem remarkably limited by comparison with the striking changes in attitude structure for the same period. And all of this limited change turns out to be concentrated within the more sophisticated half of the electorate: the lower half appears to have moved not at all!

One lesson to be gleaned, then, is that attitude consistency may become dramatically heightened without any correspondingly large increase in the active use of ordering abstractions. Similarly, these data on levels of conceptualization remain consistent with the possibility that there are in fact quite recalcitrant cognitive limitations in the least sophisticated layers of the electorate. The data do not, of course, *prove* such a case, and there are other data from the 1960s that may well serve to call such ultimate limitations into question. Most noteworthy in this regard are studies showing the rapid mobilization of black political consciousness during this period, including the Aberbach and Walker work (1970) on the impressive absorption of a black power ideology in a subpopulation cursed by persistent exclusion from the political process and generations of severe educational deprivation. These inquiries suggest that when motivational stakes are high enough, cognitive barriers can be largely overriden, even in very poorly educated segments of the population. If this is so, then we must conclude that the crises of the 1960s were simply of insufficient importance in the less attentive reaches of the electorate to produce much change in indicators of the level of ideological abstraction.[14]

If we shift our focus to indicators of attitude structure and consistency as well as to the pliable cognitive limitations that increases of education could easily remedy, then Nie presents a convincing case that the 1960s have shown such barriers to be porous indeed and rather easily surpassed by surges in public attention associated with galvanizing crises. I think this is an important lesson and one to which I can add some further evidence that may be helpful when we confront the key question of why we seem to find somewhat different responses to the same set of events when we use indicators referring to two different levels of public opinion—attitude structure versus the recognition or use of capping abstractions.

In working on the "Belief Systems" manuscript I was led by the very strong static relationships between education and levels of both conceptualization and ideological recognition to take for granted that education was a critical predictor not only of ideology but also of attitude structure. Soon after that manuscript was committed to publication I carried out what I expected to be a very routine check of that supposition. In particular I wanted to verify the assumption that more highly educated people would show more stable responses over time than the less well educated to the political issues described in that paper. When the proper data were assembled, this hypothesis was not exactly disconfirmed: there was virtually always a trend in the expected direction. But whereas I had expected to find rather large differences in attitude stability by education, the observed differences turned out to be quite trifling.

This surprising result touched off a more intensive inquiry. If education yielded only a very weak discrimination between people with more and less stable attitudes on these issues, were there any other background variables that *would* show the kinds of discrimination I had expected for education? After a rather long and unrewarding search I did find such a variable, although substantively the answer to my question was slightly deflating. The variable that discriminated at a reasonably satisfying level was a composite one that summarized individual differences in partisan political activism. Partisan activists showed notably higher levels of stability in their responses to these issue items over time than did persons less engaged in the political process. I say this was a somewhat deflating result because it merely implies that the best discriminator of the stability of these partisan political attitudes is partisan political involvement. This is not a tautology, although it is scarcely astonishing. However, when these findings are laid against the weak discriminations arising from differences in education it is easy to conclude that motivational differences represented in the more elastic term of political engagement are much more important governors of attitude stability than are the relatively inert "ascribed" characteristic of past education, even though this does not appear to be the case with respect to the use of capping abstractions.

The above results are focused on the stability of attitudes for individuals over time, rather than on the consistency of multiple attitudes at single points in time as done by Nie (1974). However, the expectation that firmer integration of attitude structures will produce higher stability in component attitudes of the structure is a compelling one. Hence we might anticipate that the unimportance of education relative to political involvement as a predictor of attitude stability might also be apparent where consistency indicators of attitude structure are concerned.

Nie shows that this is indeed the case. The differences in attitude consistency by education are typically rather small at single points in time, just as we noted was true for the attitude stability data, although the differences do go in the expected direction. More importantly, the poorly educated participate in the sharp gains in consistency between 1960 and 1964 at fully the same rate as the well educated: the crystallizing of attitude structures in the 1960s is surely no mere function of upgraded levels of education. On the other hand, when the data are examined by reports of campaign interest, the largest gains in consistency by some margin register among the most interested, and there was a rather progressive growth in such interest registered throughout the election years from 1956 to 1968 (although a significant decline by 1972). In other words the evidence seems fairly clear that consistency of political attitudes, like their stability over time, is as Nie concludes far more dependent on the salience of politics than on educational background.

While all of these data combine to suggest the considerable responsiveness of these properties of attitude structure to political events, the time points for which information is available are too widely spaced to make very clear just what events are involved. It is not hard to see in the civil rights battles, the urban riots, and great divisiveness over Vietnam in the later 1960s the kind of turbulence that draws public attention to an unusual pitch. Yet by far the most dramatic increases in virtually all of the Nie and Pomper indicators involving perceived partisan differentiation over the same public issues occurred in the period between 1960 and 1964. Moreover, for most of these indicators the 1968 levels, while much closer to those of 1964 than earlier points in the series, do appear to betray a slight decline relative to the 1964 peak. Yet it would be commonly assumed that turbulence gained greatly in its force over the 1964–68 period. Indeed, public divisions over Vietnam had scarcely begun to heat up and the urban riots had not yet occurred as of the 1964 observations.

Hence it seems likely that, as Pomper argues, the heightened differentiation of party positions which occurred between 1960 and 1964 was a very critical ingredient in forging more consistent attitude structures of the kind both he and Nie have documented. Since we have no very reliable measurements of the "objective" degree of party differentiation on key policy positions independent of public perceptions in this period, the data remain susceptible to a variety of interpretations. It could be argued, for example, that increased clarity of the public sense of differences between the parties arose because for other reasons the public began paying greater attention to politics in this period. Indeed, the data would be compatible with a claim that there was in fact no "objective" change in the differentiation of party positions whatever but that party positions were simply seen more clearly by an attentive public. In terms of such an interpretation, heightened popular interest and attentiveness would stand alone as a prime mover in fashioning the changes in the tenor of public opinion.

However, there does indeed seem to be ample if perhaps unsystematic side evidence that changes in party leadership positioning had produced a marked increase in objective differentiation between the parties on many of the issues figuring in the Nie and Pomper treatments. Perhaps the clearest contrast is in the state of party differentiation in 1956, when, according to our original judgment written in the period itself, the objective party differences were at their lowest ebb in some time, and in 1964, when the stress on sharp party differentiation was such a major theme in Goldwater's "choice, not an echo," campaign. And if such objective changes in leadership positioning did occur, particularly between 1960 and 1964, then it seems reasonable to imagine that this increased differentiation had some causal role in heightening public interest and hence was indeed a critical ingredient in the change.

Perhaps the chief remaining puzzle is how such vast change could occur in the Nie and Pomper indicators of attitude structure unaccompanied by much change in levels of conceptualization or some other measures of ideological awareness, such as public recognition of liberal-conservative distinctions between the parties, particularly in the less informed and/or sophisticated reaches of the electorate. Yet this may not be as perplexing as it seems, and a proper understanding of the discrepancy is undoubtedly important for any prognosis to be drawn.

In both *The American Voter* and my 1964 paper on belief systems we stressed the ease with which various reference group cues and other social mechanisms could help to create ideological patterning of political attitudes and behaviors on the part of individuals, even though these patterns might not be accompanied by much explicit understanding of the more overarching and abstract reasons why these patterns go together in the conventional ideological sense. Thus we presented notions of "ideology by proxy" and discussed the gap between knowledge of "what goes with what" and the contextual understanding as to "why." We also demonstrated that where group antagonisms ran high, the consistency of mass attitudes on political issues bearing on those antagonisms could be expected to show a good deal of crystallization, even in a period like the 1950s.

These discussions seem well tailored to address the apparent discrepancies in the performance in the 1960s between attitude structure indicators and indicators bearing on more explicit use or recognition of ideological concepts. If an important element was grossly underestimated in those discussions, it was the ease with which political parties themselves, when sharply enough differentiated in policy terms, can serve as the reference groups dramatizing "what goes with what," thereby producing marked clusterings and polarizations of policy positions in an attentive mass public. This is an unquestionable lesson from the earlier 1960s.

There is some evidence that differentiation between at least the two major parties (the Wallace movement aside) declined objectively after the 1964 peak. Surely one of the most potentially explosive issues in 1968—the situation in Vietnam—was severely muffled by the minimal differences between Republicans and Democrats regarding the disposition of the problem, as Page and Brody (1972) have clearly demonstrated. However, by 1968 group antagonisms within the electorate itself had reached a sufficiently politicized peak that high levels of consistency across issue domains could be maintained. There is no reason to imagine that the "silent majority" of the late 1960s had any profound contextual understanding of the explicitly ideological links that led the tiny but visible "counterculture" to call policemen "pigs," damn the war in Vietnam, and give vehement support to the cause of the blacks. However, since many in the silent majority took this set of positions packaged in the news by a vanguard group as an extremely negative reference point, it is not surprising that they drifted toward protective feelings about the police, defensive acceptance of Vietnam, and lack of enthusiasm or downright hostility to the civil rights movements. Hence they fell into positions of heightened ideological clarity without any clear recognition of the fact that they were doing so. This is simply social polarization, with the motive force being less ideological reasoning than group antagonism, or "nay-saying" to whatever the negative reference group is saying "yes" to.

Such an interpretation would fit well with other things we have learned concerning the dynamic differences between attitude structure and active use of ideological concepts. Thus, as I have recounted, it can be shown even with data from the 1950s that variations in attitude stability and consistency are not notably correlated with education in a static sense nor are they, presumably, dynamically bound to it. Instead attitude stability and consistency are largely responsive to elastic motivational characteristics such as interest and attentiveness. While more purely ideological measures are also correlated with political interest and attentiveness in fair degree, suggesting some modicum of elasticity, they are also very strongly correlated with education, a variable that for virtually everybody over twenty-five or thirty is completely inert. Hence it is not surprising that political situations that can produce in the short run vastly heightened levels of attitude crystallization and integration do not produce heightened levels of use or recognition of ideology. Indeed, whereas advances in aggregate education account for almost trivial fractions of the total gains over this period in Nie's measures of attitude consistency or Pomper's analyses of clarity in party perceptions, they do account for a very substantial proportion of the limited changes in the levels of conceptualization between 1956 and 1968.

From many points of view which I see as highly important, including system performance considerations, changes in the nature of public opinion at the level of attitude structures are of more significance than the plodding progress of ideological conceptualization over the same period. That is, relatively speaking, the elections of the later 1960s and 1972 have been highly ideological ones for the mass electorate, and this remains true whether the ideological patterning of those elections has arisen from some genuine ideological rejuvenation or from the somewhat shallower social mechanisms I have described. However, if we are to achieve any grasp of likely future outcomes, it is undoubtedly useful to know whether the underpinnings of the attitude integration of the 1960s are of the reflected social type or are in fact more autonomously ideological.

Prognosis

Any prediction of the likely state of public opinion in 1980 is bound to be hazardous and, in a sense, quite foolish without foreknowledge of the surrounding political conditions that might pertain. If we were sure that a new storm of troubles would be gripping the electorate five or ten years hence, we would have quite different expectations than if we could be certain that a period of more routine politics would develop. Nonetheless, since data from the two decades in which public opinion has been most carefully monitored seem to show quite different properties, particularly at the level of attitude structure, it seems important to ask which of these states of public opinion is the more "normal" one. Were the 1950s not only quiescent but ridiculously so? Or is it the 1960s that were abnormal in terms of these properties of public opinion?

We can wrest a few intelligent guesses from the diagnostic material we have just examined. The overall levels of education in the electorate must necessarily continue to advance in coming years. Thus while such changes in educational composition are not of great importance in understanding the short-term variations between the 1950s and 1960s, their more permanent long-term effects should not be underestimated. The degree to which political attitude structures are integrated may wax and wane, but there is something of a rising floor of explicitly ideological awareness, and thus it seems unlikely that the electorate of 1980 could look like that of 1956, however routine national politics might have become in the interim.[15]

Since there is some connection, albeit a weak one, between explicit ideological awareness and attitude integration, we would also have to conclude that even with quiescent politics and blurred party differences, indicators of attitude consistency in 1980 should not fall all the way to their 1956 levels, although they might come rather close. However, this does not fully answer the question of whether the valleys of attitude consistency in the 1950s or the high plateaus of the 1960s are the more normal case.

I know of no way to get any purchase on this question save by the device of looking at other total electorates, hoping that our data may be catching them when they are neither abnormally low nor high in these terms. This is a risky business because there are differences in political culture which may render comparisons spurious. It is particularly risky with indicators of the integration or consistency of attitude structures, since these indicators are based on averages of intercorrelations across a limited selection of current policy issues. Such measures may be highly dependent on the issues chosen and the way questions are worded. If the issues selected are distributed widely across diverse policy domains with an eye to "coverage," the intercorrelations will naturally tend to be lower, other things being equal, than if multiple items are asked within two or three issue domains to improve reliability. Hence absolute estimates of consistency based on intercorrelations are quite uninterpretable without knowing more about selection criteria. The main interest of such indicators from an analytic point of view lies rather in relative differences between groups, such as mass and elite, or within the same groups across time with the issue items held constant.

Since different political issues are central in different countries and usually come to a head in different terms in any event, few such topical issues could be held constant from country to country. Therefore cross-national comparisons are bound to be weak. However, in one instance we have issue data, from the French electorate in 1967, in which the goals underlying the survey procedures were identical with those that produced the original 1956 items that Nie (1974) has used for the United States. While these comparisons must be treated very gingerly, the data placed in Nie form and laid against the United States time comparisons (from Nie Fig. 4) are presented in Table 2.

TABLE 2   Indicators of attitude consistency for the United States (Nie) and France

| | United States | | France |
	(1956)	(1968)	(1967)
Average (gamma correlation coefficient) for all	.14	.40	.12
Average for domestic issues	.24	.51	.23
Average between domestic and foreign issues	—.01	.23	.00

Another looser comparison is available for a smaller set of domestic issues for West Germany as of 1969. Within this data set, the relevant entry for the second row above would be .22 or .23.

Even if we must take these data with a great deal of caution, they would seem sufficient to cast some doubt on any proposition that the portrait of public opinion in the United States of the 1950s comes from a period so abnormal that it is thoroughly unrepresentative of mass electorates more generally. Indeed, in these few comparisons the United States of the late 1960s appears to be the unusual case, at least with respect to these properties of attitude structure.

If we turn instead to indicators of the active use of ideological concepts there is less need to search cross-nationally for what is "normal," since the American situation did not change enough from 1956 to 1968 to be confusing in that regard (see Table 1). Nonetheless we are beginning to fill in a broader picture of the state of ideological awareness across a variety of countries. By far the most discrepant finding, on the surface at least, is that in European countries in which a "left-right" descriptive vocabulary is at its most common, this vocabulary is widely recognized in the mass public. Moreover, the vast majority of voters in such systems are willing to describe their own positions on left-right scales. And when asked to locate various parties within their nation on the same kind of scale, the voters on the average cite locations (ignoring a fair level of individual "noise" around such central tendencies) which accord quite well with informed observers' judgments, particularly for old and familiar parties.[16]

This may not be surprising in view of the widespread dependence on this terminology by the media and by politicians in these countries. However, when one moves below the surface labels, the more active use of ideological frames of reference begins to look more like that in the United States. Perhaps the most direct evidence at the moment comes from Klingemann (1973). After helping to carry out the painstaking assessment of the variable of levels of conceptualization for the United States, he did the same kind of qualitative reading of protocols for their issue and ideological content in 1969 data for West Germany. While there are occasional interesting cultural differences, particularly in some background correlates of the levels of conceptualization, the gross contours of the national distribution on the variable are quite similar to those estimated for the United States in 1968. Apparently, despite the popular left-right yardstick, the actual issue and ideological content of spontaneous political evaluations in West Germany reads roughly like the range of illustrations presented for each level of conceptualization in Chapter 10 of *The American Voter.*

In France, where again the left-right yardstick is common, almost one-quarter of the people in our 1967 sample admitted that they did not know what the terms signified, although this group included a substantial number who recognized the terms readily and were quite willing to select locations for themselves. Another 10 to 15 percent gave such lame explanations of the meaning of differences between left and right (e.g., "they do not agree") that their understandings may fairly be questioned. Thus while merest recognition in France is much higher than it is in the United States for the liberal-conservative distinction, any deeper grasp of meaning seems more developed by only a small margin. Moreover, the modal position by far of persons choosing a location for themselves was at the neutral point, a location that internal evidence shows has little significance for party choice behavior and, indeed, contains a very disproportionate number of those who do not understand the terms.

For Britain, where the left-right vocabulary does not have quite the same primacy as on the Continent, Butler and Stokes (1969, esp. pp. 174–214) have shown that only 21 percent of the citizenry claimed that they thought of the British parties in left-right terms and only 25 percent said that they ever thought of themselves personally in these terms. Politicians and journalists, asked to estimate proportions of understanding, gave vastly exaggerated guesses, as is typical. And as such data might suggest, the Butler-Stokes analyses of preference orders across the three principal parties failed to show any strong unidimensional organization.

In sum, while there are intriguing differences among nations in political culture and vocabulary which intrude on the structure of public opinion on political matters, the most general cast of that opinion seems quite similar cross-nationally and not far removed from the portrait of that opinion drawn from the United States in the 1950s. Once again, these observations are not at all intended to challenge the significance of the dramatic changes in the United States of the later 1960s and early 1970s. Whether one thinks in terms of practical political meaning or of extension of our conceptual horizons by the variation in context these changes provide. their significance is undoubtedly large. But it is too early to see them as the normal state of opinion.

To summarize, then, I would expect indicators of the active use of ideological concepts to edge forward progressively over the next decade. On the other hand, indicators referring to attitude consistency may well recede in some degree as political crisis declines. There are, however, several reasons not to expect them to return all the way to levels of the 1950s. In addition to considering the effects of a considerable intervening change in education levels, we might suppose that attitudes crystallized into integrated structures during the crisis would show greater stability over time than did many of the comparable political attitudes expressed during the 1950s. Finally, if my diagnosis of the role of information costs in the formation of public opinion is correct, then there are positive feedback mechanisms that, after the surge in attentiveness in the 1960s, should help to prevent those indicators of attitude structure from sagging back rapidly, even if the pressures of crisis were to evaporate at great speed. That is, if wider ranges of the electorate have been more attentive in recent years, such that they are bringing more recalled information to incoming political news, then they may find their information costs down and their interest in political news up correspondingly.

One factor we have seen to be very critical in the shaping of public opinion seems to remain, however, quite incalculable in advance. This is the degree of objective party differentiation on major issues which may be displayed at various points in the future. There are always some competitive ideological pressures on party elites toward differentiation and other pressures of a Downsian vote-maximizing sort which press toward convergence of positions. The net resultant of these opposing forces at any point in time is so dependent on a complex interaction between events and party elites that our predictive capacity seems very limited. The party differentiation factor appears to be important enough in determining the attitude structures of the electorate that any prognosis must remain somewhat speculative.

THE NATURE OF VOTING BEHAVIOR

Since public opinions form the main raw material for the mechanism of elections, we have come many steps toward appreciating some of the major controversies surrounding the study of voting behavior. In this section I shall begin with the briefest of resumés of the history of work in this area, for the sake of minimal background. As in the first section, however, my main attention will be directed less at organizing the staggering portfolio of literature in the area than toward focusing on a few of the controversies that seem to have attracted greatest attention in recent years among political scientists interested in the area.

I shall argue that some of these controversies are more genuine and important than others. Several turn out on examination to be pseudocontroversies, either because the root questions they are addressing are poorly formulated or because they fail to realize that answers to different questions asked of a subject matter may appear quite discrepant when in fact they are describing different but quite compatible facets of the same reality.

Of the many detailed and richly varied questions that have been asked of voting behavior, we shall limit ourselves to controversies arising in connection with the three following broad queries:

What are the main proximal determinants of individual voting choice?
What are the main macrocosmic sources of change in both partisan divisions of the vote and the historical character of voting systems?
How does mass voting contribute to public representation in the broader political system?

Background

One way of thinking of the history of empirical inquiry into voting behavior is to consider its declining enslavement over the decades to a limited armory of tools and data. The first systematic inquiries of any scope, such as that of Andre Siegfried in 1913, were dependent on hand-manipulated tabulations and shaped maps based on relatively aggregated voting returns. While a generation of brilliant scholars working more or less within the same confines, including Ogburn, Tingsten, Goguel, and V. O. Key in his earlier period, developed many hunches as to the individual temperaments, perceptions, and motivations that underlay various voting patterns, the work was by its very character rather macrocosmic.[17] And yet even here the painful restrictions on data processing kept its scope somewhat limited: to cover much time depth it was necessary to restrict the geographic area and/or the fineness of geographic disaggregation of the data, and extensions in either of the latter two terms had to be purchased through shortenings of the time axis.

The development of personal interviews within a sample survey base, foreshadowed by the work of Merriam and Gosnell (1924) on nonvoting in Chicago in 1924, had an enormous impact on the character of the field because it gave access to the individual respondent. The work of Lazarsfeld and his associates at the Bureau for Applied Social Research at Columbia University in the 1940s, and that of Campbell and his associates at the Survey Research Center of the University of Michigan since the later 1940s have been most noteworthy in capitalizing on this technological development.[18] For two or more decades the focus of inquiry underwent a kind of implosion into the act of voting choice in its most microcosmic sense, whether that meant the small group or the individual psyche.

Since the late 1950s, with the fetters of data-processing capabilities and data access falling away, the field of inquiry has exploded outward again in almost all possible directions. It has moved outward in space, with rapidly growing literature involving cross-national comparisons of voting behavior, both survey based and aggregate.[19] It has expanded its time scope, notably with more systematic examination of voting in earlier historical periods, an effort facilitated by major gains in the archiving of machine-readable historical voting data by the Inter-university Consortium for Political Research and by the continuation of the Michigan sequence of biennial election studies, allowing a wide range of scholars to work with a lengthening time series on the American electorate.[20] The pioneering work by Miller and Stokes (1963, 1964) on constituent contributions to legislative outcomes has begun to extend perspectives upward, toward the interaction of the election system with other system outcomes.

Determinants of Individual Voting Choice

The number of factors that can in one context or another be shown to bear on individual voting choice is extremely large and diverse. For crude working purposes it may be useful to group them according to whether they are (1) proximal or distal to the voting decision and (2) political or nonpolitical. Probably the bulk of work by political scientists in the past twenty years has focused on factors that are both proximal and political: the immediate political perceptions and preferences that are molded into a vote decision. These are the "public opinion" elements and will occupy the lion's share of our attention. Distal factors most notably include determinants that are not political in a direct sense, such as social class or religious and ethnic group membership. However, some distal factors such as a lengthy family tradition of a particular partisanship are more political in their substance. Factors that are on one hand proximal but on the other hand nonpolitical are rather sparse and usually left as exogenous, but they would include such situations as a person who votes against his or her private preferences to satisfy a spouse.

In recent years two quite distinctive approaches to proximal political factors leading to voting choices have been operating concurrently. The first is the empirical, or inductive, approach usually rooted in analyses of sample surveys. The second approach is more recent and involves deductive modelling. It gained its major impetus from the brilliant work of Anthony Downs, *An Economic Theory of Democracy,* published in 1957. This work has been carried on in various directions by William Riker, Otto Davis, Melvin Hinich, Peter Ordeshook, and others.[21]

The two approaches differ quite radically from one another in their starting points and initial texture but aim ultimately at some convergence. The most noteworthy deductive models relevant to mass voting behavior start with a limited set of assumptions about the determinants of the voter's behavior and the structure of the situation the voter confronts in approaching his or her decision. It is assumed, for example, that the voter assesses the relative proximity of various candidate or party alternatives to his or her own position on one or more dimensions of political conflict and then—assuming the voter will behave rationally—chooses to vote for the closest alternative. This is very much a commonsense view of the dynamics of voting, and were the matter left here the exposition would not be very exciting. However, by formalizing the assumptions about behavior and the structure of the situation in this fashion it is possible to arrive at quite a variety of strict deductions concerning competition of parties and candidates over policy positions that will maximize appeal to voters. Furthermore, details of assumptions can be varied in order to ask how optimal candidate strategies and other outcomes would differ as a consequence.

If the deductive approach imposes a structure of theory from the outset and then asks questions as to what would follow if this structure were to pertain in the real world, the inductive approach works toward theory, as it were, "from the ground up." It starts with patterns in empirical data and attempts to move toward increasingly higher-order generalizations about the causal grounds for such observed patterns.

Apparently it is often tempting to the academic mind to exaggerate differences between the two approaches by way of demonstrating that one activity is sublime and the other ridiculous. The deductive approach is frequently charged with irrelevance on grounds that the assumed conditions it delves into with such rigor are not matched in the real world. The inductive approach is similarly criticized for its lack of theoretical power or its misguided dependence on special cases, which will never replicate themselves in the same way, so that truly general causal knowledge will be very long in the discovery, if it is discovered at all. Actually, both approaches have their virtues and their sterilities, and the history of science suggests that a vigorous interaction between the two is likely to produce the most fertile advances of inquiry.

Moreover, it is easy to overstate the differences between the two once each is much beyond its starting point. While occasional deductive theorists deny they have any interest at all in the fit between their assumptions and the real world, most model development does move in the direction of relaxing unrealistic assumptions and adding more realistic conditions, within the limits of deductive or mathematical tractability. Similarly, few empirical investigations begin without rough theoretical hunches that are being tested, and beyond the first exploratory stages it is usually true that enough loose theory has begun to take shape that rough deductions from it may be made toward further testing and hence increased tightness and generality of theoretical propositions. The important point is that the two developments be kept in increasing contact, such that empirical work can show deductive theory where its assumptions are most lacking in verisimilitude and deductive theory can guide empirical work in the data it chooses to collect and organize.

While students of voting behavior have succumbed very little to the shallowest kinds of "superior-method" quarrels between the deductive and inductive approaches, different impressions created by the preoccupations of the two approaches have in fact created some sense of disjuncture as to the character of voting behavior, and most of the principal controversies in the field in recent years seem to be fuelled by this disjuncture. The terms of the controversy have almost nowhere been clearly laid out, a matter that has kept debate short of the crystalline and has produced a variety of pseudoissues as well as many contending ships passing in the night. However, the primary discussion seems to concern how "rational" voting behavior can be said to be, and it often focuses on the role that issue evaluations of the competing parties and candidates play in the determination of individual voting choice. Since the rationality assumption as well as the perception of issue "distances" are at the heart of most deductive models, the controversy has arisen because some inductive work, most notably that of the Michigan school, is often read as calling the rationality assumption into question. It is in this sense, rather than because of methodological propriety, that the debate stimulated by the inductive and deductive approaches has flourished in recent years. In order to lay out my own view of the controversy we must first briefly review the terms of the Michigan model, with emphasis on those points of its treatment of proximal political factors which overlap with the concerns of deductive modelling.

The Michigan Model of Proximal Orientations

Some of the early Michigan work, most clearly represented by *The Voter Decides*, proceeded on the assumption that the choice of votes was made by the individual on the basis of his or her evaluations of three main ingredients of an election situation: the candidates, the issues, and the parties. The study of the 1952 election reported in that volume had in fact measured orientations toward all three of these terms, and the monograph documented rather amply that all three orientations were significant determinants of the vote subsequently cast by respondents.[22]

The American Voter reported the continuation of this measurement in the 1956 election and put a considerably greater stress on the kind of multivariate analysis which could address the question of the relative weights of the three ingredients in determining individual voting choice. For the purposes of such estimation, issue orientations were by far the most troubling, because in contrast to the simple fact of two major parties and their two candidates there was a large range of potential issues, all of which struck close observers as having at least some salience. Not all could be investigated because of obvious limits on interview length. Ultimately, a battery of some sixteen issues was laid out, attempting to cover the major dimensions of policy debate shaping up in the 1956 election. For each such predetermined issue the interview was designed to measure the key variables of a commonsense, "rational" model, in which proximity of the parties to the individual voter's positions on the respective issues would be the main determinants of the parties' attractiveness. Ideally we would have liked to have measured five or six aspects of the voter-party-candidate relationship for each issue. However, the sixteen issues made too large a multiplier, and we were forced to limit the questionnaire to three pieces of information for each of the sixteen issues. These were (1) the individual's own location on the issue, (2) the individual's view as to whether the current administration fell short of or went beyond his or her own positions, and (3) the individual's estimate as to which party was closest to his or her own position on the issue.

Although sixteen issues were a rather large number, it remained a matter of concern that the identity of these issues had been determined by investigator fiat. What about other issue concerns that might be of high salience for particular individuals in the electorate? Here we depended on the fact that very lengthy open-ended questions concerning the voter's various reasons for liking and disliking each of the candidates and parties were asked. Since the commonsense view of voting at the time—and one to be welded into later formal models—was that parties and candidates were attractive or unattractive to voters as a function of issue positions they represented, these open-ended questions gave each voter a chance to express the issue bases for his or her preferences, however idiosyncratic these might be. The coding of the volunteered responses was organized in a fashion to distinguish between an issue component of these bases for preferences as opposed to other kinds of reactions.

Thus there was a direct assault on what seemed in advance to be the sixteen principal issues of the election, plus an assessment of other volunteered issue grounds for candidate and party preference. The pure issue content that came through in the volunteered responses fell a good deal short of prevailing assumptions, however, and this led us in the next major study (1960) to add a further set of questions of a "most important problem" sort, which obliged respondents to give a sense of what issues seemed most salient to them in the setting of the election, regardless of whether or not they thought to mention issues or policies in stating the main grounds for their evaluation of the parties and candidates. These materials were too late for inclusion in *The American Voter*, although more recently RePass (1971) has exploited them to good advantage, showing that such self-selected issues are quite strongly harmonized with party preference and the final voting choice.

Attempts to arrive at a sense of relative weights for the three orientations generally produced rather surprising results relative to assumptions, prevalent since the beginning of popular voting, that issue differences were the standard basis for assessing which candidates and parties were to be preferred. There was clearly a significant issue "weight" in the aggregate vote decision. However, it was rather widely outrun by sheer party loyalty in any direct confrontations involving predictive capacity.

Moreover, no satisfying estimate of the relative weight of the issue and party orientations could be completed without some understanding as to what portion of the overlap between issue positions and choice of party for allegi- ance should be credited mainly to the party or to the issue side. Empirically, as Searing, Schwartz, and Lind (1973) have pointed out, this overlap—the cor- relation between issue positions and party identification—was not as large as might have been supposed on commonsense grounds, especially for the sixteen predetermined issues. However, it was present and was stronger still where in- dividuals selected their own issues of concern. Estimates of relative weight could vary quite significantly according to whether this overlap was seen as involving mainly issue or party motivations.

This is essentially a causal question: Does the voter express loyalty to a party because it seems the best instrument for achieving his or her prior issue concerns? (Again, this is the running assumption of standard democratic the- ory, as well as many of the later "rational" models.) Or does the voter come to take up issue sides perceived to be supported by the party to which he or she feels prior loyalty? While there was evidence in the data that flows were pres- ent in both directions, the less expected flow from prior party loyalties to issue positioning seemed remarkably strong.

For one thing, party loyalties in most cases appeared to antedate the emergence of the particular issues involved, such that those loyalties would be hard to construe as being "caused" by the issue preferences. Secondly, when issue items of the structured kind tipped off the respondent as to the position of the parties, the relationship between respondents' issue positions and prior partisanship strengthened substantially. This suggested a major cue-giving function of the parties with respect to issue positioning of the respondent and implied that the relationship between issue positions and partisanship was low chiefly because partisans frequently did not know what issue positions their preferred parties took and hence what ones they should take themselves. More- over, there was usually a stronger relationship between personal partisanship and perception of which party stood closer to the individual on the issue than there was between the individual's party and his or her own issue location. In other words, Democrats tended to report that the Democratic party was closest to them, whatever their own position on the issue and whatever the "objective" reality; and Republicans reported the Republican party as closer to them, with similar lack of discrimination. Apparently having already com- mitted themselves to a personal position on these issues and lacking any real knowledge of party differences in the matter, the voters assumed that the preferred party must share their own location. Dynamics of this kind did not suggest that the issue positions were the main causal agent when party loyalty was congruent with the voting decision.

All of these findings led to a good deal of effort to understand why issue orientations, rather than being the standard basis for vote formation as common sense would suggest, appeared in reality to be so overshadowed by party loyalties. The two main explanatory terms offered—voter disinterest and inattentiveness on the one hand and lack of sharpness in actual party differentiation on policy positions on the other—have already loomed large in our preceding discussion of public opinion. And, as we have also seen, Pomper's impressive demonstration (1972) of heightened clarity in the public mind as to party locations on major issues in the 1960s made clear that one of the preconditions for stronger levels of issue voting had been fulfilled. It simply became more difficult for partisans to decide casually that their preferred party must be on the same side of a debate that they themselves were on. Not only were parties giving stronger cues than in the 1950s but the development of galvanizing crises produced more stable and meaningful attitudes among the public for many key issues. And when personally developed issue positions collided with past party preferences, as they did with increasing frequency, the weight of issue-based voting gained ground relative to that of party-based voting, as Nie (1974) and others have convincingly shown.

There seems to be no broad disagreement about the facts of this history. Controversy has seemed to settle instead on how these facts are to be viewed and in particular on the question of how "rational" popular voting can be said to be. In a general way, "rational" voting is often equated simplistically with "issue voting." By contrast, although with only limited justification, voting hinged mainly on party loyalty or on the charisma of particular candidates is taken to be irrational or at least "nonrational." In the face of this artificial opposition, the question of relative weights of party, issue, and candidate orientations is thus converted into the question of "how rational" voting behavior is. Accounts that examine partisan determinants of voting decisions are taken to favor an "irrational" view of voting behavior; accounts stressing issue voting defend the voters' rationality. Hopefully we can emerge from the ensuing pages with a clearer view of the superficiality of this controversy. We cannot proceed far, however, without first taking a harder look at the concept of rationality itself.

The Problem of Rationality

It seems self-evident that it is hard to ascertain how rational voting behavior is without first specifying rather closely just what "rationality" is to include or exclude in the voting context. Scholars of the deductive school, working with austere models limited to variables of their own choosing, can employ formal definitions which, when the total structures of their deductions are taken into account, are quite satisfying. However, the controversy as to how rational voting behavior "really" is lies entirely on the empirical side. V. O. Key (1966) was largely responsible for reinstating the popularity of the rationality discussion in empirical studies of voting, but his use of the term was quite casual. He made no attempt to specify how instances of rational and nonrational voting might be distinguished, and a succession of scholars like RePass (1971), Pomper (1972), and others have taken up the same cudgels while leaving the concept of rationality equally undefined.[23]

This lack of specification as to what rationality means in the voting context is particularly painful because if there is any answer at all to the question of voting rationality, the answer is likely to be almost entirely a creature of the definition of rationality being used. This is to say that by using one entirely reasonable—yea, classic—definition, absolutely all voting behavior is totally rational. With other definitions more limited proportions of voting behavior could be considered rational; and with some the proportion would be small indeed.

Choice behavior that "maximizes perceived (or expected) utility" for the actor is perhaps the most familiar explication of what choice behavior is "rational." The vagueness of the term "utility" is well known, but even supposing that we adopt a rough and ready set of commonsense connotations for it the definition still is next to useless, for strictly construed it can only push us into a tautology: any behavior the actor chooses to engage in must maximize his or her perceived utility or otherwise the actor would make another choice. The person who casts a vote contrary to his or her political preferences to maintain harmony with a spouse is thereby voting rationally, since the perceived utilities of marital harmony outweigh perceived utilities of one party winning over the other, and therefore a vote on such grounds is one that maximizes perceived utility, i.e., is rational. Or, to take an extreme case, the psychotic who bangs his or her head against a wall is engaged in rational behavior because if there were other more gratifying ways of spending the same time, the person presumably would choose those over head banging. This definition of rationality is scarcely a straw man, being the most conventional formal one. Yet from this perspective all voting choices are rational by definition, so that debate over the degree of rationality in elections is intrinsically pointless.

Clearly this definition is not what most scholars who find the debate an important one have in mind. Yet it is impossible to put the discussion on any firmer footing without clearer specification as to what choice patterns maximize the individual's expected utility but are being ruled out as not rational.

Since I have never found the concept of rationality sufficiently clear to be depended on in inductive work (although its value in deductive modelling is surely beyond dispute), I do not feel it is my obligation here to make the precise specifications necessary for the question of the degree of rationality in the real world to be meaningful and researchable. Moreover, it seems likely that any effort to provide such specifications would itself lead to a considerable morass, in which the definitional "solution" would probably generate more controversy than answers to the question of empirical reality.[24]

Thus, for example, the most obvious way of narrowing the rationality concept is to drop the subjective modifier "perceived" and attempt to judge whether given votes are in the "best interest" of the persons casting them in some objective sense, whatever the voters themselves may think. However, such a gambit creates fierce difficulties. For instance it could be argued with regard to aging persons that the most vital "objective" impingement of governmental decision-making on their lives has lain for some forty years in the character of social security programs. Having some program rather than none and having more generous payments rather than less represent the best objective interest of persons in or approaching old age. However, over this forty-year period it has been the Democratic party that has consistently fought to have such programs and then to have more generous programs over the resistance of the Republican party. And over the same period the older segments of the American electorate outside the South have typically cast strong majorities of their votes for the Republican party. If we code all of those votes as "irrational"—now in an objective sense—our estimates of the general rationality of voting behavior would have to be scaled down rather substantially. Yet our whole chain of reasoning, while considerably more interesting than discussions that leave "rationality" at the tautology stage, is obviously subject to vigorous dispute, which would have to be settled in itself before meaningful answers as to the more general degree of rationality in voting behavior could be addressed. I have no desire to defend the above set of propositions concerning votes among the elderly: the important point is that it is such thickets as these that must be entered and brought under control before the rationality question begins to have much intellectual interest.

Of course it is clear that much of the recent literature defending voter rationality means by "rationality" less the classic definition than simply "issue voting." In other words, it is implicitly assumed that where voting behavior is concerned there are meaningful exclusions from the category of "rational:" votes that are based on decision mechanisms other than estimates of policy and issue "distance" are taken to be nonrational. This simple equation between "issue voting" and "rational voting," however, creates a number of conceptual tangles that have gone largely unheeded.

One such tangle concerns the problem of misinformation. It is a frequently demonstrated empirical reality that some voters who have particular issue concerns at some times vote for the "wrong" candidate out of misconception as to the relative positions of the competitors. In some ways the hawkish voters in the 1968 presidential primaries who voted for McCarthy on the assumption he too was a hawk are examples of this syndrome. Now such a pattern is clearly issue voting, by definition. It is also rational voting, in the tautological sense:

such a person's vote is being cast for the candidate he believes will maximize his utility on the issue of concern. However, in the less tautological, if rather vague, sense in which "rationality" has been used in the recent literature, the mechanism of voting is clearly a shorthand by which voters or electorates that are sufficiently informed about issues and elite positions can maintain a meaningful dialogue with decision-makers about policy preferences. Of course the issue voter who is proceeding on misinformation cannot be counted as "rational" in this latter, more meaningful sense: the voter is not adequately informed, and his or her contribution to aggregate vote "message," as read by elites, is the opposite of what the voter intended and thus subversive of meaningful dialogue. Hence we cannot count this vote as an instance of rational voting in the nontautological sense: it is exactly the contrary. Yet it remains incontrovertibly an "issue" vote. Where, then, does this leave any simple equation between issue voting and nontautological rationality?

It is very easy, of course, to restore a sense of rationality to the misinformed voter. This can be done by either of two routes. One, which we have already employed in the first section of this essay, involves the imputation of information costs. It led us to the ironic conclusion that given the structure of the situation in which many voters find themselves much of the time (i.e., facing substantial information costs), voters are quite "rational" in remaining uninformed. The problem here, of course, is that this syndrome continues to contradict the meaning of voting behavior which is usually intended by the "rationality" shorthand in the recent literature: rational voters are voters who are accurately informed and maintain a meaningful communication with elites.

The other route is one chosen by V. O. Key in his posthumous monograph, *The Responsible Electorate* (1966), and is a somewhat homespun corollary of the information cost argument, although it bites in a distinctive direction: voters cannot be expected to know what elites fail to tell them, and if elites hand out misinformation, then the responsibility (or "rationality") of voters cannot reasonably be impugned simply because the misinformation is fed back into vote decisions. This is the famous metaphor of the electorate as "echo chamber."

Since *The Responsible Electorate* appears to have prompted much of the more recent "issue voting" literature, it is important for us to relate it in some detail to the current discussion. The empirical core of the book is an examination of the issue positions of persons who reported changes in their vote from one presidential election to the next. Key shows that there is a considerable congruence between the reported positions on issues most relevant to a particular election and the lines of voting change that the election touches off. Thus, for example, a major issue of the 1936 election was the social security legislation being pushed by the Democrats and resisted by the Republicans. People who had voted Democratic in 1932 but who were against social security figured prominently among "switchers" to the Republicans in 1936; and 1932

Republicans who favored social security likewise figured prominently among those switching to the Democrats. Data of this kind, given in some form or other for all elections of the period available for scrutiny, led Key to his thesis that the American electorate had been more responsible, rational, and issue oriented than earlier accounts had implied.[25]

The Responsible Electorate has been subject to certain misreadings. Some readers, for example, have concluded that the book shows that issues are far more important than party loyalties in determining the individual vote decision. Actually, the book does almost nothing to address the relative weight question. Most of the tabulations are limited to switchers—persons voting for one party in one election and the other party in the next one. Switchers are exactly the subset of the total electorate—invariably a limited minority— caught by the data at a moment in which they are abrogating whatever sense of party loyalty they may possess. Hence they are the subset for which the weight of party loyalty is effectively reduced to zero. What this necessarily means in turn is that the relative predictive weight available for issues is greatly increased. Indeed, the more important the weight of party loyalty might be in the total electorate, the more brilliantly an issue weight must appear to surge forward when the field of view is restricted to the subset of the electorate for whom, by self-selection, party constancy is reduced to zero. What is ignored in the misreadings is the fact that Key was attempting to account for *marginal change* in voting outcomes rather than the total vote. Since such marginal change can be seen as determining the flux of those outcomes, this research question is an enormously important one, and Key's treatment of it is most valuable. However, although Key himself was scarcely confused on the point, readers often feel that the details of empirical reality have been greatly turned around. In fact, most of the sense of disjuncture is a simple function of the different research question being addressed. The greatly heightened importance of issues in the Key calculations are a logical necessity of the shift in research question and not a contradictory finding.

If we may now relate the Key work to the problems in equating issue voting with rationality, it is important to recognize that the way in which Key organized his data deftly avoids one facet of the misinformation problem. That is, he dealt with gross flows from one party to the other and the attitude positions of persons contributing separately to one or another flow. This means that if one prior Democrat moved to the Republicans in 1936 and was against social security, whereas one prior Republican, also against social security, moved to the Democrats, Key's particular case for issue importance in voting change would be properly cancelled out. The case for issue importance can be documented only if—as indeed was the case—there is a net surplus of negative feelings about social security in the Democratic-to-Republican stream relative to that in the Republican-to-Democratic stream. Hence, his estimates are protected against conflicting public perceptions as to which party stood where on which issue: if total confusion had reigned, there could have been massive "issue" voting without its registering as such in the Key tables.

This is perhaps an elementary point, but it is frequently ignored. I have seen many manuscripts that in effect show that people report a voting preference for the party that they also report is most likely to do what they want on the policy controversies they see as most important. There is of course an enormous correlation here, and the magnitude of this correlation is adduced as proof that almost all voting is issue voting and hence is rational (in the implied sense of a well-informed electorate). Unfortunately, such accounts fail to recognize the phenomena of both misinformation and rationalization, although both have repeatedly been shown to occur at far from trivial rates in the electorate. Thus, for example, long-term party loyalists typically have no trouble finding a problem they can report the party they would have voted for in any event is particularly "good" on. Such reports build in a strong correlation between issue and vote preferences, even though the causal sequence may in many instances have been quite the reverse of what the investigator infers. Moreover, it is frequently true that loyalists of opposing parties who nonetheless share the same policy positions on a problem see their own party as the one more likely to do what they want on the issue. Strictly speaking they cannot both be right, and often one of them is obviously misguided, yet in the correlational format such misinformation is cumulated with genuine information to show how well informed and attentive to issues the public is! It is not surprising that such crude efforts to draw indirect inferences as to the informedness of the electorate give impressive results, which are persistently at odds with more careful and direct assessments.

If Key had some protection on the misinformation problem built into his tabulations and if those tabulations showed a significant congruence between issue positions and voting change, why did he feel obliged to invent the metaphor of the "echo chamber," which already begins to evade somewhat the purest notions of "rationality" and responsibility? We can only guess at this point. Surely Key was well aware of data on the prevalence of political misinformation and undoubtedly had read sample survey protocols in which respondents justifying a vote or vote change with an appropriate issue concern display hair-raising misinformation on the subject, even though they will be counted in tabulations as "issue voters" and well informed. The "echo chamber" provides as escape route that preserves the probity of the voter: clearly voters cannot be expected to have information that is withheld from them.

In the days of Vietnam and Watergate there is not much need to emphasize how felicitous a notion the "echo chamber" is. At numerous important junctures in the nation's history it has been apparent that the public has been concertedly misled, intentionally or otherwise, by enough decision-makers that it would indeed be unreasonable to say the public was gullible or irrational for having accepted the misinformation dutifully. This is the pure "echo chamber" phenomenon, and it is deserving of a good deal more study than it has received.

At the same time, the "echo chamber" metaphor does not come to grips with most of the misinformation problem as commonly registered in electoral competition. It argues that people naturally believe what they are told. What it obscures is the chief fact of most political competition: voters are told many conflicting things, which they could not possibly "echo" in any unitary way. They must select what is more or less probable among these claims and counterclaims, and this whole process the echo chamber says nothing about. Voters in the 1930s were told that proposed social security legislation was a plot of the Kremlin or the Pope to subvert America. They were told that if it passed, everyone would be obliged to wear dog tags. They were also told on the other side that none of these things was true and that unfamiliar legislation was necessary to cope with a problem that had hardly existed in the same form a generation earlier. If all that a voter had heard about social security had been the Kremlin story, he or she couldn't be entirely blamed for believing it, just as Key argued. On the other hand if this is all the voter had heard about it, we may wonder why this proves him or her to be well informed and responsible. If instead the voter was sufficiently informed to have heard several claims and counterclaims but found the Kremlin plot the most plausible of the set and thereby switched to the Republicans, we may still wonder at what this says about his or her adequacy of political information. It is self-evident that in the most prevalent situations of political competition the echo chamber is embarrassingly weak as an excuse for misinformation, although now and again it is sadly appropriate.

Other common facets of the information problem are even more wildly out of tune with the echo chamber metaphor. How, for example, do we adapt the metaphor to explain why so many New Hampshire voters in March 1968 assumed McCarthy was a hawk on Vietnam? Surely McCarthy had not kept his dovish position secret on the national scene in preceding months nor had the mass media refrained from reporting that position monotonously for an extended period. This is what the public had been told, in the sense of elite input to the echo chamber. If the metaphor is useful to explain information deficiencies, why was there so little recognizable echo?

To summarize, then, in my estimation Key failed to cope with his customary adeptness with the information problem, although he poked at it with the "echo chamber" idea, and he made the further mistake of importing the concept of rationality to the discussion while leaving it hopelessly undefined. His final and posthumously completed work has helped to legitimize a simplistic equation between rationality and "issue voting" which simply does not bear scrutiny. Some portion of genuine issue voting proceeds on misinformation, and hence demonstrations concerning issue voting cannot be used to show how well informed the public is nor can they be used to prove rationality, save in the sterile tautological sense in which rationality governs all behavior, which is to say the case in which proofs are irrelevant from the outset. All of these problems would fall away if the focus were on issue voting *per se,* uncluttered by the rationality concept.

There is another quite independent point of view from which the equation of issue voting and rationality, with its implied opposite—the equation of party identification or personal attraction of the candidates with non- or irrational factors—becomes extremely awkward. This is the simple truth that the factors of party identification or personal attraction of candidates can readily be represented as "proximity" terms in formal deductive models that proceed entirely on the assumption of rational decision-making. In other words, just as vote decisions may be determined in part by the citizen's estimation as to which candidate falls closest to his or her own position on various issues, so may vote decisions also be influenced by which candidate or party the voter feels closest to on other nonissue grounds. Indeed, with respect to party loyalties Davis, Hinich, and Ordeshook (1970) have suggested exactly this incorporation in their multidimensional proximity model. I know of no connotations of the root concept of rationality which make such an incorporation bizarre. Yet the frequent implication that rational voting is issue voting rules out this incorporation without any apparent reason.

It would seem helpful, then, if questions of the prevalence of issue voting were kept separate from questions of the prevalence of rationality in voting behavior. Anybody who feels the rationality question is worth pursuing is welcome to do so, of course, although hopefully I have made the point that without further specification as to what voting choices qualify as nonrational the question is impossibly formulated and not worth much debate. I would therefore prefer to pursue the issue voting question. We shall find that although setting aside the leap from issue voting to pronouncements about rationality rids us of many gratuitous conceptual tangles, the issue voting question itself is less than straightforward.

The Weight of Issues Relative to Other Proximal Factors

Perhaps the first thing necessary to recognize in talking of weights across orientations to parties, candidates, and issues is that neither precise nor entirely general solutions are possible. Occasionally investigators take a single body of data and attempt with some new and improved data-reduction technique to show what such relative weights "really" are. It seems obvious that these weights will vary from time to time, place to place, and subpopulation to subpopulation. *The American Voter* speculated that while comparable measurements were lacking, it was likely that the party weight had dominated voting decisions even more thoroughly in 1948 than it did in the 1952 and 1956 elections. Similarly, it would be surprising on simple intuitive grounds alone to find that the two Eisenhower elections were not something of a local maximum for the weight of a candidate factor.[26] And it seems clear from the work of Nie (1974) and others that the weight of issue voting advanced to relatively high levels in the later 1960s, with some decline in the potency of pure party loyalty as a predictor. Since these weights are themselves variables, rather than constants, the main research interest in them is to arrive at some orderly specification of the conditions under which they vary.

Less attention has been paid in recent years to such codification of variation, however, than to a controversy over the relative roles of party identification and issue orientations in the determination of voting choices. Part of the controversy stems rather simply from the fact that the weight of issues in the late 1960s was in reality greater and hence significantly less overshadowed by party identifications than it had been in the 1950s. But this "true change" aside, considerable dispute remains, and it helps make clear why I doubt that any precise "weight" statements are likely to be compelling, although of course rough ranges of weights or gross differences in relative weights are surely worth attention. This irrelevance of high precision would be true if for no other reason than the fact that different data reduction techniques and somewhat discrepant data bases are sure to give at least modest variation in results even for the same election situation. But it is the more obvious given the substantial overlap between issue concerns and party loyalties, which makes assignment of unique weights rather problematic.

Perhaps it would be wisest to treat this area of overlap as a variable in its own right for purposes of estimation of weights rather than to seek to partition it into "pure" issue and "pure" party components. But if such a partitioning is to be made, then as we noted earlier there seems fair agreement that it should depend on causal primacy. That is, in some cases it is clear that a voter has adapted his or her party identification to fit some issue of pressing concern; in other cases it seems likely that a voter's issue concerns are handy rationalizations for support "this year" of the party he or she has always voted for. The former case we would consider an instance of issue voting; the latter case an instance of party voting. Unfortunately, a substantial part of the overlap between issue orientations and party loyalties is not so neatly partitioned.

Brody and Page (1972) have provided an excellent discussion of the problems inherent in disentangling this kind of ambiguity in causal flow. As they show, it is a discrimination that is unlikely to be at all compelling without longitudinal data, and even then it is difficult. One or two observations on this score are worth highlighting. First, raw correlational analysis that merely assesses the covariation between issue proximity, party loyalty, and vote choice is nearly certain to *over*estimate the importance of specific issues in determination of the vote. This is true because in the area of overlap—voters whose issue position, party, and vote are congruent—there are almost invariably voters who do not have independent knowledge of their party's position on the issue. As Pomper documented, even in the era of relative clarity on these matters a significant fraction of the electorate admits on each major issue not knowing party positions, and an even larger fraction reports seeing no difference between the parties; in earlier eras both proportions were more sizable still. There is no point imagining that the issue leads to party preference when the individual does not even know that there is any relationship between the two. The party-candidate link, however, is rarely problematic in the same sense.

A second and more basic problem is the time frame within which the net direction of causal flow is being estimated. This is important because one may arrive at quite different estimates for exactly the same path of events according to the time frame chosen. The conceptual difficulty is nicely illustrated by an unusual response from a voter who planned to vote Republican in 1956 because of a lifelong Republican preference. When pressed as to what it was that was attractive about the Republicans, the answer was, in effect, "they wanted to keep Prohibition—I don't just know what the parties have been up to lately, though." Now in one time frame this vote would have been an instance of fervent issue voting: for Prohibition and against drink. However, given the utter irrelevance of this issue in 1956 or, for that matter, in the preceding fifteen years, it seems more reasonable to consider this 1956 vote best accounted for by party loyalty.

This point is an extremely general one. We cannot say that *all* party identifications are initially forged by a voter's issue concerns: there are other sources of initial preference, including attraction to charismatic political figures. Moreover, it is clear empirically that the modal single source of partisanship over the electorate as a whole is family transmission, which often occurs before the individual even knows what a political issue is.[27] But if one is asking about still more primeval causes, and is willing to take a time frame that crosses generations freely from parent to child, then it is indeed likely that a dominating primacy must be accorded to issue concerns back at the very beginning of any family's partisan tradition.

However, it is not unreasonable to ask the question of primacy in a shorter time frame in the interest of maintaining a modicum of substantive relevance for any issues seen as generating partisanship and hence a vote decision. And within such a restricted time frame—a span of several quadrennial elections, for example—party identification is likely to gain considerably in its causal primacy relative to the flux of issues occupying the nation over such a period.

There are several properties of party identification which suggest it has a potent role in shaping policy preferences, but they take on such meaning only when they are considered in combination. The first such property is a simple one: if one is restricted to a single variable with which to predict voting decisions as well as a range of other political differentiations, party identification seems to be the most efficient one to choose at almost any time in almost any political system that has any continuity of party history.[28] It would typically outrun even the most potent issue predictor by a rather wide margin in terms of variance accounted for in individual vote decisions.

This fact is a critical link in a chain of reasoning, although taken alone it says next to nothing about the importance of party voting relative to issue voting. For example it gives us no assurance whatever that the party identification measurement is, for most voters, any more than a summation as to how the individual expects to vote, that vote having been determined primarily by recent issue considerations. Indeed, this taint of momentary summation may well make the concept of party identification somewhat less useful in some countries than it is in the United States.[29] Fully as important, if we are genuinely interested in playing party voting off against issue voting, is the consideration that it is manifestly unfair to restrict an estimate of issue voting to a single controversy. As we noted earlier, the issue concerns that may weigh on one or another voter's individual decision-making are enormously multifarious, and any fair estimate of the impact of issue concerns on voting decisions must take account of all of this variety.

The most efficient way to take account of this variety and thereby achieve a maximal estimate of the influence of issues on individual vote decisions, as we have seen, is to invite the voter to say what national problems he or she feels are most important as well as to name which party he or she feels is most likely to handle the problems in the best way. It is important to keep in mind that this kind of information, while admirably adapted to estimating individualized issue concerns, can produce confusions if generalized to some other kinds of problems of concern to students of electoral systems. Thus, for example, the more that idiosyncratic issue concerns and private perceptions of party intentions on policy matters—conflicting from individual to individual in some degree—are given free play, the more remote we become from evaluations of voting as a communication system in which policy messages are being transmitted in an intelligible form. As Boyd (1972) has pointed out, the gain in accuracy of predicting individual votes comes at a cost of restricted applicability to normative theory or analytic work on theories of party competition, for which some modicum of shared perspective concerning the party system must be assumed. Nevertheless, for the specific problem for which it is tailored, it is a useful data base.

RePass (1971) has used data we collected in this form to estimate weights of such self-initiated issue concerns relative to party and candidate orientations in the shaping of individual voting decisions for the 1964 election, the period in which issue voting was beginning to gain in magnitude. The strongest *independent* weight predicting the vote (after the other two orientations had been controlled) was .39 for a candidate attraction variable. This high value is not entirely surprising, since candidate preference lies closest to the voting act itself, although the value appears to have been somewhat higher in

1964 than in some elections. The weakest independent weight of .23 was associated with the volunteered issue orientations, but RePass points out that it did not lag much behind the performance of party identification (a weight of .27 with the other orientations controlled).[30] It should be kept in mind, of course, that this low weight for party occurs only after the overlaps between party identification and candidate attitude and between party identification and issue orientation are removed. It is entirely appropriate to ask about the independent weights of issues and party, with the candidate variable controlled, since we are momentarily suspending judgment as to the direction of causal flow with respect to the overlap between these two variables. It is somewhat less appropriate, perhaps, to take out the party-candidate overlap, since there seems little question but that when abiding party loyalties are congruent with reactions to the candidates, typically new, most of the causal flow is from party to candidate assessment. However this may be, the *independent* weight of issue concerns, measured in this maximal sense involving self-selection of issues by the individual, was clearly not trivial in 1964. If we were to view a major portion of the overlap between such selected issues and party identification as one of issue primacy as opposed to party primacy (RePass does not take such a position), then our sense of the weight of issue voting in this case might catch and surpass that of party identification itself.

However, data on the long-term stability of party identification, when coupled with their predictive power, do begin to constitute a rather substantial case that much—although surely not all—of the overlap between issues and partisanship arises from a party-to-issue causal flow, although if it were possible to arrive at a neat partition of the relative flow, such a proportion would itself undoubtedly show some variation over different epochs of political history.

Evidence of the durability of party identification comes from several sources. First, and perhaps weakest, is evidence that shows that only a small proportion of people reporting an identification with a party say that they have ever identified with another party in the past.[31] This is weak because all long-term recall data of this introspective type are prey to memory decay and perceptual biases such as resistance to an admission that it was ever necessary to change parties. However, these reports of rare change are nicely enough buttressed by other data to enjoy a rough credibility, and thus they deserve mention.

More incisive evidence comes from the few longitudinal studies that have actually traced a representative sample of the electorate over an extended period of time. Principal and perhaps unique among national samples is the panel of respondents interviewed by the Survey Research Center in 1956, 1958, and 1960 (twice in 1956 and 1960). The five interviews in this panel yield a multiplicity of estimates of individual change in party identification over various short- and medium-term lapses of time, ranging from six weeks to four years. Quite naturally, the shorter the time lapse, the higher the correlation of party identification as measured at the two points involved. Four estimates are available for what is roughly the two-year period between our biennial national elections, and these show a narrow range between .82 and .85 (Pearson correlation coefficients), with an average value across the estimates of slightly greater than .835. If we take as an index of stability the temporal covariance (r^2) of measurements, the value over this time lapse is almost .70 (actually, .697).

If left in a vacuum these figures may not have much meaning to many readers. They make clear that party identifications are not immutable over time: there is at least a minor but continuing edge of change in the adult population as a whole.[32] On the other hand, it is not necessarily clear just how impressively stable a temporal correlation of .84 is, particularly since such a value is specific to a particular lapse of time. Perhaps we can lend it meaning most rapidly by observing that we have found *no* other political attitude of any type which shows a two-year stability that is as much as *one-third* as great (in terms of proportions of temporal covariance) as party identification, and if we restrict our attention to political *issue* responses, the same observation would be true even of combinations of the kinds of structured issues being measured in the 1956–60 period. In other words, relative to other political attitudes measured across time, party identifications are not simply stable: they are fantastically stable.

Furthermore it can readily be shown that on more than one count the data we have cited are *under*estimates of the effective stability of party identification, at least in this period. For example, if we decompose the 1956–60 panel data along lines of past electoral participation for voters over thirty (i.e., old enough to have a history of participation to report) and ask about party identification stability within these classes, we find the data of Table 3. This display makes very clear that instability in reports of party identification

TABLE 3   Stability of party identification, by electoral participation
(respondents over thirty, 1956–60 panel)

In presidential elections, have voted in	Two-year party identi-fication correlation (r)	Percentage of sample
All		
Plus other participation	.93	7
Voting only	.91	27
Most	.85	43
Some	.78	19
None	.42	4
		100

over time becomes greater, reasonably enough, the less closely the individual relates to the electoral process. Moreover, although the "never-vote" category amounts in these data to only 4 percent of the sample, a very disproportionate amount of the total instability in these identifications is concentrated in this group. Of course people who never vote also never figure in empirical estimates of issue and party weights in voting, and people who vote only in some presidential elections are going to be relatively underrepresented in such estimates. Therefore we can reasonably conclude that total-population estimates of party identification stability, high though they are, systematically understate the stability that pertains for voters in any given presidential election, which is to say for the subset that actually figures in issue voting estimates.

It is also obvious that there is bound to be a certain amount of measurement error or unreliability in these party identification reports in their compiled versions on data tapes. This means that even if there were never any true change in partisanship, cross-time correlations would not be perfect. With the five-wave data available for party identification over different lapses of time it is possible to estimate what proportion of observed change is due to unreliability as opposed to true change. Very exacting analyses of this kind lead to the suggestion that if it were possible to eliminate the edge of unreliability that fogs any such measurement, the "true" correlation in party identification over a two-year lapse in this period would have been .953 for the total population, with a still higher value pertaining for the active electorate.

It must be stressed that all of these estimates are drawn from the 1956 to 1960 period in the United States and cannot with certainty be generalized across all periods. It is known, for example, that the proportion of voters considering themselves to be relatively independent of any party loyalties showed a significant, if not enormous, increase starting abruptly between 1964 and 1966 and progressing through at least 1972. Such a loosening of party ties surely means that rates of defection from party increased during this crisis, and it would seem plausible that actual changes in partisanship may have occurred at an increased rate also. However the latter conclusion need not follow in any strict way from the growth in independents. Quite apart from the fact that a disproportionate share—although by no means all—of the increase in independents has come from entering cohorts, a tendency for the proportion of independents to increase on the Republican-Independent-Democratic continuum merely shrinks the absolute variance of the frequency distribution without necessarily changing people's relative positions in the way required to diminish a cross-time correlation coefficient.

It is therefore a great pity that we lack major panel data from the later 1960s to document by how much, if at all, the rate of change in party identification may have been stepped up under the pressure of critical events during this period. The one shred of longitudinal data on a national sample which exists for any part of the period since 1960 is a small adjunct subsample of persons reinterviewed in 1966 after having participated in the 1964 election study. Yet this is a useful shred of information since it falls in a period after the most marked changes had already occurred in indicators of the Nie and Pomper type and after the full sense of crisis had begun to grip the nation. It also includes the beginning of the period in which the number of independents had begun to rise. We find, however, that the temporal correlation of party identification in this tiny panel (128 cases) for the two-year interval, 1964–66, stands at .862, or a value that is absolutely higher than estimates drawn from the 1956–60 panel! To be sure, the sample is small and the correlation could not be distinguished with any confidence from the .84 that characterized the earlier period. But it would be very hard to argue from these data that the 1956–60 panel estimates fell in an abnormal period when party attachments were at some pinnacle of stability that was soon to be washed away by the crises of the mid-1960s.

Similarly, the retrospective reports of identifiers whether they had ever changed from one of the major parties to the other do not show any startling advance in the later 1960s, despite the rise in proportions of independents. The gross figure for such party changers at any point in a lifetime was just under 17 percent in 1964, before the weakening in aggregate party identification began, a figure close to data from the 1950s; it was 18 percent in 1968 and 17 percent again in 1970. For what they are worth, then, these reports give little hint of accelerated conversions from one party to the other.

It is when taken together that the high predictive power and extreme stability of party identifications begin to have a rather obvious significance for the riddle as to which has caused which, when we observe that issue positions and party identification show a heightened congruence, as they did in the later 1960s. The literature defending issue voting tends to see issue positions as causing partisanship when the two overlap or are congruent for individuals at any point in time. Yet this amounts to arguing that a set of variables in flux (issue positions) cause partisan feelings that are in fact known to be quite constant, an interpretation that seems at the very least logically awkward. Issues emerge and disappear from election to election, and individual positions on those issues that do endure for any time at all are manifestly much less stable over time than is partisanship. It is therefore hard to contend that positions adopted on this flux of issues create the sense of location on the party identification continuum, when the latter locations typically have greatly antedated any cognition of these policy debates.

Indeed, this matter is most clear at exactly the point at which issue voting can be made to appear the most impressive: in data in which the respondent chooses his own salient issues. It is such issues that are by far the most transient. RePass (1971) shows that the issues selected as most important by the electorate in 1960 bear little relationship to those deemed most important in 1964. Some 6 percent of the 1960 sample referred to racial difficulties as the most important national problem; by 1964 this had become the choice of well over three times as many people. Other policy concerns multiplied by factors as great as ten over this period or shrank by equal factors. Even when the disparate set of 1960 and 1964 domestic issue concerns are all bundled together as one, which they are clearly not, there was a change in mention from less than 40 percent to over 60 percent between the two years. If in the face of such flux we discover that most people feel the party they identify with is also by some coincidence the one most likely to "do what they want" on the problem selected, it would be strange to suppose that these newfound issue concerns have "caused" people to become Democrats or Republicans, especially since we know they were almost invariably of the same party persuasion before the issue attracted their attention.

It is for reasons such as this that we have tended to assume that prior partisan loyalties are *typically* responsible, in the sense of being causally primary, when party preferences turn out to match with issue positions. This is not to say they *always* are. As Goldberg (1966, 1969) has pointed out, for some limited fraction of the overlap between party loyalty and issue positions in predicting vote decisions, policy feelings have clearly been primary, causing at least temporary adjustments in partisanship. Moreover, if with V. O. Key we contemplate only the marginal changes in vote preference which produce variation in outcomes from election to election, then the psychological significance of the policy-to-party causal flow is correspondingly increased. But none of this changes the conclusion that for the vast bulk of the overlap between policy positions and party choice in voting, party loyalties constitute the prior, or causal, term.

It is for such reasons as well that I have suggested (Campbell *et al.*, 1966) that the impact of current issues on current voting might be estimated better in terms of the capacity of those issues to deflect voters from their normal partisan voting habits than by the more conventional direct correlations between issue positions and voting choice with no account taken of the effects of prior partisanship in shaping both of these elements. Such "normal vote analysis" has been used to advantage by Boyd (1972) and others. It provides only a rough approximation of the independent impact of current issues since it implicitly considers party identification to be causally prior to issue positions when the two are congruent, whereas we know that this is not true in every case but only in the vast majority of cases. However, it is an approximation that seems rather obviously preferable to the more conventional procedures, which either implicitly or quite explicitly take issue positions to be prior in the area of overlap, an assumption known to be very wide of the mark. Estimates that are still more satisfying could be achieved on the basis of longitudinal data that would permit instances of issue-to-party causal flow to be sifted out of the area of overlap and properly assigned. But longitudinal data of the requisite time depth are virtually never available.

All told, then, our discussion has made two facts clear. One is that the relative weights of issues and party loyalties show significant variation over time, with issue concerns taking on heightened importance in periods of crisis and in the degree that objective party differentiation on policy matters permits. The second is that even in such periods of crisis, party identification continues to be the dominant causal force in explaining the totality of individual voting choices, at least within any short or intermediate time frame. However, as Key has reminded us, explaining the totality of individual voting choices is scarcely the only important question facing the student of voting behavior; several other questions of manifest importance can do a great deal to restore our appreciation of the role of issues in the functioning of electoral systems.

The Role of Issues in the Aggregate Voting System

We have already touched on one such question in dealing with Key's *The Responsible Electorate.* Any examination of voting *change,* as opposed to the totality of vote decisions, is bound to give a prominent place to issues. A phenomenon like party identification is naturally of limited value in accounting for change since it is by definition an inertial factor. But it is not totally irrelevant to the study of voting change since we know that when people defect from their preferred political party in a particular election or series of elections they are very likely to return "home" to the original party when the immediate factors inducing defection obsolesce. Since returning "home" is a form of voting change, even an inertial factor like party identification may be seen as a relevant predictor of it, and indeed this homing tendency is the basic reason why the predictive power of party identification holds up as well as it does over longer reaches of time. Nevertheless, while the strength or intensity of partisanship predicts how probable it is that a defection will occur, the fact of an identification cannot in itself predict that a defection *will* occur.

Of course it is such temporary desertions, when they occur asymmetrically between the parties, which constitute much of the story of change in aggregate election outcomes. These defections are not the entire story, since the motions of the minority of independent voters, along with differential turnout between party camps, make a contribution to voting change as well.[33] But in a system like that of the United States the phenomenon of defection seems to be the principal component of aggregate voting change. Since the role of issues in producing defections is far more pronounced than its role in accounting for the totality of individual vote decisions, the general importance of issues in determining whether incumbent administrations are reconfirmed or thrown out (a problem of voting *change* rather than voting *per se*) is of course substantial. This should not be taken to mean that issue concerns are the sole source of defections. In fact the evidence is that in most election situations in which individual candidates have considerable visibility, as in American presidential voting, the personal appeal of the candidate of an opposing party or the unattractiveness of the candidate selected by one's own party is usually a more important source of defection than issue grievances (Boyd, 1969). On the other hand, since candidate pairings are relatively transient from election to election, candidate-based defections normally terminate in a return to the home party. It is likely that a significant proportion of defections that harden into more permanent "conversions" as time wears on are those that stem from issue grievances. While as we have noted that such conversions seem to be rare, they are also the most significant form of voting change in the long run, a fact that lends added importance to their frequent issue base.

There is another related sense in which issue concerns lend stronger patterning to aggregate vote outcomes than might be expected given the somewhat underdeveloped levels of issue determination of vote decisions at the individual level and the wide range of relatively idiosyncratic issue orientations and perceptions flowing into the vote. This involves a mathematical consequence of aggregation, which must be kept in mind in reading studies of voter rationality based on aggregate voting data, such as the excellent work by Kramer (1971). To make the point vivid let us erect a hypothetical case. Suppose that we have a set of voting districts, each of which contains an electorate in which 90 percent of all voters are totally uninterested in the kind of political issues pursued by investigators inquiring as to the rationality of voting behavior; or, if interested, the 90 percent scatters itself across a bewildering range of such issues and demonstrates high levels of aggregate confusion as to which party stands where on these issues. Suppose that the other 10 percent are highly alert pocketbook voters, who gauge recent trends in their local economies with exquisite care, voting for the incumbent if recent performance is favorable or against the incumbent if it is not. In such a setting, if we take measures of objective economic performance by district and relate them to aggregate vote divisions, either across districts at single points in time or for the same districts across time, we can find some spectacular correlations in either direction. In fact, the more pure the "noise," in a statistical sense, which is being contributed by the 90 percent of each constituency, the more perfect these correlations should be. And of course it is almost irresistible to leap from such high-magnitude correlations to the belief that one is dealing with an enormously rational electorate, when by construction in this hypothetical illustration almost the opposite is the case.[34]

To the student concerned about the functioning of democratic systems and in particular about their grounding in intelligible policy debate, these simple observations should be enormously gratifying. For there can be major gain in intelligibility through aggregation, since aggregation is an excellent means of driving out "noise." We shall see later that aggregation is probably quite critical in the generation of an intelligible "representation function" as well. At the same time, however, we should not conclude that the state of affairs at an individual level can thereby be written off as totally irrelevant. While there are probably respects in which it is much less consequential than many observers have taken for granted, there is a very real sense in which voters whose preferences have been purged from consideration as "noise" by aggregation have been effectively disfranchised, at least in a collective sense, and this naturally remains a matter of ethical concern. Moreover, I observed at the beginning of this essay that popular elections are admittedly a rather blunt and sluggish instrument of control, and of course how sensitive they are—at least with respect to how far the vote swings between parties in response to an objective stimulus of the type identified by Kramer—is in no small measure a function of what proportion of voters are "alert" to the stakes of popular elections, with common frames of reference.

Summary

Over the course of this extended section I have tried to address what seem to be the major controversies that have arisen in recent years regarding proximal political determinants of individual voting choice. In spending my space in this fashion I have been obliged to ignore many delightful minor controversies, including some that bear on the major ones. There is also a rather large trove of both findings and methodological developments which I have left unrecognized. Indeed, in tracing controversies that stem in an indirect way from a clash of traditions between the mainstreams of inductive empirical work and deductive "rational" modelling, I have entirely neglected constructive areas of work which aim at a smoother marriage between the two, such as empirical work on the spatial representation of party competition.[35]

My chief aim in reviewing these controversies has been to suggest that the empirical realities of voting behavior are nowhere nearly as disjunctive and confusing as cursory readings of the literature imply. It is not hard to contrive contradictory impressions from data assembled on different bases for the purposes of asking quite different questions. But few of these data turn out on examination to involve contradictory findings that are genuine enough to excite scientific curiosity. Usually it is rather easy to see that the divergent impressions are a necessary product of the divergent questions or, in some instances, of even simpler mathematical necessity.

Macrocosmic Change in Voting Systems

There turns out to be a point of rather attractive fit between much of the work on the psychology of the voting act and some of the more intriguing features of long-term voting change in the political system of the United States. Most notably, students of historical American voting statistics have noted for some time that the party division of the national presidential vote across several generations shows the properties of what is often called a "quasi-stationary equilibrium." That is to say, the division of the vote seems to oscillate for an extended period of time around a central value like 48 percent Democratic. Then there is a rather abrupt change to a new central tendency like 56 percent Democratic, around which the vote oscillates for the next extended period of time.

This particular aspect of highly aggregated votes taken as a time series, one of the few features that distinguishes voting data from other irregular time series like wheat yields or stock prices, is naturally of rather profound significance. Politically, in our two-party system, it means that save for rare periods in which the central tendency of the vote division is at equilibrium very close to 50 percent, one party seems to enjoy a natural majority over the other. This does not imply that the party suffering only minority support cannot win a majority of presidential or congressional votes in a given election: favorable oscillations away from the equilibrium level can provide occasional victories. But a conjunction of especially favorable circumstances is needed for the minority party to win power, and the minority party has little hope of holding power for as long as half of the time of the period during which the equilibrium level of the vote division disfavors it. Naturally enough, the more widely the equilibrium level departs from a 50–50 division in a given epoch, the more difficult it is for the minority party to win any given election and the smaller the fraction of time that it can expect to have power during the epoch.

Critical Realignments of Party Strength

In a classic essay V. O. Key (1955) drew the attention of scholars to the set of "critical elections" which lay at the transition from one equilibrium level of the party vote division to another. He pointed out that such junctures were times of high intensity of political feeling and represented not merely a change in the partisan division of the vote but also a considerable reshuffling or realignment of the social bases of party support. Such realigning processes vary widely in both their rapidity and their geographic scope. Key (1959) came to distinguish between the sudden realignments associated with critical elections and what he termed "secular realignments": more gradual and long-term redistributions of party support across social groupings in particular geographic areas. Similarly, the evidence seems to be that even fairly rapid realignments of very localized scope are scarcely rare events in American political history, at least in the sense that in any given decade some number could be found on the national political map. However, for any given area such rapid realignments are surely rare, and only very infrequently do they involve a large enough electorate to be very perceptible even in regional returns, particularly as they may be actively obscured by some small countermovement in some other locale.

Naturally, most scholarly attention has been given to realignments that are relatively rapid and massive—typically more or less nationwide—in their scope. And there seems fair consensus that the past 150 years of American history has featured three such national realignments fitting these specifications, at intervals spaced roughly a generation apart: (1) in the decade just before the Civil War, (2) around 1896, and (3) the period between 1926 and 1936.[36] In each case the national division of the two-party vote underwent an alteration fundamental enough to reshape the terms of party competition.

There is no particular mystery as to the proximal causes of the three major realignments in American party history. In each case a major polarization developed on a policy issue that excited abnormal passions and crosscut the traditional positions of the major political parties, leaving them attempting to straddle the issue or breaking into warring factions. Burnham (1970) has provided a useful account of many regularities that seem to attend periods of realignment, including the fact that they are usually heralded by the emergence of third-party movements that win surprising mass support by articulating new grievances that the traditional parties have been unwilling or unable to express. He also attempts to account for the rough periodicity of such critical realignments in terms of the likelihood that party positions forged by such crises gradually lose their relevance as time passes as well as their flexibility to adapt to new polarizations that run along different lines. More recently, Sundquist (1973) has reconstructed details of the policy maneuvering that actually took place within the leadership of the existing parties at the time of each of the three major realignments and has offered a set of "scenarios" as to outcomes, according to different modes of response by party and faction leadership, which might be expected in the face of realigning pressures.

There is similarly little difficulty at the mass level in understanding how individual-level models of voting choice based on party identification can produce lengthy periods of constancy in the equilibrium level of the popular vote division, punctuated by occasional step changes in that level. While a very feeble rate of individual shifting of party loyalties goes on continually, mostly due to the adjustment of a person's loyalty to fit that of a spouse, such changes are very thinly scattered over an aggregate and run in both directions between the parties, thereby leaving the net division of national party strengths quite undisturbed. This abiding division, as measured by party identifications, is obviously the equilibrium level that tends to endure for an extended period. The shifts in vote division observed during such periods, taking the form of oscillations around the stable central value, spring in some degree from vote-switching by true independents but are rather considerably amplified by defections on the part of identifiers. It would be logically possible for both types of change to occur at a substantial rate without much net change in the observed vote division, if the changes largely compensated for one another. However, the evidence is strong that in a typical election, short-range circumstances—including the relative charisma of current candidates and salient issues of the moment—do favor one party over the other. Independents move toward the favored party, which suffers few defections among its own flock; the disfavored party, meanwhile, loses heavily in defections and to some degree in abstentions by others of its normal loyalists. Thus the net change may have considerable amplitude, although the change is merely a temporary oscillation since the defectors will return home as soon as circumstances warrant.

These internal dynamics of such short-term oscillations have been massively documented by election studies of the past twenty or thirty years and are subject to little dispute. Against such a backdrop it is natural to imagine that a period of true realignment involves not merely defection but a much more permanent conversion to the favored party, so that there is no question of "returning home," and the underlying division of party loyalties is thereby more durably altered. Yet this is pure surmise, for the simple reason that no such periods have been available for study in depth since sample surveys became a common methodology.[37] Sundquist (1973), in addition to his direct reconstructions of leadership change in realigning periods, has made a commendable effort to envision the currents of conversion at the grass roots, utilizing indirect indicators such as data on party registration from those states requiring such a commitment. Yet, as he recognizes, these data are, for a variety of reasons, including the gamesmanship of cross-filing in some states, only an uncertain reflection of what a cross section of the electorate might have reported concerning its party attachments at the time.

What little work has gone forward toward the reconstruction of these internal dynamics makes the surprising suggestion that even a very marked national realignment can occur with only an extremely limited rate of full-blown conversion of individuals from one political camp to the other side. A good example of a "marked realignment" is that which occurred sometime within the period from 1924 to 1936, since the magnitude of change in apparent equilibrium levels of the party division of the national vote was surely as great in this period as in any of the earlier periods identified as realignments. That is to say, a reasonable estimate of the underlying national party division in the period leading up to this realignment puts it at about 42.5 percent Democratic.[38] After the dust had settled the same division emerging in the later 1940s and early 1950s was about 53 percent Democratic and inching forward. This before-after difference of greater than 10 percent in the underlying party division in the country seems if anything to be larger than any comparable estimates for earlier realignments.

It is naturally tempting to conclude that over 10 percent of the electorate must have become genuinely converted from a Republican party identification to a Democratic one in the course of this realignment. It is easy, however, to sketch a model of what was going on in this period which requires a proportion of true conversions scarcely more than a percentage or two of the electorate as a whole.

First let us review the known contours of the vote division in this period. After massive shifts toward the Democratic party in the 1932, 1934, and 1936 elections there was a slow but steady erosion of apparent Democratic supremacy, which stretched at least through the election of 1946. There was a good deal in this later period that remained constant, the most notable being the charisma of Franklin Delano Roosevelt, as evidenced by his election to unprecedented third and fourth terms as president. It would not be surprising if Republicans enamored of Roosevelt were seduced into a rather lengthy continuation of the defections they had first launched in the 1932–36 period. Indeed, the erosion of support for the Democrats in national elections after their high-water marks of 1934 and 1936 was visibly more rapid at other levels of office than the presidency. Sundquist has noted this fact and pointed out that the realignment from a Republican to a Democratic majority appears to have been consummated below the presidential level only in delayed fashion, with a first surge in the 1928–36 period, followed by a visible if relative sag in Democratic fortunes until a new surge of Democratic support below the presidential level consolidated the realignment in the 1950s. He attributes this pattern to the slow maturation of a cadre of vigorous and charismatic young Democrats, inspired by the New Deal, to an age at which they could take over pre–New Deal local Democratic party structures and compete for national office.[39]

All of these patterns smack rather suspiciously of a very large mass of Republican identifiers who were never actually converted to a Democratic allegiance but who had supported Roosevelt and the Democrats in the 1932–36 period and thereafter with varying speeds drifted back to their mother party. This raises the possibility that very little full-blown conversion occurred in the 1930's. At first glance it might seem difficult to understand why, short of large-scale conversion, the equilibrium level of underlying party loyalties had not by the late 1940s reverted to the same massive Republican advantage that had pertained before the crisis with its waves of defection began. Nonetheless, it turns out that this is not at all difficult to explain.

The simple demographic fact left out of most thinking on the subject is that the turnover in the composition of the national electorate—its rejuvenation with younger cohorts—is a good deal more rapid than meets the eye. For example, rough estimates from Census data suggest that within the American electorate of 1940 about one-third were persons who had been too young to have figured in the electorate of 1928 (the election on the threshold of the new era) and hence had no necessary connection to the partisan coloration of that electorate or its preceding era. Similarly, the electorate of 1950 was *in majority* new (about 55 percent) relative to the electorate eligible to vote in

1928! Now it is well known that in periods when change is stirring, the young are much more clearly stamped with new outlooks than the old; and given the general discrediting of the Republican party and the resurgence of Democratic popularity in connection with the Great Depression, it would be reasonable to suppose that younger cohorts in this period were markedly Democratic in their sense of identification as well as in their votes, although for most of them this meant no conversion or even defection whatever.

In fact, given the known parameters of turnover in the composition of the electorate, it is quite easy to calculate the party division that would need to have characterized the newer, post-1928 voters in order for a realignment from 42.5 percent Democratic to 53 percent to have been accomplished without imputing any lasting conversions to the aging members of the original 1928 electorate. For example, if the remainder of the 1928 electorate had by the election year of 1944 still been 42.5 percent Democratic, then a 68 percent Democratic division in the post-1928 portion of the 1944 electorate would in fact aggregate to the necessary Democratic majority. As of 1952, the point for which the first reliable estimates of party identification based on nationwide probability samples are available, post-1928 voters, by then a majority of the electorate, would need to have been only 60 to 61 percent Democratic to account for the parameters of the realignment without invoking any conversions whatever in the older electorate. In fact the set of post-1928 voters in the 1952 Survey Research Center sample yielded an estimate of aggregate party loyalties of 58.6 percent, only a tiny shortfall relative to expectations that ignore the possibility of conversion completely.[40]

It is scarcely our intention here to argue that no lasting conversions did occur during the 1930s on the part of persons old enough to have voted in the 1928 election. Changes in party registrations in some areas in the 1930s as shown by the Sundquist (1973) data are surely more rapid than can be accounted for by the entrance of new Democratic cohorts. Even though the behavior of these registration proportions by party over the 1930s imply both short-term strategic choices and temporary registrations with the Democrats by Republicans anticipating a defection, the pro-Democratic swings portrayed must have included some true converts.

Similarly, retrospective reports of such party conversion collected after 1950, while generally thin in the aggregate to begin with and scattered across time as well as between parties, do show a telltale bulge favoring the Democrats in the earlier 1930s. The problem is that this bulge seems far too small to account for a shift in the loyalties of the total electorate by more than 10 percent in that period. Such long-term retrospect is notoriously unreliable, and the inadequate number of such reports has usually been written off as mere forgetting. But the purpose of our discussion is to show that true conversions may indeed have been much more limited than meets the eye, since large-scale defections coupled with steady turnover in the composition of the electorate do not fall far short of reconstructing the known change between the state of these matters in the 1920s and the situation as it became revealed by sample surveys in the early 1950s. It helps account as well for what Sundquist has noted as the delayed consummation of the realignment.

There is one other cluster of findings which is thoroughly fascinating with respect to these internal dynamics of party realignment and which also happens to blend very smoothly with our revisionist account of the character of the realignments of the 1930s. That account has placed heavy weight on the sharply Democratic coloration of cohorts entering the electorate during the 1930s. While such an assumption is bountifully supported by such loose data as are available from the period, it implies an occurrence of Democratic children of Republican parents on an uncommonly large scale. Naturally, when change of this magnitude occurs, disjunctures must present themselves at one point or another, and since we have been arguing that disjuncture in the form of personal conversion of deeper party loyalties was probably rather limited, much of the weight of disjuncture is pushed off on a generational cleavage.

However, two pieces of newer data hint strongly that "cleavage" may be a thoroughly inapt term for the process as it was acted out. One piece of data involves almost archaeological reconstructions that I have carried out with cohort analyses of all relevant data on party identification collected by the Survey Research Center since 1952. These data show a bulge of Democratic strength associated with cohorts born in roughly the 1905–12 period relative to cohorts born at earlier dates, which is perfectly timed to represent the young voters at the beginning of the 1930s.[41] However, let us suppose that we duplicate such a cohort analysis no longer with voters themselves but rather with the general partisanship they associate with their parents. Such an analysis is weakened by two facts: (1) the parental partisanship question has been posed less frequently than the item of personal identification, so that much larger sampling error clouds any detailed estimates, and (2) we do not have specific reports as to the birth years of parents, so that we can array them in cohorts only on the basis of their children's age and can relate them to chronological years only by making a standard assumption of a 30-year generational difference, parent to child. Since there is obviously substantial variance around a central tendency in the vicinity of 30 years, we can expect our analysis to suffer further clouding on this score.

Therefore we may not be too surprised when such an analysis is completed to find that it simply lacks the fair clarity of features found in cohort analyses, organized by birth year, of the respondents' own identifications. There is not, for example, any reliable trace of a Democratic bulge beginning with cohorts born in the 1905–12 period, although we would have a right to expect such a bulge in view of the fact that there is no strong reason to suppose that our indirectly located sample of "parents" should differ much from their immediate age peers more directly located as children of some earlier generation of parents. What is surprising, therefore, is that the one discontinuity resembling the expected bulge is not found in the 1905–12 cohort but rather seems to be pushed back into the 1890s!

This discrepancy, which at first glance seems perplexing, would appear to have a very straightforward explanation. We should first refresh our memory as to who the people are who were born in the discrepant 1895–1905 period. They are parents who were in their thirties during the 1932–36 epicenter of the realignment. All of them had been eligible to vote prior to 1928, and probably a substantial majority of them had voted in the relatively Republican ethos prior to 1932. They must have been mostly Republican themselves, although if data from more recent swings in the partisanship of American voting are any guide, they are precisely the set of "experienced" voters most likely to have defected to the Democrats under the pressures of the Depression. At the same time they are parents whose children were in what Hyman (1959), Greenstein (1965), and others have seen as the crucial period for political socialization with respect to parental transmission of party identifications. And it is these children who were reporting, in the 1950s and 1960s, that their parents were relatively Democratic, when the other more incisive cohort analyses of the parents themselves suggests that these parents would have reported themselves to be "generally" relatively Republican.

The obvious solution to the riddle lies in the likelihood of misperception. We have a parental generation containing disproportionate concentrations of Roosevelt Republicans, whose children took them to be Democrats. In other words, if we merely assume that the chief cue concerning parental partisanship for many children is how their parents are voting in a given year or period, especially at the presidential level, such that a vote the parent might consider as a temporary defection is taken to be "true" partisanship, then we find ourselves with a cohort of Americans, about ten years "wide," who could enter the electorate in the later 1930s and 1940s and consider themselves as Democrats without any particular sense of disjuncture with the partisanship of their parents, at least as they perceived that partisanship.

The above speculation is strongly buttressed by data of a different kind arising from a different epoch but carrying exactly the same message. In 1965 a study of a national sample of high school seniors conducted by Jennings included independent interviews with the parents of the students involved. Both the children and the parents were asked their own party identification, and children were in addition asked to report the party identification of their parents.[42] Analyses by Denney (1971) show that the children's reports of their parents' partisanship correlated much more strongly with the presidential vote cast by the parent in the 1964 election than with the parents' own testimony as to their primary party loyalty. Since the typical defection in the Democratic landslide of 1964 involved Republicans temporarily switching to vote for Lyndon Johnson and against Barry Goldwater, this means we have a set of children who coded their parents as Democratic on the basis of the presidential vote cue although their parents continued to regard themselves as Republicans, undoubtedly voted Republican at other levels in 1964, and returned home to the Republicans in subsequent elections. Since these were children who, at eighteen, were in the main about to leave home definitively before another major election, it is easy to see that many would never have much chance subsequently to correct their impressions.

From some points of view these findings may seem bizarre since it would seem reasonable to suppose that a child in a generally Republican home would be aware that his or her parents were crossing party lines in a given defecting vote for president. However, the trend of findings from parent-child studies, especially by Jennings and Niemi (1968), indicates that while family partisanship is communicated early and exerts a heavy influence on the child's later partisanship as an adult, it is difficult to demonstrate much transfer of other political orientations and values from parent to child. What these more recent data imply is that even the transfer of partisanship itself, while demonstrably effective, rests in many cases on amazingly superficial cues—mainly the most salient parental vote preference for the most visible office in the land, without any nuances of contradictory political philosophy or general partisan dispositions. And such evidence in turn lends strong support to the surmise that many children of Roosevelt Republican parents in the later 1930s and 1940s suffered no sense of repudiation of family tradition as they began to establish their own personal voting histories of Democratic predilection.

In sum, then, we have hypothesized that neither generalized party convictions of individuals nor the high continuity of the parent-child partisanship bond need suffer much dislocation in order to account numerically for the relatively massive shift in aggregate partisanship which is the net result of a critical realignment. The key element is instead the temporary defection, a behavior not experienced as a generalized partisan disposition by the parent but perceived as such by the child.[43]

The Prospects of a New Realignment

If one puts any stock at all in the seeming periodicity of major partisan realignments in the United States, then one might think the country is already overdue for such an event, which might be expected to occur thirty to forty years after the one that centered in 1932—that being some time roughly in the 1964–72 period. Indeed, Burnham (1968) and other scholars have been hinting ever since the results of the 1964 election began to be scrutinized that such a phenomenon may be impending. Moreover, as we have seen, there has been substantial fodder in the later 1960s for the belief that public opinion was unusually galvanized and basic change was intruding on the fundamental parameters of the American voting system. Most noteworthy where realignment is concerned, perhaps, has been the coupling of a decline in levels of loyalty reported for the two major parties with intense public feeling concerning a circle of issues that seemed to crosscut the standard battlegrounds on which the Democrats and the Republicans had waged war since the last realignment of the 1930s.[44] Nevertheless, as of this writing there is not much compelling evidence that any clear partisan realignment, at least in its classic or ideal-type form, has occurred or even is as yet well under way.

On the other hand the concept of a critical realignment involves a syndrome of events, elements of which may tend to but need not necessarily co-occur. For example, two defining criteria seem to involve (1) a relatively marked shift in the central tendency of the national two-party vote division, and (2) a realignment of the bases of party support, typically defined in social terms, with new coalitions replacing older ones. Historically, these two events appear to have co-occurred with some regularity. However, it is not hard as a logical matter to imagine a considerable reshuffling of party coalitions which might sum to very little net change in the partisan coloration of the nation as a whole. Nor is it inconceivable to think of a marked gain in popularity of one party over the other which has an "across-the-board" flavor without any noteworthy realigning of bases of support. It remains true, of course, that the frequent coincidence of these phenomena is a fact of primary importance, but it is perhaps too much to expect that they must always coincide.

Burnham (1970) is correct in observing that many of the elements familiar from past realignments have been evident in the later 1960s. In 1968 George Wallace formed the most successful national third-party movement in several decades, a group created to express grievances crosscutting the traditional postures of the two major parties. In a galvanizing crisis, levels of loyalty for the traditional parties fall off; this occurred in the late 60s and continued through 1973, leaving ground fallow for the formation of new attachments. In both 1968 and 1972 the Republicans, although a distinct minority in the land, captured the presidency and in the second of these elections by a major landslide. All of these elements hint at realignment, and they have emerged roughly "on time": about a generation after the preceding realignment. At the level of obvious indicators, all that has been missing is the culminating shift toward a new partisan coloration of the country of the sort that has typically accompanied such events in the past.

Perhaps such a shift is in the immediate offing, and surely we would be wise not to consider the continued dominance of the Democratic party in statements of party identification as any warrant that major realignment is not under way. As Price (1968) and others have argued, the nature of party identification is such that it will inevitably be a lag term rather than a lead term as an indicator of change.[45] Indeed, our earlier arguments have implied in the most straightforward way that if party identification measurements in the modern mode were available for 1932 and 1934, they would have continued to show about the same Republican majority they had shown in 1928 or 1924, apart from the very young. What would have heralded the more permanent realignment that subsequently emerged, if we limit ourselves to hypothetical data from the early 1930s, would have been continued defections not simply for president but at all levels of office, along with cohorts of new voters showing marked Democratic biases in party identification as well as vote.

There is no particular counterpart for this configuration of elements in the 1972 election. It is true that the minority party won the balloting at the presidential level by a landslide, an event that required large-scale defection by Democratic identifiers. It is also true that both parties have engaged in some effort to redefine themselves in response to the new pressures of recent years: the Republicans with the "Southern Strategy," the Democrats in the maneuvers over the composition of the nominating convention that helped to produce the McGovern candidacy.

But the similarities with the preceding realignment terminate roughly at this point, and beyond it there are nothing but sharp contrasts. For example, the defections of Democrats in 1972, unlike those of Republicans in the early 1930s, were very dramatically contained at the presidential level, and at other levels of the ballot voting nationwide was quite normally Democratic. More striking still are the data concerning younger voters. Instead of the votes of the young running with the defections of older citizens, as was the case in the early 1930s, young voters in the 1972 election seem to have been headed in the opposite direction. While it is hard under the landslide conditions of the 1972 presidential election to find any segments of the population other than blacks who actually contributed a majority of their votes to Mc-Govern, one other population category fitting this description was made up of voters in the 18–24 age range, according to data for that year from the Center for Political Studies. And the reported party identifications of younger citizens at that time are if anything more massively pro-Democratic than even the vote divisions reported by the young in the 1940s or early 1950s. In short, if we absolutely insist on some kind of large-scale shift in partisan sentiment occurring as a function of this critical period in American history, it would be about as easy to argue that the shift would be further in a Democratic direction as to claim that the period would eventuate in a Republican majority.

However, taking all of these conflicting trends together, it seems clear that no marked change in the partisan division of the nation has as yet manifested itself. Even the evidence for change in the social bases of party support over this critical period is rather unimpressive. To be sure, a South in which blacks are predominantly Democratic in national-level voting and in which a strong current of Republicanism has built up among whites represents a signal change by comparison with the distribution of party strength in the South as of 1948 or 1952. These developments may even have shown some acceleration in response to the crises of the late 1960s. However, they were well under way long before the crisis began its rise to a crescendo, and they seem to fit Key's description of a gradual "secular realignment" far better than they fit the specifications of a critical realignment. This slow evolution of the region is apparent in Axelrod's (1972) interesting calculations for the social bases of electoral coalitions in the 1952–68 period, but there are no other abiding changes of any magnitude, either of the secular variety or sudden shifts associated with the pressures of the 1964–68 period. Miller, Miller, Raine, and Brown (1973), in their report of the 1972 election, also note that apart from this regional change and a drift associated with education, the social bases of party support in 1972 look very similar to those of twenty years earlier, despite upheavals and wild swings of the presidential vote in the interim.

Burnham (1970) has argued that two major factors have prevented the turbulence of the later 1960s from producing an electoral realignment in classic form. One is the absence of a sudden "triggering event" comparable in scope and penetration with the collapse of the stock market in 1929. The other is the "onward march of party decomposition," an erosion of the hold that American political parties have on the minds and affections of the electorate. Burnham feels that such indicators as the increase in self-professed independents since 1966, particularly among the young, along with evidence over a long time span as to continuing increases in split ticket voting represent a general deterioration of parties as an instrument of politics in the public mind, which has been going on with only temporary reversals since the turn of the century. If indeed we are approaching "the end of American party politics," then the question of what party realignment might emerge from the pressures of the current period becomes largely academic.

Sundquist (1973) expresses doubts about this point of view. Much of his own treatment, as we have seen, anticipates rather different party outcomes resulting from a period of realigning pressures according to a variety of different ways in which the several leaderships of the parties and their internal factions respond to these pressures. Indeed, one of his five principal scenarios as to leadership responses has the outcome "no major realignment." Recent years have surely demonstrated the degree to which large partisan displacements rest on an intricate conjunction of events and the full mosaic of decisions and nondecisions at the level of party strategists and other political elites from a variety of prominent and powerful factions at the national level. Even the most stray events, such as the crippling of George Wallace by an assassin, may vitally intrude on the probabilities that events may sweep toward any one of several realignment outcomes. Therefore while a major partisan displacement has typically been the most enduring result of past crises in American party history, it now seems plausible that such a crisis, even one that is "on time," may come and go without it.

Conclusion

In this section we have discussed some of the ways in which microcosmic theories of voting behavior fit into the most central discussions of macrocosmic voting change. Most readers will be aware that in so doing we have left numerous relevant topics unmentioned. The independent decodings by Campbell (1960) and Glaser (1962) of factors underlying the long-standing rule of thumb among politicians that the party occupying the White House loses congressional seats in the off-year election constitute an excellent example of microcosmic regularities being applied to macrocosmic riddles. On a broader front the work of Burnham (1965), Jensen (1968), and other scholars interested in the reconstruction of American voting history is extending our horizons regarding basic ranges of variation in political culture at a mass level in the United States and the impact of these variations on the gross contours of voting behavior. On an equally sweeping canvas, the germinal studies of Lipset and Rokkan (1967) on the emergence of mass electorates and party systems in Europe command the closest attention.[46] Since the focus of much of this work is on turnout and political participation, a topic that I have been spared in order to avoid an encyclopedic catalogue or a much longer essay, I have not undertaken to weave it into my discussion here. However, it contains much that is basic to an understanding of voting systems and the macrocosmic institutional and historical factors that bear even on their partisan outcomes.

Voting Systems and the Representation of Public Opinion

I suggested at the outset of this essay that the prime purposes of a system of routinized mass balloting are to provide some communication and control upward from a population or a rank and file to a decision-making leadership. Studies of public opinion and voting behavior have often been criticized for becoming too engrossed in the details of individual decision-making or in the outcomes of specific votes or even in larger changes in the character of popular voting over time and thereby losing sight of the broadest questions of "So what?"—in what way does the existence of such a communication and control mechanism affect other features of the political system and the social order, including most notably the policy outcomes that are the supposed targets of the voting mechanism from the start?

   The first step in this direction is the development of studies that examine the interaction between the mass voting system and those elite actors who are in some sense dependent upon it. Such studies have increased in numbers in recent years. The deductive tradition in a Downsian mode focuses on one aspect of elite decision-making which is naturally dependent on the state of opinion at the mass level: Given one or another distribution of voter opinion as an election situation approaches, what are the optimal strategies for policy positioning of the parties and their candidates? An intriguing empirical application is provided by the Rosenthal investigations (1970) into the dynamics of coalition formation among the multiple political parties of the French Fourth Republic for purposes of the second, or runoff, vote as a function of the vote division pertaining in the initial balloting. Other studies, such as that by Kingdon (1966), have addressed the way in which successful and unsuccessful candidates perceive the electorate and facets of the vote message that are being communicated by the election.

Works of this kind are refreshing because they begin to incorporate in a more systematic way the elite side of the communication process known as the popular election. However, they remain contained within the immediate context of elections rather than attempting to discern how the nature of the mass-elite interaction bound up in elections goes on to influence policy outputs or other critical features of the political process.

Some studies focusing on policy outputs or elite decision-making, such as Dahl (1961), do use election data in a backdrop sense, and quite a large number have attempted to draw systematic relationships between some aggregate demographic characteristics of voting constituencies and variations in the contributions of their representatives to the policy formation of the legislative process.[47] But very few studies are reported which involve independent but interlocking investigations between the grass-roots citizens of political constituencies and the leadership delegated to represent them, with emphasis on the policy outcomes that arise as a result of popular elections.

It is not surprising that such studies are rare, for they are large, complex, and costly. As of this writing only two exemplars at a national level have been reported for the United States involving interlocked investigations with elites and their constituencies. One is the pioneering study in 1958 by Miller and Stokes of American congressmen and their constituents.[48] The other is the more recent work by Verba and Nie on the citizenry of sixty-four small American communities (under 50,000 population) and their local leadership.[49] Fortunately, both studies have numerous cross-national replications, which in coming years should begin to provide some sense of the degree to which differences in history and institutions impinge on the fundamental processes of representation.

The two studies have in common a focus on elite responsiveness to citizen wishes as expressed through democratic participation in general and popular voting in particular. Both studies are based on interviews carried out on both the mass and elite sides, with samples organically related to each other in the political representation sense. Both studies contain data on elite perceptions of mass wishes, and at least the Miller-Stokes study contains mass perceptions of the policy aims of the candidates competing in the election studied. Both studies depend most integrally on measures of congruence ("concurrence" in Verba-Nie terminology) between mass wishes and elite preferences or policy-making behavior. And both studies are devoted to an examination of the conditions under which such congruence is strong or weak.

These two studies are, however, in dramatic contrast in many other particulars. Most obviously, the setting is the local community for Verba and Nie and relatively small communities at that; for Miller and Stokes the arena is that of Congress and national-level legislation. While both studies measure a kind of mass-elite congruence, each is devoted to a different one of the two major facets of representation and responsiveness. The Miller-Stokes study deals with the congruence between constituent policy position and the policy positions of the candidates for representative roles. Verba and Nie focus instead upon mass-elite agreement with respect to problem priorities, or the agenda-setting face of decision-making, with only limited attention to the specific ways in which such problems should be resolved. Miller and Stokes operate entirely within the context of popular elections on the mass side but extend their view past representative preferences on policy to actual behavior—role-call voting in the House of Representatives—which is determinant of official policy outputs. Verba and Nie do not go beyond subjective elite statements of priorities to ask whether differences in such statements actually eventuate in objectively different political outcomes. On the other hand the data that they report extend well beyond popular voting as a mechanism for mass input to elite decision-making and hence provide a useful opportunity for setting elections into some perspective against other familiar forms of democratic participation.

All told, then, the Verba-Nie work is in no sense a replication or in any direct way an amplification of the Miller-Stokes study. Nevertheless the two studies do converge with respect to their most fundamental and global finding: there is indeed a detectable and under some conditions substantial "representation function" that is furthered by the mechanism of popular elections. While such a finding so broadly stated may strike some as being self-evident and trivial given widespread acceptance of elections as a means of accomplishing exactly these ends, the efficacy of elections is occasionally called into question from various ideological perspectives. Moreover, the fact that these empirical demonstrations can be carried off in such different venues with the same global finding begins a sort of triangulation on the effectiveness of popular elections that is well worth continuing.

Of course such a demonstration in itself is hardly the main point of either study. Rather, given that some quite visible representation function can be observed with this kind of interlocking design, the interesting part of the inquiry is to begin to examine the chief features of this representation by asking under what conditions the representation bond seems robust or feeble. And both studies provide considerable analysis of this conditional variation.

Before we briefly recount some of the major results it is worth standing back and reviewing why such a complex design seems indispensable to the study of representation and elite responsiveness. While it does not seem important here to review normative theories of representation, which in any event are being discussed elsewhere in these volumes,[50] it is clear that our whole view of the meaning of any kind of congruence in political preferences or action between leaders and the led hinges rather dramatically on the causal dynamics of the processes involved. This is not to say, of course, that the fact of congruence

in and of itself lacks interest, since absence of congruence and even a more active *in*congruence are empirically possible and typically assumed to be the case
in thoroughly elitist or tyrannical regimes. Nevertheless it is clear that any observed congruence might have arisen purely through successful indoctrination
of a mass by the elite.

In addition, there are abundant mechanisms that might create a congruence that is in a sense unconscious or accidental, at least from the point of view
of the two parties to the transaction. Perhaps the most frequently discussed case
is that in which the delegate is like other persons in his or her constituency
simply because he or she shares their past experiences and perspectives. Thus
the delegate's political reflexes are congruent with the constituents even though
he or she may take no interest in hearing their views and feel no compunction
about a posture of responsiveness to them. Such a configuration is one of "congruence" and fits easily under most definitions of "representation." But it has
little to do with any current motivations toward "elite responsiveness" and addresses the control and communication functions of popular elections only in a
rather oblique and perhaps even trivial sense.

Thus mass-elite linkage designs, as represented by our two examples, are a
first crucial step in examining the processes that underlie any observed congruence, since they permit at least the collection of relatively precise evidence concerning where both parties to the transaction stand and, as importantly, where
each party thinks the other party stands. Once again, these matching data
taken alone hardly cinch the case for mass control/elite responsiveness, but
they are indispensable in isolating certain obvious forms of "unconscious" representation. Moreover, other data such as elite eagerness to be responsive or
mass determination to have delegates attentive to their instructions, while subject to obvious biases that require careful interpretation, have some bearing on
the matter as well. All told, then, while the question of causal dynamics is, as
always, extremely difficult to resolve, it is only with such designs that even presumptive evidence can begin to be assembled.

Both sets of investigators are commendably cautious about the question of
actual causal influence. Their key dependent variables are modestly labelled
"congruence" and "concurrence" to avoid gainsaying the case, and both have
invested considerable analytic energy in attempting to reconstruct causal relationships as thoroughly as any nonlongitudinal study design will permit. In
each case there is a reasonable demonstration of at least a presumptive sort
that a significant portion of the observed congruence is a matter of elite responsiveness to perceived mass wishes and that this flow of influence does depend rather vitally on the existence of popular elections.

Verba and Nie show not only that there are positive levels of concurrence
between the priorities assigned to local problems by citizens and by their local
leadership but, much more importantly, that concurrence strengthens when
citizen participation levels are higher. This key finding can be demonstrated at

both the individual and collective levels. That is to say, individual scores on concurrence of priorities with local leadership are greater the more highly participant the individual is politically. And when all the individual scores are averaged within communities, the general trend in concurrence is upward (save for one wrinkle rather neatly explained) as one moves from less to more participant communities.

Such a pattern would exist if community leadership is responsive to citizen messages about problem priorities in the degree that they are communicated from the grass roots. But as the authors recognize, this pattern would remain consistent with other causal dynamics as well. For example, highly participant citizens tend to be of higher socioeconomic status and hence more similar to community leadership than the less participant. Thus the heightened degree of concurrence might be an artifact of this similarity rather than an active form of influence and response. However, the authors are able to show by controls on status that it is mainly the fact of participation rather than of status which is important in accentuating concurrence.

Still more important as a counterhypothesis is the possibility that the more participant a citizen is, the more exposed to and influenced by leadership priorities he or she is, so that the causal flow creating increases in concurrence with participation is a matter of leadership shaping of such political assessments rather than leadership attention to popular demands. Here the authors introduce a measure bearing on the degree of activity reported by leaders in communicating with citizens and working with community groups, on the assumption that if concurrence were mainly created by leadership influence efforts, there should be dominant positive correlations between leadership activism and concurrence. Reasonably enough, such correlations (with various forms of leader activism) turn out to be positive, but they are only of very modest magnitudes and far smaller than the correlations linking citizen activism and concurrence. Although the evidence necessarily remains somewhat circumstantial, the data patterns fit more comfortably with the assumption that the flow of influence is upward rather than downward.[51]

The Miller-Stokes study permits us to examine the question of causal dynamics at two rather different levels. The first level is most conceptually comparable to the Verba-Nie analyses in that it takes an existing leadership for granted—in this case, members of the United States House of Representatives—and attempts to gauge their responsiveness to the distribution of opinion in their respective constituencies. Let us keep in mind that, unlike the Verba-Nie case, we are dealing here with issue positions rather than problem priorities and that the case is carried not simply to attitudinal statements by elite respondents but onward to actual policy-determining behavior: the role-call votes of the House members in the policy domains on which constituent opinion has been observed.

As in the Verba-Nie case, however, there is a general cast of agreement (or positive correlation) between variations across congressional districts in citizen opinion and the direction of roll-call votes cast in the Congress by the diverse representatives of these districts. With respect to these correlations, at least two observations should be drawn.

The first observation relates to a point we stressed earlier in this essay concerning the benign effects of aggregation in highlighting lines of coherence (or "rationality") in voting systems. Miller and Stokes were confronted with a choice not unlike the option exercised by Verba and Nie: Should analyses proceed at an individual or an aggregated level? The key unit of observation in such a study is the constituent-representative bond. However, constituents are vastly more numerous than representatives, a fact that raises the problem of how many such bonds are being observed. From the individual point of view, each of (say) 10,000 constituents has such a bond with his or her representative, so that there are 10,000 bonds. If we wish to view the matter in this light, then the congruence or lack thereof of each constituent with his or her representative is a separate datum, and we more or less ignore the fact that many sets of constituents are relating to the same representative. From the more aggregate point of view there are far fewer such bonds: only the limited set made up of a representative's relationship to his or her aggregated district. This view not only is very realistic but also fits congenially with democratic theory: the representative cannot hope to vote in accord with the wishes of all of the members of his or her constituency at once, since conflicting opinions exist. If the representative is truly eager to follow the dictates of the district, he or she must reflect the majority or some central tendency of its opinion on a given issue. Therefore it makes sense to deal with bonds between the representative and the aggregated district and not with each individual in the district.

In point of fact the Miller-Stokes analyses are cast in this latter format. However, it is of interest to note that some unreported analyses have been conducted in the disaggregated, individual form. The correlations between individual opinion and representative vote turn out to be quite chaotic and, on the average, much closer to zero than some of the fairly robust relationships that emerge when representative behaviors are merely correlated with aggregated, "mean" opinion by district. In other words, the process of aggregation here is once again driving out great quantities of idiosyncratic or individual-level "noise" on these issue opinions, and without this step we might feel considerable despair at the triviality of the "representation function." However, the aggregate form seems to be the conceptually crucial one in any event.

The second observation that must be made concerning these typically positive correlations between policy sentiment in congressional districts and roll-call votes cast by district representatives in Congress is that the general magnitude of these correlations varies quite widely. On matters of foreign policy these positive correlations are quite faint, whereas on racial issues they are very strong, with social welfare activism falling somewhere in between (Miller and Stokes, 1963). These variations by issue domain in the general robustness of the representation function are, of course, of great conceptual importance in sorting out conditions under which representation varies. However, for the purposes of this general overview the global observation that there is a positive cast to relationships linking district opinion with representative vote shall suffice.

As with the Verba-Nie observations of positive concurrence, these signs of congruence are just a beginning if we are to address causal dynamics. The Miller-Stokes data are rich enough to address the issue from several sides, but perhaps the most straightforward analysis involves taking account of the representative's own issue position and his or her perception of the district's issue position. Whereas these tend to be correlated, the relationship is far from perfect, and it can be shown that the representative's assessment of district sentiment usually has some independent impact on his or her roll-call behavior apart from that behavior predictable from his or her own position. While there is another problematic link in the chain between actual district opinion and the representative's estimate of it, the correlation referring to the representative's accuracy of perception tends to be sufficiently large that a reasonable chain from district opinion to roll-call behavior can usually be established quite apart from the representative's own views. The causal case remains presumptive, of course, since some other unknown third factor may jointly shape both the representative's assumptions as to district opinion *and* his or her roll-call behavior. Nonetheless, despite substantial variation in the strength of the evidence across issue domains, the data configurations are such as to be compatible with the hypothesis that the representative's cognizance of district opinion does influence his or her own voting behavior in policy legislation within the House of Representatives.

All of the above is with respect to the leadership sitting in the Congress and, like Verba and Nie, takes the composition of this leadership as a given. However, it is perfectly fair to push causal questions back one step and ask how the composition of this particular leadership was determined. Such a question throws us squarely into the mechanism of the popular election, since it takes no elaborate causal analysis to know that most of these representatives have their seats because they succeeded in winning more popular votes than their competitors. This is the control function of elections, and it is possible that legislative outcomes would have been vastly different if even some fraction of local majorities had switched their votes to the opposite candidate.

The Miller-Stokes study includes interviews with unsuccessful as well as successful candidates. We cannot tell from these interviews exactly how the unsuccessful candidates would have cast their votes in House roll calls, since they never had the opportunity to do so. However, their opinions on the issues are known, and it is possible to contrast them with opinions among the set of successful candidates to see whether the public purchased more agreement with its votes in the election than it would have if the outcomes of races had been reversed. While of course there are exceptions with respect to some candidates on some issues, in general the levels of agreement with winning candidates are much higher than they are with losing candidates over the issue domains covered. In other words, constituencies were much better represented by the set of candidates selected than they would have been by the set of candidates rejected. This screening is true popular control, and while the causal case does not remain perfectly unequivocal even in this case it is surely rather compelling.

The Verba-Nie study examines the importance of election participation from a rather different but complementary angle. While some of their community leader sample involves elected officials and while undoubtedly there is intracommunity competition between some of the leaders interviewed, the context is not narrowly that of elections and the leadership does not split neatly into competing factions. However, a great deal of information was collected on types of mass political participation, of which voting participation is but one possibility. The authors show that some of the other forms of participation, such as nonpartisan activities in community organizations, or individualized initiation of contact with political officials, or even partisan campaign activity, are not as tightly correlated with voting participation *per se* as might be thought and are reasonably discussed as distinctive inputs (Verba and Nie, "Political Participation," this volume).

This scope in assessing forms of participation permits a comparative evaluation of the role of elections in enhancing concurrence in problem priorities between citizens and their local leadership. As we have seen, such concurrence increases generally with omnibus indices of local participation. However, when we isolate the four component types of political participation, which seems most effective in advancing this kind of agreement? The importance of high voting participation stands out rather clearly from the start, but its role is intriguing. As the authors demonstrate, in communities in which voting participation is relatively vigorous all of the other forms of participation contribute quite an additional effect in increasing concurrence. But in communities in which voting is relatively low there is no reliable gain in concurrence as a function of aggregate increases in any of the other three forms of political participation. The authors assume that while elections by their very nature convey relatively limited amounts of information in and of themselves, the "messages" that do come through are more truly representative of the community at large than are the other forms of political input, most of which are chiefly engaged in by relatively high-status segments of the community. Moreover, elections seem to play a rather key role in the representation process: where they are vigorously attended they appear to constitute a kind of generalized pressure on leadership, rendering it more attentive to other citizen inputs that carry more detailed demands and directives.

Conclusion

Since public opinion is a prime ingredient of popular elections, some scholars have taken evidence concerning the limited attentiveness of the public to politics, low levels of information, and the absence of ideological frames of reference among a substantial fraction of the electorate to mean that democratic elections are "full of sound and fury, signifying nothing." Over the course of this essay I have contested that any such conclusion need follow, even if the initial data have been properly construed.

We began with the bleakest portrait of public opinion, developed mainly in the 1950s. We then considered modifications of this portrait required by the surge in public attentiveness to politics during the crises of the later 1960s. Such modifications begin to give us a sense of how elastic various parameters of public opinion may be, even when the level of education remains roughly constant in an electorate, as a function of short-term changes affecting involvement in the political scene.

I have argued that these modifications have high theoretical and political significance at the same time that I have expressed doubt that they proffer a totally new portrait. With respect to public opinion, the difference between the two periods is scarcely that between the blackness of midnight and the total illumination of high noon. It is rather the difference between the earliest moments of dawn, when the first shapes and colors can barely be discerned, and the state of affairs a half hour later, when light is still somewhat dim but shapes have taken on clear relief and colors have begun to be vivid. Even in the 1950s and, presumably, back through other troughs of routine politics in the nation's history, there was always a cadre of attentive activists of sufficient size to lend currents of public opinion and their polarizations a great deal of overall policy coherence. And even in the 1960s, with ideological orientations more salient, these orientations still had only limited penetration in the public, and misinformation and misperception remain prevalent enough to flaw the processes of electoral communication on this or that point from time to time.

While hypothetical numbers risk being taken too literally, the difference between the two periods might well be thought of in terms of a first period in which some 10 or 15 percent of the electorate is attentive and engaged enough to fit the expectations of the most naive assumptions about democratic participation, whereas in the second period the proportion of the attentive electorate has risen to 25, 30, or even 40 percent. Given such illustrative figures, it is legitimate to be awed at the magnitude of the change, a doubling or a tripling in a very short time. It is also legitimate, relative to naive assumptions that a quasi totality of the electorate looks like the 15 percent of the first period or the 30 percent of the second period, to find even the second figure rather small and the portrait still rather bleak. Thus interpretive emphases remain the creature of expectations more than the direct product of the data themselves.

In the second section we turned to elections and voting behavior. We dealt first with controversies surrounding the issue bases of individual vote decisions, attempting to find a middle path of truth between exaggerated claims and counterclaims. As we moved to more macrocosmic treatments of aggregate marginal changes in election outcomes and the whole phenomenon of realignments, we may well have noted a step change in the apparent significance of issue and policy impacts. I think it is no accident in the epistemology of study in this area that those who work with aggregated voting data often treat elections with different emphases than those who cope with a fair degree of Brownian motion at the level of individual decision-making. Neither picture is inaccurate, and it should be obvious that something approaching a statistical necessity offers a comfortable bridge between the two.

Perhaps the observation that "elections matter" and hence that public opinion is important is too simple a moral with which to end. Surely we have not shown that the impact of elections on elite decision-making even vaguely approximates total determination: the very studies that demonstrate the effects of elections show at the same time that a variety of other factors beyond popular demands contribute to such outcomes. Nor have we shown that inputs from public opinion and elections are invariably benign. It is not hard to cite numerous instances in which the outcomes of popular elections would, with the benefit of hindsight, be considered by most to have been tragic errors of judgment. Yet when compared with the histories of political systems whose leaders were disdainful or ignorant of public opinion or who stage rigged elections with no sense of accountability to their populations, such a communication machinery seems to claim high value. And if such machinery exists, it is useful to have some warrant other than hope that the messages flowing through this communication system do in fact have some impact. Without some such assurance, the study of public opinion and voting behavior would be little more than an esoteric curiosity.

Overall, I have tried to emphasize not only that public opinion and popular elections do matter but that in the large, they have some shape and sense that may seem out of keeping with the portrait of public opinion in either period we have surveyed. While I have tried throughout to highlight some of the transmutations that can link even a very bleak portrait of individual opinions in times of routine politics to elections with shape and sense, I have not attempted to draw an exhaustive catalogue of such mechanisms. Some have simply been ignored. For example, the very study by Miller and Stokes that shows a fairly satisfying degree of congruence between mass wishes and ultimate, official policy outputs achieved largely through popular elections also shows that most voters under the routine conditions that pertained knew next to nothing in policy terms or otherwise about the specific figures they chose to represent them. Here the mechanism that intervenes to salvage meaning, of course, is the system of political parties, with the gross policy images that specific parties have come to evoke over time. What is important is that a variety of such mechanisms exist, including the simple one of aggregation, such that the discrepancy between a bleak portrait at the individual level and elections of shape and sense is no perplexing contradiction.

NOTES

1.   Several basic works reviewing all or major portions of the area include Lipset, Lazarsfeld, Barton, and Linz (1954), Rossi (1959), and Stokes (1968). Sears (1969) provides the most recent and commendably encyclopedic organization of the public opinion and voting behavior literature.

2.   Sidney Verba and Norman Nie, "Political Participation," Chapter 1 of this volume.

3.   These questions were the motivating ones that lay behind V. O. Key's treatise, *Public Opinion and American Democracy* (1961).

4.   With the rise of electrical and electronic communication nets blanketing the country, the suggestion is often floated that the nation should consider establishment of a "push-button" participatory democracy, in which the totality of the nation's citizens could vote daily on important issues of governmental policy. Examples such as that above are, of course, extremely sobering in this regard. However painfully fallible the foreign ministries of the world may show themselves to be, it is minimally assuring to know that their calculations do take into account the simplest and most obvious parameters of a situation. There would be no such assurance with push-button legislation.

5.   Converse, Miller, Rusk, and Wolfe (1969).

6.   Converse (1970). For a counterstatement, however, see John C. Pierce and Douglas D. Rose (1974), as well as my rejoinder, which follows.

7.   A large panel study in France was conducted in 1967, 1968, and 1969 among a sample of French candidates for the National Assembly in 1967 and of their constituents at the mass level. A monograph on these studies is in preparation by the author and Roy Pierce. As a sample of differences between mass and elite in temporal stability of political locations, perhaps the most stable attitude on both mass and elite sides other than party identification is the individual's selection of personal position on a continuum ranging from extreme left to extreme right. After a year's lapse of time, elite self-locations showed a correlation of .93, or about 86–87 percent temporal covariance. Mass self-locations on the same scale showed a correlation of .63, or about 40 percent covariance. These findings may appear quite discrepant from those reported by Brown (1970), who found no significant differences in attitude stability over two-, four-, and six-week time lapses between contrasting groups of 18 persons deemed to be politically articulate and 18 judged as inarticulate. However, given the vastly different time lapses, not to mention discrepancies in the "eliteness" of the upper groups, comparisons between the two findings are of dubious value.

8.   The centrality axis in its simplest geographical sense appears to have the expected effects in the work of Norman Luttbeg (1968, 1971). An early study showed that in one setting, at least, public opinion on *local* issues showed considerably higher integra-

tion than public opinion on national issues had in my work. A second study involving state-level issues showed weaker integration, however, which more nearly resembled my national-level issue estimates.

9. A more detailed distribution of responses across the levels of conceptualization in 1956 is presented in Table 1.

10. For the moment we are contrasting the in-depth interview with the most conventional and abbreviated "soundings" of public opinion in a fixed-alternative or closed-ended mode. The differences begin to blur, of course, in sample surveys that elicit richer open-ended responses to more generalized questions.

11. This fact, laid out with perfect clarity by Pierce (1970), risks becoming lost in secondary accounts. For example, Pomper (1972, p. 416) summarizes Pierce's use of three measures of ideological awareness in a way that seems to imply that all three marched steadily upward from 1956 through 1960 to 1964. In fact, one of the three measures was available only for 1964. Of the two that might have shown change, the one that is essentially Field and Anderson's *did* show a gain; the informational measure, essentially the recognition figure discussed above, did not show a gain.

12. In a thoughtful discussion of Pomper's paper and of the more general question of issue voting, Kessel (1972) has mentioned a variety of methodological problems that might influence the appearance of change, and quite rightfully suggests that these problems must be examined before ultimate conclusions are drawn about change. All of Kessel's points are apt, including one that never ceases to pain us in preparing the election studies: we feel great obligation to upgrade the incisiveness of our measurements as we learn more and more about their shortcomings; yet changes of this sort can threaten to exaggerate or obscure true change in the reality being observed. My feeling is that the changes registered in the Nie and Pomper cases are sufficiently numerous and too well geared into other things known independently of the surveys themselves to evoke any major reservations about the fact that something has happened "out there," although details of the change, including its general locus within the electorate, may be vulnerable to methodological variations.

13. A possible exception of interest in the late 1960s involved the issue of school busing, in which there was frequently in metropolitan areas an all-or-nothing cast to the apparent policy options.

14. The Aberbach-Walker work, along with other studies of black mobilization in this period, have much the same "limiting-case" significance as had the 1958 congressional election in the Fifth District of Arkansas, cited earlier. That is, these studies were generally carried out locally at sites of urban riots, where sudden politicization was at its maximum, even for blacks. Hence they demonstrate partial change in a fraction of a subpopulation (blacks) that is itself but one-tenth of the total electorate. Thus the changes registered are nearly invisible in summary data for the total electorate, although the theoretical significance of the findings, in terms of what may happen when conditions are extreme, remains intact.

15. Similarly, of course, certain segments of the electorate with particularly high education are likely to show uncommonly ideological responses. Bicker's work (1972) on the California electorate is a good case in point: in the later period covered, nearly half of that electorate seemed to be college-educated as contrasted with the one person in five or six with some college education in the national electorate of 1956.

16. See the summary for France, Italy, and West Germany included in Klingemann (1972). For other descriptions see Barnes (1971), Pierce and Barnes (1970), and Sarlvik (1971).

17. Some of the chief works in this tradition include Siegfried (1913), Ogburn and Talbot (1929), Tingsten (1937), and Goguel (1951).

18. The primary Columbia volumes were Lazarsfeld, Berelson, and Gaudet (1944), Berelson, Lazarsfeld, and McPhee (1954), and McPhee and Glaser (1962). Main monographs from Michigan include Campbell, Gurin, and Miller (1954), and Campbell, Converse, Miller, and Stokes (1960 and 1966).

19. Some of the earlier works involving such comparisons include Lipset (1960), Alford (1963), and various collaborations of Survey Research Center personnel with colleagues in Norway, France, and Britain, some of which are collected in Campbell *et al., Elections and the Political Order* (1966); where political participation is concerned, see Almond and Verba (1963).

20. Particularly seminal early works of this kind for the United States have been those of Lipset (1963, 1964), Burnham (1965, 1970), and historians Lee Benson (1961) and Richard Jensen (1968); for Europe, Stein Rokkan (e.g., 1970).

21. Key references, in addition to Downs, include Davis and Hinich (1966), Riker and Ordeshook (1968), and Davis, Hinich, and Ordeshook (1970).

22. This is, of course, a highly truncated account of the substance covered by *The Voter Decides*. Among other things, the monograph developed measurements of other orientations, such as political efficacy and citizen duty, seen as bearing on the choice whether or not to participate in the election. We sidestep these developments because they are more relevant to the subject of political participation, treated in Chapter 5 of this volume. See Campbell, Gurin, and Miller (1954).

23. One pleasant exception is Shapiro (1969), who does indeed take care to explain the conception of rationality he uses. However, the definition is borrowed from deductive work and is in a form that resolves few of the assignment ambiguities with which real-life instances of voting seem saturated.

24. David E. RePass is undertaking such a theoretical effort to clarify what rationality means in the voting context, an effort that is surely overdue and welcome. Personal communication, 1973.

25. Numerous commentators have pointed out rather severe problems in the Key data, including the dependence on what is almost certainly biased recall of vote choices four years earlier and insensitivity to the possibility that "issue" positions had been brought into line with candidate preferences that had been formed on nonissue grounds. One or two of these problems will occupy us shortly; for the moment, however, it is useful to discuss the conceptual argument, taking the data at face value.

26. The great short-term importance of the identity of presidential candidates in electoral change in the United States is well demonstrated in Stokes (1966).

27. See the discussion of political socialization by Sears, Chapter 2 of Volume 2 of this *Handbook* series.

28. An exception with respect to the vote itself may frequently be attitudes toward the candidates, since this is virtually the vote preference itself. That is, when a voter is attracted to a candidate from an opposing party, the likelihood of defection from his or her normal party seems at a maximum, whereas the voter preferring the candidate of his or her own party is extremely unlikely to defect.

29. Butler and Stokes (1969) encounter a problem of this sort in dealing with party identification measurements in Great Britain. Similar problems have been noted for Germany by Shively (1972) and others working with current survey data there, as well as by Thomassen (1974) for the Netherlands.

30. The weights cited are standardized partial regression coefficients.

31. The figure is about one identifier out of six for reports covering respondents' lifetimes to date. Furthermore, some of these include identifiers who had defected in the current election, had given their normal identification in a preceding statement, and when asked if they had "ever" thought of themselves in terms of the opposing party felt obliged to say "yes" and to describe their current momentary defection. With these persons discounted, only about one identifier in eight or nine reports a change of parties "ever" in the past. Of course a somewhat greater proportion of people reports motion between "independence" and identification with a particular party.

32. It has often been pointed out to me in some surprise by scholars working with our panel data on party identification that the proportion of respondents who give exactly the same response to the items involved (i.e., are coded as strong Democrats, weak Republicans, etc.) over the 1956–58–60 period is quite modest. The observation in itself is correct: there is quite significant movement of individuals between adjacent categories, reduced movement over as many as two steps, and extremely limited movement over any noteworthy distance across the scale, as from one party camp to the other. But this fact does not in itself mean, as it often seems to be interpreted, that hence it is erroneous to describe responses to the measure as highly stable. The best summary measure of the stability is the correlation coefficient between repeated measurements of the variable over time; and the best frame of reference to help in judging whether a given temporal correlation suggests high stability or something less is to compare this temporal correlation with temporal correlations for other kinds of political attitudes and evaluations, as we proceed to do in the paragraph above. At the same time it is important to keep in mind that such correlational estimates deal with the *relative* stability of persons arrayed on the party identification continuum, rather than with stability of their absolute locations in specific categories. Thus, for example, while the aggregate partisan division of identifications has been remarkably stable over time, numerous scholars have noted that this division wobbles slightly over time in response to short-term tides favoring one or the other party. Thus, for example, the distribution was slightly more Republican in cast at the time of Eisenhower's 1956 election triumph than it was two years later, when short-term tides seemed favorable to the Democrats. Any correlational treatment of the variable over time, by implicitly equating mean values that may in fact be slightly disparate, clearly sets aside these short-term absolute fluctuations and focuses instead on the degree to which respondents have changed their *relative* positions on the scale. For a good discussion of these absolute short-term fluctuations in the Survey Research Center 1956–58–60 panel study, see Brody (1974).

33. For an interesting method of measuring the individual voter's contribution to voting change which takes into account both defection and nonvoting, see Shanks (1970).

34. Kramer himself avoids this pitfall of inference with conclusions that are quite carefully worded, dealing with "election outcomes," rather than individual votes, and events that are not "*solely* the product of past loyalties and habits" or random or irrational (Kramer, 1971, p. 140, italics added). Unfortunately, his work is often cited as proof of the high prevalence of "rational voting" at the individual level. The simple fact is that the Kramer data are compatible with an enormous range of possibilities where such prevalence is concerned.

35. Among excellent recent examples see Weisberg and Rusk (1970) and Rabinowitz (1973). Another central work in the intersection between these traditions is provided by Shapiro (1969).

36. Important early efforts to identify the major American realignments include, in addition to Key (1955), MacRae and Meldrum (1960), and Sellers (1965).

37. As we shall discuss shortly, a new realignment has in one sense become "overdue," and, as Burnham (1970) has demonstrated, there was much in the crises of the later 1960s that fits the configurations of prior critical realignments. However, as of this writing no genuine realignment of conventional scale has emerged.

38. This rough estimate is based on the average national two-party division of the vote over the six elections to the House of Representatives between 1918 and 1928.

39. It seems fair to see this explanation as rather nicely complementing the description I shall develop.

40. The 1952 estimate is based on a normal vote calculation for respondents age forty-four and under.

41. An example is provided by the graph on p. 154 of *The American Voter* (Campbell *et al.,* 1960), although updatings of the same graph continue to show essentially the same effect.

42. Of several reports from this study the most central for our immediate purposes here is Jennings and Niemi (1968). See also Jennings and Niemi (1974), especially Chapter 2.

43. After this passage was written I became aware of a somewhat parallel set of suggestions by Beck (1974). However, there are several points of divergence, if not contradiction. For example, Beck offers the interesting hypothesis that children growing up during periods of routine politics are less strongly socialized into party loyalties than those growing up in periods adjacent to critical realignments and hence are fertile terrain for the defections that will mark the next realignment. This hypothesis would embrace the observed increase of independents starting in 1966 and would also suggest a device producing some periodicity in the occurrence of such realignments.

44. This clash of old and new issues has been prominent in election reports from the Center for Political Studies since 1968. See Converse, Miller, Rusk, and Wolfe (1969), Weisberg and Rusk (1970), and Miller, Miller, Raine, and Brown (1973).

45. Somewhat more responsive to changes over time are the images held of the strong and weak points of the major parties by the public. Following initial work of this kind by Matthews and Protho (1966), several scholars have been plotting change over time in these perceptions, using data from the Center for Political Studies series of election surveys. A good example, covering the full period from 1952 to 1972, is provided by Trilling (1974). The authors show considerable evolution of these perceptions during this period, although the link between these image changes and shifts in party identification itself remains speculative.

46. Other important recent macrocosmic studies include Rose and Urwin (1969) on cross-national comparisons of stability in voting support for major parties during the postwar period.

47. Some of the most noteworthy studies in this vein include Turner (1951), MacRae (1952), Sorauf (1962), Froman (1963), and Rieselbach (1966). A summary of much of this material, incorporated in a simulation of roll-call voting in the House of Representatives, is provided by Cherryholmes and Shapiro (1969).

48. Certain of the basic results are reported in Miller and Stokes (1963), and Miller (1964).

49. The mass-elite sample is part of a larger study reported by Verba and Nie (1972). See especially chapters 17–19.

50. See Polsby, "Legislatures," Chapter 4 of Volume 5 of this *Handbook*. For a more extended theoretical treatment of representation see Pitkin (1967). Empirical works with valuable discussions of the representation process include Bauer, de Sola Pool, and Dexter (1964) and Wahlke, Eulau, Buchanan, and Ferguson (1959).

51. Verba and Nie 1972, especially pp. 328–32.

REFERENCES

Aberbach, Joel D., and Jack L. Walker (1970). "The meanings of black power: a comparison of white and black interpretations of a political slogan." *The American Political Science Review* 64:367–88.

Alford, Robert (1963). *Party and Society*. New York: Rand McNally.

Almond, Gabriel, and Sidney Verba (1963). *The Civic Culture*. Princeton: Princeton University Press.

Axelrod, Robert (1972). "Where the votes come from: an analysis of electoral coalitions, 1952–1968." *The American Political Science Review* 66:11–20.

Barnes, Samuel H. (1971). "Left, right and the Italian voter." *Comparative Political Studies* 4:157–75.

Bauer, Raymond A., Ithiel de Sola Pool, and Lewis A. Dexter (1964). *American Business and Public Policy*. New York: Atherton Press.

Beck, Paul A. (forthcoming). "A socialization theory of partisan realignment." In Richard Niemi (ed.), *New Views of Children and Politics*. San Francisco: Jossey-Bass.

Benson, Lee (1961). *The Concept of Jacksonian Democracy*. Princeton, N.J.: Princeton University Press.

Berelson, Bernard, Paul F. Lazarsfeld, and William N. McPhee (1954). *Voting*. Chicago: Chicago University Press.

Bicker, William E. (1972). "Ideology is alive and well in California: party identification, issue positions and voting behavior." Paper presented at the 1972 Annual Meeting of the American Political Science Association, Washington, D.C.

Boyd, Richard W. (1969). "Presidential elections: an explanation of voting defection." *The American Political Science Review* 63:498–514.

—————— (1972). "Rejoinder to 'comments' by Richard A. Brody, Benjamin I. Page and John H. Kessel." *The American Political Science Review* 66:468–70.

Brody, Richard A. (1974). "Change and stability in partisan identification: a note of caution." Mimeographed.

Brody, Richard A., and Benjamin I. Page (1972). "Comment: the assessment of policy voting." *The American Political Science Review* 66:450–58.

Brown, Steven R. (1970). "Consistency and the persistence of ideology: some experimental results." *Public Opinion Quarterly* 34:60–68.

Burnham, Walter Dean (1965). "The changing shape of the American political universe." *The American Political Science Review* 59:7–28.

_____ (1968). "American voting behavior and the 1964 elections." *Midwest Journal of Political Science* 12:1–40.

_____ (1970). *Critical Elections and the Mainsprings of American Politics.* New York: Norton.

Butler, David, and Donald E. Stokes (1969). *Political Change in Britain.* New York: St. Martin's Press.

Campbell, Angus (1960). "Surge and decline: a study of electoral change." *Public Opinion Quarterly* 24:397–418.

Campbell, Angus, Philip E. Converse, Warren E. Miller, and Donald E. Stokes (1960). *The American Voter.* New York: Wiley.

_____ (1966). *Elections and the Political Order.* New York: Wiley.

Campbell, Angus, Gerald Gurin, and Warren E. Miller (1954). *The Voter Decides.* Evanston, Ill.: Row, Peterson.

Cherryholmes, Cleo H., and Michael J. Shapiro (1969). *Representatives and Roll Calls.* New York: Bobbs-Merrill.

Converse, Philip E. (1964). "The nature of belief systems in mass publics." In David E. Apter (ed.), *Ideology and Discontent.* New York: Free Press.

_____ (1968). "The concept of a normal vote." In Angus Campbell, Philip E. Converse, Warren E. Miller, and Donald E. Stokes (eds.), *Elections and the Political Order.* New York: Wiley.

_____ (1970). "Attitudes and non-attitudes: continuation of a dialogue." In Edward R. Tufte (ed.), *The Quantitative Analysis of Social Problems.* Reading, Mass.: Addison-Wesley.

Converse, Philip E., Warren E. Miller, Jerrold G. Rusk, and Arthur G. Wolfe (1969). "Continuities and change in American Politics: parties and issues in the 1968 election." *The American Political Science Review* 58:1083–1105.

Dahl, Robert A. (1961). *Who Governs?* New Haven: Yale University Press.

Davis, Otto A., Melvin J. Hinich, and Peter Ordeshook (1970). "An expository development of a mathematical model of the electoral process." *The American Political Science Review* 65:426–48.

Davis, Otto A., and Melvin J. Hinich (1966). "A mathematical model of policy formation in a democratic society." In J. L. Bernd (ed.), *Mathematical Applications in Political Science,* vol. 2. Dallas: Arnold Foundations, Southern Methodist University Press.

Denney, William Michael (1971). "The intra-family transmission of partisanship." Unpublished term paper, University of Michigan.

Downs, Anthony (1957). *An Economic Theory of Democracy.* New York: Harper & Row.

Erskine, Hazel G. (1962). "The polls: the informed public." *Public Opinion Quarterly* 26:669–77.

_____ (1963a). "The polls: textbook knowledge." *Public Opinion Quarterly* 27:133–41.

_____ (1963b). "The polls: exposure to domestic information." *Public Opinion Quarterly* 27:491–500.

_____ (1963c). "The polls: exposure to international information. *Public Opinion Quarterly* 27:658–62.

Field, John O., and Ronald Anderson (1969). "Ideology in the public's conceptualization of the 1964 election." *Public Opinion Quarterly* 33:380–98.

Froman, L. A., Jr. (1963). *Congressmen and Their Constituencies*. Chicago: Rand McNally.

Glaser, William A. (1962). "Fluctuations in turnout." In William N. McPhee and W. A. Glaser (eds.), *Public Opinion and Congressional Elections*. New York: Free Press.

Goguel, Francois (1951). *Geographie des Elections Francaises de 1870 a 1951*. Cahiers de la Fondation Nationale des Sciences Politiques. Paris: Armand Colin.

Goldberg, Arthur (1966). "Discerning a causal pattern among data on voting behavior." *The American Political Science Review* 60:913–22.

_____ (1969). "Social determinism and rationality as bases of party identification." *The American Political Science Review* 63:5–25.

Greenstein, Fred I. (1965). *Children and Politics*. New Haven: Yale University Press.

Hyman, Herbert H. (1959). *Political Socialization*. New York: Free Press.

Jennings, M. Kent, and Richard Niemi (1968). "The transmission of political values from parent to child." *The American Political Science Review* 68:169–84.

_____ (1974). *Families, Schools and Political Learning*. Princeton: Princeton University Press.

Jensen, Richard (1968). "American election campaigns: a theoretical and historical typology." Paper delivered at the 1968 meetings of the Midwest Political Science Association.

Kessel, John H. (1972). "Comment: the issues in issue voting." *The American Political Science Review* 66:459–65.

Key, V. O., Jr. (1955). "A theory of critical elections." *Journal of Politics* 17:3–18.

_____ (1959). "Secular realignment and the party system." *Journal of Politics* 21:198–210.

_____ (1961). *Public Opinion and American Democracy*. New York: Knopf.

_____ (1966). *The Responsible Electorate: Rationality in Presidential Voting, 1936–1960*. Cambridge, Mass.: Harvard University Press (Belknap Press).

Kingdon, John W. (1966). *Candidates for Office: Beliefs and Strategies*. New York: Random House.

Klingemann, Hans D. (1972). "Testing the left-right continuum on a sample of German voters." *Comparative Political Studies* 5:93–106.

_____ (1973). "Dimensions of political belief systems: 'levels of conceptualization' as a variable. Some results for USA and FRG 1968/69." Preliminary handout prepared for the European Consortium for Political Research Workshop on Political Behavior, Dissatisfaction and Protest, April 12–18, 1973, Universitat Mannheim.

Kramer, Gerald H. (1971). "Short-term fluctuations in U.S. voting behavior, 1896–1964." *The American Political Science Review* 65:131–43.

Lane, Robert E. (1962). *Political Ideology: Why the Common Man Believes What He Does*. New York: Free Press.

_____ (1973). "Patterns of political beliefs." In Jeanne N. Knutson (ed.), *Handbook of Political Psychology*. San Francisco: Jossey-Bass.

Lazarsfeld, Paul F., Bernard Berelson, and Hazel Gaudet (1944). *The People's Choice*. New York: Duell, Sloan and Pearce.

Lippmann, Walter (1922). *Public Opinion*. New York: Macmillan.

Lipset, Seymour Martin (1960). *Political Man*. New York: Doubleday.

_____ (1963). *The First New Nation*. New York: Basic Books.

_____ (1964). "Religion and politics in the American past and present." In R. Lee and M. Martin (eds.), *Religion and Social Conflict*. New York: Oxford University Press.

_____ (1967). *Party Systems and Voter Alignments*. New York: Free Press.

Lipset, Seymour Martin, Paul F. Lazarsfeld, Allen H. Barton, and Juan Linz (1954). "The psychology of voting: an analysis of political behavior." In Gardner Lindzey and Elliot Aronson (eds.), *Handbook of Social Psychology*. Cambridge, Mass.: Addison-Wesley, pp. 1124–1175.

Lipset, Seymour Martin, and Stein Rokkan, eds. (1967). *Party Systems and Voter Alignments*. New York: Free Press.

Luttbeg, Norman R. (1971). "The structure of public beliefs on state policies: a comparison with local and national findings." *Public Opinion Quarterly* 35:114–16.

MacRae, Duncan, Jr. (1952). "The relation between roll-call votes and constituencies in the Massachusetts House of Representatives." *The American Political Science Review* 46:1046–55.

MacRae, Duncan, Jr., and James A. Meldrum (1960). "Critical elections in Illinois: 1888–1958." *The American Political Science Review* 54:669–83.

Matthews, Donald R., and James W. Prothro (1966). *Negroes and the New Southern Politics*. New York: Harcourt, Brace and World.

McClosky, Herbert (1964). "Consensus and ideology in American politics" (1964). *The American Political Science Review* 58:361–382.

McClosky, Herbert, P. Hoffman, and R. O'Hara (1960). "Issue conflict and consensus among party leaders and followers." *The American Political Science Review* 54 (June 1960), No. 2.

McPhee, William N., and William A. Glaser (1962). *Public Opinion and Congressional Elections*. New York: Free Press.

Merriam, Charles E., and Harold Gosnell (1924). *Non-Voting*. Chicago: University of Chicago Press.

Miller, Arthur H., Warren E. Miller, Alden S. Raine, and Thad A. Brown (1973). "A majority party in disarray: policy polarization in the 1972 election." Paper presented at the 1973 meetings of the American Political Science Association.

Miller, Warren E. (1964). "Majority rule and the representative system of government." In Eric Allardt and Y. Littunen (eds.), *Cleavages, Ideologies and Party Systems: Contributions to Comparative Political Sociology.* Helsinki: Transactions of the Westermarck Society.

Miller, Warren E., and Donald E. Stokes (1963). "Constituency influence in Congress." *The American Political Science Review* 57:45–56.

Nie, Norman H., with Kristi Andersen (1974). "Mass belief systems revisited: political change and attitude structure." *Journal of Politics* 36.

Niemi, Richard, and M. Kent Jennings (forthcoming). *Families, Schools and Political Learning.* Princeton: Princeton University Press.

Ogburn, W. F., and Nell S. Talbot (1929). "A measurement of the factors in the presidential election of 1928." *Social Forces* 8:175–83.

Page, Benjamin I., and Richard A. Brody (1972). "Policy voting and the electoral process: the Vietnam issue." *The American Political Science Review* 66:979–88.

Pierce, John C. (1970). "Party identification and the changing role of ideology in American politics." *Midwest Journal of Political Science* 14:25–42.

Pierce, John C., and Douglas D. Rose (1974). "Non-attitudes and American public opinion: the examination of a thesis." *The American Political Science Review* 68:626–49.

Pierce, Roy, and Samuel H. Barnes (1970). "Public opinion and political preferences in France and Italy." A paper presented at the 1970 Meeting of the American Political Science Association, Los Angeles.

Pitkin, Hanna Fenichel (1967). *The Concept of Representation.* Berkeley: University of California Press.

Pomper, Gerald (1967). "A classification of American elections." *Journal of Politics* 29:1–40.

——————— (1972). "From confusion to clarity: issues and American voters, 1956–1968." *The American Political Science Review* 66:415–28.

Price, Douglas (1968). "Micro- and macro-politics: notes on research strategy." In Oliver Garceau (ed.), *Political Research and Political Theory.* Cambridge, Mass.: Harvard University Press.

Rabinowitz, George Burt (1973). "Spatial models of electoral choice: an empirical analysis." Dissertation at the University of Michigan.

RePass, David E. (1971). "Issue salience and party choice." *The American Political Science Review* 65:389–400.

Rieselbach, Leroy N. (1966). *The Roots of Isolationism.* Indianapolis: Bobbs-Merrill.

Riker, William H., and Peter Ordeshook (1968). "A theory of the calculus of voting." *The American Political Science Review* 65:25–42.

Rokkan, Stein (1970). *Citizens, Elections, Parties.* Oslo: Universitets-forlaget.

Rose, Richard, and Dereck Urwin (1969). "Persistence and change in western party systems since 1945." Paper presented at the Conference on Comparative Social Science, Cologne.

Rosenthal, Howard (1970). "Size, winning coalitions, and outcomes." In Sven Groenings, E. W. Kelley, and Michael Leiserson (eds.), *The Study of Coalition Behavior.* New York: Holt, Rinehart and Winston.

Rossi, Peter (1959). "Four landmarks in voting research." In Eugene Burdick and Arthur Brodbeck (eds.), *American Voting Behavior.* New York: Free Press.

Sarlvik, Bo (1971). "The Swedish party system in a developmental perspective." University of Gothenburg.

Schattschneider, E. E. (1960). *The Semi-Sovereign People.* New York: Holt, Rinehart and Winston.

Searing, Donald D., Joel J. Schwartz, and Alden E. Lind (1973). "The structuring principle: political socialization and belief systems." *The American Political Science Review* 67:415–32.

Sears, David O. (1969). "Political behavior." In Gardner Lindzey and Elliot Aronson (eds.), *The Handbook of Social Psychology,* vol. 5, 2nd ed. Reading, Mass.: Addison-Wesley.

Sellers, Charles G. (1965). "The equilibrium cycle in two-party politics." *Public Opinion Quarterly* 30:16–38.

Shanks, John Merrill (1970). "The impact of voters' political information on electoral change: a reexamination of the quality of American electoral decisions." Dissertation at the University of Michigan.

Shapiro, Michael J. (1969). "Rational political man: a synthesis of economic and social-psychological perspectives." *The American Political Science Review* 63:1106–19.

Shively, Phillips W. (1972). "Voting stability and the nature of party attachments in the Weimar Republic." *The American Political Science Review* 66:1203–25.

Siegfried, Andre (1913). *Tableau Politique de la France de l'Ouest sous la Troisieme Republique.* Paris: Armand Colin.

Smith, M. Brewster, Jerome S. Bruner, and Robert W. White (1956). *Opinions and Personality.* New York: Wiley.

Sorauf, Frank J. (1962). *Party and Representation.* New York: Atherton Press.

Stokes, Donald E. (1966). "Some dynamic elements of contests for the presidency." *The American Political Science Review* 60:19–28.

————— (1968). "Voting." *International Encyclopedia of the Social Sciences,* vol. 16. New York: Macmillan.

Sundquist, James L. (1973). *Dynamics of the Party System.* Washington, D.C.: The Brookings Institution.

Thomassen, Jacques (1974). "Party identification as a cross-cultural concept: its meaning in the Netherlands." Paper presented at the Workshop on Participation, Voting and Party Competition. European Consortium for Political Research Joint Sessions, March 28–April 2, 1974, Strasbourg.

Tingsten, Herbert (1937). *Political Behavior: Studies in Election Statistics.* Stockholm Economic Studies. London: P. S. King.

Trilling, Richard J. (1974). "Party image, party identification and partisan realignment." Manuscript, Duke University.

Turner, J. (1951). *Party and Constituency: Pressures on Congress.* Baltimore: Johns Hopkins University Press.

Verba, Sidney, and Norman H. Nie (1972). *Participation in America: Political Democracy and Social Equality.* New York: Harper & Row.

_____ (1975). "Political participation." Chapter 1, this volume, *Handbook of Political Science.*

Wahlke, John C., Heinz Eulau, William Buchanan, and Leroy C. Ferguson (1959). *The Legislative System.* New York: Wiley.

Weisberg, Herbert F., and Jerrold G. Rusk (1970). "Dimensions of candidate evaluations." *The American Political Science Review* 64:1167–85.

3

INTEREST GROUPS

ROBERT H. SALISBURY

INTRODUCTION

The investigation of interest groups presents a number of problems requiring preliminary clarification and boundary settlement. So many disputations have occurred and so much, polemical and analytical, has been written that a brief review of the main issues involved in defining the field is in order.

Theory of politics or political phenomena? Much of the best-known literature associated with interest-group analysis deals with the meaning, application, and utility of group theory (or theories) of politics. Important empirical and theoretical statements about interest groups are contained in many of these works, of course, but Bentley, Truman, Latham, Hagan, and some others present themselves as political theorists arguing for an analytic framework in which the group, however defined, is taken as the basic unit of observation and description. Whether conceptualized as a comprehensive scheme or a partial effort, the idea of group in these works is essentially an analytic construct used to order and interpret observed phenomena and not necessarily identical with what the real world would identify as interest groups.

This essay will not be concerned with group theories of politics. Its scope will be limited to the phenomena of formally organized associations which attempt to influence governmental decisions. No assertions are made and no inferences are warranted regarding the relevance of group theories of politics. Even the comparative significance of interest groups as a variable in a comprehensive analysis of politics will receive only indirect attention. These questions are examined elsewhere in the *Handbook* (Greenstone, Vol. 2), and the boundaries set by their omission are hardly severe.

Culture-bound or general? A common criticism of interst-group analysis has been that it purports to be a general theory of politics, or at least to deal with universally observable phenomena, whereas interest groups are, in fact, a peculiarly American cultural artifact (LaPalombara, 1960; Macridis, 1961). We may omit consideration of the theoretical argument, but we shall be concerned with the empirical issue. Are interest groups relevant only to the experience of the United States? Hardly any political scientist would any longer suppose so in the face of the considerable descriptive literature describing interest groups in other countries. Are interest groups a feature of advanced industrial societies and found only thinly, if at all, in underdeveloped and primitive systems? A stronger case can be made for this proposition, but the same case can be made regarding many other institutional and behavioral components of such polities. Thus we shall regard the relationship between interest groups and political cultures as a matter for investigation, not of definition, and we may expect to find a relatively complex set of connections between two such richly textured variables.

A normative question? Are interest groups desirable? Perhaps it does not need to be said that the focus of discussion here will be analytic and empirical, but both the professional literature and the political reality related to interest-group politics have so often been preoccupied with the normative dimension that we cannot altogether ignore it, even if we would. The moral legitimacy of legislative bodies is nowhere disputed. The political party, once of dubious standing, seldom any longer has its existence called into question, though of course the position of particular parties may often be challenged. But interest groups, as a class, continue to play a morally uncertain role in quite a wide variety of polities. Thus legitimation of their existence, as well as their behavior, becomes a matter of concern and hence of action. Group leaders and members behave in particular ways in order to gain acceptance for their organization. Decision makers shape their actions in contexts that are given meaning by the culture's estimate of the moral worth of organized group pressures. In short, this basic normative issue is transformed into empirical questions of great importance.

In another sense also the analytic position accorded interest groups is affected by a normative context. Several writers have traced the intellectual origins of interest-group analysis to the English pluralists, who sought to establish voluntary associations as legitimate political units intermediate between the individual and the state (Latham, 1952). Wedded to American pragmatism (Crick, 1959; Smith, 1964), pluralism came to have broad currency, especially among Americans, as a comprehensive doctrinal defense of political systems committed to stability, consensus, and toleration. Pluralist arguments have not always employed the organized association as the "moving part" responsible for maintaining system equilibrium. Grouping, interest, class, and other terms of somewhat vague reference have been used, but there is no doubt that the analysis of organized groups has often been closely tied to pluralist evaluations of political systems and processes. Accordingly, recent critics of pluralism have sometimes seen studies of interest groups as implicitly committed to pluralist normative postures. Our discussion will attempt to incorporate some consideration of the normative implications of research findings and hypotheses contained in interest-group research and, as well, to consider as interest-group phenomena some of the disputatious activity concerning the appropriateness of interest-group analysis.

Definitions

It was Bentley (1908) who said: "Who likes may snip verbal definitions in his old age, when his world has gone crackly and dry." The sentiment has style, and Bentley was regrettably faithful to it, with the result that Bentley's arguments were metaphorically powerful but analytically muddy. One often cannot tell whether to take him seriously, because it is seldom clear what he meant. Subsequent scholars have found it necessary to make distinctions and define terms. Indeed, in many discussions of interest groups there is such a preoccupation with definition and *a priori* classification that the wisdom of Bentley's view seems confirmed. Here we shall examine the notions of group, interest, and pressure. There are some divergent views on how to employ these concepts, but they need not hamper our later discussion so long as we are clear about how the words are to be used.

The group. Almost the only student who tries to avoid using the term "group" in discussing the phenomena we shall examine is Finer (1966). He prefers the term "lobby," but his objection to alternative names is to the modifiers "interest" and "pressure," not to the word "group." We may conclude therefore that whatever manifold areas of definitional disagreement remain, the concept of group lies at the core of this body of work.

At least six variants of meaning may usefully be distinguished in the use of the term "group." First is the *categoric* group, referring to a set of "individuals who have some characteristic in common" (Truman, 1951, p. 33). When the characteristic in common is associated with a socially significant role, it may lead to the imputation of values or goals believed to be held by those who share the characteristic. Farmers, students, and Catholics are among the many terms used to denote sets of people whose political identity as a group is inferred from their social roles, and we may refer to them as *inferential* groups. Categoric and inferential groups, however, are analytic shorthand devices designed to ease the identification of relevant divisions in the system. Clearly, the common assumption is that such sets are politically meaningful groups primarily because they display attitudes or values in common. It is the *shared attitudes* rather than the shared social characteristic which are important. Wealth more often than hair style gives rise to group activity, because until very recent times people rarely have developed meaningful value patterns or shared attitudes about hair styles. In passing, however, we may note that inferential groups have another kind of importance. A political actor may anticipate that an inferential group will develop common values and act on them. He may suppose, for example, that old people will oppose public spending for ice skating rinks. The actor may then behave in anticipatory response to this "potential group" (Truman, 1951, pp. 345, 51–2). Nevertheless, it is the values held, or prospectively held, that give potentiality to such a group.

In Truman's discussion no real distinction is made between a shared-attitude group and a group formed through *interaction* among its members, because he seems to say that it is interaction which generates common attitudes. In his theoretical discussion, however, it is interaction which receives the greater attention and is seen as the sine qua non of a "proper group." Thus "interactions, or relationships, ... are the group" (p. 24; and see Ziegler, 1964: "It is the interaction process that is vital" p. 31). Interaction may be regarded as sufficiently flexible to include both primary and secondary modes of interaction (Truman, pp. 3, 5–6). A minimum frequency and duration of interaction is assumed before a group can be said to exist, but no particular pattern of relationship, such as hierarchical, leader-follower, or buyer-seller, is mentioned. For Truman the significance of interaction as the defining characteristic of group is, first, that it allows the identification of potential groups by observing sets of people who share a particular attitude but do not interact (p. 35; note that here Truman places attitudes as prior to interaction). Second, the stress on interaction enables the observer to evaluate the significance of formal organization, "merely a stage or degree of interaction" (p. 36).

A somewhat different conception of the term is implied by a stress on *activity* as the defining characteristic of group. Bentley, though eschewing clarification, refers to the "mass of activity" that is the group, and Hagan (1958) emphasizes this side also. This positivist approach to the identification of groups declines to assume that social characteristics, interactions, or even shared attitudes will necessarily result in relevant behavior expressing the claims of one group upon another. The activity-based concept of group begins with the behavior and works back to discover such characteristics as the actors may have in common. The activity-based concept leads to a rather broad notion of any particular group. By including *all* the activity directed toward a common policy goal, the group may be said to include decision makers, activist associations, and marginal participants. Both formal organizations and isolated individuals may be part of "the group." It may be well to note here that in this usage the term *interest* is sometimes taken as synonymous with group (cf. Bentley, 1908; Hagan, 1958; Peltason, 1955) and sometimes as the "directional aspect" of the mass of activity (cf. Young, 1968, pp. 81–2). In either case one may speak of the "anti-segregation interest" or the "anti–capital-punishment group" and have the same kind of referent in mind.

Finally, group may be defined as *formal association*. Conceptually, this is the most restrictive meaning used, and, contrary to the wishes of those advocating an "interest-group approach to politics," this conception leaves much politically meaningful activity out of its ken. Moreover, although there are still marginal uncertainties over when and whether particular activities are formally organized, this conception of group is considerably less ambiguous than the alternatives. Formal associations identify themselves to the observers, and that is a great help. Perhaps it is for that reason that nearly all students of interest groups—though not so much group-oriented students of other political phenomena—in fact study formal associations. In this essay so shall we. In addition to the relative clarity and ease of this usage, concentration on formal associations has other advantages. It facilitates examination of group internal life and comparison among groups regarding organizational forms and internal processes. More important perhaps, this conception makes the study of interest groups a subfield of organization theory generally, and this relationship may promote useful dialogue toward the development of more encompassing theory.

Interest and pressure. We have noted already one way in which commentators have employed the term "interest": namely, as a synonym for group, with both words referring to activity. For Bentley the activity is the interest, and no teleological additions are in order. For Truman, on the other hand, it is the "shared attitudes [that] constitute the interests" (p. 34). These attitudes include both "frames of reference for interpreting and evaluating" and "attitudes toward what is needed or wanted in a given situation, observable, as demands or claims upon other groups in the society" (pp. 33–39). A third usage is expressed by MacIver (1932) when he says that interests are "the objects toward which . . . [attitudes] are directed." Although Truman chooses to interpret MacIver's "objects" in a curious way, suggesting that "oil interests" would refer to attitudes toward the physical substance of petroleum, MacIver's is, in fact, the most common usage, and by "objects" is meant "actions of governmental authorities." The interest is in public policy broadly defined. The characteristic which implicitly distinguishes an *interest* group from other kinds of groups is the organization's concern for and activity regarding some issue involving governmental action. Truman chooses to distinguish between interests, defined as noted above, and *political* interests which involve claims made upon or through governmental institutions. Virtually no one else has made this distinction, however, and in the empirical literature deviation is rare from the following usage: *An interest group is an organized association which engages in activity relative to governmental decisions.* There remains a deliberate ambiguity in this conception, however: to wit, whether the association must be private and voluntary. This issue remains open, as witness the discussion below of coercion and of institutional and official groups.

One major objection to the prevailing conception of interest is raised by British scholars who point out that in British political tradition the concept of interest is an old one and refers to a sector of society (cf. the discussion of inferential groups, above) rather than any particular organization. There may be groups organized to express a particular interest or "stake in society," and Finer (1966) calls such organization "interest groups" whereas Stewart (1958, p. 25) calls them "sectional groups." This usage has seldom appeared in America, however, among either political scientists or politicians, and it is mainly the American vocabulary which has dominated this field of investigation.

The principal competitor to "interest" as the key modifier of "group" has been "pressure." From Odegard's landmark study (1928) to the present, the term *pressure group* has been used by distinguished scholars, primarily for two reasons. First, it is a popularly familiar term, needing little explication to place its referent in a recognizable context. Second, pressure connotes that which is politically meaningful about organized groups: their activities designed to influence governmental policy. The objections to the word "pressure" are also twofold. Pressure is thought, first, to conjure up all too much popular association, most of which follows the rather lurid forms of journalists' exposés. The term conveys images of corrupt practices and narrowly self-interested behavior that are inadequate pictures of empirical reality. Pressure also implies the use of sanctions by the group in order to persuade governmental officials to act in the desired fashion. This image, too, is wholly inadequate to represent the complex relationships among organized groups and public officials. Those scholars who continue to employ "pressure group" as their generic term mean by it the same as those who prefer the emotively more neutral term "interest group," however, and it may be hoped that disputation over words may give way before the apparently widespread consensus on what is to be studied.

The scope of coverage. The empirical phenomena which fall within the scope of a concern with organized interest groups are of huge proportions. All the work on labor movements, for instance, is of central interest. So is the burgeoning literature that deals with student organizations. Professional associations, organizations of business firms, and farm groups, along with the myriad of cause, promotional, and protest organizations, provide a store of data so rich as to intimidate all but the most courageous investigator. Political parties, legislatures, and armies provide tiny numbers of cases for study, whether done within one country or cross-nationally, compared with the numbers involved in the interest-group universe. Sociologists employ a still more inclusive term when they consider voluntary associations (Sills, 1968), but the range of interest groups is still very great. One consequence, not surprisingly, is a nearly total absence of any comprehensive compilation of interest-group data of even the simplest kinds. There is no serious effort to describe organized associations except within particular political systems, and even single-country studies are highly uneven in scope and theoretical potential.

Despite the thinness of empirical base, however, and perhaps contributing further uncertainty about how to enrich the descriptive stock, there has been considerable discussion which, in one way or another, concerns how to conceptualize interest groups as components within the larger framework of the political system. Some of this discussion deals with organized groups only by implication, but there is enough direct consideration given to enable us to distinguish four principal modes of analyzing interest groups, and to these we now turn our attention.

MODES OF ANALYSIS

The analysis of interest groups has its main origins in the work of American scholars and mostly in work devoted to political phenomena in the United States. One consequence of these origins has been, as noted, a prolonged dispute over the relevance of interest groups in non-American settings. Another consequence, however, has been to impart an essentially American perspective to the analysis of groups wherever they are, to see them primarily as mechanisms which make policy demands on governmental decision makers. A number of conceptual and research implications follow. One is that groups are assumed to be *outside* government and that their power over policy lacks legitimacy therefore. Pains are taken to differentiate parties and interest groups. Further, each group is assumed to be a unit in which leaders and followers are cohesive in their values. Internal processes, however interesting, are assumed to be of minor impact on their efforts to influence public decisions. In this section we shall try to show that there are several alternative modes of study which lead to rather different research strategies and diverse empirical findings.

Groups as input units. A considerable portion of the literature that attempts some kind of comprehensive statement about the characteristics of political systems identifies interest groups as component units which contribute a significant portion of the demands to the decision-making segments of the system. In this literature, groups, like other components, are conceptualized functionally, and although the functions associated with group activity are given somewhat diverse names, they are almost entirely input functions. We shall take the writing of Gabriel Almond and associates (1960, 1966) to stand for this category of work.

In his best-known formulation of essential political-system functions (Almond and Coleman, 1960) Almond identifies interest articulation as one of four input functions, and he suggests that in many political systems this function, the formulation and expression of political demands, will be performed by organized interest groups. Almond and Powell (1966) differentiate four types of articulation mechanisms, however, of which organized associations constitute only one. They use the more general term "interest group" to mean "a group of individuals who are linked by particular bonds of concern or advantage, and who have some awareness of these bonds" (p. 75). The four types of mechanism can be arranged in a kind of continuum of self-awareness, as follows: (1) *anomic interest groups,* "the more or less spontaneous penetrations into the political system from the society, such as riots, demonstrations, assassinations, and the like"; (2) *nonassociational groups,* such as kinships, or ethnic, regional, or status groups which articulate interests intermittently and without formal organization through individuals, family heads, or other such spokesmen; (3) *associational groups,* characterized by orderly procedures, professional staff, and explicitness concerning their specialized and manifest function of interest articulation; and (4) *institutional interest groups,* formal organizations or persistent informal groups within social institutions that have manifest functions other than interest articulation. A military or bureaucratic clique, a legislative caucus, or a faction in a union would all illustrate the last type.

Almond and Powell go on to distinguish various means of access, styles of articulation, environmental factors affecting articulation patterns, and they suggest some of the consequences of weak, diffuse, rigid, or affect-laden articulation patterns. Essentially their argument is that political development depends on the emergence of differentiated infrastructures. Among these may be associational interest groups, although in authoritarian systems political leaders may try to control and dominate such groups to prevent them from becoming autonomous. Even so, however, such groups, along with the other types of articulation mechanisms, are seen to become progressively more important as the overall system becomes more complex, tension and conflict increase in volume and severity, coordination and control become more difficult, and demands for political action are thereby generated in growing numbers and accelerating urgency.

Almond and Powell do not claim that organized groups invariably gain importance as demands increase in intensity. Other articulation mechanisms may also play a larger role—e.g., riots to express black demands. Leaders may anticipate rising demands or otherwise displace interest groups by taking over the articulation function, a point Almond and Powell make but do not fully discuss in conjunction with the position of groups. Indeed, the result is to leave quite unclear just what functional development to expect regarding interest groups. Presumably social differentiation, a hallmark of development in this formulation, leads to the creation of more interest groups, but it is not clear that groups will perform the articulation function.

The functional importance of interest groups is not confined to articulation, however. Almond and Powell mention groups as among the mechanisms involved in political socialization, for example, and although the socialization literature does not give extensive treatment to interest groups, there is mention of this function in the monographic studies of particular interest-group associations. Confining ourselves to the Almond-Powell list of functions, we still find groups mentioned in connection with communication (p. 169, for example), the recruitment of political elites (see Seligman, 1971), and even interest aggregation. In short, interest groups are assigned roles of some significance with regard to all the input functions of a political system. The principal factors suggested as constraints on the operation of groups are (1) the extent of structural differentiation in the system and (2) the amount of subsystem autonomy. The more differentiated the system, the more groups are expected to exist, and if these groups are relatively autonomous, they may be expected to play important input roles. Even if they are not autonomous but are effectively dominated by a political party, for example, the associational group may still be a significant agent of socialization, communication, and mobilization. On the other hand, there is a good deal of writing which contends that if there is sufficient differentiation and autonomy of subsystems, such other structures as political parties or official elites will force interest groups with their narrow demands into a subordinate or peripheral functional position. This somewhat old-fashioned party-reform tradition implicitly shares with the newer system-function school the view that groups are input mechanisms making demands upon government, and this view leads to a preoccupation with such matters as access and influence, resources of power, styles of articulation (lobbying), and interaction with other input structures, notably political parties.

Before we leave this discussion of groups as input mechanisms, we should note a rather important piece of evidence concerning the importance of this function as perceived by the citizenry. Almond and Verba (1963) found that only a fraction (1.7 percent) in any of their five nations would work through a formal group in order to influence either local or national government. A far larger proportion expressed a preference for *informal* collaboration, especially in the United States and Britain. From one-sixth to one-half of organization members in the Almond-Verba sample would use the group as an input mechanism, but, again, this is a small portion indeed of the total electorate. One reasonable conclusion, which the authors do not draw, would be that organized groups do not gain their principal significance from their political-input activities and that consequently an input orientation may lead to some misunderstanding of the nature of such organizations.

Groups as system outputs. A very different set of questions arises if one chooses to regard interest groups mainly as one form of result from political action. For example, we may stress, with Rose (1954), the effect of industrialization processes on social organization and see the rise of labor unions and business associations alike as one consequence of industrial growth and the accompanying social differentiation. In this connection, interest groups are one of the more commonly cited illustrations of the shift, proclaimed by Tönnies, from *Gemeinschaft* to *Gesellschaft*.

At a less comprehensive level of analysis it is common to argue that, for example, a "weak" party system produces, or at least facilitates, a strong pressure-group system (see, e.g., Schattschneider, 1942; Ziegler, 1971). A fragmented decisional system is widely thought to encourage associational groups. Returning to the functional language of Almond and Powell, political cultures which value pragmatic bargaining styles of interest aggregation are thought to grant a legitimacy to interest groups that absolute value orientations and traditionalist styles would deny.

At still another level the descriptive literature provides a number of cases wherein public-policy decisions have created or at least subsidized the formation of associational groups. Trade associations have been encouraged (Fishbein, 1955), labor unions have been given special advantages for organizing (Taft, 1964), and farm groups have been given public money to help recruit members (McConnell, 1953; Block, 1960). Professional and quasi-professional groups frequently receive official authority to limit entry to their profession by means of licensing and examining procedures. The reverse has also been known. Labor unions have been opposed by public policy. Many types of protest groups have been harassed and in a good many instances prosecuted as organizations. The point is that associational groups are the objects and consequences of political actions as well as mechanisms for the articulation of demands.

If one regards groups in this light, quite different questions come to mind. One wants to know which groups are favored by what policies and who (which other groups?) formed those policies. To what extent are interest groups the more or less inevitable result of the broad social forces let loose by industrialization, or alternatively, how much of this array is the product of political choices that might have turned out differently? From another angle, how much effect would particular alterations in policy have on the interest-group configuration in a system? Suppose that such associations were taxed instead of subsidized, persecuted rather than tolerated, locked out of legislative halls and denied access to the bureaucracy. These were the conditions under which many nineteenth-century pluralists in fact operated, and this perspective has provided one important criterion for describing and evaluating totalitarian regimes. It is important to remember that this mode of analysis does in fact deal with interest groups and should be juxtaposed with the input analysis previously discussed.

Groups as authoritative decision makers. Although the logically restrictive theories of sovereignty may be confounded thereby, it is nevertheless clear that in many advanced industrial systems private voluntary groups have assumed or been given de facto authority to make or participate in public decisions. There are varying degrees of certainty associated with these group-authority roles. One pattern is illustrated by the apparently secure consultation and advice sought and taken by the relevant ministries from the British Medical Association (Eckstein, 1960) and many other British interest groups (Beer, 1965) prior to taking major policy steps. Even more authoritative is the situation where the group nominates members to sit on official government bodies. Finer (1966) reports that the Trades Union Congress as such was represented on 62 government committees, and the Confederation of British Industries was surely not far behind. Indeed, TUC has threatened nonparticipation as a political weapon to force concessions from a Tory government.

In the United States there is much less official recognition accorded to private groups. Economic sectors or interests may frequently have a clear de facto claim to official representation on certain bodies, but seldom is this claim exercised formally by organized groups as such. More characteristic of official incorporation into authority roles are the patterns of formal clearance and rating given to prospective judicial appointees by the American Bar Association (Grossman, 1965), and the nomination of slates from which state appointing officers make their selection (Watson and Downing, 1969). For certain local community programs, such as those organized to combat poverty, voluntary organizations like NAACP and CORE have often been granted seats on the boards in either advisory or governing capacities. In general, though, whatever influence private groups may have on U.S. policy-making, they are not often given formally acknowledged authority to participate in the decisions.

Yet the American system, which relegates private groups mainly to informal roles, is perhaps more the exception than not. De jure authority to appoint members of the Economic and Social Council in France lies in the hands of major economic organizations (Ehrmann, 1968). In West Germany the occupational *Kammern* not only function as interest associations but also "exercise derivative governmental functions over their members" (Edinger, 1968) in terms laid down formally by law. We shall return to this issue later. Here our concern is to establish the variety of roles and functions which private interest groups play, and particularly to make it clear that in many systems certain of these groups, as formal organizations, possess significant fragments of official decision-making authority.

Groups as organizations. Quite a different perspective on interest groups is revealed if one regards them in the first instance simply as a variety of formal organization characterized by voluntary membership and the absence of production or distribution of goods or services for an external market. One result of this view is to make the matter of their political concerns problematic. That some groups are political, others not, is something to be investigated and explained, not a defining characteristic. A second consequence is to encourage the observer to turn his attention quickly to matters of internal organization and patterns of relationship. The question of oligarchy comes up early, and many related issues of leadership selection and control accompany it. Membership, recruitment, satisfaction, turnover, and involvement are quickly identified as problematic issues to be investigated, whereas an input orientation tends to regard the group as highly cohesive and variations in membership attitudes as a peripheral concern. The consequences of this orientation are not trivial. Such scholars as Olson (1965) and Lipset, Trow, and Coleman (1956), for example, have reached conclusions with profoundly important implications for any analysis of lobbying and other input efforts.

TYPOLOGIES

Typologies, like definitions, have little point unless they are employed to guide research and provide touchstones of theory construction. The numerous classifications of interest groups developed by scholars in recent decades have not always contributed very much to either theory or research. This disappointment may result from the fact that so many of the extended discussions of interest groups are directed toward beginning students rather than professional political scientists. Textbooks on American or comparative politics and the specialized volumes on interest groups utilize their typologies rather more as outlines of the arrangement of their material and as means for making some introductory points about groups than as guides to research or self-conscious contribution to theory. Nevertheless, there are some useful distinctions to be made among the many catalogues of interest-group types, useful in the sense of allowing us to be more explicit about the questions and the data which are likely to be turned up if one catalogue is used rather than another.

Typologies based on interest content. Probably the most common classificacation used by American writers has been based on socioeconomic sectors. The interest-group universe is typically divided into such sectors as agriculture, labor, business, the professions, and "others" with each susceptible to much variation in subdivision. British writers, on the other hand, have usually adopted a more general set of categories. They distinguish between *sectional* groups, such as labor or business, which reflect the great "interests" of society and *cause* or *promotional* groups organized to express a particular policy objective.

The American practice has mainly pedagogical tradition and convenience to recommend it. It is not apparent that powerful theoretical statements are likely to emerge from treating labor unions as a group subset distinct from business associations, although Key and McConnell make interesting efforts to develop sector-based theory. On the other hand, the descriptive and heuristic convenience of differentiating among sectors is enormous. There is a useful tradition of scholarship devoted to comparative labor movements, and comparable cross-national analysis of other sectors might persuade us that theory could indeed be enriched by further utilization of this basic classification.

Meanwhile the distinction between sectional and promotional groups does give rise to some hypotheses of general application. For example, sectional groups are more durable and are more likely to enter into quasi-official consultative relationships with governmental agencies. Promotional groups face more severe problems of goal adaptation when political climates change. In the British literature, indeed, substantial influence over policy is attributed to sectional groups, but promotional groups, even when they mobilize a large following, tend to be regarded as having only rather minor impact in public decisions. This difference in impact reflects not only the differences between the two types of groups but also most importantly the ways in which government officials relate themselves to the private organizations. As a consequence of the great increase in formal participation by sectional groups in official bodies and the parallel rise of formal consultation with these groups by administrative agencies, sectional-group tactics and strategies have become very different from the means used by promotional groups. The Trades Union Congress still holds parades, and the Confederation of British Industries or affiliated business groups might still conduct public-relations campaigns, but the protest demonstration and other *public* or *open* strategies are certainly more commonly pursued by promotional groups. Meanwhile, few officials would feel it necessary as a matter of course to consult these organizations before making choices that affect them.

In the American literature this distinction is much less clear. Sectional groups do not enjoy the same semiofficial status as in Britain (or on the Continent), and although there are certainly different strategies for gaining access, they would not necessarily be different for a cause group (Anti-Saloon League, Committee of One Million Against Recognition of Red China) than for a sectional organization like the American Medical Association or the National Association of Manufacturers.

A somewhat different basis for classifying groups may be observed in Cohen's distinction (1957) between tangible interests and intangible interests. This distinction is based on the motivations of group members rather than on the policy objectives as such. The latter may be identical for both kinds of groups, but an organization devoted to reducing tariffs in order to promote increased exports of cotton is regarded differently than is a group of economists with a philosophical commitment to free trade but no investments in firms which will benefit from it. This distinction has its uses, and it is incorporated in the more general scheme based on member benefits discussed below.

A number of discussions have attempted to distinguish among groups on the basis of the domain of their chief policy interests. The most common line of demarcation is between groups concerned with foreign policy and those which concentrate on domestic policy. This distinction has some descriptive use since, particularly in the past, the congeries of political forces and institutional processes involved in, say, the treaty-making process on foreign-aid programs were rather different from those by which most domestic decisions were reached. The massive interpenetration of military, diplomatic, fiscal, and mass political pressures and forces has undermined the effectiveness of this distinction, and if policy domain is to retain its analytic utility for classifying interest groups, a more refined scheme is required.

It may sometimes seem that policy domain signifies little more than the output side of sectional interests, as implied, for example, by such terms as agriculture policy or labor policy. The existence of a policy domain, however, is an empirical question. It depends on the persistent operation of a relatively autonomous set of interest groups and decision makers interacting to produce a distinguishable set of policies. It is the existence of an observable subsystem of activity that indicates the presence of a policy domain, and interest groups may be integral parts of this subsystem. When they do exist, such policy domains invite useful comparisons, both with one another and across political-system boundaries. This kind of comparative policy analysis does not always incorporate interest groups explicitly, and *some* of these omissions are warranted. But from the point of view of the student of interest groups, the linkage of group organizations to policy types, where policy typologies are based on action subsystems, promises important descriptive advantages and perhaps some theoretical potentialities, as it links this subject more firmly to the burgeoning field of policy analysis.

A somewhat different approach to the group-typology question bases its classification not on the policy objectives pursued by the organization but on the kinds of benefits or values which are exchanged *within* the organization and which provide the basis for the group's existence as an organization (Salisbury, 1969). This approach begins with a distinction between the leaders of the group and the members or followers, and it postulates an exchange relationship between them. In a labor union or a business trade association, the content of the exchange—what the leaders offer the members as inducements to membership—may be primarily *material* economic benefits. In a predominantly social organization the benefits may be chiefly *solidary,* the pleasures of close association. Clark and Wilson (1961) include among the solidary rewards such things as "socializing, congeniality, the sense of group membership and identification, the status resulting from membership, fun and conviviality, and so on." In what some call cause or promotional organizations, the benefits of membership are *expressive.* That is, the members of such an organization gain through their membership the expression of their values in the form of public statements and other actions taken by the leaders of the group.

Any particular organization may in fact rest on a mix of these three types of benefits, and the variations in recipe are doubtless very wide. But a considerable number of hypotheses can be derived from an analysis of interest groups based on this typology. Moreover, it appears that this three-variable typology of groups subsumes several of the other variations we have discussed. It has one clear advantage over the sectoral-promotional distinction. The latter depends entirely on the ability of an observer to decide whether a group truly "represents" a significant sector of society or merely claims to do so in order to promote a cause. A great many causes are promoted by sector organizations. It is therefore a rough and ready distinction at best. The initial classification of groups according to the material/solidary/expressive-benefits typology may be only a little less impressionistic, but in principle the categorizations may be based on research. Members and nonmembers can be interviewed and their motivations assessed, and a variety of indirect measures can be adduced. The resulting patterns may display a great variety, and the possible richness of detail in classification in itself is encouraging. Thus, as a research strategy this approach seems to have merit.

The theoretical potential of the membership-benefit classification is also substantial. For example, the hypothesis that sectional groups are more durable than cause groups (see above) is incorporated as: Groups based on material benefits are more durable than those organized around expressive benefits. This is made into more than an observation, however. It is now related to the ease of organizing and hence of factionalizing expressive groups and to the inherently tenuous connection of any individual's commitment to a cause and his membership in any particular organization which gives voice to that cause. The uses of introducing the distinction between leaders and members into the basic typology of interest groups will be explored further in discussing group formation and growth and a number of other topics. We may note in passing, however, that this orientation depends on the mode of analysis discussed above which views an interest group, first of all, as an organization.

Typologies based on organizational forms. Truman devotes considerable attention to discussing the importance of organizational form in group operation, and his primary distinction is between federally organized groups and those whose structure is unitary (1951, pp. 115ff). Federations tend to be less cohesive, though as Truman points out, there may be inescapable social facts or preexisting constituent-organization identities which preclude greater centralized control. Where the constituent units are organized geographically rather than functionally, Truman suggests, cohesion in the parent body will be less severely threatened. It may also be noted that federated forms in which the constituent units are geographical are well adapted to the divisions of authority in a federal political system and are mainly to be found in such systems as those of West Germany and the United States.

Olson (1965) presents a classification which is rooted in a theoretical argument and essentially is one of structural differences. He differentiates among small, intermediate, and large groups. In small groups a single member may support the provision of a collective benefit by the group if his share of the benefit is at least equal to the cost of his effort. Members of small groups lack anonymity. The impact of each on the welfare of others is great, and the connection between each individual's self-interest and the interests common to all is close. In large groups (cf. oligopoly and competitive markets), on the other hand, these conditions do not hold. There, Olson argues, no individual, if he is rational, will support action for collective benefits because he will receive the benefit anyway. Unless there is coercion, selective benefits, available only to members of the group, must be provided to persuade people to join unions or march for a cause. Olson's argument is essentially a logical one, however, rather than a basis for classifying observable groups. He says that people would not join groups unless they were small or perhaps of middle size, and size is left unspecified, without selective benefits. But groups exist, and Olson's subsequent discussion is devoted to analysis of the selective benefits by which members were induced to join.

Another approach to group classification based on organizational forms looks at the type of control relations between leaders and followers. Truman discusses the "democratic mold" by which interest-group organizations have attempted to meet "the 'democratic' expectations of the community, including of course, most of their members" (1951, p. 129). The elements of this mold include the election of officers, the vesting of ultimate authority in conventions, and often the use of referenda to determine the group's position on policy questions. Truman contrasts these structural devices with what he calls "corporate tendencies," structural features whereby a relatively small, stable oligarchy is enabled to retain effective control over the organization, especially its finance but also much of its other activities, pretty much regardless of the "democratic" procedures used. Truman suggests that organizations might even be ranked on the basis of adoption of "corporate" forms. But this approach assumes quite explicitly that the structural norm is one of popular control. Among existing interest groups this norm is by no means consistently observed. In what may be called managerial groups (Eldersveld, 1960; Scoble, 1967), there has never been any pretense that contributor-members would control the organization. In such well-known organizations as Common Cause, members have the opportunity to support the cause, but the members of the self-perpetuating board of directors have full authority to determine the organization's policies and choose its staff. This is true, also, of a large proportion of the expressive groups, which, like retail merchants, offer customers the opportunity to patronize their enterprise but no chance to select either the clerks or the management or to do more than request a new line of goods. Democratic forms are widespread, of course, and both their utilization and their evasion are important features of interest-group activity. But they are far from universal, even in a political system where democratic norms are fundamental in conferring legitimacy on any organization that claims, as most interest groups do, to represent some important community sentiment.

The theoretical and research potential of a classification based on these internal organizational variables is not entirely clear, since we have so little research even partially cast in this framework. At the very least, however, one might hazard the assumption that popular control procedures would be more elaborate in long-established organizations and in those which involve more central values of the members—a labor union, for instance, rooted in the job of the member as compared with an organization whose activities are peripheral to the everyday concerns of the "operating units." Truman advances the hypothesis that corporate devices are more common where one organization is in sharp conflict with another and needs to keep secret some of its organizational life to protect itself against the enemy. But our systematic knowledge of structured variations is meager, and therefore the possibilities of research along these lines can hardly be anticipated.

Typologies based on membership types. The interest-group literature provides almost no analysis whatever of a rather important and certainly not an obvious question, namely, what are the units of membership? Discussion of "joining" and group participation assume that it is individuals who belong, and, of course, it is often so. But not always.

Wootton (1970) has observed that most industrialized systems display an interest-group pattern with at least three organizational levels. First, there is the "operational unit," whose members are individuals and whose primary activity as an organization is to serve the needs of those individuals. Obvious examples would be a local union or a corporation. Some groups would themselves have no further superstructure, but many would be parts of "second-order" groups, such as an international union or a business trade association, whose "members" are the operational units. At still a third level are the "peaks," such as the AFL-CIO or the Confederation of British Industries. Wooton does not claim generality, or even clear and differentiating criteria, for this formulation, but it is probably true that many sectoral (or material-benefit) organizations are structured in approximately this three-tiered manner. A large share of the expressive or cause groups are not so arranged, however, perhaps because they rarely last long enough to develop such complexity.

The term "peak association" has been used by Key (1964), among others (see also Brady, 1943), to refer to sector-wide organizations which embrace a comprehensive array of constituent sector organizations. The AFL-CIO and NAM are examples in the United States; the American Farm Bureau Federation would suffer a vigorous challenge from rival groups as anything more than a second-order enterprise. In Britain the National Farmers Union, the Trades

Union Congress, and the Confederation of British Industries are clear examples of peak "organizations of organizations." Peak groups typically play a different political role from that taken by their constituent organizations. Theirs is a problem more of coordination, information exchange, and representation to other groups and the general public than of the provision of direct, selective, material benefits to members. The peak group may act essentially as a central staff to the constituent groups for certain purposes, especially regarding political action in its many forms.

Riggs (1950) used the term "catalytic group" to denote still another type of "organization of organizations." Catalytic groups are typically formed ad hoc to deal with a particular policy issue or special political occasion. They have short organizational lives and are established by leaders of constituent groups to stimulate attention and coordinate resources for a short-term campaign. Either as another category or as a variety of catalytic group, we can add the many "front" groups which may consist of other organizations or individuals, or may perhaps have no members at all but serve only as an organizational straw party, precisely as does a dummy corporation. One must note whether those who actively support a group—with money or signatures, let us say—thereby become formal members of the organization or whether they remain outside as "fellow travelers."

Another dimension of group membership involves the question of who is eligible to belong. Expressive groups commonly invite the support of everyone who supports their particular cause, but open membership is not characteristic of many other types. Labor unions share with other sector groups a membership restricted to those who "belong" to the sector, and "belonging" is most frequently defined by one's employment. Many professional groups, though not all, limit their membership to those who have certain requisite training and/or are engaged in practicing the profession. There are important interest-group organizations, such as the U.S. Conference of Mayors, in which the membership unit is formally the municipality, and membership is exercised by the holder of an official role, the mayor (Farkas, 1971). Similarly, the National Institute of Municipal Law Officers, the Conference of Chief Justices, the Association of School Boards, and many others are organized around formal roles rather than individuals as such (Vose, 1966). In general, one suspects that the proliferation of organized interest groups in the twentieth century has been primarily a proliferation of role-based organizations and has been both the consequence and a partial cause of increasing differentiation of social, political, and economic roles.

Role-based organizations have potentially interesting characteristics. If the city pays the dues, membership costs the public official nothing out of pocket. What effect does this have on his calculation to participate or to demand services from the organization? We would suppose that open organizations would be more fragile and have greater membership turnover than those with restricted membership. We might also guess that membership based on individual characteristics, whether job, training, or value commitment, would show more volatility than would membership of which the unit was in a formal sense the role itself.

GROUP ORIGINS AND GROWTH

Arguments about the functional significance of interest groups in political systems depend to an important extent on assumptions about the factors that give rise to group formation and the patterns of growth displayed by organized groups in the system. In particular, the view that groups serve to articulate political demands and transmit them to decision makers, either directly or through the aggregating mechanisms of parties, is rooted in the notion that groups arise in order to give expression to politically relevant demands. This theory of group formation has been given its fullest expression by David Truman and has been contested by Olson and Salisbury, among others. So much interpretation of the role of interest groups depends on the position taken regarding their origins and growth that we shall examine this question in some detail.

Truman's position begins with his conception that shared attitudes growing out of and reinforced by interaction constitute the group, and that it is increasing interaction which becomes stabilized by the formation of formal associations. Organization is thus a stage, relatively advanced but still a stage or phase, in the growth of concerned interaction. Organization is especially important, however, because it is visible, it is a stabilizing agent, and it adds political weight to the group. Pursuant to this basic perspective, it is necessary to ask what produces shared attitudes leading to interaction and, especially, what accounts for the growth in frequency and intensity of interaction that leads to association formation.

For Truman the basic factor is "disruption of established patterns of behavior." He postulates an equilibrium condition which, at some stage in time, is disturbed, dislocating and usually disadvantaging a particular sector of society. In order to reassert a viable equilibrium, the group, intensified in its interaction, forms an association which seeks to stabilize the "relationships of their members to one another and to other groups." In this connection Truman uses the phrase "tangent relation," referring to interaction whereby members of one group are brought into contact with another and they develop common attitudes toward the issue or problem that gave rise to the interaction. It is not clear how this concept differs from the somewhat simpler idea that associations are organized by shared-attitude groups which experience increased interaction, unless perhaps the notion of tangency is intended to suggest the basis on which attitudes come to be shared in the first place. If so, then the argument would be as follows: Tangency results in interaction; interaction leads to shared attitudes; intensification of interaction leads to association. But inasmuch as increased interaction may also be accompanied by a growth in *conflicting* attitudes and behavior, this is clearly not a sufficient interpretation. Perhaps, however, the argument should be put thus: Tangency results in interaction; interaction combined with disturbances leads to intensified interaction *and* common attitudes among those *similarly affected* by the disturbance; intensified interaction leads to association. In any case, Truman clearly means to combine the ideas of disturbance and interaction, and he seems to view them as reciprocally related.

The catalogue of disturbances Truman provides in specific illustration is substantial. The increased "division of labor within industry, the growing differentiation between employer and worker, and the consequent major changes in the status and rewards of both workers and managers..."; changes in transportation and communication, in economic organization, and in technology; market fluctuations, the needs of economic planning during war, depression, or other emergencies; alterations in family structure; population immigration—the list of factors includes virtually every major element of social change one can think of. The formulation is not very precise, but its essential meaning is clear. Interest groups are organized when people become dissatisfied, the dissatisfaction resulting from some disturbing process of social change. "The associations function to restore a previous equilibrium or to facilitate the establishment of a new one ... [either by] imposition of claims directly upon another group ... [or with the assistance of] the wider powers of some more inclusive institutionalized group [most commonly government]" (Truman, 1951, pp. 104–5).

There are several important implications of this argument. First, the fundamental variables giving rise to interest-group formation are macro–social forces of change. Second, groups will be organized primarily under circumstances of disadvantage and will seek to use their organized strength to improve their position relative to other groups. Third, associations seek to stabilize the internal relations among members, but both internal stability and restored intergroup equilibrium are achieved primarily by means of satisfying claims made upon other groups. That is, the goals of group incorporation and the essential activity that characterizes these associations involve conflict among groups. Indeed, a key supplementary factor promoting group organization is the threat of countergroups, and because of this tendency toward competitive organization, Truman suggests that there often is a "wave-like" pattern of organization. Fourth, there is a "gravitation toward government" as groups find they cannot satisfy their need to stabilize things without the help of more inclusive authority. Note, however, that Truman does not say that groups will always and only seek governmental assistance or that they are not truly interest groups unless they enter the political arena. It is possible, within his terms, for interest groups to confine their efforts to economic or social action, and here

Truman differs from some less thoughtful commentators who appear to assume that all interest groups are formed in order to influence government. Such a view, as we shall see, does great violence to the historical facts and leads to some fundamental misunderstandings of interest-group phenomena. Truman's approach is more probabilistic and presents a more complex view of how and why organized groups begin.

Before leaving the Truman argument, let us examine one other feature. Truman provides two slightly different hypotheses concerning the historical pattern of group formation in society as a whole. One, the wave theory, says simply that the formation of one group may cause disturbances or accentuate cleavages among other groups and lead them to organize in response. As Key (1964) puts it, "Organization begets counterorganization." The clearest examples of "such waves of association-building" are the rise of employer associations to combat labor unions in the latter part of the nineteenth century.

The second, and probably more fundamental, macro–social pattern is that of *proliferation* growing out of the rapid pace of change, specialization, and diversity of interests in modern society.

> With an increase in specialization and with the continued frustration of established expectations consequent upon rapid changes in the related techniques, the proliferation of associations is inescapable. So closely do these developments follow, in fact, that the rate of association-formation may serve as an index of the stability of a society and their number may be used as an index of its complexity. Simple societies have no associations . . . as they grow more complex . . . societies evolve greater numbers of associations. (Truman, 1951, p. 57)

In this statement Truman projects a pattern of association growth for complex societies with the following characteristics: an upward secular trend, rising in proportion to the pace of social and economic change; spurts of growth following marked periods of change and destabilization; and, incorporating the earlier hypothesis of wave-like growth, additional secondary spurts following the primary association-growth periods. Truman does not hint at the existence of any societal upper limit, so presumably as long as the process of social fission goes on, group formation would continue apace.

Now it must be stressed that Truman's entire emphasis in the discussion of group origins is on macro–social forces and processes. Moreover, virtually every commentator who has considered the question in general terms—and not many have done so explicitly—has likewise stressed social forces as the causes of interest-group formation. The classic analytical pluralists generally assumed that if people are disadvantaged and are aware of it, they will inevitably organize themselves to set things right. They further assumed that the individuals who join a group all share attitudes/interests and that the group will act to defend or advance those interests (e.g., Latham, 1952a, and the critique in Olson, 1965, especially pp. 123–26). In the hands of some, this apparent automaticity of group formation is seen as a benign invisible hand that keeps the "special interests" under constraint (Galbraith, 1952). Others, denying that any such inevitability of organized self-expression can be counted on to help the disadvantaged, come therefore to be critical of interest-group pluralism, either as political analysis or as a political ideology (Schattschneider, 1960). In any event, the line of argument that leads from broad processes of social change to interest-group formation is surely the prevailing one among those who have dealt with the problem.

Recent criticism of this perspective has raised doubts regarding both the logic and the historical data employed. Olson has dealt particularly with the logic. He has shown that insofar as an interest group is organized in order to bring influence to bear on government (lobbying) or in any other way to make claims upon other groups, no rational self-interested person will join unless he must or unless he is persuaded to join for some other reason. The reason is simple. If influence is achieved and the group secures its claims against others, the individual who shares the interest involved will benefit fully without joining. In rational-choice theory and analysis this is the "free rider" problem. A worker will get his wage increase. A businessman will get his tax loophole. A veteran will get his pension. And so on. Therefore interest groups will not be successfully formed unless one of three conditions obtains. One is philanthropy, which Olson discounts as a sufficiently widespread force to account for the extant multitude of groups. A second is compulsion, which Olson notes is characteristically employed to sustain membership in labor unions, through closed or union shop and occasional physical intimidation, and in one form or another, including primary-group pressure, coercion may be observed in a good many other groups. The third and most common is the use of selective benefits, those benefits offered only to members of the organization and not available to others who may share the group attitudes but do not formally belong. Common illustrations include the health and recreation fringe benefits of labor unions, insurance and cooperative programs of farm organizations, technical business assistance of trade associations, and so on.

Now the point of Olson's argument is that without the use of selective benefits (and compulsion may, for simplicity, be understood as a sort of negative selective benefit), and regardless of the commonality of attitudes or intensity of interaction, no viable organization can be formed which imposes any cost on members as a condition of joining. (We are deliberately overlooking Olson's distinction between small groups, which he believes may be organizable without selective benefits other than the pressures arising from small-group interaction, and large groups. Olson does not seem to regard this distinction as crucial to the analysis of interest groups, though it is so to the development of his logical case, because nearly all groups of concern to political analysis would qualify as large. In Salisbury's elaboration and revision of Olson's argument, the small versus large distinction is not even logically necessary.)

The importance of Olson's point can hardly be exaggerated, for it quite fundamentally undermines virtually all the extant theories of group formation, even if one recognizes that, apart from Truman, most writers have been content with implicit rather than explicit theoretical foundations. Olson is saying that social forces cannot be the sufficient cause generating interest groups to propound or defend the values of their members. If there is a correlation between social change and group formation, it depends on the presence of whatever additional factors are required to account for the introduction of selective benefits. It is really to this problem that Salisbury (1969) addresses himself.

Salisbury's analysis of group formation is laid at the micro level, and his basic orientation is derived from economic theories of the firm. He suggests that the formation of organized interest groups requires the active presence of organizers (see also Wagner, 1966; Frohlich, Oppenheimer, and Young, 1971). These organizers, or entrepreneurs, invest some form of capital resources in a set of selective benefits to be made available to those who join the organization. The prospective benefits may include any combination of material, solidary, and expressive incentives, though, as we shall note later, some combinations are easier to offer than others. Potential members may be considered as a market which may or may not respond to the entrepreneur's efforts with sufficient enthusiasm to create a viable organization. The concept of organizational viability is not easy to render with precision, but it is clear that if an organizer is to provide a flow of benefits satisfactory to members, there must be a sufficient return flow of support from members in order to sustain the organizer. This return flow may also be any combination of the three types of benefits (goods, incentives, rewards) so long as it satisfies the entrepreneur's needs. If the flow of benefits in either direction of this exchange relationship should fail, the organization cannot survive. If potential members are not attracted to a particular entrepreneur's offering, his organization must collapse. The assumption here is that the entrepreneurial effort is autonomous. If, as is often true, one organization is subsidized by another, then failure is not so inexorable but depends on the maintenance of support from the parent group.

The interpretation of interest-group formation is thus a theory both of origins and growth and of decline and death. No other extant theory of groups seems to concern itself with the mortality of organizations, perhaps because, like Truman, they regard formal organization as "mere technique," an almost superficial expression of more deeply rooted interest/attitude groupings. If the interests are truly there, their organizational expression is bound to come, and if one association dies, another will soon take its place. Salisbury argues that there is neither inevitability nor automaticity in the process. Organization and growth are highly problematic. A complex set of hypotheses must be employed to account for these processes, instead of the rather simple dislocation/proliferation concepts reviewed earlier. These hypotheses involve the emergence of entrepreneurs, the provisions of organizing capital, the significance of various "benefit packages," and the character and response of potential markets. We shall here attempt only to indicate some of these hypotheses to illustrate the kind of substantive interpretations that follow from this line of argument.

Entrepreneurs/organizers tend to emulate others who have been successful. American farm organizations were established in profusion once the example of the Grange was recognized (Saloutos, 1960). Student protest groups greatly increased in number following the organizational success of SDS and Mario Savio's protests in Berkeley, California (Lipset, 1971). These and countless other examples illustrate a familiar entrepreneurial process: Investment tends to follow demonstrations of market potential. At some point there must be an innovator who breaks new ground, identifies a new market, or assembles a new set of appeals. Once the breakthrough occurs, and only then, others will enter the new market to generate organizational proliferation.

Group organizers tend to be recruited by means of their own participation in previous organizational efforts. Farm-group organizers in the late nineteenth century tended to have experiences as subordinates in the Grange. CIO organizers in the 1930s generally came from other unions. The American peace movement in the 1960s drew entrepreneurial talent from a long sequence of peace-organizational efforts reaching back to the mid-1930s (Wittner, 1969). A corollary to this proposition is that *group organizers tend to remain within a social sector or expressive issue/policy domain.* That is, labor organizers do not branch out to establish farm groups. Conservationists do not take up the cause of the armed-forces veterans. Organizers, many of whom are involved in establishing more than one group, generally confine their appeals to markets with which they are familiar and types of benefits with which they have had experience. At the same time, however, the role of interest-group organizer is a durable one in modern societies. Particular individuals tend to remain in this role and its successor, the role of organizational leader, over long periods of time. The notion that group leaders are recruited by virtue of socialization within a context of experience with related organizational activities seems at least a necessary precondition to the hypothesis that postulates an agitator personality type as the factor responsible for the emergence of particular individuals as group organizers (Lasswell, 1930).

The concept of organizing capital may easily be misconstrued to imply a more strictly economic form than is intended. What is meant, rather, is that an organizer must offer something to induce people to join his group. Moreover, his organizing efforts are costly to him, in time, in energy, and usually in money. If the benefits projected are mainly material—insurance, cooperatives health services, wage hikes, technical guidance, etc.—the actual money capital required to inaugurate the flow may be considerable. If so, it must be provided either by the savings or borrowings of the entrepreneur or by subsidies. The latter are probably the more common source of initial capital. United States government resources were employed directly in establishing the American Farm Bureau Federation, for example, and in sponsoring trade associations during the three periods of strongest growth, the early 1920s, the NRA period of 1933–1935, and World War II. Other examples of partial government subsidy are too numerous to list, but private group subsidies are probably more numerous still. Labor unions commonly subsidize cognate unionizing campaigns. Catalytic groups and "front" groups are both types of formal associations supported by other organizations. The NAM promoted the establishment of the Chamber of Commerce. And so on.

One reason that underdeveloped systems have relatively few formal associations is also the reason that they have less economic development. They lack capital resources. In developing societies there is a capital-formation stage in industrial growth which must be reached before effective durable organizations can be created, especially insofar as these groups depend on an exchange of material benefits. Given a sufficient communications technology, expressive-benefit groups can be organized more cheaply and therefore earlier in the development sequence. It is this point that Beer (1965) reflects in observing that promotional groups were prominent in Britain in the early nineteenth century but sector groups did not gain real strength until later. Much the same is true of the United States.

Expressive-benefit groups are less capital-intensive and thus, as noted, cheaper to organize. What is required is an appeal, a cause, an issue, or a "line" that, being articulated, finds receptive hearers who are willing to contribute to the support of that position. Postage, letterheads, and mimeograph machines are key items of expense, rather than insurance schemes or sponsored charter flights. By joining an organization proposing to promote such a viewpoint, the members gain the satisfaction of making contributions, either material via dues or expressive via petition signatures or their names on a letterhead, to the public presentation of that perspective. It may be a comprehensive ideology. It may be an eccentric cause of the narrowest significance. But it gains support, and it achieves publicity and sometimes political weight through the interplay of entrepreneurial initiative and responsive support from those who join.

Now it may appear that expressive groups do not fit under Olson's theory. Olson himself is inclined to think they constitute an exception in that the orientation toward and support of a cause need not be rational in economic terms. It is possible for such groups to seek collective benefits beyond their own self-interests because group members motivated by philanthropy, religion, or ideology may join together without insisting on a parity of personal benefits and costs. But this does not account for why one organization in a field is supported rather than another, or why in some periods many groups flourish but in others the same cause is moribund. It must be that organizational members insist no less on satisfaction from expressive groups than from material groups. People join *a particular organization* because they derive from supporting it benefits of some kind which are not available to them outside that organization, privately or from some other membership. These benefits may be partly solidary in many organizations, but insofar as the group is expressive, the benefits come from giving support to the cause as formulated and publicly expressed by some specific entrepreneur.

Olson contends that rational men will not in fact benefit from supporting a public cause, since its achievement in governmental policy will be equally satisfactory to them whether they belong to the organization or not. But this contention overlooks the undoubted "benefit" which many, though not all, people desire from backing a "good old cause." Moreover, Olson assumes that the individual member of a large group makes no significant contribution to the achievement of the policy objective. Yet the size necessary for an interest group to achieve its policy desires is almost always a matter of great uncertainty. Until the critical threshold of numerical strength is reached, the contribution of each additional member is potentially crucial to success. Therefore, within very broad limits and in addition to the personal satsfactions obtained, it may be quite rational politically to join a cause-oriented group in the hope of adding the critical increment of political strength.

Of course, a very large number of the "causes" of politics are never finally achieved. They remain forever in one stage or another of becoming. If political success were the sole basis of appeal to the membership, many otherwise durable groups would disappear. But success remains elusive, and outcomes are uncertain. Therefore it is of importance to those who believe to have their cause effectively expressed in the hope that additional supporters will be attracted. Public expression of the cause is thus in and of itself a benefit of value which may earn membership dues in the organization created by an articulate entrepreneur.

Before considering other implications of the type of benefits involved in a group, let us briefly examine the notion of the membership market. Who responds to organizers' appeals and under what circumstances? To begin, the answer to these questions is squarely rooted in the value patterns of a community. People do not join organizations in pursuance of attitudes they do not have or causes they have never heard of. Appeals to form an industrial union fall flat in a rural society. Self-sufficient farmers do not join marketing cooperatives. Moreover, the value patterns that may lead to organizational support are rooted in the structure and dynamics of the society. It is surely this to which Truman refers when he speaks of the importance of social dislocation in giving rise to new groups. Such disturbances alter value patterns in the society and thereby provide potential markets for entrepreneurs. This may also be what Macridis (1961) and others have in mind in citing political culture as a critical variable in determining the extent to which organized groups will be formed.

The impact on individual values of economic and social change is obviously profound, and because of this impact, such changes must be regarded as important factors in determining rates and directions of group activity. Nevertheless, they are mediated by the variables of capital resources and entrepreneurial initiatives.

Attitude patterns are neither constant over time nor shared uniformly throughout a society. Vertical cleavages may split the system so deeply that no groups can be organized so as to bridge the gap. Thus in Italy and France "ideological families" constitute differentiated markets which union organizers or student leaders find almost impossible to transcend. The United States is divided less deeply, perhaps, but along many more different lines, and these cleavages also constitute market barriers to would-be organizers. Class, age, region, occupational role, party connection, place of residence, primary-group contacts, and a host of other factors serve to limit the scope of various types of interest groups. It is not just professional and economic-sector organizations which are so constrained. The market for "peace groups" has displayed a remarkably consistent shape since the 1930s, even though its size has fluctuated greatly. The letterheads and mailing lists of right-wing organizations look much the same from one decade to the next, even though the formal names of the associations change and many of the causes have been transformed (Vose, 1972; Dudman, 1962). The delineation and shadings of the interest-group markets of a political system may well tell us more richly of the politically relevant value patterns in that system than comparable analysis of partisan orientations (Braungart, 1971). But without the relatively simple and durable structure that party identification provides, the scholar's descriptive task is far more difficult.

There are other factors of significance operating to affect the market potential of interest-group organizers. One that is of great theoretical and practical importance is the business cycle. Here there is direct conflict in the expectations which follow from Truman's social-disturbance hypothesis and Salisbury's entrepreneurial hypothesis. Truman must argue that economic-group activity varies inversely with prosperity, and, for example, he does so explicitly with regard to farm organizations. So also do Key (1964) and Ziegler (1964). The latter says, for example, that farmer "movements achieved their greatest numerical strength during periods of economic distress and declined as soon as the effects of the immediate threat were alleviated." * The evidence of membership strength among farm organizations points in the opposite direction. The numbers of farm organizations and the numbers of members alike have risen during prosperity and declined during depression. In the face of hard times the leadership often could not sustain the cooperatives and other sources

---

* Ziegler's revised edition, with G. Wayne Peak (1972), omits this discussion but does not offer a substitute formulation on the point.

of material benefits, and members could not afford the dues. The same is true of virtually every other type of organization. Labor-union strength in the United States and Britain has consistently grown with high employment and fallen in recession. Business associations have prospered especially well during prosperity and also, like labor unions, have been substantially augmented during wartime. Expressive groups appear to lose members at a very rapid rate when economic conditions falter. The militance with which organization leaders press their causes may, to be sure, increase as circumstances worsen, but this is quite a different thing. The organizations themselves quite consistently suffer in periods of economic adversity. Economic depression is not the only form of social disturbance referred to in Truman's argument, but this kind of dislocation is given an important role and one which is contrary to the evidence.

There are exceptions. The U.S. Conference of Mayors was created in 1933 at the very bottom of the Depression. Many state leagues of municipalities flourished in the same period (Browne and Salisbury, 1972). The reason was that the organizations began to provide quite tangible benefits on an expanded basis—federal funds from USCM lobbying and such things as legal services from the state leagues—that actually saved the city members considerable money. Most interest groups were not so happily situated with regard to their members' material needs. Consequently, they lost membership.

Another societal factor affecting the formation and growth of organized groups is the framework of law. Legal norms affect the costs of organizing and operating many types of organizations. In pre–Clayton Act America the application of antimonopoly doctrines was a major barrier to trade-union organization because it made it so difficult for the organizers to develop meaningful wage benefits by means of collective-bargaining action. A permissive legal setting during the NRA period of 1933–1935 encouraged the formation of business trade associations, whereas the revival of antitrust prosecutions in the post-1935 period slowed them down. Union organizing was encouraged by the Wagner Act (1935) and made somewhat more costly by the Taft-Hartley Act (1947). Legal norms are always operative one way or another, but they are altered from time to time, and the changes may facilitate or retard the formation and growth of various types of groups. Indeed, the alteration of the formal rules affecting interest-group organizations is often a prime concern of group political activity. We shall speak of this again later.

Other relevant societal variables may be mentioned more briefly. Communication and transportation technologies have great importance in allowing organizers to reach larger membership markets and, especially with expressive benefits, extend them more cheaply. Urbanization, by increasing population density, has quite similar effects, enabling formal organizations to be established more easily. Thus Wright and Hyman (1958) report more memberships among urban dwellers than in rural areas. Industrialization has led to the increase of leisure time and the greater stress on consumption. Group membership is not always a particularly active phenomenon though for some members it may become so. It is often a form of consumption, especially of expressive-group benefits. Accordingly, we would expect membership in such groups to be drawn disproportionately from more affluent sectors of society, and the population of organized groups generally should expand with rising levels of prosperity.

Industrial society is characterized by more complex structures of roles, and as we have already noted, many organized groups derive their members from those who occupy particular roles in the social or political system. Familiar examples include veterans' organizations, parent-teacher associations, associations of school principals and of sheriffs. But organizations do not only follow the emergence of differentiated roles. They may also help to create or at least more clearly define the role so that its occupants come to have a more developed sense of who they are and how they differ from others. Municipal leagues for several decades devoted much effort to this task, holding conferences and producing literature designed to induce self-conscious differentiation and self-improvement (which they called professionalization) among municipal officials (Browne and Salisbury, 1972; Vose, 1966). As the role structures of city government gained in complexity and definition, the number of specialized organizations likewise increased. Meanwhile the older, more general leagues either adopted new activities and provided new kinds of benefits or went out of business. Role differentiation may destroy organizations, too.

Finally, we may note an upper limit on interest-group development which may be viewed as a structural or systemic variable. We refer to density, the proportion of a potential membership market which actually belongs to organized groups. As density increases in a system, the prospects for future growth must decline as an asymptote of both size and number of groups is reached. Further, it seems to be true that within a given sector or membership market there is a long-run tendency toward organizational consolidation. Monopoly may not result, but a modest decline in the overall number of groups is not uncommon after a density peak is reached.

We will conclude this discussion by expressing in summary form some additional hypotheses and descriptive findings regarding interest-group formation and growth. To begin, membership in interest groups is a minority taste. In the Almond-Verba (1963) study the United States is reported to have a bare majority of members over nonmembers, but the United Kingdom, Germany, Italy, and Mexico, in that order, all have fewer members. It appears generally that political and economic development is strongly associated with the incidence of voluntary group membership. Within systems, membership is associated with socioeconomic status, urbanization, and civic involvement. Cross-national patterns of membership within particular sectors vary considerably. Some 90 percent of the commercial farmers of Britain belong to the National Farmers Union. In the United States the proportion of farmers belonging to some general farm organization is considerably smaller, though there are great difficulties in determining who, for these purposes, is to be included as a farmer and what constitutes a general farm organization. Virtually all British trade associations belong to CBI, and the latter thus represents all but a handful of British firms. The American counterpart, the NAM, is generally estimated to represent less than 10 percent of the business world, though again there are enough uncertainties about measurement to suggest that this figure is suspiciously low. Membership of workers in labor unions is not so very different in Britain and the United States, though Britain appears marginally higher. Membership of unions in the peak associations, however, is much higher in Britain. British sector groups are thus more centralized in their organization, even where the density of membership is more or less comparable. We noted earlier that group organizations often display a structure paralleling that of the political system in which they operate, and this may help account for the greater centralization of British groups at the peak level. Relevant governmental decisions are far more likely to be made centrally. The National Union of Teachers in Britain must be able to bargain at the national ministry, whereas in America there are some 3000 school boards with autonomous authority. Other relevant variables would certainly include the structure of the socioeconomic base from which members are recruited. American agriculture is more diverse in both commodity patterns and size of farm than British. For that matter, so is American industry. Consolidation of the sector in a single organization is thereby made more difficult. Systematic cross-national comparison may reveal more precisely the variables and relationships of most significance in determining the patterns of group membership in different types of political systems.

One other hypothesis may be offered regarding the broad pattern of change in the group structure of a system over time. Beer (1965) suggests that in Britain there has been a progression from promotional-group politics (Anti–Corn Law League and the like) to sector-group politics. In the sense that there were many promotional groups about before there were well-organized labor unions or organizations of business firms, this is quite true. It also seems to be so today that although British sector groups bargain with the appropriate ministries over policy, promotional groups tend largely to be confined to Trafalgar Square demonstrations, petitions of protest, and private member bills. In America, however, protest and other expressive groups hardly appear to have faded away, and in other industrialized societies, including Britain, there is no lack of vitality in the organization of new groups to promote new causes.

Another way of approaching Beer's point may be in the analysis Browne and Salisbury (1972) offer of the organizational sequence in a particular sector, American municipal officialdom. Briefly, they suggest that the first major organization in the field, the National Municipal League, was largely expressive in the benefits offered and open in membership to everyone interested in cities.

City officials, however, were leery of reform and seldom joined the NML. They did respond in some measure to another organization, the League of American Municipalities, which devoted its efforts in considerable measure to encouraging officials to improve their skills and develop a more professional capacity in their roles. In a sense, this role cultivation was an intermediate step between the open-membership, cause-oriented NML and later organizations, like the state leagues of municipalities and the National League of Cities, which provided quite tangible material services to their members. But the members, city officials in this case, had first to develop their ability to recognize and appreciate the value of such services as sophisticated legal advice or help in filing applications for federal grants before they could respond to organizations which offered them as inducements to membership. Finally, once the roles of city officials had achieved firm definition, there was pressure to consolidate organizations which sought to serve essentially the same role set. The U.S. Conference of Mayors and the National League of Cities both aimed at top city officials and ranged across all the major urban problems. Their partial merger in 1969 came in recognition of the fact that when the ambiguity in role structures is reduced, the potentialities for organizations of role occupants also undergo constraint.

INTERNAL PATTERNS

Students of interest groups have frequently given attention to the internal arrangements by which the organizations conduct their affairs. Studies of specific groups are particularly rich in descriptive material regarding group leadership, leader-follower relations, the role of executive staff officers, and the like, and Truman splendidly summarizes a broad range of this material. In other more general discussion of interest groups, however, internal patterns have received only tangential attention. One may suppose that this has occurred because the modes of analysis employed in most of these discussions provide little theoretical reason to expect that attention to the internal life of the group will yield much understanding of the group's power in the society. It may therefore suffice to assume (per Michels, 1915) a general tendency toward oligarchic control of most interest-group organizations and a general tendency for most group members to accept as satisfactory such policy statements and influencing efforts as the group leaders may undertake. These assumptions allow the observer to treat the group as a unit and to use the actions of the leadership as behavioral indicators of group intentions. As we have noted, however, to view groups as organizations, especially as structures of benefit exchange, renders these unitary assumptions highly problematic.* The congruence of leaders and followers in

---

* Rogin (1967) makes an interesting analysis of the political implications of the assumption that labor unions were unitary organizations.

attitudes is an important question for investigation, not assumption (Luttbeg and Ziegler, 1966). Cohesion and factionalism, their causes and consequences, are given greater significance. All the interesting questions about power distribution within organizations can be asked of interest groups. Groups are there and have important effects on their members and on society, and this fact alone has long led students of labor unions to give major attention to internal union affairs. In addition, we expect the variables of internal group life to affect their efforts to influence public policy.

Role Differentiation

The variety of organizational arrangements and types among interest groups is sufficient to confound any effort at simple characterization of role structures. In an earlier section we discussed the distinction between the entrepreneur or organizer of a group and the member. This role distinction has literal referents in the formation of every organization and therefore provides a baseline for examining subsequent role developments. Salisbury's analysis tends to merge the historical role of group entrepreneur with the conceptual role of group leader, and this undoubtedly confuses the issue. Let us therefore pass over the problems of role differentiation in the formation phases of interest-group organizations and consider them only as ongoing organizations.

The most serviceable formulation of the basic roles to be found in most interest groups is threefold: leaders, members, and staff. By leaders we mean those members who are designated or acknowledged as leaders by their fellow members. In most cases this designation takes the form of election to formal leadership positions, although in some unions, for instance, some formal leaders are installed by other leaders, as when a local or a regional unit is taken over by the international. Moreover, in managerial groups, as we have seen, the acknowledged leaders are not elected. Instead, a recognition of the legitimacy of the manager's leadership role is one of the initial conditions of joining the organization.

The role of member is relatively unambiguous so long as one defines an interest group as a type of formal organization. If the organization is indeed formalized, it must have explicit criteria for distinguishing members from non-members and for defining the act of joining. The membership unit may vary a good deal, however. Many groups have both individual and organizational members. In some interest groups there is a differentiation among members; for example, many professional associations have full and associate members, with the latter paying lower dues and having a lesser voice within the organization.

A further differentiation among members with interesting research potential separates those who are formally active, attending meetings, serving on committees, and generally paying attention to the organization from those who are not. Sometimes, indeed, there is a formal class of members designated as inactive, but in every group we would expect to find a range of participation. In general, the fragments of available research indicate that participation varies in association with identification with the group and that both participation and identification are related to agreement with official organization policy and value position (Smith and Freedman, 1972).

But there are complicating factors. For example, factionalism indicates active participation by members who must disagree with some part of the formal leader's stewardship. If an organization has relatively low salience for its members, they may choose inactivity or withdrawal following disagreement with leadership actions. In a highly salient organization, however, such attitude conflict might reasonably be expected, *ceteris paribus,* to lead to increased participation. What this suggests, of course, is that interest-group organizations vary greatly in the salience they hold for their members. Some voluntary associations are more voluntary than others. Many labor-union members have no effective choice but to join, and neither do the members of many professional associations. It may partly be a matter of coercion, legal or otherwise. It may partly be a matter of the importance of the benefits which the organization distributes to its members. The more substantial these are and the more central to member value patterns, the more salient the organization.

A final point regarding the role of members involves the hanger-on or fellow traveler who identifies with the organization and may even contribute to it but does not formally belong. Scoble (1967) has noted that most of the National Committee for an Effective Congress support was derived from this category, and it would probably be common in other managerial groups. On the other hand, the Farm Bureau and the AMA have few hangers-on. Many nonmembers may identify one way or another with such an organization and evaluate its policy statements accordingly, but this ought not to be regarded as a variety of membership unless accompanied by some reasonably regular form of activity, such as a subscription to the organization's publication or attendance at its meetings. A third category of groups presents greater complications, however. Many cause organizations have a relatively small organized core and a much larger periphery of nonmember followers. Unions have sometimes drawn expressive support from large segments of the public. The point here is that the nonmember supporters must be kept clearly differentiated from the members if the analysis is to be effective.

The role of interest-group staff has received only sporadic and mainly anecdotal attention. Garceau (1941) discussed the role of Dr. Morris Fishbein, executive director of the American Medical Association for many years and, as editor of the *AMA Journal,* a dominant figure in developing and enunciating AMA public policy views. In many other associations, too, the personnel appointed by the elected officials to administer the affairs of the organization have a most influential voice in determining the activities of the organization, allocating some of the benefits to members, and articulating the group's policy views as well as representing those views to official decision makers (Thorp *et al.*, 1971). It must be made clear that we are distinguishing between the elected leaders of the organization and the appointed staff. Where the elected leaders serve as full-time paid officials, as labor-union and farm-organization leaders usually do, we expect staff officials to take a more subordinate position. In a very large number of groups, however, elective officers either are unpaid or serve only a short term or both. In these circumstances the opportunity for any full-time official to take effective leadership is substantial.

Much of the power of staff officials results from their great superiority in information regarding the membership and its concerns and, if the group is attentive to public policy, governmental affairs as well. On the one side, this enables the staff to make suggestions to a nominating committee concerning who might be useful members of the executive committee. On the other side, the staff sees more quickly and clearly the opportunities and necessities for lobbying action and intergroup alliance, and in many organizations the staff receives explicit discretion from the elective leaders to use its initiative. In groups that offer members an array of material benefits, it is often the staff that serves as entrepreneurs, initiating programs and cultivating the development of the benefit programs.

In the Soviet Union the role of staff member is especially important. Skilling and Griffiths (1971) report that organized groups are commonly dominated by functionaries who "arrogate to themselves the authority to express group interests . . . [but] their initiatives may be subsequently endorsed by group members." In some organizations the staff entrepreneurial role has been made virtually autonomous, as in the creation by the National League of Cities–U.S. Conference of Mayors of a separate staff corporation to administer a variety of programs under federal contract, and simultaneously to more than triple the financial and personnel resources available one way or another for NLC and USCM programs (Browne and Salisbury, 1972). It is not uncommon for an interest-group staff to engage in the sale of special services to members and thereby become independent of membership dues. It would be wrong, however, to suppose that possession of such initiative and even financial autonomy removes group staff from the constraints of member demands or elective-leader directives. Such evidence as there is suggests quite strongly that interest-group staff officials generally espouse and adhere to traditional doctrines of popular control and a responsible bureaucracy. If a staff member transgresses the norms, he is likely to be put down. Even the legendary Dr. Fishbein was finally instructed to stick to his administrative last and leave policy questions to the elective officials. That there are relatively few major cases of outright conflict between staff personnel and elective interest-group officials suggests not only the substantial apathy of most group members and the effective performance of many staff officials, but also the willingness of the staff to accept subordination whenever this kind of tension has threatened group cohesion.

The role of lobbyist is one of increasingly clear definition and sharp differentiation (Dexter, 1969). This differentiation is aided in the United States by the widespread requirements that persons who spend money to affect the passage of legislation must register as lobbyists. Although some groups are represented before governmental bodies by their elected officers and some by staff executives, a large proportion of the American groups operating at the national level employ specialized personnel to conduct their lobbying activities. Seventy percent of Milbrath's (1963) sample of lobbyists either were employed as full-time lobbyists by particular organizations or were independent or free-lance representatives who worked for whatever groups might find their services useful. In the four states studied by Ziegler and Baer (1969) more than half of the lobbyists were officers of the organizations they represented, a finding that suggests a smaller degree of role differentiation at the state level. Holtzman (1970) has described the recent emergence of the legislative liaison officers of federal executive departments, another example of a lobbyist role.

Political folklore insists that the ranks of lobbyists are mainly filled by former legislators and capital-city lawyers. In fact, only three of Milbrath's sample of 114 were former legislators, and 12 percent of Oklahoma lobbyists had served in the legislature (Patterson, 1963). In Nebraska a larger ex-legislator group was observed, however (Kolasa, 1971). Lawyers constituted some 20 percent of Milbrath's sample and somewhat larger fractions of the various state lobbying groups studied. Still, the proportion of lawyers among lobbyists was, if anything, smaller than that proportion among legislators.

Ziegler and Baer report that in the four states they studied lobbyists averaged more years of experience than the legislators. In other states, too, relatively long service seems to be characteristic of those who register as lobbyists. More than half of the Ziegler and Baer group reported a sense of belonging to a lobbying profession, an orientation that was especially strong among those who invested more fully of their time and personal commitment in their jobs.

All the recent studies point to a reasonably well-defined set of individuals occupying the lobbyist role, seeing themselves as a distinct group with an identity and a legitimate function. There are complaints, to be sure, at the frequent public misunderstanding of the lobbyist role, and some evidence that, despite the growing clarity and consensus about lobbying norms, the role is still marginal and accordingly subjects its occupants to some tensions.

Lobbyists can be divided into subgroups, depending on the patterns of activity in which they engage (Jewell and Patterson, 1973). One such type is the Contact Man, whose primary conception of his task is to contact decision makers, cultivate their goodwill, and maximize personal influence with them. At the state level the proportion of Contact Men is fairly high, ranging from one-third to three-fourths of the lobbyist total. In Washington, on the other hand, three-fourths of Milbrath's sample report spending less than 10 percent of their time in contact work. The Contact Man orientation tends to be more common among spokesmen of organizations with large memberships and potential electoral power, such as labor unions, than among smaller groups, such as those from the business sector.

A second major subrole is that of Informant. Informants seek primarily to convey information to decision makers in the hope that it will be persuasive. A third subrole is the Watchdog, who keeps a close watch over the decision makers and informs his clients of any developments which may affect them. Informants and Watchdogs spend a high proportion of their time in their own offices engaged in research, writing, and long-distance communication. Ziegler and Baer report that these two groups make up from one-third to nearly two-thirds of the total lobbyists in the four states they studied, but that the closer to full-time the lobbyist, the more likely he was to stress a Contact Man orientation. They may be at variance with Milbrath's finding that in Washington, contact activity is given less attention than research and intraorganization work. One other type of lobbyist is the strategist, who specializes in planning broad legislative campaigns and serving as a "lobbyist's lobbyist."

In general, interest groups in other political systems have not displayed such highly differentiated role structures. In Britain, for example, there are some individuals who have served as free-lance lobbyists or "parliamentary advisors" (Potter, 1961), but they hardly constitute anything approaching the differentiated profession which Ziegler and Baer suggest is emerging in American politics.

In general, too, interest-group organizations in Britain have considerably smaller staffs and fewer paid officers than comparable groups in the United States. British labor-union bureaucracies, for example, are very much weaker, and many British professional associations have no paid executives whatever. Such organizations must operate quite differently from highly bureaucratized groups in order to bring pressure to bear on governmental decision makers. The modes of interaction between group and government will inevitably be affected by the role structure of the group. Having explored aspects of group role structure and role differentiation, we will turn now to modes of group-government interaction.

MODES OF INTERACTION

The ultimate focus of nearly all political-science discussion of interest groups is the effect of group activity on governmental decisions. Earlier we observed that one of several modes of analysis was to consider groups as input functions. In fact, however, although it falls within this mode, most of the literature is narrower in scope and largely implicit in theoretical orientation. The emphasis is on description of observables taken on their own terms. What do organized groups do in order to influence public decisions? What are their tactics? What are the strategic options? How effective are they? How much of the total policy result can be explained in terms of group activity?

These questions raise several problems. Some are conceptual and definitional, and we have already examined many of that set. Others involve matters of measurement, and they are very difficult. The case-study literature of group activity frequently attributes influence to a lobbying campaign on the strength of the testimony of participants, such as lobbyists and policy makers, or of close observers, such as newspapermen. Systematic interviews of these same kinds of people (Teune, 1967; Francis, 1971) may be used to form more generalized estimates of group influence, but interview studies also depend largely on reputation rather than direct observation of influence at work. And the diversity of perspectives held by decision makers about lobbyists and pressure makes it exceedingly difficult to identify when influence has occurred and when there is really only parallelism of purpose and action between lobbyist and government official (Bauer, Pool, and Dexter, 1963; Garceau and Silverman, 1954).

Parallelism can be observed, and it serves as the basis for much attribution of influence. Noting that particular groups desire particular policy results, that they engage in activities designed to influence policy makers toward the desired goal, and that policy makers in fact choose the policy in question, the observer concludes that a significant causal connection must have existed among the three observables. Plainly, such attributions are often fully warranted. It is equally evident, however, that they are not always so, nor is it very often warranted to generalize about influence relationships at the system or subsystem level solely on the basis of imputations derived from parallelisms.

The difficulties involved in measuring amounts of group influence over policy make comparisons among systems, among groups, or among policy domains very risky. Yet it is not at all uncommon to find such comparisons and to see them used as components in an argument about the relationships among other variables. For example, Ziegler (1971) was able to relate the estimates of pressure-group strength in each American state made by political scientists to the strength of party competition, and he found the relationship generally to be inverse. The data were exceedingly weak, but the observed relationship was consistent with traditional arguments that strong parties tend to aggregate demands and subordinate pressure groups.

Let us accept that most research to date has not successfully solved the problem of measuring group influence. Yet we do not wish to fall back on anecdotes about particular instances of group activity or simply present a cafeteria of tactical options, lobbying techniques, and diverse policy goals for the reader to select from as the spirit may move. Instead, let us explore some of the major types of interaction between interest groups and governmental decision makers. This focus may enable us to develop a more effective set of categories and thus organize a range of literature that is wider than the extant alternatives.

The principal alternative is institutional. That is, group efforts to exert influence on policy makers are arranged, in a large proportion of the major studies, according to the institution, or set of decision makers, toward which the influencing efforts are directed. Thus Truman writes chapters on public opinion, parties and elections, and the major branches of government in his section on the "Tactics of Influence." So, indeed, did Bentley. So does Ziegler (1964). So does Holtzman (1966). So, recognizing the differences in institutional arrangements between Britain and America, does Finer (1966). The primary consequence of this way of organizing material is to stress adaptations in group tactics necessitated by differences in rules, norms, and procedures of the particular institution. Thus efforts to influence the American judiciary require very different methods than do efforts to influence the legislature. But an examination of these differences tells us more about the policy-making institutions than about the interest groups in question. To be sure, some groups, such as the NAACP during the long struggle for civil rights, find more opportunities for success in one institutional arena than another (Vose, 1959). But any rational organization today which desired to influence judicial policy would follow, if it could, the tactical pioneering of NAACP lawyers, utilizing test cases, *amicus curiae* briefs, friendly law reviews, and so on. And so it seems that within some limits group tactics tend to be dependent on institutional norms.

A related point in extant literature is that interest groups tend to gravitate toward the effective centers of power in a given political system. Thus in Britain (Beer, 1965; Rose, 1964), and to a considerable extent also in the United States (McConnell, 1966), groups are said to have concentrated increasingly on influencing administrative agencies in the detailed implementation of policy, with a relative diminution of efforts to mobilize the electorate or influence the legislature. Surely in important ways this assertion is correct. At the same time, however, groups do not always have equally effective leverage in every institutional arena, as the NAACP example illustrates. Civil-rights lobbying turned to the federal courts because state arenas and Congress were unresponsive, blacks could not mobilize enough electoral strength to alter them, and the language of the U.S. Constitution offered some opportunities for effective judicial argument. Similarly, many cause or expressive groups go to the streets, not because it represents a rational tactic for optimum effectiveness, but because it is the only tactic the group knows how or is able to employ.

Not only are there within-group constraints on the institutional targets groups seek to influence; there is also much complexity as a rule in the distribution of effective power within an institutional structure. It is true enough but far too simple to say that power has shifted from legislative to administrative hands in modern industrial societies. Important decisions are made, or affected by what happens, in many places. A particular group, desiring to influence a specific policy outcome, may well find it necessary to conduct not one set-piece campaign but many, spread over considerable time, employing diverse tactics and even resulting in multiple outcomes insofar as the policy process comes to rest sufficiently to identify outcomes as such.

Practical lessons can be learned, of course, from examining interest-group tactics vis-à-vis particular institutions. Certainly many groups have profited by studying some of the classic campaigns (Odegard, 1928; Hacker, 1962; among others). The heuristic value of such a focus may also be considerable, especially if, as is so often true, the ultimate subject matter of instruction is the institutional structures of government. But by the same token, comparison across institutionally diverse systems is made much more difficult thereby, and this seems an especially high cost to pay when the groups themselves, especially those from the major economic sectors, are so eminently comparable. Accordingly we shall consider another way of categorizing group-influence tactics based on the modes of interaction between groups (always to be understood as a shorthand expression referring to the behavior of leaders, staff and/or members) and governmental decision makers, in whatever institutional forms the latter may be organized.

The assumption underlying our classification is that lobbying, as the term is ordinarily understood, is not the most characteristic mode of group-government interaction. Rather, lobbying is seen as one of three major categories of strategic activity, one that is defined by the relative specificity of its policy objectives. Lobbying involves explicit efforts by a group spokesman, the lobbyist, to secure (or block) some particular decision or action on the part of governmental officials. A second mode we may call representation, wherein the group spokesman seeks to be represented explicitly in the institutional mechanisms by which a class of policy decisions is to be determined. The third mode of interaction we shall consider is that of comprehensive mobilization, whereby interest groups are integrated with other organizations, such as political parties, in a more or less long-term effort to mobilize broad community support and, in turn, gain control of the full array of governmental policy-making machinery.

Lobbying

The effort to secure specific policy decisions or the appointment of favorably disposed government personnel we define as lobbying. We have already discussed the role of lobbyist, especially as it has developed in the United States, and it is clear that in the United States the activities of lobbying are increasingly differentiated and specialized. That is, they are performed by people clearly designated as lobbyists—legally, politically, and in social interactions. Nevertheless, by no means all lobbying is conducted by lobbyists. A considerable share of the efforts of interest groups to influence public policy is conducted by group elites interacting with governmental elites in what the former hope is a persuasive way.

Elite interaction. The type of lobbying characterized as elite interaction is ex-
emplified by the relationships between labor-union leaders and a favorable
White House or a congressional committee. Such relationships have become
commonplace in America since the 1930s, and the important thing about them
is that each party occupies such a powerful status that either one can, in effect,
summon the other to a meeting at almost any time. At such a meeting the two
may explore a situation, exchange information, or simply maintain a rather
perfunctory contact. Or they may bargain with each other, using as resources
whatever strengths they can draw upon from their respective organizational
authority (McConnell, 1963). Thus the President has some substantial bargaining resources in that he may threaten or withhold an antitrust prosecution, a
direct television appeal to the public, or an action in the legislative arena. But
the head of AFL-CIO or a spokesman for the steel industry also has organizational resources, not the least of which is refusal to cooperate in some administration program designed to promote such goals as economic growth or infla-
tion restraint.

In Britain and a number of other European systems, elite interaction has
been sufficiently institutionalized to provide an additional type of formal representation of organized groups in the official authority structures of the regime.
It may be that the much more informal style of elite interaction in the United
States is moving in this same direction. For the present, however, American
interest-group elites may still be expected to contact government officials primarily when they have something specific to discuss, some policy question to
talk over, or some decision to influence. The contact is irregular and ad hoc,
and it is quite often shielded from public scrutiny. Indeed, in American politics
the informality is likely to be accentuated by having both the official and the
nongovernmental elite insist that their visit was only a social encounter between old friends.

Informality and ambiguity, however, also affect the social perceptions of
this form of lobbying. On the one hand, elite interactions, being at least partially hidden from view, may be supposed by some to be vastly extensive and
of great effect on public-policy outcomes. Correlatively, within an intellectual
perspective that explains policy in terms of who influenced whom, any elite interactions that can be observed or imputed are endowed with causal import,
usually running from group leader to government official.

In another respect, informality and ambiguity present a severe analytic
difficulty for the student of interest groups. When a corporate executive speaks
to a governor, does he represent an organization which can reasonably be included in some list of interest groups? Or is his position itself more ambiguous,
part of a general structure of influence relationships but not necessarily an example of interest-group lobbying? Clearly, the answer depends on how one defines the range of one's concerns, and within that range how one labels the
various categories. It may serve the cause of clarity to confine the label "inter-

est-group lobbying" to activities undertaken by organization leaders, but the line separating the head of a labor union from the head of a corporation is hardly a firm one. The latter may act slightly less as a representative spokesman for his organizational base and perhaps more as spokesman for his class or social stratum. But how far such a distinction between formal organization and informal social structures will be truly useful for these problems is yet to be seen.

Professional lobbying. Lobbying by professionals presents a complex and diverse array of activities. These activities encompass direct efforts to persuade officials and indirect efforts to influence constituents, reference groups, public opinion, or whatever, in the hope that officials will, in their turn, be affected. However, in this discussion we will consider indirect lobbying under the heading of mobilization. Professional lobbying encompasses formal and informal methods of influence. Its techniques include bribery or social entertainment, as well as testimony before legislative committees on research studies. Moreover, Milbrath and others have shown that a considerable amount of lobbying activity is not immediately directed toward specific policy decisions but is aimed rather at keeping communications channels open, building a trustful relationship with decision makers, and in general cultivating a context in which future policy requests will be sympathetically received.

It has already been noted that the specific tactics of lobbying depend heavily on the rules and norms of the institution whose formal policy decision is at issue. The *amicus curiae* brief is a relevant tactic before the U.S. Supreme Court (Krislov, 1963), for example, whereas buttonholing members in the lobbies and corridors may be more productive in a legislature (Palamountain, 1955). Other factors affect the choices of tactics, too. For example, predominantly expressive groups may derive much satisfaction from advertisements in the *New York Times*, but solidary groups may prefer rallies in Trafalgar Square or protests on the Pentagon steps (Parkin, 1968). It is seldom clear that these tactics are the most influential available, but they provide returns within the organization (or movement), and they are familiar activities in which the group's leaders are relatively skilled, as they often are not in more conventional lobbying.

Tactical choices may depend on the quality of argument available to particular protagonists. Some lobbying causes may be advanced through the sober presentation of research findings to a legislative committee, a court, or an administrative agency, but other causes, less persuasive on their obvious merits, may be served more effectively by bribery or the trading of favors. Evidence from the United States generally supports the proposition that the more professionalized the lobbying—that is, the more differentiated and stable the role of lobbyist—the more time is devoted to developing research materials, negotiating coalitions of support within and outside the decisional bodies, and cultivating the support of the group's own members for particular policy positions developed in this process of negotiation. To put it differently, the more professional the lobbying, the more symbiotic the relationship between lobbyist and decision maker.

We are speaking here of those lobbying activities which are sustained over some substantial period of time, and it is important to distinguish these from the ad hoc lobbying of a group whose policy interests are relatively short-lived and narrowly focused, or, indeed, whose very existence as an organization is too brief to permit stable lobbying relationships to develop. Much ad hoc lobbying employs professional lobbyists to serve as spokesmen or tacticians, and much of the other activity of this kind follows routinely the conventional modes of action. Nevertheless, it is primarily ad hoc lobbying which is likely to generate the most egregious violations of institutional norms, whether out of ignorance, incompetence, or wanton disregard of the rules of the game.

Mobilization. An important mode of interaction between interest group and decision maker involves the mobilization by the group's leaders of constituency support sufficient to constitute a potential sanction, usually electoral, over the public official. Mobilization strategies may be comparatively indirect: utilizing public-relations campaigns, for example, in the hope of generating broad and diffuse public support for the group and its policy objectives. Some campaigns are directed toward specific policies but seek nevertheless to persuade, or at least to neutralize, the general public through broad mass-media appeals. Mobilization may be employed in narrower fashion, however, such as aiming to arouse the group's own members to take direct action to influence policy makers. Inspired letter or telegram campaigns and the use of "bus tripping" to bring large numbers of agitated constituents to visit legislators are among the many examples of mobilization strategies.

The utilization of these strategies by a group's leaders presupposes that the organization has (or can attract) substantial numerical strength, that its strength is sufficiently well distributed to carry weight with a significant number of decision makers, and that the leadership can in fact "deliver" the membership: to protest, to journey to the state capital, perhaps to vote contrary to past habit in the next election, and generally to act so as to induce uncertainty and anxiety about the political future in the mind of the decision maker. Many interest groups are too small, too poorly distributed, or of such marginal interest to their own members that they are unable to deliver in pursuance of mobilization strategies. Altogether, mobilization is risky, since a recognized commitment to such a course, if it fails, can well discredit the organization on grounds of both political strength and trustworthiness. Particularly when electoral sanctions are the intended objective, group leaders have often found themselves unable to affect the voting habits of their members enough to make a crucial difference (Bernstein, 1941). Accordingly, mobilization tends to be approached with caution by most groups, especially those with multiple policy objectives and a long-term presence in the political arenas.

Representation

In a considerable number of systems, economic- or social-sector groups seek a mode of interaction with decision makers which is designed to affect a broad range of particular policies and which is intended to provide generalized, long-term influence over a class of issues. This type of interaction we shall call representation since the strategies by which groups seek to achieve stable generalized influence are essentially strategies for securing representation, whether de jure or only de facto, in the decision-making process.

Sponsored membership. A common representation strategy finds an organized group sponsoring the campaign and, if successful, the membership of decision makers in authoritative institutions. A substantial proportion of the members of the British House of Commons, for example, have explicit and acknowledged ties to organized groups, and the groups, in turn, clearly perceive the election of some of their members as advantageous to their general policy interests (Stewart, 1958; Millett, 1956; Finer, 1966). To a very much lesser degree, some groups in the United States undertake open sponsorship of candidates for public office. Labor unions in particular have assisted the election and sustenance of some of their members to legislative bodies (Greenstone, 1969). Residency requirements for American legislative elections make group sponsorship more risky, however, since the group must be able to mobilize voting strength in a particular district. In all but a rather small number of American legislative districts, explicit ties to particular organized groups may prove a handicap with nonmembers, who generally far outnumber the members. Official sponsorship, therefore, is comparatively rare.

More common in the United States, however, is active group involvement in the informal recruitment and electoral support of candidates. The motives are not very different. In either case what is wanted is generalized policy support from office holders. But whereas in Britain group sponsorship is official and even tends to be quasi-monopolistic—Mr. Pryce-Jones serving as *the* spokesman for the arrowroot industry, for example—American group-legislator relationships tend more to be characterized by mutual sympathy, shared understandings in policy issues, and reciprocal support at critical junctures. Seldom, however, would a congressman be willing to accept a label as *the* spokesman for any organization not specific to his district, and seldom could the group count on his support in any and all circumstances. Electoral support generates friendship and influence, to be sure. But representation when it is so derived is much more informal and problematic than when explicit sponsored membership is involved.

Occupying authority roles. In a number of European countries an organized group obtains explicit representation on decision-making bodies either by having the group designate one of its members to serve or by vesting certain formal authority in the group itself. To illustrate the latter method first, in Germany the occupational chambers, or *Kammern,* have considerable formal regulatory authority over their members, and most lawyers, doctors, and independent producers in business or agriculture must belong to the appropriate chamber (Edinger, 1968).

More common is the explicit membership of organizational representatives on public bodies. For example, according to Finer (1966), the Trades Union Congress in Britain was officially represented on 62 government committees. The counterpart peak organization of business, the Confederation of British Industries, was not much less active. For the most part, this participation inhered in the group, not in the individual member, and it is common practice for the interest-group leaders to designate which of this number is to sit on the committee, board, or commission. Moreover, one of the sanctions utilized by major interest groups like the TUC is the threat of refusal to serve on government committees. The legitimacy of the extensive structure of advisory and inquiry committees depends sufficiently on the participation of major sector groups for the threat to be both credible and politically serious.

In sharp contrast, there is virtually no explicit organizational representation on American governmental bodies. Economic sectors are often included, of course. Medical doctors serve on licensing boards and advisory bodies, and they direct the administration of public health service and medical care and research. But neither in form nor in fact is it thought legitimate for the American Medical Association, state or local medical societies, or specialized organizations to designate the key officials. Labor members may sit on certain bodies, such as the Presidential Pay Board created in 1971. But although the labor members all held top positions in the U.S. labor hierarchy, the selections were made by the President, not the labor groups.

The point at issue is whether organized associations as such possess legitimate claims to speak for their sectors on public bodies. European practice generally acknowledges this legitimacy, and the associations thus can dominate the representational machinery. Moreover, this position of dominance can be used to enhance the group's appeals to prospective members. By increasing its proportion of the total sector membership, the group's claim to representativeness is further legitimized, and so on toward institutionalization. In this situation the significance of the organization and its internal authority structure is enhanced with respect to its relationship to the affairs of the state. In the absence of such formal incorporation, not only are the legitimacy of the organized association and its claims of representativeness called into question; the association may also be more vulnerable to schismatic tendencies and competitive group formation. Contrast the British National Farmers Union, to which nearly 90 percent of British commercial farmers belong and which serves as effective spokesman, consultant, and quasi-bargaining agent in dealing with government officials (Self and Storing, 1962), and the myriad of American farm organizations, some stable and some ephemeral, none of which has hegemony and which altogether do not include more than one-third of the commercial agriculture sector as members (Talbot and Hadwiger, 1968). The American Farm Bureau Federation would rank high among American interest groups in terms of formal ties between it and governmental agencies, but never did it approach the position of sector dominance of the British NFU. Moreover, its formal ties to government had to be severed precisely because they were so widely regarded as politically improper (Block, 1960).

Consultation. Consultative relationships linking policy makers and interest-group leaders may range from official and explicit group participation on policy boards through membership on advisory boards, regular but informal discussions, and finally to ad hoc opportunities which, however valuable, cannot always be depended on. Beer (1965) and others have emphasized the importance to organized groups in Britain of dependable consultative relationships. They particularly stress the significance of consultations with administrative agencies and the special importance of *timely* consultation, that is, consultation prior to the making of policy decisions. It may fairly be said that in Britain, at least with regard to the main sector organizations—and, be it recalled, there is little uncertainty over which peak group legitimately represents a given sector —prior consultation by the ministry has not only become standard practice; it is widely thought to be a necessary step to legitimize any important policy decision a ministry might take or propose affecting the sector. On matters which involve mainly the adjustment of administrative practice, the consultative process tends to be institutionalized in the form of association representatives on advisory committees. More substantial policy adjustments, however, including most of those requiring new legislation, utilize informal means of communication. Sometimes, as, for example, when a Tory government attempts to revise industrial relations, the consultative process gets badly tangled up with party politics. Nevertheless, the norm appears to call for full consultation as an integral part of the process of developing policy proposals.

The position of cause or promotional groups is much less clear. Many of these groups are concerned with a single issue, of course, and often are too short-lived to develop regularized consultative arrangements. Many are organized to protest against existing policy or the very lack of a voice in the policy-making process. Some of these groups may be coopted into long-term advisory or participatory relationships. But many cause groups are organized around an exchange of expressive and solidary benefits, and they depend for much of their appeal on protest activities. Such groups cannot be transformed into advisory committee service without alienating their own membership. Moreover,

except when a cause fits into the structure of partisan concerns, it is often difficult for a cause group in Britain to find points of access or leverage in the
governmental system. The relative centralization of authority means, among
other things, that such diverse institutional devices as legislative investigations,
floor amendments, or *amicus curiae* briefs, so familiar to American group tacticians, are not so readily available to British group pressures.

In the United States there are multiple points of access for all kinds of
groups, and at the same time the extent of prior consultation with sector organizations is highly variable. It depends on such considerations as partisan
interests and the idiosyncratic relationships between particular policy makers
and particular group spokesmen. Consultation occurs, certainly. It is commonly
formalized in appearances by group spokesmen to give testimony to congressional committees. Beyond this, however, regular consultation with organized
associations is not generally recognized as legitimate, and when it occurs it may
become a liability, making adoption of a particular policy more difficult. In
general, it appears that in other western European countries, relationships between interest groups and policy makers display substantial similarities to those
in Britain, especially on matters of economic-sector policy and planning (Shonfield, 1965). There are, however, some important differences which reflect not
only differences in governmental structures and political culture but also variations in political-party systems and the ideological context of partisan conflict.
Let us look briefly at the effects of some of these elements.

Comprehensive Mobilization

Comprehensive mobilization refers to a situation where an interest-group organization is an integral part of a larger unit of political action, usually a political party, and directs its own political energies mainly to the broad campaigns of election and ideological persuasion of the general public. The group
attempts to mobilize the populace, and it does so in terms of a broad platform
of policy objectives rather than a more narrowly defined set of interests.

LaPalombara's description of Italian interest groups (1964) provides perhaps the clearest example of what we mean. Although there are important exceptions, a substantial portion of the major sector organizations in Italy enter
into a *parentela* relationship with bureaucratic agencies and political parties.
What this means is that the interest group becomes part and parcel of a "political family," ideologically united and sharing the broad range of political
objectives held by the "family," whether Catholic, Socialist, or Communist.
The interest group plays a part in the efforts of the family to mobilize the
public for elections and for direct action, as well as for maneuver within the
institutions of Italian government.

When interest groups are caught up in *parentela* relationships, bargaining
for ad hoc policy advantages cannot readily be undertaken. Rather, the group
rises or falls with the success of its family. Group leaders may wish to avoid

this fate and seek to disentangle their fortunes from those of the party. In Italy, for example, there are many *clientela* relationships between groups and bureaucratic agencies wherein the group becomes the acknowledged representative of a social sector, and there develops a symbiosis for the mutual protection and advantage of group and agency. But *clientela* arrangements depend on the existence of cohesion in the sector, and *parentela* tendencies, dividing sectors into families, constitute a continuous threat to the survival of *clientela*.

The contrast between Italian *clientela* and *parentela* and American group-party-government relationships reminds us that in the United States there is little that resembles a political family and therefore no very significant tendency for sectors to divide organizationally according to sociopolitical or ideological considerations (but cf. Bailey, 1950). It does not altogether follow, however, that sector organizations always behave as maximizers of group self-interest, eschewing alliances with party groups or avoiding the espousal of ideological causes with a fervor that makes bargaining with opponents a most difficult task. Labor organizations at every level of American politics have often worked very closely with the Democratic party, providing some 15 percent of its campaign funds and in some cases coming to dominate the local party machinery altogether (Greenstone, 1969; Scoble, 1963). To some extent, the American Farm Bureau Federation has enjoyed such close ties to national Republican administrations and, even more, the Farmers Union has been so intimate with Democrats as to jeopardize each group's ability to work with the other party. In Britain the consultative relationships between ministry and sector organization are frequently jeopardized by partisan and/or ideologically uncompromising activities on both sides. Especially is this true of the TUC under a Conservative party regime.

In general, it appears that sector organizations, particularly the peak associations, are most often tied into partisan families, with the more specialized interest groups and most cause groups remaining comparatively aloof from party entanglements. In the case of cause groups it may often be only within one party that any sympathetic response is achieved (Parkin, 1968), but neither absorption nor merger of group with party is likely to follow. Typically, neither component wishes to taint its organizational reputation by formally acknowledging ties to the other. Direct representation of group members in legislative bodies may frequently be accomplished and the cause thus introduced into party caucuses and the like. But no identity of party and cause necessarily follows from a moderate overlap of membership; the members of each and the larger public remain able to tell the difference.

Close party-group relationships occur in many systems, often simultaneously with the more conventional "American" or perhaps "Samuel Gompers" mode of group-government interaction, which stresses a nonpartisan electoral strategy of "rewarding friends and punishing enemies" and a lobbying strategy of attempting to work closely with anyone with authority to exert an important influence over policy outcomes. The likelihood of prominent *parentela* arrangements is surely strengthened by the presence of sharp ideological and class cleavages in the society. It is sharply reduced by the presence of party organizations which are decentralized, self-sustaining, and oriented toward capturing the prerequisites of governmental office. The stress in American interest-group ideology on nonpartisanship may be tied to the dominance since the Civil War of party organizations devoted to material-benefit exchanges between leaders and followers. And, to the extent that such party organizations atrophy, the possibility grows of interest-group–candidate "families" with distinctive ideological hue, not disposed to accept as legitimate the bargaining tactics of traditional lobbying.

The Importance of Opposition

We will conclude this section by noting briefly that both the form and the content of interest-group–governmental interactions are affected by the nature and extent of conflict over the policy objectives at issue. Notions of conflict are central to some interest-group theories, but it seems more in keeping with the main thrust of the empirical literature to regard conflict as problematic. The application of the idea of conflict to interest-group activity implies opposition to the demands of a group. Opposition may vary not only in intensity and scope but also in form, and for our purposes the variations in form are significant. At one level a group may encounter opposition or resistance from the officials acting as individuals with divergent values. At another level the opposition may arise from such general considerations as bureaucratic inertia or overall limits on available public funds. More specific opposition to a particular policy objective may arise from a countergroup, devoting its activities toward achieving the opposition-policy result. And, in situations characterized by comprehensive mobilization strategies, opposition would typically be expressed by rival partisan or sector "families."

The existence of opposition should not be assumed. In consultative relationships with administrators, for example, it often happens that no articulate opposition exists, especially where the group represented includes a high proportion of the sector whose interests are involved. Conventional lobbying does not always confront organized opposition, though systematic inertia may still prevent group success. In general, however, where opposition does exist, we would expect it to occur in the following way. Representational modes of group-government interaction would least often encounter explicit opposition. Lobbying modes would often encounter countergroup lobbying. Comprehensive mobilization modes would be expected to be involved with counterpart mobilization efforts and hence comprehensive political conflict. Even here, however, not every mobilization must encounter opposition directly. Some mergers of labor unions with the Democratic party in American local areas have illustrated that mobilization may sometimes achieve monopoly.

THE IMPACT ON SOCIETY

We have reviewed several analytic modes employed in the analysis of interest groups and considered some of the central findings of research. Most of this research has been concerned with the more or less direct impact of group activity on public policy, and a secondary theme of attention has involved the internal dynamics of group life. We have said little, however, about the impact of interest groups on the lives of their members or, more generally, on the life and culture of the larger society.

English and continental pluralists of the late nineteenth century and the early twentieth century emphasized the legitimate contributions and stressed the importance to society of having exclusive groups to serve their members as objects of loyalty and as functioning agencies of social action and civic life intermediate between the citizen and the state. In America, where even the autonomous state itself was not accorded unqualified legitimacy, this intermediate role of organized interest groups has received less attention. Instead, their alleged threat to individual liberty, as with labor-union coercion, or to benevolent public policy, as with excessive lobbying power, has received more discussion and has constituted some basis for normative evaluation of interest groups in the society.

Nevertheless, the empirical questions are important, and our descriptive data are in embarrassingly scant supply. What have been the economic benefits distributed to organization members by labor unions, farm organizations, trade associations, and professional bodies? To what extent has the availability of benefits to members of private groups depressed the demands for those benefits from the government, thus penalizing nonmembers and, quite possibly, perpetuating deprivation. It is this kind of argument which permeates much of the modern criticism of pluralist analysis. Pluralists are alleged by their critics to contend that all significant needs and interests in the society will be met by group formation and pressure. Whether this charge is really warranted need not detain us, because we so lack adequate information about who derives what benefits from group membership. Since we do not know the extent to which participation in voluntary organizations leads to increased benefits—material, solidary, or expressive—we cannot assess the personal or social costs of nonparticipation. We cannot adequately judge the consequences to individuals or to the society of whatever "mobilization of bias" may inhere in a particular pattern of interest-group membership. It should be noted that we are talking here about quite a different question from what is perhaps the more familiar one—namely, to what extent do organized interest groups furnish effective vehicles for mobilizing political strength and securing public-policy response? Our concern is rather to stress that in the universe of voluntary associations there are immense effects on the lives of group members about which we know relatively little. They are surely of great sociopolitical significance, and unless we know more than we do at present, we will continue to be quite unable rationally to evaluate the impact of interest groups on society.

Consensus or Fragmentation

A widely circulated hypothesis employed to account for the alleged stability and consensus of the American political system is based on overlapping group memberships. As David Truman formulated it, "membership" was not confined to dues payers but included all those who identified with a particular value position. Truman gave much attention to the difficulties of maintaining cohesion within organized groups. He observed that group members did not devote all of their loyalty to a single organization and in fact were affiliated with several different interests. With member loyalties divided, and in several different directions, group leaders had to moderate their policy stands in order not to offend any major segment of their following. Moderation of group stands would be brought about by the underlying network of multiple cross-cutting affiliations. And this moderation of the claims of one group upon another would help keep political tensions in the system to manageable proportions.

This general interpretation has been incorporated into many of the standard statements about the American political system, and it seems to give organized groups a pivotal role in accounting for system stability. Truman himself did not really hold this view. He says that "multiple membership in organized groups is not sufficiently extensive to obviate the possibility of irreconcilable conflict" (1951, p. 510), and he rested his interpretation of American stability much more heavily on an underlying attitude consensus, which he termed the unorganized potential interests in the rules of the game and which others subsume under the heading of the political culture. Yet Truman did suppose that multiple memberships would, as far as they went, reduce intergroup hostility. They could be expected to cross-pressure the members by exposing them to diverse views. In certain other cultures, on the other hand, organized associations are largely confined within ideological "families" or subcultures, Communist, Catholic, Socialist, and so on. In these situations multiple group membership would be expected to reinforce the hostility between subcultures since, as Verba notes, cumulative memberships are expected to increase political involvement, reinforce views, and increase their intensity. The data are not adequate fully to test these alternative hypotheses, but Verba's analysis (1965) is strongly suggestive that although in Italy group memberships are cumulative and tend to reinforce hostile views of other political sectors, in the United States the effects of multiple memberships were rather slight. Apparently, the member of several organizations tends either to stay generally within a politically homogeneous set or to screen out enough of the conflicting information to minimize most of the cross-pressuring effects of multiple memberships.

It should be noted further that formal organization membership altogether is considerably less extensive in the United States than political folklore traditionally has held. The Almond-Verba study (1963) shows that although marginally more Americans than Britons belong, the differences are not enormous, and the number of nonmembers is substantial in every system studied. Moreover, in some sectors of society the proportion of role occupants who belong to formal interest-group organizations is much greater in Britain than in America. Business associations and farm organizations enroll nearly all of their potential members in the United Kingdom but only a modest fraction in the United States (Beer, 1958). Labor-union membership varies somewhat less. The extent of membership density in a given sector obviously must affect the extent to which group affiliation can shape public attitude preferences and behaviors. High density would contribute added legitimacy to claims by the leaders to speak for the sector. It might also add some weight to the recommendations of the leaders *to* the members since high density would presumably reflect a social norm that formal group membership was appropriate for those in a particular sector.

Clearly, membership density is related to sector-wide (class?) consciousness. In some cases high densities of sector membership may lead to problems in maintaining cohesion in the enlarged and perhaps more heterogeneous group. Yet the comprehensive organizations of a high-density system may lead, through enhanced intrasector interaction and leader-to-member communication ("farming the membership" in American interest-group parlance), to greater agreement on values throughout the sector. Values are not fixed; organizational life affects them (Putnam, 1966). It remains problematic, therefore, whether high-density membership patterns result in lower group cohesion. A reasonable hypothesis might be that socioeconomic heterogeneity within a sector and organizational density interact with each other in shaping sector cohesion, and the two factors should not, therefore, be considered separately.

Interest Group Liberalism and Normative Judgment

To conclude this essay, let us consider a major critique of what is thought of as being at once a conception of how the American political system operates (and, by reasonable extension, other Western democratic systems also) and an analytic orientation toward political systems generally. Under the influence of Theodore Lowi's provocative formulation (1969), this double-edged point of view has come to be known as interest-group liberalism. Lowi's argument and those related to it cover a great deal of analytic and historical ground. Here we shall focus on one element only, albeit one of great importance to the normative side of the argument. Lowi contends that in a system of interest-group liberalism, public policy is mainly the result of the bargaining and pressures of organized groups. He argues that there is no effective power standing aside from the contending groups that is able to judge which one is to be preferred or to impose some criterion or rule on the policy game other than political strength.

Whereas such observers as Galbraith (1952), Herring (1940), and Dahl (1967) have regarded this system as benign, Lowi joins Schattschneider (1960) and many others in finding it deficient. In Lowi's view, when policy is made in response to group pressures, it typically fails to meet the social needs for change. Interest-group–derived policies tend to be conservative, preserving or enhancing the status of articulate groups that are already in relatively strong position by virtue of their organized self-consciousness. Unorganized or inarticulate interests lose out, and no "invisible hand" operates to ensure effective counterorganization by dissatisfied people. Lowi insists on the need for firm, clear rules by which public authority could judge whether to respond to a policy demand or to adjust to a special case. Flexibility is bad in public authority, says Lowi, because it really means giving in to the politically strong, i.e., those who are organized for effective political action.

Lowi is not altogether clear about where his objection to interest-group liberalism really lies. Is it primarily the effective exclusion of the unorganized that is the problem? This argument, centered on quasi–class conflict, is a familiar part of much contemporary criticism of pluralism and of interest-group work as a part of the pluralist intellectual camp. Lowi mentions this point but does not dwell on it, and it does not seem central to him.

Is his concern one of disappointment over who wins and who loses? That, too, might serve to motivate an attack on any system or paradigm of analysis. Lowi's contention, however, is mainly to the effect that under interest-group liberalism hardly anybody wins while nearly everyone is less well off. To the extent that the public officials act reflexively, acceding to the demands of the well-organized and articulate, they fail truly to solve problems or meet genuine needs. Only by reasserting autonomous regulatory authority, by "taking charge of the interests," can Pareto-optimal welfare criteria be met. Bargaining will never do it.

Here, then, is Lowi's central objection. It is his fundamental distrust of bargaining—continuous negotiation and trading over limited objectives, with a view toward optimizing short-term benefits to the players and acting so as to maintain enough mutual trust to keep the game going—as a useful process for solving social problems. In a sense, Lowi objects to "politics." He regards it as less satisfactory than juridical processes or even bureaucratic implementation as ways to achieve rational solutions. He is thus in fundamental opposition to such social theorists as C. E. Lindblom (1965) and other incrementalists, who contend that marginal adjustment is virtually always the optimum way to effect change.

The operational side of Lowi's objections might be to enlarge the authority of quasi-judicial officials and rigidify the criteria by which they were to act. It is not clear whether this would mean that the post–interest-group-liberalism state would thus become more responsive to the unorganized interests of society or simply less the captive of the organized. On the whole, Lowi tends to stress the latter. Many antipluralists, however, have given special weight to the former.

In any case, the ghost of Arthur Bentley may still haunt the observer. If organized groups come to play a less decisive role, *whose* interests exactly will be strengthened? Which substantive political values will be enhanced by Lowi's juridical democracy? Who wins, and what do they win, in the antipluralist society? These questions must still be asked. The political terrain must be mapped, and the political score must still be kept. An interest-group perspective continues to be of great help in these essential descriptive functions, without which normative evaluation of political life lacks its empirical anchor.

REFERENCES

Almond, Gabriel, and James Coleman, eds. (1960). *The Politics of Developing Areas.* Princeton: Princeton University Press.

Almond, Gabriel, and G. Bingham Powell (1966). *Comparative Politics: A Developmental Approach.* Boston: Little, Brown.

Almond, Gabriel, and Sidney Verba (1963). *The Civic Culture: Political Attitudes and Democracy in Five Nations.* Princeton: Princeton University Press.

Bailey, Stephen K. (1950). *Congress Makes a Law.* New York: Columbia University Press.

Bauer, Raymond A., Ithiel de Sola Pool, and Lewis Dexter (1963). *American Business and Public Policy: The Politics of Foreign Trade.* New York: Atherton Press.

Beer, Samuel (1965). *British Politics in the Collectivist Age.* New York: Knopf.

——————— (1958). "Group representation in Britain and the United States." *Annals of the American Academy of Political and Social Sciences* 319:130–40.

Bentley, Arthur (1908). *The Process of Government.* Chicago: University of Chicago Press.

Bernstein, Irving (1941). "John L. Lewis and the voting behavior of the C.I.O." *Public Opinion Quarterly* 5:233–49.

Block, William (1960). *The Separation of the Farm Bureau and the Extension Service.* Urbana: University of Illinois Press.

Brady, Robert (1943). *Business as a System of Power.* New York: Columbia University Press.

Braungart, Richard G. (1971). "Status politics and student politics." *Youth and Society* 3:195–211.

Browne, William P., and Robert H. Salisbury (1972). "Organized spokesmen for cities: urban interest groups." In Harlan Hahn (ed.), *People and Politics in Urban Society*. Beverly Hills, Cal.: Sage Publications.

Clark, Peter B., and James Q. Wilson (1961). "Incentive systems: a theory of organizations." *Administrative Science Quarterly* 6:129–66.

Cohen, Bernard (1957). *Political Process and Foreign Policy*. Princeton: Princeton University Press.

Crick, Bernard (1959). *The American Science of Politics*. Berkeley: University of California Press.

Dahl, Robert A. (1967). *Pluralist Democracy in the United States: Conflict and Consent*. Chicago: Rand McNally.

Dexter, Lewis Anthony (1969). *How Organizations are Represented in Washington*. Indianapolis: Bobbs-Merrill.

Dudman, Richard (1962). *Men of the Far Right*. New York: Pyramid Books.

Eckstein, Harry (1963). "Group theory and the comparative study of pressure groups." In Harry Eckstein and David Apter (eds.), *Comparative Politics: A Reader*. New York: Free Press of Glencoe.

——————— (1960). *Pressure Group Politics: The Case of the British Medical Association*. Stanford: Stanford University Press.

Edinger, Lewis (1968). *Politics in Germany*. Boston: Little, Brown.

Ehrmann, Henry (1968). *Politics in France*. Boston: Little, Brown.

Eldersveld, Samuel (1960). "American interest groups: a survey of research and some implications for theory and method." In Henry Ehrmann (ed.), *Interest Groups in Four Continents*. Pittsburgh: University of Pittsburgh Press.

Farkas, Susanne (1971). *Urban Lobbying: Mayors in the Federal Arenas*. New York: New York University Press.

Finer, Samuel E. (1966). *Anonymous Empire: A Study of the Lobby in Great Britain*, Revised edition. London: Pall Mall Press.

Francis, Wayne (1971). "A profile of legislator perceptions of interest group behavior relating to legislative issues in the states." *Western Political Quarterly* 24:702–13.

Frohlich, Norman, Joe A. Oppenheimer, and Oran R. Young (1971). *Political Leadership and Collective Goods*. Princeton: Princeton University Press.

Galbraith, John Kenneth (1952). *American Capitalism: The Concept of Countervailing Power*. New York: Houghton, Mifflin.

Garceau, Oliver (1941). *The Political Life of the American Medical Association*. Cambridge: Harvard University Press.

Garceau, Oliver, and Corinne Silverman (1954). "A pressure group and the pressured: a case report." *American Political Science Review* 48: 672–92.

Greenstone, J. David (1969). *Labor in American Politics*. New York: Knopf.

Grossman, Joel (1965). *Lawyers and Judges: The A.B.A. and the Politics of Judicial Selection*. New York: Wiley.

Grupp, Fred W. (1971). "Personal satisfaction derived from membership in the John Birch Society." *Western Political Quarterly* 24:79–84.

Hacker, Andrew (1962). "Pressure politics in Pennsylvania: the truckers vs. the railroads." In Alan Westin (ed.), *The Uses of Power: Seven Cases in American Politics.* New York: Harcourt, Brace and World.

Hagan, Charles B. (1958). "The group in a political science." In Roland Young (ed.), *Approaches to the Study of Politics.* Evanston, Ill.: Northwestern University Press.

Herring, E. Pendleton (1940). *The Politics of Democracy.* New York: Rinehart.

Holtzman, Abraham (1966). *Interest Groups and Lobbying.* New York: Macmillan.

_____ (1970). *Legislative Liaison: Executive Leadership in Congress.* Chicago: Rand McNally.

Jewell, Malcolm E., and Samuel C. Patterson (1973). *The Legislative Process in the United States,* 2nd edition. New York: Random House.

Key, V. O., Jr. (1964). *Politics, Parties and Pressure Groups,* 5th edition. New York: Crowell.

Kolasa, Bernard D. (1971). "Lobbying in the nonpartisan environment: the case of Nebraska." *Western Political Quarterly* 24:65–72.

Krislov, Samuel (1963). "The *amicus curiae* brief: from friendship to advocacy." *Yale Law Journal* 72:694–721.

LaPalombara, Joseph (1964). *Interest Groups in Italian Politics.* Princeton: Princeton University Press.

_____ (1960). "The utility and limitations of interest group theory in non-American field situations." *Journal of Politics* 22:29–49.

Lasswell, Harold D. (1930). *Psychopathology and Politics.* Chicago: University of Chicago Press.

Latham, Earl (1952a). *The Group Basis of Politics.* Ithaca: Cornell University Press.

_____ (1952b). "The group basis of politics: notes for a theory." *American Political Science Review* 46:376–98.

Lindblom, C. E. (1965). *The Intelligence of Democracy.* New York: Free Press.

Lipset, Seymour Martin (1971). *Rebellion in the University.* Boston: Little, Brown.

Lipset, Seymour, Martin Trow, and James Coleman (1956). *Union Democracy.* Glencoe, Ill.: Free Press.

Lowi, Theodore (1969). *The End of Liberalism.* New York: Norton.

Luttbeg, Norman R., and Harmon Ziegler (1966). "Attitude consensus and conflict in an interest group: an assessment of cohesion." *American Political Science Review* 40:655–67.

MacIver, Robert M. (1932). "Interests." In E.R.A. Seligman (ed.), *Encyclopedia of the Social Sciences* 14:144–48.

Macridis, Roy C. (1961). "Interest groups in comparative analysis." *Journal of Politics* 23:25–46.

McConnell, Grant (1953). *The Decline of Agrarian Democracy.* Berkeley: University of California Press.

_____ (1966). *Private Power and American Democracy.* New York: Knopf.

_____ (1963). *Steel and the Presidency—1962.* New York: Norton.

Michels, Robert (1915). *Political Parties: A Sociological Study of the Oligarchical Tendencies of Modern Democracy.* Translated by Eden and Cedar Paul. Reprinted. New York: Free Press.

Milbrath, Lester (1963). *The Washington Lobbyists.* Chicago: Rand McNally.

Millett, John H. (1956). "The role of an interest group leader in the House of Commons." *Western Political Quarterly* 9:915–26.

Moodie, Graeme, and Gerald Studdert-Kennedy (1970). *Opinions, Publics and Pressure Groups.* London: Allen and Unwin.

Odegard, Peter H. (1928). *Pressure Politics: The Story of the Anti-Saloon League.* New York: Columbia University Press.

Olson, Mancur (1965). *The Logic of Collective Action.* Cambridge: Harvard University Press.

Palamountain, Joseph C., Jr. (1955). *The Politics of Distribution.* Cambridge: Harvard University Press.

Parkin, F. (1968). *Middle Class Radicalism.* Manchester: Manchester University Press.

Patterson, Samuel C. (1963). "The role of the lobbyist: the case of Oklahoma." *Journal of Politics* 25:72–93.

Peltason, Jack W. (1955). *The Federal Courts in the Political Process.* New York: Doubleday.

Potter, Allen (1961). *Organized Groups in British National Politics.* London: Faber and Faber.

Putnam, Robert D. (1966). "Political attitudes and the local community." *American Political Science Review* 60:640–55.

Riggs, Fred W. (1950). *Pressures on Congress: A Study of the Repeal of Chinese Exclusion.* New York: King's Crown Press.

Rogin, Michael (1967). "Voluntarism: the political functions of an antipolitical doctrine." In Charles M. Rehmus and Doris B. McLaughlin (eds.), *Labor and American Politics.* Ann Arbor: University of Michigan Press.

Rose, Arnold (1954). *Theory and Method in the Social Sciences.* Minneapolis: University of Minnesota Press.

Rose, Richard (1964). *Politics in England.* Boston: Little, Brown.

Salisbury, Robert H. (1969). "An exchange theory of interest groups." *Midwest Journal of Political Science* 13:1–32.

Saloutos, Theodore (1960). *Farmer Movements in the South, 1865–1933.* Berkeley: University of California Press.

Schattschneider, E. E. (1942). *Party Government.* New York: Farrar and Rinehart.

_____ (1960). *The Semi-Sovereign People*. New York: Holt, Rinehart and Winston.

Scoble, Harry (1967). *Ideology and Electoral Action*. San Francisco: Chandler.

_____ (1963). "Organized labor in electoral politics: some questions for the discipline." *Western Political Quarterly* 16:666–86.

Self, Peter, and Herbert J. Storing (1962). *The State and the Farmer*. London: Allen and Unwin.

Seligman, Lester (1971). *Recruiting Political Elites*. New York: General Learning Press.

Shonfield, Andrew (1965). *Modern Capitalism: The Changing Balance of Public and Private Power*. London: Oxford University Press.

Sills, David (1968). "Voluntary Associations." In David Sills (ed.), *International Encyclopedia of the Social Sciences* 14:357–79 New York: Macmillan and Free Press.

Skilling, H. Gordon, and Franklin Griffiths, eds. (1971). *Interest Groups in Soviet Politics*. Princeton: Princeton University Press.

Smith, Constance, and Anne Freedman (1972). *Voluntary Associations: Perspectives in the Literature*. Cambridge: Harvard University Press.

Smith, David (1964). "Pragmatism and the group theory of politics." *American Political Science Review* 58:600–11.

Stewart, J. D. (1958). *British Pressure Groups: Their Role in Relation to the House of Commons*. London: Oxford University Press.

Taft, Philip (1964). *Organized Labor in American History*. New York: Harper & Row.

Talbot, Ross B., and Don F. Hadwiger (1968). *The Policy Process in American Agriculture*. San Francisco: Chandler.

Teune, Henry (1967). "Legislative attitudes toward interest groups." *Midwest Journal of Political Science* 11:489–504.

Thorp, Bruce, *et al.* (1971). *The Pressure Groups: A National Journal Intelligence File*. Washington: *The National Journal*.

Truman, David B. (1951). *The Governmental Process*. New York: Knopf.

Verba, Sidney (1965). "Organizational membership and democratic consensus." *Journal of Politics* 27:467–98.

Verba, Sidney, and Norman H. Nie (1972). *Participation in America: Political Democracy and Social Equality*. New York: Harper & Row.

Vose, Clement E. (1959). *Caucasians Only: The Supreme Court, the NAACP, and the Restrictive Covenant Cases*. Berkeley: University of California Press.

_____ (1972). *Constitutional Change: Amendment Politics and Supreme Court Litigation Since 1900*. Lexington, Mass.: Heath.

_____ (1966). "Interest groups, judicial review, and local government." *Western Political Quarterly* 19:85–101.

Wagner, Richard E. 1966. "Pressure groups and political entrepreneurs; a review article." *Papers on Non-Market Decision Making* 1:161–70.

Watson, Richard, and Randal Downing (1969). *The Politics of Bench and Bar*. New York: Wiley.

Wittner, Lawrence S. (1969). *The American Peace Movement, 1941–1960*. New York: Columbia University Press.

Wootton, Graham (1970). *Interest Groups*. Englewood Cliffs, N.J.: Prentice-Hall.

Wright, Charles R., and Herbert H. Hyman (1958). "Voluntary association memberships of American adults: evidence from national sample surveys." *American Sociological Review* 23:284–94.

Young, Oran (1968). *Systems of Political Science*. Englewood Cliffs, N.J.: Prentice-Hall.

Ziegler, Harmon (1971). "Interest groups in the states." In Herbert Jacob and Kenneth Vines (eds.), *Politics in the American States*, 2nd edition. Boston: Little, Brown.

——————— (1964). *Interest Groups in American Society*. Englewood Cliffs, N.J.: Prentice-Hall.

Ziegler, Harmon, and Michael Baer (1969). *Lobbying: Interaction and Influence in American State Legislatures*. Belmont, Cal.: Wadsworth.

Ziegler, L. Harmon, and G. Wayne Peak (1972). *Interest Groups in American Society*, 2nd edition. Englewood Cliffs, N.J.: Prentice-Hall.

4
POLITICAL PARTIES

LEON D. EPSTEIN

Political parties have occupied so large a place in modern political life that there is now a vast scholarly literature both on the subject itself and on the relationship of parties to governmental institutions and to political behavior generally. All of this literature cannot be reviewed in a single essay. This becomes most obvious with the recent extension of inquiry from the United States and other Western nations to parties in Africa, Asia, Latin America, and Eastern Europe. It is therefore necessary to set boundaries for the analysis while also stating the great breadth of the field. This is done in the first two sections of the chapter by first defining the subject and then by describing the ways in which the subject has been studied. Each of the next sections is devoted to a conventionally important aspect of political parties: interaction in what is usually called a party system, the various degrees of organization for campaigning and other political activity, the closely related party process of selecting candidates, and the role of parties in government and especially in governmental policymaking. Finally, returning to methodological questions raised early in the chapter, the relative importance of political parties is reconsidered in light of limitations indicated by recent experience and study. Here, as elsewhere in the essay, the theme is one of concern for the possibility that political parties need not be so highly developed as many scholars have thought desirable and necessary for the success of a democratic system.

DEFINING THE SUBJECT

Settling on the definition of political party is not as easy as it first seems. Nor is it unimportant (Ranney, 1968). How one defines "party" determines the subject and the method of study. Since party is derived from the word part, it is clear that a political party is a group within the larger whole of the political community. But what kind of group? Surely not every political group. Labor unions and business trade associations, veterans organizations and peace mobilizations are examples of the many important political groups that are not political parties under any common definition. They may be large and highly influential with respect to governmental decision-making; they may even expend money and effort during an election campaign in behalf of endorsed candidates for public office. But they fall short of being political parties in the usual sense as long as they do not provide the labels with which such candidates are primarily identified either on official ballots or through quasi-official literature. This criterion may appear a rather technical means for excluding from the party category an interest group that participates in every other way in the electoral process. But the labelling distinction is useful, as well as analytically defensible, in limiting the subject to what is commonly understood as the party phenomenon.

In positive terms, the definition remains a very broad one in that political parties are all the otherwise varied groups that provide the labels under which candidates seek election to governmental office. Parties may give candidates a good deal more than their labels. Often, but not always, they contribute organized memberships and financial resources. Or they may constitute the effective structure of government policymaking by mobilizing a majority, perhaps virtually all, of the elected public officeholders. But whether or not these additional activities are involved, the crucial defining characteristic is the provision of labels for candidates seeking elective public office. Customarily, it is true, even the smallest label-providing party will also have at least a degree of organization, perhaps only a skeletal structure of nominal officers, so that the label represents a group of citizens. This much, along with some stability of electoral support, seems characteristic of virtually all modern entities called political parties, as distinguished from the more ephemeral faction of an earlier time. It is, therefore, tempting to insist that parties be defined as relatively stable, organized, label-providing groups. But such a definition unnecessarily raises difficulties about the status of the less stable, the loosely organized, and even 'the small or minor entity that we customarily call a party when it presents candidates under its label. It is simpler to have a broader definition to fit all parties presenting candidates. Admittedly most scholarly concern is with the relatively stable, organized, and large parties.

Such parties are modern phenomena appearing no earlier than the nineteenth century. Previously, groups of political leaders, notably in parliamentary bodies, acted collectively as critics or as power holders, and these groups loosely presented themselves to limited electorates. In eighteenth-century Britain and elsewhere such groups, while often termed mere factions, were also called parties, as indeed they would be called under the broad definition already stated. But they were not modern. There was no need for stability, organization, and size when seeking office in predemocratic times. Modern parties arose only with the substantial enlargement of electorates following expansion of the right to vote, and political parties as we know them are distinctively a response to the new mass electorate of the nineteenth and twentieth centuries.

Understandably the United States, as the first nation to extend the franchise to very large numbers of its citizens, was also the first nation to have modern political parties. The approximate date is 1800, when Jeffersonian Republicans successfully won sufficient electoral support from the less popularly organized Federalists to control the national government. The Federalists too can be regarded as a modern party without significantly changing the date of origin (Chambers, 1963). It is more usual to start with the Jeffersonians if only because they first used a party organization to mobilize an electoral opposition (Robinson, 1924; Binkley, 1943; Charles, 1956). There is an argument, however, that modern parties even in the United States were not established until a few decades later, after a non-party period that followed the disappearance of the Federalist-Jeffersonian cleavage. Not only had the American electorate become substantially larger between 1800 and the 1830s, approaching white manhood suffrage as did no other nation's electorate at the time, but political leaders of the Van Buren generation now accepted opposing parties as permanent and legitimate (Hofstadter, 1969, Chapter 6). And, as we know, one of the actual American parties of the 1830s turned out to be so extraordinarily long lasting that it is still with us. Whether the date of origin is 1800 or 1830, the precedence of party development in the United States is evident. Britain, for example, did not have parties on a similar scale until the 1860s, when its electorate was enlarged sufficiently to justify the organizational effort already accepted in the United States. So the parties previously established in the British Parliament, joined eventually by a major party originating outside of Parliament, developed organized followings. In certain respects these were more highly structured and larger than their earlier American counterparts. Other Western European nations followed roughly similar patterns at about the same time.

The rise of modern parties coincident with the mass franchise, if not the universal franchise, leads to the question of the inevitability of parties at least in nations whose officeholders are subject to large-scale competitive elections. This is another way of asking if parties should be defined as essential elements of democratic politics. They *seem* so, since there is no instance of a twentieth-century democracy that functions without political parties. (Nor, for that matter, is there a twentieth-century dictatorship, resting on mass participation, that functions without at least one, but usually only one, party—distinctive though its role is.) Conceptually, however, it has to be granted that elections can be contested by individual candidates or by ad hoc candidate slates that do not possess most of the characteristics of parties. In fact, such contests are not unknown even in fairly large municipalities, especially in the United States

(Adrian, 1961), and there are approximations of these nonpartisan contests in other constituencies where parties are so loosely structured as to have little impact and to qualify only barely as definable parties. This involves more than the absence of meaningful organizations. It also means that parties are able to do little to orient the votes of an electorate that regards itself as independent and as attracted primarily by individual candidates. Should these instances be put aside as residuals from a pre-party age or as transient products of progressivism and clean-government movements? The obstacle to doing so is the persistence and reemergence of such party weakness in the very country, the United States, where modern parties first developed and where they ought by now to be most clearly dominant as an essential response to competitive democratic politics. Moreover, a limited party activity and the no-party situation on which it verges are often characteristic of American communities appearing to be advanced economically and educationally. The evidence is admittedly only enough to raise a question about the inevitability of parties in democratic society. What can still be said with certainty—and it really says a good deal—is that parties have existed, so far, in every nation with a mass electorate.

More uncertain in defining parties is whether to include those entities, operating under the name of parties, that exist in noncompetitive electoral systems. This question is raised entirely apart from any question concerning an authoritarian or totalitarian party that functions within a competitive system. When such a party proposes candidates for public office, even though simultaneously seeking power by nonelectoral means, there can be no serious doubt that it (the Communist party in France or Italy, for example) has to be included along with other parties competing in the same nation. Its inclusion does not preclude recognition of the party as antithetical in principle, and presumably in practice, if it won an election, to the very system in which it competes. The difficult case is posed in a nation, communist, fascist, or otherwise authoritarian, that is already without competitive elections but that has an organization monopolizing various political activities that would, in Western democracies, be performed in some degree by two or more parties.

The Communist party of the USSR is now the oldest, one of the most important, and perhaps the most fully studied contemporary example of the monopolistic party (Fainsod, 1953; Armstrong, 1961). The type is a striking phenomenon of the twentieth century, appearing as an accompaniment of communist government both in Eastern Europe and spectacularly in China, and in various noncommunist authoritarian regimes. Western Europe of the interwar years provided two prime examples, in Fascist Italy and Nazi Germany, where *the* party had first been one of several competitors electorally in a democratic system (Neumann, 1942). The Falange in Spain had a different origin and also a less pervasive role (Linz, 1970). Recent noncommunist party monopolies have been most evident in some developing nations, especially in Asia and Africa, when a single party either emerged from a preindependence national movement or was developed soon after independence as an instrument of the new powerholders (Almond and Coleman, 1960; LaPalombara and Weiner, 1966). The several monopolistic parties, communist and noncommunist, European and non-European, differ from each other in many respects, even to the extent of the fullness of their monopolies. But they are alike in seeking to mobilize political support and leadership recruits for the regime. However much they vary in effectiveness as mobilizers or in other governing or quasi-governing activities, these parties accompany every dictatorship that seeks popular support. They are aptly called "mobilist" by LaPalombara and Weiner (1966, p. 425). The mobilist party is almost as characteristic of twentieth-century dictatorship, and only of twentieth-century dictatorship, as competitive parties are of twentieth-century democracy. Dictatorships still exist, it is true, without parties of any developed kind, and such regimes even reappeared in Africa after an effort at party organization (Wallerstein, 1966). But the nonparty situation seems much less typical of the twentieth century's dictatorship than does the mobilist party.

From this much discussion of the monopolistic party it is evident that it is awkward to leave so modern a phenomenon outside the definition. Some of its activities, at least, are plainly the counterpart of those performed elsewhere by competing parties; the Communist party of the USSR, for example, does present candidates for elective public office (uncontested, to be sure) and also seems to recruit prospects for nonelective public office. Of course, like most mobilist parties, it does much more besides, and it is these other activities—particularly any that are incompatible with electoral competition—that provide a strong case for regarding such a party as different in kind from Western democratic parties (Cassinelli, 1962). The party that is legally and actually coercive in its monopoly is surely distinguishable even from a party that happens, in a region of a Western nation, to enjoy a virtually uncontested domination. Nevertheless, after recognizing this distinction in all of its political significance, there is no harm in maintaining the breadth of definition. It is surely more convenient than searching for a new word to describe an entity that its members, along with most of the rest of us, are accustomed to calling a party. Furthermore, we do no violence to the source of the word. Even a monopolistic party is still only a part of the political whole in the sense that the community contains other political groups—military, technocratic, and government bureaucratic, for example—even if no other party. There may even be, as in contemporary Poland, another party or two consistent with a virtual monopoly of power by a "hegemonic" party (Wiatr, 1970).

Having defined the term generously in accord with common usage, it is imperative to limit the subject of most of this article to a more readily manageable area. The chief concern is with American political parties, understood in a comparative perspective afforded by the experience of Britain, the English-speaking Commonwealth nations, and the nations of Western Europe. Other references are few even though there are now in Latin America, Asia, and Africa several substantial experiences with party competition as well as with the equally modern monopolistic parties. These instances are excluded not for analytical reasons but because of limited knowledge and space. Consequently, whatever is said about American parties or about Western democratic parties should be understood to be a discussion of only a segment of the experience with modern political parties. The segment is important in itself, but knowing about it is by no means to know about parties in other areas of the world. We are long past the time of assuming that the Euro-American experience with parties or anything else is a pattern to be followed in Asia and Africa, and we are also past the time of assuming that a pattern developed in Asia or Africa, or in Russia, is about to disappear under the impact of westernizing influences.

APPROACHES TO THE STUDY

Large and important portions of the research contributing to an understanding of political parties are conventionally (and in this *Handbook*) subsumed under other headings like public opinion, ideology, and legislatures. Notably this is true with respect to voting behavior and related attitudes of the electorate, in which areas the sample survey and ecological analysis of election data have provided most of what we know about the extent, the nature, and the durability of popular support for parties. Leading examples are Campbell *et al.* (1960) and Butler and Stokes (1969). These and other similar studies cannot be ignored in any discussion of political parties, but a sensible division of intellectual labor means that they receive less attention here than in other chapters. The same holds for the role of parties in governmental agencies; again obviously the topic is much too significant to be ignored in studying parties, but the scholarly literature belongs primarily to specialists in legislative or executive behavior. Here the topic, while receiving considerable emphasis near the end of the chapter, is not fully explored.

What remains as the presently separate study of political parties is often divided, as it is by Schlesinger and Eckstein in the *International Encyclopedia of the Social Sciences* (1968), between party units and party systems. The first focuses on parties as organizational responses to different socioeconomic and governmental situations and the second on competitive interaction patterns among party units. An accompaniment of this arrangement, under the second heading, is a concern with the number of parties in given nations or constituencies and with explanations of the causes and the significance of the variations in number. Often this has led to concentration on the impact of election provisions and thus on the provisions themselves: one type of electoral system (single-member, simple-majority) is believed conducive to two-party competition and another type (proportional representation) to multiparty competition. Naturally the subject is intriguing for political scientists. Not only does it allow the use of mathematical techniques but it seems to provide a basis for expert recommendations of electoral legislation to encourage a preferred party system. Often these recommendations rest on the challengeable assumption that electoral laws are fundamentally the cause rather than the result of the number of parties. Even without the assumption it is possible that the issue of number of parties receives the wrong kind as well as too much attention from political scientists. In what follows, particularly in the next section, the number of parties is treated as an aspect of party competition generally. Only brief reference is made to the well-established school of thought that concentrates on the number and the related consequences of election laws.

A basic but not irreconcilable difference in approach is between those who regard parties as independent variables, likely to influence other political phenomena including governmental forms and outputs, and those who regard parties as dependent variables, likely to be influenced by constitutional and governmental structures and by socioeconomic conditions. In many studies the approach is not solely and strictly one way rather than the other. Often the distinction is not made clear at all. But, self-consciously or not, there is almost always one emphasis or the other. At one extreme, for example, some political scientists eager to reform parties can be observed to treat parties largely as causal agents in the political process. They assume that it is possible not only to change parties radically, without first changing anything else, but also thereby to effect changes in government and in electoral behavior. Or, to cite an example at the other extreme, a few scholars, often but not always trained in sociology, can be observed to treat parties as little more than the consequence of social and economic forces producing constellations of leaders, followers, and voters. This sociological reductionism, while by no means uniformly characteristic of political sociologists, has been a more prominent tendency in the last few decades than has the other main dependent-variable approach, which treats parties as functions of constitutional orders, governmental structures, and even (as noted previously) election laws. The sociology of parties, partly because of its association with the quantitative and innovative studies of voting behavior, has seemed less old-fashioned than constitutional or structural analysis. Only lately has it come under serious criticism, and then for what are said to be excesses already abandoned (Sartori, 1969).

The last comment points toward a moderate if less clear-cut position. It is to study parties both as independent and dependent variables, that is, as intervening variables that are both influenced and influencing. In fact, almost everyone can agree that such treatment corresponds with reality. Parties are responses to circumstances of many kinds, *and* they are also, once existing, among the circumstances that determine political life. A party can simultaneously be viewed as the product of a given economic class and a given constitutional order and as a continuing organizational and structural channel through which politics is conducted. Not often, however, does anyone thus study parties simultaneously as dependent and as independent variables except in a synthesizing text rightly seeking balance and completeness. Most studies of parties have particular themes that make it desirable to treat parties primarily if not exclusively in the one way or the other. For instance, a study of social class and political parties will, with good reason, consider parties as dependent variables. So will someone seeking to estimate the impact on parties of federalism or of the separation of executive-legislative powers. On the other hand, parties often become mainly independent variables for those focusing on factors affecting legislative roll-call voting, on the role of party organizations in election campaigns, or on the impact of party loyalty on election outcomes. This too is a legitimate and useful approach as long as its practitioners remain aware of its limitations. Parties are not always the prime political movers. Nor are they capable of activities and roles regardless of the social and institutional circumstances in which they have developed and now exist.

There is a methodological issue that cuts across the dependent-independent variable distinction. This is whether parties should in any sense be the principal foci for analysis. A fully functional approach seems to deny the validity of analyzing parties as a distinct subject matter. The basic consideration is the performance of certain system-serving functions, like political communication, mobilization, and rule making; subsidiarily, parties along with other agencies are observed to perform these functions. What parties do, by way of aggregating interests, for example, may remain of great concern; the practical methodological result, then, is to consider the usual party topics but within a new and broad context (Almond and Coleman, 1960). A different consequence of the approach is to deemphasize parties by regarding many of the functions ordinarily attributed to parties as just as successfully performed, in terms of system maintenance, by other political groups or agencies. It is true, however, that one does not have to be a full-fledged functionalist in order to adopt that kind of perspective. Even a scholar who criticizes functionalism, partly on the grounds of its ambiguity, can argue that parties should not be assumed to perform any given functions in a given political system (Sorauf, 1967). It follows, in this criticism, that the word "functions" is dropped altogether in favor of the nontechnical term "activities" associated with particular party structures. Much is to be said for this terminological simplification, but the important point here is its association with the view, shared by some functionalists, that parties ought not be treated as though they necessarily were the agencies doing certain things in order to sustain a political system. Other agencies might do those things, or they might not be done at all. We cannot be sure that the result of ineffective parties would be the failure to sustain a particular system.

So bland or neutral a conception of party is unusual among those who have studied the subject. Like scholars in other fields, political party specialists have naturally conceived their subject as important. Also, understandably, they have often argued that parties are crucial factors in democratic politics.

Especially by the mid-twentieth century this view became characteristic of most historians and political scientists working in this area. Among the political scientists are those of the responsible-party school, which was led by Schattschneider (1942), embraced at one point by a prestigious committee of the American Political Science Association (1950), and reasserted in literary-historical style by Burns (1963). Their concern is to strengthen parties through greater centralization, issue-oriented memberships, coherent programs, and disciplined legislative behavior (Kirkpatrick, 1971). Rejecting both the old patronage machines and the more recent weakly structured American organizations, the responsible-party school has tended to regard British parties of the mid-twentieth century as its model. The American reformers thus share in certain respects the preference of Duverger (1954) for the highly articulated, mass-membership party, which he declared as he concluded his comparative study to be increasingly typical of advanced democratic nations except the United States. Neumann asserted similar opinions in his well-known anthology of studies of parties in Western nations (1956).

The common ground here is the conviction not only that parties are vitally necessary for effective democracy but that they must be strong in certain significant ways if they are to perform as necessary. Perhaps the fervor and to some extent the assurance of this faith has receded since the early 1950s (Kirkpatrick, 1971), but at least a modified belief in the efficacy of parties has remained influential despite recent challenges.

It is useful to contrast this belief with the older perception of parties as unfortunate aberrations from desirable democratic politics. Scholarly views of this kind were preceded by those of leading political figures, the best known of which belong to the founding fathers of the United States. They hoped either to do without parties or to deal with them as apparently necessary evils; certainly they did not welcome parties as had their famous British contemporary Edmund Burke in his praise of the predemocratic parliamentary factions of the eighteenth century. Rather, the first generation of American political leaders, Jeffersonian as well as Federalist, thought of the respective parties as no more than temporary instruments designed to absorb the opposition by conciliation or annihilate it by electoral success (if not by repression). Permanent party contest, with alternation in office, was not yet settled in the belief system (Hofstadter, 1969, p. 8). Even when party was fully legitimized in the minds of the next and succeeding generations of American politicians, the intellectual or academic reception of the new kind of organization remained unfavorable during much of the nineteenth century. Indeed, it was studied hardly at all while legal and constitutional approaches dominated the study of government. However inevitable it was in accompanying the democratic franchise, party in its first highly developed American form seemed too strong, too dominant, and, since it was characteristically a patronage machine, often too corrupt. So it seemed to James Bryce (1891), the most influential British student of American politics in the nineteenth century. He hoped for a less formidable organization in Britain's newer democratic order.

Much more pessimistic about party organization ever becoming benign either in Britain or the United States was Ostrogorski (1902), the author of the first large comparative study of parties. After an immensely detailed account of the activities of American and British parties organized outside of formal governmental structures, Ostrogorski concluded that any such permanent organization was tyrannical in relation to elected public officeholders. His extreme individualistic view, it should be noted, was nevertheless a democratic one and therefore distinguishable from the antiparty attitudes of those who opposed any mass electoral basis for governmental authority. More to the point here is that Ostrogorski was denying the legitimacy not just of the boss-ridden American patronage machine, but also of the newly organized British party association, which was composed of issue-oriented, program-committed local members who sought to determine the position of parliamentary representatives. Nor was Ostrogorski the only early scholarly critic of the nonpatronage party organization which was developing near the turn of the century in Western Europe generally. Better known is the thesis advanced by Michels (1915) that even the most democratically intentioned political organization—in Michels' view the Social Democratic party—suffered from the workings of an iron law of oligarchy that caused power to be concentrated in the hands of a bureaucratic leadership. Of course, Michels expected nothing better in any other kind of organization—the iron law held always and everywhere or it was hardly of iron—and he was generally disillusioned with democracy. Nevertheless it is fair to say that he belongs to that substantial and once apparently dominant scholarly tradition that approached parties in an adversely critical if not destructive spirit.

Whether that spirit is again rising, late in the twentieth century, after a period of optimism and occasional glorification of parties, is worth discussion at the end of this article. In the meantime, from an admittedly skeptical middle position, the chapter treats the importance of parties both as uncertain and as varying with circumstances.

COMPETITIVE PATTERNS

The common and deceptively simple classification of party patterns is according to the number of substantial parties competing for offices in a given nation or constituency, and this classification most often presents one-party, two-party, and multi-party "systems." The three-fold classification has the virtue of including every party pattern, even that which is only intraparty competition. All that is excluded is a no-party situation, which might or might not be competitive. There are questions about fitting certain marginal cases in one rather than another of the three patterns, but these tend to be settled by a reasonably acceptable arithmetic formula. For example, a nation with three or more actual parties seems to have a two-party competitive pattern instead of a multiparty pattern as long as only two parties secure most of the votes and especially most of the elective public offices over a period of years. "Most" is defined as enough to provide either of the two parties, at different times, with a governing majority. So Britain, apart from one recent election, is almost universally regarded as having a two-party national pattern despite a persistent consequential third party plus other minor parties. Similarly, a constituency (like an American state) with one of two principal parties maintaining majority control over a long period is still said to be two-party competitive if the second party either wins once in a while or polls a defined substantial percentage of the vote. On the other hand, an American state whose dominant party has no substantial competition from a nearly nominal opposition is classified as having a one-party pattern (Ranney and Kendall, 1956).

A somewhat more difficult problem for this classification, as well as for any other classification of party patterns, concerns the constituency to which the criterion of competitive elections is to be applied. Should it be a limited area—state, province, region, county, city, or even smaller unit—instead of the larger political whole of which that area is a component? One aspect of this problem is readily illustrated by an American state that has virtually no interparty competition for its state offices but sharp two-party contests for its presidential vote. Then the classification depends on which level of competition one is analyzing. But there is another aspect of the problem. Even a state without meaningful interparty competition at any level is still part of a larger nation in which there is two-party competition for the presidency and for congressional control. So from the standpoint of the larger body politic, the one-party state is contributing to the two-party competition. The same, of course, holds for all one-party constituencies within larger competitive wholes. Looking at it the other way around, the larger units (nations in relation to their states or provinces, states to their county or district subdivisions, and so on) seem to be composed of many constituencies likely to have much less interparty competition. Higher level two-party or multiparty competition may be largely the result of aggregating different one-party patterns. In fact, as can readily be observed, this is usually the case. The threefold classification is not thereby destroyed, any more than any other method of classification, but it assumes an additional dimension by taking into account the scope of the constituency being characterized.

Even thus modified the threefold classification can be sharply challenged for the significant differences that it seems to conceal. The one-party category includes at least two analytically different types found within the confines of the old American South's Democratic party dominance. One type exhibited a well-defined bifactionalism, with each faction possessing most of the characteristics of a party within a party and thus leading to the virtual equivalent in a direct primary election of regular two-party competition (Sindler, 1956). The other type, lacking clear-cut factions, presented electoral contests only between personalities (Key, 1950).

A two-party pattern also includes sharply different types not only with respect to the degree to which the two leading parties actually dominate elections but also with respect to the nature of the two parties themselves. Two-party competition plainly means something very different when each of the parties is able to perform as cohesively as a British parliamentary party rather than when parties perform as uncohesively as Republicans or Democrats in American national politics. In the latter case there is the *form* of two-party competition, perhaps more fully achieved than in Britain, but each major American party is so loose a coalition that an electoral majority for it has a meaning for the exercise of governmental power altogether different from the meaning of an electoral majority in Britain.

This difference suggests that the whole idea of classifying by number of parties is useful only within limits, as is evident also in a close look at the variety of one-party systems outside the United States (Fainsod, 1968). So too within the multiparty category there are such different types as to challenge the general relevance of the threefold classification, as opposed to a continuous scale of relative competitiveness (Rae, 1967). In continental Europe, where multiparty patterns have been usual in democratic regimes, one pattern is fairly described as moderate and the other as extreme, corresponding in high degree with workability of a parliamentary regime in the first instance and with failure, or at least great difficulty, in the other (Sartori, 1970). Moderate multipartism, involving about three or four substantial parties, none of them of an authoritarian, antisystem bent, characterizes Scandinavian nations, Belgium, West Germany, and perhaps the Netherlands (Lijphart, 1968). It is associated with a capacity to form stable cabinet government either through a single majority party or a limited, relatively secure coalition. Extreme multipartism, involving a greater fragmentation and at least one large party dedicated to the destruction of the democratic regime, may be observed in Italy, the French Fourth Republic, and Weimar Germany.

Again it is plain that something other than number of parties is being introduced in order to produce an analytically useful classification. The presence of the antisystem party does seem crucial (Taylor and Herman, 1971). It makes for doubt whether multipartism as such should be condemned for its supposed contribution to, or at least association with, unstable parliamentary regimes. If only one distinct kind of multipartism can be so associated, then much of the previously assumed significance of the line between the two-party and the multiparty types will have disappeared. After all, the significance derived from the belief in the desirability of stable and effective parliamentary government and from the belief that the way to achieve it was through two-party rather than multiparty competition. To some extent this reflected an Anglo-American bias, but it has been shared by many European scholars, some of whom have sought electoral laws that would encourage dualism in existing multiparty nations. Bolstering this view has been the belief that there is a natural dualism flowing from responses of voters and politicians, who are either for or against a given policy (Duverger, 1954).

Although scholars occasionally defend multipartism, particularly a successful working model like that of the Netherlands (van den Bergh, 1955), many political scientists during the postwar decades showed a decided preference for the two-party competitive pattern. The preference appears to accompany the now-established desire for the strong party capable of governing, presumably through the achievement of a majority position following from bipartism. As such, this preference differs sharply from an older conception, popular among liberal intellectuals of the last century, that sought to widen the diversity of group representation in legislative bodies, often through election devices designed to reduce or eliminate the possibility of any one party winning majority control. By the mid-twentieth century that conception had suffered from its association with the unfortunate experiences of the larger continental European nations, each of which had had an unstable multiparty parliamentary regime that proved unable to survive. Always, of course, there were other and perhaps more fundamental factors available to explain the failures, as well as other nations (however small) whose multiparty regimes survived and even prospered. But France of the Third and Fourth Republics, Italy of the old monarchy and of the later republic, and Weimar Germany provided monumental examples of the apparent vicissitudes of at least "extreme" multipartism and so of the election device, chiefly proportional representation, that helped maintain the multipartism if it did not actually produce it. The contrasting success of "moderate" multipartism may even reinforce the preference for bipartism since the moderate multiparty pattern is observed to succeed insofar as its operation approximates that of the two-party pattern.

American studies of American politics have dealt with the two-party pattern in a different context. Multipartism has appeared only sporadically in the United States. The numerous and persistent minor parties, by definition, do not transform the pattern to multipartism; their existence is in principle and in practice entirely compatible with the substantial dominance of two parties or of one party. "Third" or even "fourth" parties, on the other hand, do signify by their very name, as distinguished from minor parties, a discernible variation. A few of these larger parties have even won electoral votes in presidential elections of this century, specifically in 1912, 1924, 1948, and 1968, but significantly it was a different third party in each of those years. American states have had occasionally successful third parties, but when such parties secured any large number of offices, as in Minnesota, Wisconsin, and North Dakota in the interwar years, they did so by practically displacing, for a time, one of the two traditional major parties. The more recent Liberal and Conservative parties of New York State have not succeeded in the same degree, and even their occasional triumphs appear to function as pressures converting one or the other of the major parties to a more congenial ideological position. So far at any rate they do not appear to produce, or even threaten to produce, European-style multipartism. So political scientists concerned primarily with the United States naturally think of the more familiar one-party pattern, which has prevailed in various degrees in many states, as the alternative to bipartism. Like most other political scientists, they too prefer bipartism.

A certain amount of intellectual energy has been spent in making the American case for this preference. One-party domination, however, is not in all ways as easy a target as multipartism. It would not contribute to instability of executive authority even in a parliamentary-cabinet system, and such a consideration is irrelevant in American government, where stability of executive authority is assured regardless of the party pattern. On the other hand, the one-party pattern appears to have the serious deficiency of precluding electoral competition and so of being unsuitable from a democratic standpoint. But this obvious criticism holds only if there is no direct primary election in which large numbers of voters have the opportunity to choose the dominant party's candidates. Almost all American states have provided this opportunity during most of the twentieth century. The legal forms for primary voter participation have differed from state to state, but they have generally become consistent with a mass franchise in the one-party states. Naturally it is in such states that the direct primary tended to be first developed and subsequently to attract the most electoral attention. In fact, when established successfully in one-party states, the direct primary may, as an effective electoral opportunity for new competing groups and candidates, discourage the building of a large second party. Yet, despite some evidence in one state of fairly frequent use of the primary to defeat incumbent legislators (Epstein, 1958), the weight of American experience seems to be against meaningful primary contests in congressional and legislative elections (Turner, 1953; Key, 1956, Chapter 6). Gubernatorial and United States senatorial primary contests may more often be competitive, but the argument against one-party domination remains unless congressional and legislative offices are as frequently contested in a significant way in primaries as they are in two-party competition. One is tempted to say "as they would be" in two-party competition until remembering that such competition cannot simply be decreed for a one-party constituency lacking the socioeconomic bases for local organizations of the existing national or state parties. Usually, therefore, the argument against the one-party pattern has to rest on bipartism's superiority (as measured by voter turnout, office turnover, and meaningful contests) in those states or other constituencies in which bipartism can and does exist.

A similar intellectual difficulty appears to have been encountered in the impressive effort to demonstrate bipartism's superiority in terms of policy outputs. American one-party and two-party states have been ingeniously compared in their respective responses to what are conceived to be publicly demanded and needed policies, often of a welfare nature. The first such study, showing a positive correlation of bipartism and favorable policy outcomes in the six New England states, was believed by its author to support the advantages of two-party competition (Lockard, 1959). Subsequently the hypothesis has been challenged by more extensive and more refined analysis demonstrating that the admittedly positive correlation between bipartism and certain policy results is less than the positive correlation between degree of socioeconomic development (particularly wealth) and the same policy results in the several states (Dawson, 1967). The findings strongly suggest that socioeconomic factors explain both interparty competition and policy outcomes and that bipartism is itself one of the results that follow at a given stage of development. By no means, however, is this showing universally accepted as conclusive (Lockard, 1968). An extensive literature now exists on the topic (Greenstein, 1970, pp. 76–77n).

Any conclusion of this sort would reduce the general importance of party patterns, particularly as causal agents, and consequently would direct attention to what are believed to be underlying bases for electoral competition. In this perspective, bipartism, however strong the remaining preference for it, can be seen to fit only some circumstance but not others. And it can also be seen to take radically different forms—not just the usually cited standard British form of highly organized, cohesive, and programmatic parties, alternating in governing, but also the American form of loose, accommodating, and heterogeneous parties that must often, under the separation-of-powers formula, share in governing. Or two major parties, although much closer to the British variety in their organization, cohesion, and program commitments, may be perceived to share governing power in the kind of coalition that lasted for two decades in postwar Austria (Secher, 1958). Thus the two-party pattern, which even in all of its forms taken together is by no means prevalent, falls well short of characterizing democratic electoral competition when considered only in the standard British form. It is that form, however, that has really been preferred most often by political scientists in the United States as well as elsewhere.

Turning away from this matter of preference for a given competitive pattern allows one to concentrate on trying to understand the factors responsible for the various patterns. This partly involves the question of what makes for a certain number of parties rather than for another number, but it also involves the broader question of the nature of electoral cleavages even if one is not interested in the relation of cleavages to the number of parties. An example of the attempt to deal with the first question has already been cited with reference to the largely economic basis for two-party rather than one-party politics in American states. There are other American studies analyzing the relevance of urbanization for the maintenance of two-party competition, but there is no agreement about the degree of urbanization, if any, necessary to sustain such competition (Eulau, 1957; Gold and Schmidhauser, 1960). Certainly some

American states as well as other constituencies have had periods of two-party competition without large urban populations, and it could even be argued that until such populations become so large as to be entirely dominant they might provide a sufficient base for an urban party facing a rural party in a given state. A significant urban-rural cleavage could exist only as long as there was a substantial population for each of the two interests.

It is not, however, this kind of cleavage that is usually meant by the connection of urbanization with party competition. Rather than a cleavage between urban and rural interests, the more regularly discussed cleavage is between two primarily urban groups: one composed mainly of wage earners and the other centered about middle and upper income earners. This is the familiar class cleavage assumed to characterize an electorate at a given stage of industrial development. For this cleavage to provide the basis for party competition there must be not only a sufficient number enfranchised to vote in each broadly defined class but also leaders available to build a party representing each class. Usually the leadership emerges once there are sufficient numbers of potential voters of a given class. But situations have existed, even over substantial periods of time, in which a fairly large working class does not have effective enough leadership for much of a party organization, especially at a local or regional level. In other words, large numbers of industrial wage earners appear not to be a sufficient cause for a major working-class party to exist. There are important advanced industrial areas where such a party does not exist in the usual sense of the term although significant class voting may nevertheless be found. On the other hand, large numbers of wage earners, especially manual workers, obviously constitute a necessary condition for the existence of a working-class party in competition with a largely middle-class party, linked to entrepreneurial interests in a capitalist economy, or with any other parties. This is not to say that there must be a large working class in order to have two-party or multiparty competition. Interparty competition has operated in a meaningful way on bases other than the now-familiar class lines. Nineteenth-century American politics provides abundant examples, and so does the party pattern of Canada.

Nevertheless class cleavage has been widely regarded as by far the most important, if not the entirely dominant, basis for interparty competition in advanced industrial nations. This view prevailed especially during the middle decades of this century. Many studies illustrate this emphasis. The degree of class voting, that is, the association of class status with party preference, has been found in a careful comparative study to vary in descending order in Britain, Australia, the United States, and Canada, but important enough in each case to be used as the benchmark for analysis of other factors (Alford, 1963). More pointedly for Britain's party links to the class cleavage, there are two books that seek to explain why approximately one-third of the working class does *not* vote for the Labour party but chooses the Conservative party instead (Nordlinger, 1967; McKenzie and Silver, 1968). Another recent and broader study of British voting behavior suggests that this old Tory working-class vote is diminishing in proportion as, in succeeding generations, the Labour party attracts higher percentages of its "natural" working-class following (Butler and Stokes, 1969, pp. 109–11). The evidence, it should be noted, is not at odds with the belief that the intensity of class antagonism is decreasing with relative affluence or with the fact that the industrial working class is itself a declining (though still a very large) percentage of the total population of an advanced Western society.

The findings of class-based voting in Britain, despite some doubts raised by electoral behavior in the 1970s, remain important. But Britain may be unusual in having now or in the recent past no other broad cleavage rivalling that of class. To project the British experience to other nations is risky in at least those instances in which other electoral cleavages remain important. Those cleavages cannot be assumed to be giving way to class. On the other hand, no one denies that there is a great deal of class-based voting in Western Europe and the United States (especially in northern industrial states). There is little to suggest its long-run diminution, although there are data indicating a decline from 1955 to 1965 in class-based partisanship among voters in Germany, France, and Italy, but not in Britain (Abramson, 1971). The better-known, current view is to stress an impressive stability in the class-based behavior of voters in Western nations since 1945 (Rose and Urwin, 1969 and 1970). Of course the class voting varies not only in degree but also in the number of parties dividing the vote. What is thought to be general is a large and significant correlation of voting behavior with socioeconomic class stratification. Thus there is even one bold and imaginative attempt to predict how Spanish citizens would vote, if they could vote in a free election, by assuming that Spain's socioeconomic classes would follow much the same broad party cleavages as those followed by Italian voters of similar socioeconomic classes (Linz, 1967).

The consequence of even a considerable emphasis on the generality of class-based voting need not be the neglect of other factors relating to electoral divisions. Indeed it is often the starting point for an analysis of factors accounting for variation in degree of class voting between different nations or constituencies as well as for the occasional absence of class voting altogether. Thus the relatively low correlation of class with party voting in Canadian national elections leads to explanations of regionalism, religion, ethnicity, and language. Similarly in the United States most of these factors, plus those of race and related historical events, are used to account for voting that often, in regions and states, deviates from a projected national pattern derived from class divisions. It must be admitted, however, that there is a tendency in this approach to treat nonclass voting as though it were the consequence of residual and diminishingly important factors; in a kind of democratized Marxism, the cleavage between middle and working classes is assumed to be naturally and eventually paramount in an industrial society. Two disadvantages can flow from this approach. The first is that it downgrades the long-run relative importance of nonclass factors; it really also downgrades those class factors involving different and more complex stratification than that of propertyless wage earners versus property owners and associated middle and upper income groups. The second disadvantage, while more hypothetical, is that the simple division between two classes may be less characteristic of the highly developed societies of the late twentieth century than of societies at a slightly earlier time when industrialization was both newer and more dominant with respect to employment. In other words, the electoral division between working class and middle class, even if still demonstrable on a large scale, might be a declining force in a postindustrial society.

A treatment of socially derived cleavages in relation to party alignments which avoids the indicated disadvantages of strictly class-centered analysis is presented by Lipset and Rokkan (1967). In their view, four cleavage lines help to explain differences in Western democratic party patterns. Besides the owner-worker cleavage, making for similarity among the national patterns, significant cleavages are found to exist along center-periphery, state-church, and land-industry lines. Each of these is already familiar from well-known European or American experience except perhaps the center-periphery cleavage that Rokkan himself amply illustrates from Norwegian political history (Chapter 8). The remarkable feature of these party patterns in Western Europe generally is that each appears to have been established by the 1920s and to have endured into the 1960s, even to the extent of reappearing in Italy, Germany, France, and Austria after substantial interruptions during periods of suppressed electoral competition. The effect, as Lipset and Rokkan stress, is to have party alternatives and often party organizations that are now much older than most members of the electorate. They may seem to have an anachronistic quality, dating as they do from a different time.

If this is so in Western Europe, what about the even older American parties? It should follow that the party alternatives would derive from the cleavages of a much earlier time. In a way, something like this is the thesis of an analysis of American party development (Chambers, 1967), in which the whole century after 1865 is regarded as a derivative stage in which the Republican and Democratic parties, already in a virtually completed pattern, simply adapted to circumstances first through the patronage machine, then through progressive procedural reform, and finally (after 1932) through the politics of welfare and the mass media. This thesis does not claim that the electoral cleavages between the two parties have remained stable over the whole century in the manner suggested for Western European alignments during a forty-year period. The socioeconomic bases of American parties shifted, especially as the industrial working class became heavily Democratic in those northern states that had been Republican after the Civil War, and as various racial, ethnic, and regional alignments were substantially modified (Sundquist, 1973). Yet the point remains well taken that at least a great deal of the American party pattern is a very old one (Burnham, 1970). And it would not be difficult to make the case for the persistence of much of the electoral alignment, as in Europe, over about forty years.

Such persistence is likely to be deplored by many critics who see almost everything else, including the relevant governmental policy questions, so drastically changed in the last forty years as to require similarly great changes in party politics. On the other side, the persistence of electoral alignment, since it does not have to be equated with the maintenance of outdated policy positions or even of old organizational procedures, can be welcomed as a sign of democratic stability. Moreover, what is called persistence or stability need not imply a completely static electoral behavior; at a minimum, small, short-run voting shifts are assumed to take place, and they often are sufficient to displace one party's officeholders with another's, especially but not only in a two-party pattern. Or the evidently persistent electoral alignment may conceal certain important changes. For example it has been shown that American congressional voting patterns, while still subject to less national and more constituency influence than Britain's parliamentary elections, have nonetheless changed markedly in a nationalizing direction over the last half century. A careful analysis of variance between presidential and congressional voting leads to the conclusion that there has been a "secular decline of constituency forces" in the United States (Stokes, 1967, p. 202). If continued, as seems likely, this trend will almost certainly have a great impact on American party politics. Various cleavages of a local or regional kind will have been largely displaced by others of a national character, and so each party will, in that event, be based much more largely on a national electorate and less on a coalition of local and regional electorates. The movement in this direction may be too slow and halting for those who are ready for radical change and whose impatience with the existing pattern is hardly lessened by knowledge of historical trends established by statistical analysis. Nevertheless any such trend is evidence of a type of important change that can take place beneath the surface of an apparently long-established electoral alignment.

One likely explanation of the slowness of change in electoral behavior is based on the party itself as a factor in maintaining voter loyalty in successive elections and even in successive generations. Once in existence as a substantial force, a given political party is obviously a factor in determining how citizens vote. The party label alone is an influence, and so is any organized following committed to active campaigning for labelled candidates. Even a small organization ordinarily seeks self-perpetuation, which, in the process, helps to sustain the party's electoral support. It is in this context that the argument is made for considering party as a key independent variable determining election patterns rather than as only or mainly the result of socioeconomic circumstances (Sartori, 1969). Certainly analysts of voting behavior have amassed impressive evidence for the significance of party identification. They have done so especially in the United States, where the strength of the identification has most often been doubted. Elsewhere it is unusual to question the primacy of the party label; voters in Western Europe are simply assumed to vote according to their party preferences rather than to a personal or other identification of candidates. The question arises and can be explored in the United States because at least some voters are believed to use nonparty criteria. But at least until the 1970s, their numbers, while substantial, were found to be a small proportion of the electorate (Miller and Stokes, 1963; McPhee and Ferguson, 1962). Party identifiers, while declining slightly in 1968 and apparently more sharply after 1970, ordinarily compose the bulk of the American electorate (Merelman, 1970). And until now a particular American party identification, once established, has not readily changed (Campbell *et al.,* 1960). Moreover, in a pioneering cross-national sample survey, a significantly larger percentage of American respondents identified with parties than did French voters (Converse and Dupeux, 1962). On the other hand, more American identifiers than French or other European identifiers may not regularly vote their identifications (Campbell and Valen, 1961; Valen and Katz, 1964); Americans split their tickets or otherwise deviate from their supposed identification. Nonparty voting is encouraged by the structure of American government. Having so many offices to fill in elections is one such structural feature. Another is that American voters choose their executives, notably president, governor, and mayor, to hold office separately from elected legislators—that is, with an independent electoral mandate. Not only is the individual quality of the candidate for executive office thus likely to be salient, but there is really no compelling reason for voters to follow their usual party preference for executive as for legislative candidates when the governmental system can function with an executive of one party and a legislative majority of another. Plainly, then, ticket splitting might become both general and habitual, as some observers believe to be happening in the 1970s, along with a so-far unarrested decline in party identification during the same period.

ORGANIZATION

The commonly understood referent for the term "party organization" is the structure of leaders and followers beyond the strictly governmental apparatus. Of course, government officeholders may also occupy important positions in those external organizations: the president of the United States is the leader of his party outside of government as well as in it. And there are party organizations of officeholders, which often antedate the external organizations and remain crucial in policymaking. Parliamentary and congressional parties or caucuses are familiar examples. Separating them from the analysis of external organizations is not to minimize their consequence. On the contrary, the governmental parties can well be considered more durably consequential in competitive democratic politics. It is simply convenient analytically to start with the external organizations. One reason is that many political scientists consider these organizations to be the characteristically modern feature of parties, marking the response of political leaders, often already in public office, to an emerging mass electorate whose votes must be sought. This approaches the definitional suggestion, put aside here, that a party can be said to exist, in any modern sense of the term, only when it does have a substantial external organization. In any such perspective attention is naturally focused on the importance of the organization (Schlesinger, 1965). Interestingly, during recent decades scholarly study of this kind has been less prominent in the United States than in Western Europe, and for the very good reason that the really large external organizations of the mid-twentieth century have been European, including British, phenomena rather than American. It is true that the earlier and occasionally persistent patronage machines of American cities have been studied (Gosnell, 1937; Peel, 1935) and that later more ideological organizational efforts in certain American constituencies have received attention (Wilson, 1962). But in the United States there is simply much less to study as long as the European-style mass-membership party, organized nationally, does not exist. This situation has led many American political scientists to join their European colleagues in arguing that the mass-membership party should exist in the United States.

The best-known work proposing as well as projecting the spread of the mass-membership party is by Duverger (1954), and it relies heavily on the growth and apparent dominance of this kind of large-scale organization in the postwar politics of Western Europe. Duverger's case was bolstered by trends in this direction over the previous half century and also by a broader perception that the modern age generally demands large-scale organization for any substantial achievement. So he could contrast what he observed of mid-century European parties, especially in France, with the more individualistic politics of an earlier parliamentary experience. The contrast was not only to the period before the mass franchise but more particularly to a slightly later time in most European nations, before the development of major socialist working-class parties. These were the parties that Duverger believed to have pioneered in building mass-membership organizations, presumably out of the necessity imposed on a working-class movement to mobilize its numbers against the other resources of middle and upper class parties. Then, in what he called a "contagion from the left," the working-class parties so demonstrated the superiority of mass organization as to require nonworking class parties to develop a similar mechanism instead of relying almost solely on a cadre of politicians and notables (Duverger, 1954, p. xxvii). As May points out, Duverger's classification is more complex than this mass-cadre distinction, especially in its presentation of an organizational type characteristic of certain nondemocratic parties and most highly developed in the cell-based structure of large Communist parties (May, 1969). But it is chiefly for the emphasized modernity of the mass-membership party, as opposed to the supposedly obsolete cadre party, that Duverger's organizational analysis is known and understood.

The kind of mass-membership party that Duverger and many of his contemporaries describe and to a great extent also advocate is not just large. In addition it is characterized by definite programmatic, if not doctrinal, commitments and by mechanisms for members to articulate policy preferences, choose leaders, select candidates for public office, campaign for these candidates in general elections, and otherwise politically participate in an organized fashion. There are supposed to be large numbers of activists, or militants, among the still larger total of dues-paying members, and their input of ideas and energies is to appear at each organizational level, from the local constituency to the national arena, through representational bodies, if not directly. Thus the modern mass-membership party is distinguished from the once-prevalent American patronage organization. The latter, while a good deal more than skeletal, seems a kind of extension of the cadre-type organization because its members have been mainly public officeholders, aspiring public officeholders, or clearly linked in other ways to the spoils of office. Moreover the patronage machine has not been organized to encourage (or even allow) its members, no matter how actively they campaigned, to make party policies—for the very good reason that the patronage machine by definition is not programmatic. It is understandable, then, that this American organization, far from being the type desired by party reformers, has been rejected by those who wanted the United States to have parties with organized European-style memberships (Schattschneider, 1942). Only well after the demise of most of the machines did political scientists begin to see their relative virtue (Banfield and Wilson, 1963, p. 345; Greenstein, 1970, p. 62). At least they mobilized large numbers of voters, many of them newly immigrated citizens, at a time when no other nation had yet faced a comparable task.

It can even be argued that patronage organizations have been the functional equivalents of the later European working-class parties, both of them developing at a relatively early stage of the mass franchise and then remaining in existence well after serving the original purpose of mobilizing huge categories of new voters. It would follow in this perspective that the European mass-membership party, despite its apparent dominance at mid-century, should now be undergoing a slow decline as the American patronage machines had a few decades sooner. This possibility, which reverses Duverger's projection, is explored at length in another place (Epstein, 1967, Chapters 5, 6, 9). Here it is enough to suggest that the thesis, while surely inconclusive at this point, rests on the evidence of some decline in memberships of several European (including British) parties during the late 1950s and the 1960s, the continued absence of large-scale membership parties in the United States (which cannot be viewed forever as politically retarded, especially in light of its early experience with the mass franchise), and the relative electoral success of cadre-type, catchall parties (with ad hoc rather than large stable membership structures) in Western Europe as well as the United States. Modern means of communication, preeminently television, may be displacing the campaigning methods associated with membership organizations, be they programmatic or patronage in their base. Simultaneously the socialist ideology and the working-class solidarity on which the European mass-membership party originally rested may have declined in intensity, at least for large numbers of workers, so that the party becomes organizationally less imposing even while it prospers electorally.

Nothing, however, indicates the early disappearance in Europe of this prototype mass-membership organization or of that kind of organization generally. Even if it is not the wave of the future that it seemed to Duverger and even if it has passed its peak of relative importance, it retains a durable bureaucratic structure, especially where the mass-membership party serves many purposes in addition to electoral ones. These purposes are not merely social, although those too can be impressive. They are also economic. Parties may operate businesses, and certainly several of the most successful European parties are so closely tied to trade unions that they can count on a durable, if no longer growing, membership. Furthermore, a party's political candidates, in or out of public office, continue to have the incentive to maintain membership organizations. Even if the campaign efforts of these organizations are less influential than earlier, they remain useful enough so that politicians surely prefer their availability. Despite the possibility of reaching voters through the mass media, a candidate might as well also have as large and as effective an organization as can be mustered. Accordingly, American politicians plainly use any existing party organization, be it a residual patronage machine, a new membership group, or something in between, although many candidates have had to become accustomed to building their own ad hoc campaign followings because of the absence of an effective mechanism provided by a party as such.

There is probably a tendency to perceive American party organization in its postpatronage stage as almost nonexistent when contrasted to the European mass-membership party. This is especially likely when the contrast is to the British Labour and Conservative parties, whose millions of dues-paying members are organized—from wards, through parliamentary constituencies, to annual representative conferences on a national level (McKenzie, 1963). Admittedly American parties generally do not fulfill such organizational criteria. Only occasionally in certain states, or parts of states, are there regular dues-paying memberships at all. And there is as yet, despite a Democratic proposal, no national party membership in any literal sense. Yet paying dues, after all, is only one organizational method. We assume it to be *the* method not just because of

the European party pattern but because everywhere most nonparty groups—
trade unions, business associations, and social clubs—are similarly organized.
Thus, "real" American party organizations were seen to begin only during the
1950s, when strongly programmatic dues-paying clubs, outside of the old statutory party structures, appeared to flourish in California, Wisconsin, and a few
other constituencies. They were observed, however, to be almost entirely middle class, whether Democratic or Republican, and also to be limited in their
growth (after an original impetus) and in their capacity to spread much beyond their first areas of development (Wilson, 1962; Sorauf, 1963).

Granting the now-apparent, although uncertain, limitations of these mass
dues-paying efforts, organized membership still exists in various forms in American parties. It may fall short of a mass dues-paying base and yet have enrolled
campaign workers in sufficient numbers so as to be considerably more than a
skeletal structure. This kind of organization is fully described and analyzed
for metropolitan Detroit, where Republicans and Democrats both maintain
fairly substantial precinct-based campaign networks despite the absence of any
large amount of patronage (Eldersveld, 1964). It is true that this study also
showed that there was doubt about the efficacy of the organization and especially about the adequacy of nonpatronage incentives. But such doubts must
almost always exist even when there are mass dues-paying memberships of a
strongly ideological character. Perhaps no nonmaterial incentives can be as reliable as the old patronage arrangement. Strictly social incentives, involving
group solidarity, may be inadequate to win and maintain membership activity,
especially between election campaigns, when various nonparty associations appear more attractive. Programmatic or ideological commitments, while effective
at certain times and places, may not assure continuity of organizational effort
when the commitments, as seems likely, are compromised by party leaders or
otherwise frustrated by political, often electoral, exigencies. A different kind of
incentive, however, may account for at least some active members at or near
the leadership level. Actual and potential candidates for elective public office
plainly have an interest in maintaining some degree of organization. So do
those who aspire to certain appointive offices that have remained outside of
civil service requirements. And others sufficiently enjoy, perhaps only honorifi-
cally, a sense of proximity to power and public affairs so that they maintain an
organizational effort for this purpose. The types of incentives, it is plain, help
account for variations in organization as in political participation generally
(Payne, 1968, pp. 5–24).

Accompanying the American party organizations, built on these several
bases, are certain structures prescribed by state laws. The consequence is the
statutory party, as distinguished in certain states from a voluntary organization
of dues-paying members which calls itself a party but functions extralegally.
In many states the statutory party is the only party, and it may or may not
include within it a membership of some kind. The very existence of the statu-

tory party reflects the nearly unique legal recognition and regulation of parties in the United States. American parties, while gaining official status by name on election ballots, in effect pay for that status by legal stipulation not only of their nominating procedures but also of their own internal arrangements and financing. When regulations are especially constricting the statutory parties cease to be effective campaign organizations, being superseded in this role by ad hoc candidate organizations, if not also by extralegal parties (Hennessy, 1968, p. 11). Yet the statutory party remains the official structure, having at least a cadre of officers who often, as described for North Carolina, maintain effective small groups of campaign workers (Crotty, 1968). Technically the statutory party is what most American partisan voters "belong to" when they register as Republicans or Democrats, when they merely cast votes in the primary election to nominate party candidates, or when they elect convention delegates who will subsequently nominate party candidates. And it is these party voters to whom party leaders—at precinct, ward, city, county, district, and state levels—are supposed to be responsible, usually through legally established but little used official election procedures.

Associated with the American statutory party, whether or not it includes an active campaign organization, is the party label that appears on the election ballot. Control of that label is crucial as long as large numbers of voters are accustomed to choosing candidates according to party preference. It is possible for candidates to seize the label by winning primary nominating elections although they do not simultaneously control the statutory party; notably this can be accomplished through individual ad hoc organizations or extralegal parties in constituencies in which the statutory party is a mere shell without any campaigning capacity to control its own nominating outcomes. Generally, however, control of the label and of the statutory party will go together since even an organizational shell is likely to be taken over by those who secure the party label (if they did not control the statutory party to begin with).

There are at least a few legally-based political advantages in securing the official party machinery. Often it is curiously easy for previously inexperienced citizens to do so. Of course, this hardly holds in the case of a statutory party whose organization is large and effective, as Chicago's Democratic party has remained, with its still-massive patronage, or as the Detroit area's Democratic party has become on the basis of its trade union connections. But in many places the party organization, especially but not only that prescribed by statute, has so few participating members that its leaders can readily be displaced by a relatively small but determined mobilization of activists to secure majorities at a few critical meetings. The very absence of a dues-paying membership arrangement probably simplifies a takeover since ordinary voter status, plus a party pledge, is then likely to be enough to qualify participants. To be sure, something worthwhile has to be at stake to produce a takeover. Control of the selection of delegates to nominating conventions, including state and state-based presidential nominating conventions, is one incentive. Another is control of any organizational campaign resources. If contests of this kind are limited in frequency and in the number of involved citizens, as they are widely believed to be, the explanation need not be ascribed only to political apathy. Often there may be little significance in controlling a party organization; certainly this is so when only a shell exists and it is more convenient, legally or politically, to conduct political campaigns through other means.

These other means deserve attention. They include organizations that are not strictly party organizations. Indeed it would be strange if American politics, unlike other activities in the United States, made less use of organizational techniques than did European politics. What seems probable is that the techniques are simply different. For one thing, American politics is characterized by a larger *number* of campaign organizations. In addition to whatever party organizations exist, with fewer and less regularized memberships than the European, there are many campaign organizations built around individual candidacies, occasionally more than one organization for a given individual. Each of these, it is true, is ordinarily ad hoc—that is, it exists for a single candidate and also often for a single campaign. Even if revivable and actually revived from election to election, there is no appreciable intercampaign organization. But at election time, as Americans can readily perceive by the sponsorship of campaigns, the candidate-centered organizations are alive and active at every level of constituency. They are characteristic of general elections as, of course, they are of contested primary elections. They do not entirely supersede party organizations, and they often overlap and collaborate to a considerable extent in their general election activities, notably in canvassing. Money raising, however, can be competitive both between individual candidate organizations and between these and the party's organization. Occasionally a party organization is strong enough to preempt virtually all of the effective fund raising in behalf of its candidates (Adamany, 1969), and the Republican party in many northern states has attempted at least to unite fund raising for its candidates (Heard, 1960, pp. 214–24).

The second organizational technique strongly characteristic of American parties is large-scale financing of political campaigns. No one has ever suggested American backwardness in this respect. Membership dues have seldom been necessary, or forthcoming on a sufficient scale, to finance either party or individual campaigns. Most of the time fairly substantial contributions have been made by numerous but not massive numbers of donors. The very large individual amount (often distributed among several committees) has been important and so have less spectacular but more frequently received sums from middle-income sources. Recently small sums from very large numbers have been collected by issue-oriented presidential candidates and some others. Such contributions will now be encouraged by federal legislation that limits the size of individual contributions, allows tax deductions, and provides advantages by way of public funds to match small contributions to presidential primary candidates. But any new reliance on numerous donors to individual campaigns does not require a regularized set of party contributors approximating dues-paying members. It is true that financing campaigns from many contributors is likelier to mean a greater organizational effort than that needed to raise funds from only a few large contributors. At any rate, individual candidates, like parties that run campaigns, must have staffs and offices not just to collect but also to spend money, however it is raised. But these staffs and offices, except for volunteer canvassers who may be recruited for particular campaigns, involve a small number of people who decide how even large sums are spent for mass-media advertising and for the specialized professional and technical services that can now be purchased from existing firms. Although the party or candidate campaign organization is thus limited in size, it would be a mistake to regard it as less significant or less effective than the traditional membership apparatus. Campaigns do reach voters without having to rely on a regularized enrollment of members in a party. Financing the vote-getting effort may well be facilitated by the adoption in the United States of the already established European practice of public funding of campaigns.

The case for membership organizations, it ought to be said, never rested only on their relative efficacy in winning elections even when the claim for that efficacy was made. Rather, or in addition, it has been claimed that active participation in party affairs by substantial numbers of citizens is itself a virtue in a democratic political system. Whether a mass membership helps a party secure public offices is, in this perspective, an incidental matter. The valued participation is not primarily campaign activity, although it is assumed to follow, but the discussion and development of party programs and policies. Plainly the basic premise here is that a party should have a broad program, perhaps amounting to an ideology, and that it should also, at election time, commit itself to governmental policies it would enact in order to carry out its program. One could believe that a party should so behave even without a mass membership, but it is really unlikely that a cadre organization, consisting principally of aspiring officeholders and their auxiliaries, would be programmatic. Thus American parties nationally and to a large extent generally are regarded by their critics as deficient because they have neither programs nor highly organized memberships. Developing the latter is advocated as a means to achieve coherent party programs (Burns, 1963, p. 323).

For even if programs without memberships are conceivable, they would lack the legitimacy associated with their development by large numbers of active participants. Furthermore, these organized participants are perceived as capable of requiring the party's elected officeholders to observe programmatic commitments or at least of exerting strong pressure in behalf of those commitments when governmental policies are being made. The larger and the more fully organized the membership, the more effective such pressure is thought to be. The prototype organization, in this respect, has been the socialist working-class party, whether its membership is in party branches or more heavily in affiliated unions (as in Great Britain). Substantial numbers are involved, if only to choose delegates who will develop programs and policies at regional or national meetings. And these numerous participants seem to represent a majority or potential majority of the whole electorate insofar as the working class itself constitutes the predominant interest. Thus the claim for organizational programs and policymaking is asserted most strongly and definitely in behalf of a class whose party began as a movement of nongovernmental forces seeking to gain power from established parties associated with other classes.

The British Labour party is frequently cited as a leading example, but there is considerable controversy over the actual influence of its large and highly organized membership in the making of policy. A very strong case is presented in the leading study of British parties that Labour's external organization is much less consequential (and ought to be) in determining policies of parliamentary party leaders, especially when Labour constitutes the government, than party doctrine proclaims (McKenzie, 1963). Even when the British Labour party along with the Conservative party is treated as significantly more coherent in its policymaking than an American party, it is not clear that the external organization as such is primarily responsible for this coherence (Beer, 1965). The case is fairly crucial since American party reformers have often cited British experience as a favorable precedent for building membership organizations that will be associated with commitments to programs and policies. Therefore, skeptical critics of this kind of party reform, whether or not they think it theoretically desirable, argue that evidence from Britain indicates severe practical limits to the usefulness of organizational policymaking.

These limits, it can also be argued, are becoming more clearly apparent as the socialist working-class party, while not diminishing as an electoral force, becomes more like other parties. There may then be a smaller total membership or a less active membership accompanying a lessened intensity of class feeling as well as a smaller proportion of manual workers in the total population. The mass-membership party even looks a little like the product of an earlier time in advanced Western nations (Barnes, 1968). An increasingly middle-class population, salaried and formally educated, is thought to be less likely to be mobilized or to want to or need to be mobilized in regularized party organizations. This does not mean, it has to be emphasized, that middle-class citizens and others as well are not politically mobilized at all. They may indeed be organized in many ways at least as effective as the mass-membership parties. In addition to the ad hoc individual candidate organizations and the financial contribution arrangements previously noted, there is the highly meaningful political participation through interest-group affiliations (Wilson, 1974). Such participation seems a most direct means to influence governmental policy.

CANDIDATE SELECTION

Closely related to the topic of party organization is the method of selecting party candidates for elective public offices. Candidate selection can be distinguished from the broader subject of leadership recruitment. Most of the recruitment for appointive governmental positions is now done through civil service procedures with which parties have little or no connection. Even with respect to elective offices, parties are only among the agencies through which leaders are recruited. And there are many aspects of such recruitment, including social class and personality, that make the subject of leadership recruitment much broader than a party focus would suggest.

Candidate selection is the aspect of recruitment that conventionally and analytically belongs to a discussion of parties. This is so despite the fact that parties do not always monopolize the selection of candidates. Obviously they do not do so when there are elections that are nonpartisan, in fact as well as in law. Nor do they really "select" candidates in any organizational sense when individual candidates, probably backed by organized followers of their own, are able to win official nominations (that is, the party label) through primary election campaigns. Candidates can then be said either to have selected themselves or to have been selected by party voters acknowledging no organizational tie. Or, in a less individualized but still unregularized party process, candidates are often correctly perceived to have been chosen by formal or informal groups of leaders who may be in or out of any existing party organization. When the effective selectors are the official or unofficial managers of a party, as has been true of patronage machines, then there is certainly an organizational determination. The choice is often subject subsequently to the approval of a party convention, itself plainly an organizational mechanism, or of a primary electorate, but as long as the leadership's choice regularly prevails even in a primary, as it does in some constituencies, there is good reason to consider an organization, however loose, to be effectively in control of the selection process. Considerable American experience suggests that this occurs even in the absence of patronage and of anything like the old-style party based on patronage. But where it appears is by no means universal or constant. In many American states and sections of other states effective party leadership does not exist (Key, 1956, p. 271). Not only does this allow individuals, interest groups, or newspapers to control the bestowal of the party label, but it also leads to situations in which a minority party has no candidates at all for many offices. Party leaders, even of skeletal organizations, usually help to fill the tickets if they do nothing else.

So far the context is narrowly American, and it ought to be stressed that candidate selection in the United States is almost unique among Western democratic nations. American parties are not supposed to control their candidate labels as ordinary private associations might be expected to do and as parties elsewhere are able to do. This flows partly from the already observed fact that American parties have an official public status accompanied by legal regulations. The direct primary is the mark of this status and regulation since voters belonging in no usual sense to an organized party can bestow the party label on particular candidates. But even the old American party convention delegates, who selected candidates, were themselves often chosen by rather loosely defined adherents. Significantly, the usual American term for the selection process, whether by primary or convention, is "nomination" of party candidates. It means the award of the party label for the general election ballot. For almost all American offices except the presidency this now requires a primary election. Any organized party support for a candidate contesting a primary is called an "endorsement," and it may in some constituencies virtually settle the outcome or in other situations be merely one of several factors influencing the result. The organized party, in other circumstances, may choose to make no endorsements at all and simply stand aside ready to campaign for those who win the nominations.

The equivalent elsewhere of American party nomination is simply (to use the British terms) the selection, or adoption, of party candidates, which each party, as a private organization, settles for itself. British practice is notably clear-cut in this respect, but other Western European parties operate similarly despite occasional legal regulation of procedures. The point is that the party is assumed to have a regularized membership that chooses, on its own or through its leaders, the candidates it will support for elective public office. ("Nomination" in Britain is not a party process but rather the official filing of candidacy by an individual who may or may not have been selected by a party as its candidate.) In Britain and elsewhere the parties selecting candidates vary greatly in their size and structure. There may not even be the substantial regularized membership that tends to be assumed. The major Canadian parties, for example, have ordinarily had only loosely defined external organizations at the constituency level, without uniform dues-paying memberships, and yet party leaders and activists of one kind or another in each constituency have effectively chosen candidates (Scarrow, 1964; Engelmann and Schwartz, 1967, p. 167). Even in Britain, with elaborate dues-paying organizations, some constituency associations have limited membership and activity, and yet they too select candidates in the sense that a small number of leaders do so. These are not the typical or the most important cases, as revealed in a broad analysis of the British process of candidate selection (Ranney, 1965). Especially when the selection is meaningful (that is, when it can lead to an election victory based on a party's majority or potential majority in a given constituency), there is a representative basis for the leadership committee or executive body, consisting of several dozen activists, which effectively makes the choice for the local party members. Regardless, however, of the size of the membership base, the important point remains that organized partisans are the selectors.

It should be noted that these partisans belong to local branches of national parties and so, despite occasional divergencies for either local or other reasons, they act customarily as national party members in selecting candidates for the British Parliament. They do so without being subject to strong central party administrative direction but only to rather gently offered advice except in rare instances (Ranney, 1965). The point has an importance for American students since it indicates that the crucially different feature of British candidate selection is not a much greater centralization of decision-making relative to American practice. The central party organization in Britain does not dictate local candidate selection any more than a comparable authority does in the United States; at most it might be said to exert a somewhat greater influence. Elsewhere, too, central control does not appear crucial to an achievement of working agreement among a party's successful candidates (Ozbudin, 1970, p. 339). The significant element is the difference in the nature of the respective local or constituency selectors: in the British case (as is generally true elsewhere as well) selectors are leaders of organized national partisans, in contrast to the various party and nonparty elements that prevail as selectors in the United States. Understandably the American arrangement is uncongenial to reformers who want to develop a national or a state party whose candidates will be firmly committed to a common program and policies. Having organized partisans to select such candidates seems a means to the desired end, but these partisans would themselves have to share the common objectives, as do British activists, unless, as is most improbable, they were subject to some kind of central direction.

Building a sufficiently monolithic membership party in a nation as large and diverse as the United States seems a formidable task. Even if such a party existed, so that it endorsed candidates, there would be no certainty that the candidates would subsequently secure the party's nomination—in other words, really become the party's officially selected candidates on the general election ballot. The American primary, however limited its use on many occasions, does provide an opportunity for voters to reject the choices of programmatic partisans as well as of machine bosses. It is an open question whether the primary is thus the cause of party fragmentation, by discouraging organizations that cannot readily control their own candidate selection processes, or whether it is itself one consequence of an American preference for relatively open political arrangements and for less exclusive political reliance on a party organization as such. In any event, the American methods of candidate selection, taken as a whole, are surely consistent with the uncertain organizational status of American parties. The point is well-illustrated even in presidential nominating processes; the national party conventions consist of many forces besides organized partisans. (Polsby and Wildavsky, 1971). It is fair to assume that more fully effective party organizations would exert greater control of candidate selection. Or, stated differently, really large numbers of organized partisans would have a better chance to win primary elections for their candidates.

GOVERNING ROLE

Whether or not elected public officeholders bearing a given party label are effectively the agents of an organized external membership through its control of candidate selection, they maintain an organization of their own within the government. This refers mainly to the caucus of all legislators acknowledging a certain party label, almost always the same one under which they were elected, but there is also a sense of party organization within the executive branch of government. This organization may be linked to the legislative organization bearing the same party label and exerting leadership over it, or it may represent a largely separate force. The point is that public officeholders have a mechanism enabling them to act together as a party in the government (or, more simply, as a governmental party, be it majority or minority). They would need such a mechanism not only to act as agents for an external party organization but also to act in concert on their own volition or on any other basis. Within an executive branch, considered to be independent in a separation-of-powers structure, the means would seem to be presidential direction of a hierarchical kind. In a legislative body, however, a more clearly collective method is required in any governmental system. Legislative representatives elected under a major party's label are sufficiently numerous to impose the need for a degree of organization. Thus universally there are legislative parties. Within a parliamentary system a party, if constituting a majority or a portion of a coalition majority, provides the cabinet officers. Under the American separation-of-powers formula a majority legislative party provides only the organizational leadership of the chamber. As we know, it may or may not bear the same party label as the executive branch's leadership, and even if it does there is no overwhelming likelihood that it will provide consistent and full support for the policies of that executive leadership.

This structurally based difference needs fuller exploration, but before that it is useful to say a little more about the general nature of the party's position in government. Not only does party almost always appear where there are legislative bodies, including those that are competitively elected and those that are not, but historically, as noted earlier, a party of legislative (and to some extent executive) officeholders appears often to have preceded the organization of external supporters in the electorate. The latter holds in two senses. First, many existing parties (although not most European socialist working-class parties) did literally start with groupings of officeholders sharing certain common interests and principles, on which basis they organized electoral support for themselves. Secondly, such groupings, especially in legislative bodies, existed for considerable periods of time without any substantial external organizations. The governmental party, therefore, can be said to have a basis of its own, presumably in the need for legislators and also executive officials to act together in regularly structured groups when seeking to manage public affairs or trying to conduct public business of any kind. An organized following of supporters may be highly useful, perhaps even necessary, for returning the members of the governmental party to office. But an external organization is hardly required in order for a party of officeholders to have reason to exist. This is not, however, to neglect the fact that an external organization does sometimes precede and so in a sense produce a governmental party. So it was with the British Labour party and many continental social-democratic parties that originated in popular movements outside of parliaments. Other kinds of parties have similar origins too, but none of this experience refutes the observation that governmental parties could maintain themselves now as in the past without substantial external organizations. Admittedly the practice is to have some regularly organized supporters if only because of their anticipated usefulness in election campaigns.

Looked at from the standpoint of the popularly elected legislative or executive members of a governmental party, the policy preferences of their organized followers are but one set of influences to be taken into account. This is true even in the most opportunistic sense unless the external organization controls effectively both the candidate selection process and the general election itself and is willing to use such controls to deny the candidacy of an incumbent who defies its policy preferences. These latter conditions are no doubt faced occasionally by individual officeholders, and in various forms. The external organization that controls the selection process may be national, regional, state, or local, or some combination of these. The national organization may even exert an influence for a policy preference different from that of an organization at the local or constituency level, and then the likely crucial question is which level of organization controls the selection.

In Britain, for example, the national external organization can, but rarely does, expel an M. P. from the party or otherwise prevent a constituency association from adopting him as a candidate. And a constituency association on its own can, but also rarely does, refuse to readopt an M. P. candidate (Ranney, 1965). Offending either or even both by violating their policy preferences is understandably troublesome, but hardly fatal for any large number of M.P.s. It cannot really be so for M.P.s whose departure from policy preferences of their party's external organizations is a collective decision of the parliamentary party, often following its own leadership. Here it is the governmental party that decides policy without yielding to the influence of its external organization, and, as has already been observed, this is a not uncommon British practice despite the claims of a programmatic mass membership. The British experience is most instructive at this point because in the Labour as in the Conservative case the parliamentary party, especially through its leaders, insists in principle that it should determine voting behavior in the House of Commons. Members of the parliamentary party (that is, all M.P.s bearing a given party label) ordinarily have no difficulty in following their own collective decision, or their own collective understanding to follow their leaders' decision, to vote as a bloc for or against a measure. But this is very different from following the preference of an externally organized mass membership. The most that is usually conceded on that score is a commitment to a general program favored by the mass membership and, of course, in practice to take into account the policy preferences expressed by what are, after all, the party's own supporters.

The operative principle here is of a constitutional or democratic representational character by no means peculiar to Britain. Publicly elected officeholders, even if selected by membership organizations, are supposed to represent voters generally, or at least that portion of the total electorate that voted for them. Many of the latter, while party-minded voters, are not among the smaller number of citizens who are organized party members and certainly not among the still smaller number of active party members. Therefore an elected representative, in disagreeing with organized party opinion, can claim to be taking into account the desires, explicit or presumed, of a broader public. So, it can be argued, should a governmental party take into account the desires and interests of voters outside of the party's external organization. Principle often unites with electoral expediency since the unorganized voters tend to include the marginal or swing voters who determine close elections. Furthermore those holding public office reasonably assert the need to develop policies in response to events or circumstances unknown to others. A governmental party and particularly its leadership may have more than one kind of reason for maintaining an independent policymaking role. But doing so often involves tensions with active organized external memberships, notably in labor and social-democratic parties, whose traditions appear to justify policymaking by mobilized activists.

What it would mean in practice to follow the policies of these activists is not certain. One cannot assume that activists would always or even most of the time insist on extremist policies much less acceptable to a broader public, although there appear to be instances of this kind. In the Fourth French Republic external party activists were perceived to have pulled their respective parties away from one another in the National Assembly, thus making coalition bargains more difficult to achieve and maintain (MacRae, 1967). Elsewhere, however, there is less systematic evidence on this point despite a widespread impression of disadvantages for a party's elected public officeholders and for the effectiveness of the political system in having to meet the demands of an organized external membership.

On the other side, any supposed advantage of an organized external membership for the achievement of a united policymaking governmental party is really no advantage at all when it is appreciated that a united policymaking governmental party exists without an organized external membership to help make the policy. Concluding otherwise is a false deduction from a comparison of American phenomena with what have been believed to prevail elsewhere. It is true that the United States does not have either generally cohesive legislative parties, certainly not national ones, or many large highly organized programmatic membership parties. It is also true that Britain and many European nations have both. But it does not follow that the membership organization produces the cohesive governmental party or that it is essential to such a governmental party's existence. British parliamentary parties were cohesive before there were large membership organizations (Lowell, 1901), and they are so without accepting direction from such organizations now that they do exist. The most that can reasonably be argued is that mass-membership organizations tend to reinforce or bolster the commitment of a governmental party's members to common policies, and even that argument becomes uncertain when the policies of the external organization are at odds with those chosen by the governmental party. In that case, the external influence works against cohesion in the governmental party since some of its legislative officeholders can find in the external organization's position a justification and support in breaking with the majority of their fellow officeholders. A different argument appears more valid but less relevant for the present discussion: a large-scale membership organization is feasible only as an affiliate of a governmental party that is collectively committed to policymaking on a broad programmatic basis. This does not suggest that such a governmental party will always have or absolutely needs a mass external organization but merely that the mass organization, in order to exist, needs the focus provided by a collectively committed group of officeholders or aspiring officeholders. The point is really an obvious one in light of the usual assumption that a mass membership is organized around programmatic objectives. Unless there is a governmental party capable of enough coherence to serve these objectives as a collective entity, what programmatic purpose of a citizen would be met by joining the external organization?

Returning to the view that a policymaking governmental party can and does exist without a mass-membership organization, we still are faced with the question of what explains its existence. Or, put in a more realistic form, what explains the substantial variation among governmental parties with respect to their capacity to engage in collective policymaking? All governmental parties play some role in policymaking even if sporadically or with limited unity in their ranks. Some, however, are almost always much more cohesive than others, and there is a well-established contrast in these terms between British and American parties or between parties almost everywhere and those in the United States. The contrast is usually in national terms—parliamentary parties as against congressional parties. Within the United States there are differences among state legislatures since some have parties that act with considerably more cohesion than others (Wahlke, 1962; Dye, 1965). Even American congressional parties should not be understood as being without cohesion although they can hardly be counted as regularly unified behind a given set of policies. The absence of strict regularity in legislative party voting is, of course, what is meant in describing behavior as relatively uncohesive. The description is consistent with the view that party in the American Congress might still be the most important single determinant of legislative voting (Turner, 1951; Truman, 1959). It is just not as overwhelmingly important a determinant as it is in a parliamentary system.

The plain fact about the American separation-of-powers structure is that the legislative party, when a majority, does not have to assume responsibility for governing in the manner of a majority party in a parliamentary system. It does not have the same incentive regularly to sustain an executive authority; the American president, unlike a prime minister and cabinet, is in office as the result of a separate electoral mandate and will remain there no matter how many of his policies are rejected by the Congress. Thus he survives legislative defeat at the hands of a loosely disciplined majority party bearing the same label as his own, just as he survives defeat at the hands of an opposition party majority that exists from time to time in one or both houses of Congress. On the other hand, the American executive may well succeed in persuading a cross-party legislative majority to support his policies, or such a majority might develop independently of the executive. In either case the absence of the regularly cohesive legislative party is what allows the cross-party majority to be formed. Something like this is required if American government is to work. If instead an American president of one party were confronted by an almost perfectly cohesive legislative majority of another party, itself committed to a different set of policies, it is hard to see how there could be any effective enactment of policies. Often it is the absence of cohesion in an opposition party's legislative majority that makes the system operable. This does not mean that an American president would not prefer to have his own party majority in each house of Congress and that he would not also prefer to have this party act cohesively—in support of his policies. But ordinarily he can and does function with a good deal less by way of clear-cut party support.

More to the point here, an American legislative party is able to function without providing the support for an executive that is taken for granted in the case of a majority party in a parliamentary system. It is much less of a collective governing agency. In fact, we usually speak of an American governing party, insofar as we do at all, as the strictly executive apparatus that serves the president. A Republican or Democratic government (or "administration") means a Republican or Democratic presidency with or without a majority of the same party in Congress. But it might better accord with the real situation to speak of American government as without control by party as a collective entity. At best a party only incompletely exercises governing authority, and at times it seems almost completely nongoverning despite its status within government. Instead, individual officeholders, notably the chief executive, assume governing responsibility, which elsewhere more fully belongs to a party.

The case for accepting the limited governing responsibility assumed by the American party as a response to the separation-of-powers system would be strengthened if the much more cohesive party turned out to be everywhere associated with the parliamentary-cabinet system. This still would not demonstrate the inevitability of the uncohesive party flowing from the separation of powers; so much cannot be claimed anyway. Some American state legislative parties have been remarkably cohesive, and perhaps others, as well as the national congressional parties, might also become more cohesive given more nearly uniform social and economic circumstances—in other words, despite the separation of powers. All that is argued is that the separation of powers is an institutional arrangement that makes it possible, in the sense of workable, for parties to be uncohesive. The opportunity, not the necessity, is provided.

The parliamentary system surely provides no similar opportunity, and so we should expect cohesive parties to prevail. In fact, they do clearly prevail wherever two-party or moderate multiparty competition exists in a parliamentary system and often, but not always, when there is extreme multipartism (Ozbudin, 1970). The evidence is almost uniformly impressive. Britain provides the best-known examples, but the stable parliamentary democracies of Western Europe and of the Commonwealth are basically similar in party cohesion despite considerable differences in many other respects. Norway, for instance, has highly cohesive parties in a parliament whose formal legal structure is unlike Britain's, in that it has no executive power to dissolve the legislative body, while it possesses, as Britain does not, powerful specialized standing committees and more than two consequential parties, elected by proportional representation (Eckstein, 1966, pp. 19–21). Or, to cite a still different set of circumstances for a parliamentary system, Canada has always had strongly cohesive parliamentary parties despite the nation's size, diversity, and federalism, and despite the maintenance of substantial third and fourth parties in recent decades (Engelmann and Schwartz, 1967, p. 116; Kornberg, 1967). It should also be noted in passing that Canadian parliamentary parties maintain their cohesion in the absence, in most instances, of large external membership organizations. The parliamentary system's incentives alone appear sufficient to produce cohesion in Canada, where almost all other circumstances resemble those of the United States more closely than of Britain. Socioeconomic explanations do not appear crucial.

It is easy to understand why this should be so, given two-party competition or something as close to it as Canada's modified pattern. Either one of two parties can envision itself, and be envisioned by the electorate, as occupying now or in the future a majority parliamentary position and thus having the responsibility for providing and supporting the executive. Thus a party while in opposition has strong political incentives to be cohesive, both as a simple response to the cohesiveness of the majority party supporting the government and as a sign that it is sufficiently united itself to support a future government and its policies. With multipartism the incentives for cohesion seem less apparent. Yet, as already indicated, multiparty parliamentary regimes in Scandinavia, Belgium, and the Netherlands have had cohesive parties. Mainly these are nations whose multipartism often sufficiently resembles bipartism, because they have either few parties or one that itself is close to majority status, so that the incentives for cohesion are similar to those in two-party competition. The same probably holds for the West German Republic. But among the more extreme multiparty patterns, parliamentary party cohesion has also often prevailed. Weimar Germany and, to some extent, the Italian Republic are cases in point. France of the Third and Fourth Republics is exceptional in that cohesion was not uniformly characteristic of the center parties although there was a good deal of it on the left. (The Fifth French Republic is so much of a hybrid presidential-parliamentary regime that its experience is not taken into account here.)

Legislative party cohesion, supporting an executive leadership when there is a party majority, appears characteristic enough of parliamentary systems. Especially in two-party competition this does fix governing responsibility on a party in a way that does not occur regularly in the United States. So the governing role of the American party usually appears less important. It would be wrong, however, to conclude that the governing role of American elected public officeholders is also less important than that of officeholders in a parliamentary system. The American chief executive may provide more of a policymaking governing authority than does a parliamentary party. The cohesiveness that unites a majority parliamentary party with its executive leaders (prime minister and cabinet) cannot itself be assumed to mean an especially effective policymaking process. Lately the effectiveness in this respect of British party government has been seriously questioned (Rose, 1969; Waltz, 1967).

RECONSIDERATION

As has just been indicated, American parties are not alone in being subject to a new skepticism concerning their efficacy and relative importance. Parties generally in democratic societies have become targets for those who are dissatisfied with the performance of political institutions. Thus, in addition to those political scientists already observed to have proposed particular party reforms or new kinds of parties, there are others who now look to nonparty agencies to perform the tasks for which they regard parties as unsuited or at any rate unlikely to perform. Unlike the American party reformers of the last few decades, the more recent critics show little preference for the British or European style party as opposed to the American. They may not perceive relative virtues in American parties, or even in the American political process as a whole, but neither do they follow the slightly earlier generation of European and American scholars who thought of the cohesive, programmatic, mass-membership, and responsible party, especially its British variant, as a model for the United States. In the new and still unconventional view, existing parties almost everywhere are regarded as deficient instruments of the popular will and of effective policy-making, and often inevitably so because of their very development as parties. Their actual abolition is not seriously advocated. Rather their continuation, more or less as they stand, is usually assumed, and consequently so is the use of other political means to accomplish many of the purposes formerly expected of parties.

It is well to understand that this critical perspective is different from that of most earlier opponents of political parties. In the late eighteenth century parties were seen as instruments of factional strife destroying a hoped-for social and political unity, and in the nineteenth century and the first decades of the twentieth century parties were thought to be corrupt and too monolithic in their authority (Hofstadter, 1969). Such attitudes were alike in that they reflected an objection to the strength of parties, to their activities and power, and not to any perceived weaknesses or lack of capacity. Parties were thought bad because of what they did, not because of what they did not do or could not do. It is true that this strand of criticism persists in more recent decades and even currently. There are many, in the spirit of the old critics, who seek to elevate their cause above party, occasionally substituting an heroic leader for a party. Their activity may become literally nonpartisan or it may assume the shape of a national movement that is embryonically a party in all but name. But the newer criticism, while also leading to an emphasis on politics outside of parties, reflects no belief in a presumed social harmony that parties might disturb by divisiveness or corruption. In fact, now parties are criticized, as Hofstadter (1969, p. 271) has remarked, for contributing to a false harmony by failing to present clear and significant alternatives of program and policy. Although this is recognizable as a long-standing major complaint voiced by the responsible-party reformers against American parties, what is different is the new absence of belief in the capacity of parties to reform themselves. The reasons for the absence of belief derive not only from the continuation of American parties in their established patterns, despite two decades of reform advocacy, but also from the observed status of parties in other Western democratic nations.

Why do these once more highly regarded parties of other nations, notably those of Britain, now seem less appealing? Partly it is because the European parties are thought to have changed in significant ways. In particular, the socialist working-class parties, which had been the compelling models, are no longer perceived as so heavily participatory and programmatic (or ideological) as they had been in the first half of the century. Membership and membership activity have evidently declined or at best stabilized, and the socialist party's old organizational integration is less impressive than its pragmatic electoral successes. The characteristic late-twentieth-century party even in Europe is taken to be the "catchall" type, whose limited structure and looseness of clientele tend to exclude far-reaching programs involving a mass-membership basis. That conclusion has been reached even by an eminent scholar deploring the impact of the new politics on the old socialist working-class party (Kirchheimer, 1966). Insofar as politics has become consensual rather than ideological, there is less of the intensity that built and sustained large-scale party activity in addition to voting (Chalmers, 1964). Perhaps, as has been suggested in a Norwegian study, this is a more usual state of affairs over the last 150 years than the sharper ideological conflict of a few of the early decades of the twentieth century (Torgerson, 1970). In that case any perceived waning of intense party commitments would not represent a new trend but only a restoration of "normal" politics, which had been interrupted by a conflict peculiar to time and place—say, the early twentieth-century Western Europe of the recently enfranchised and recently created industrial working class.

Another way of answering the question about the lessened appeal of the old responsible party models is to stress not so much what has actually happened to European parties but rather what we have learned about their past as well as present performances. Even when thriving, the socialist working-class model may not have worked as had once been assumed. Its oligarchical tendencies were detected early (Michels, 1915) but not clearly established as universal or as damaging to organizational effectiveness. Later scholarship, however, has substantially qualified the belief that the most prestigious working-class party, British Labour, has customarily drawn its governmental policies from its mass-membership organization (McKenzie, 1963). Here and elsewhere, as already noted, scholars have also questioned whether any external organizational policymaking would be workable in terms of the democratic principle and practice that make public officeholders responsible to the electorate more generally. In any event, it is hard to find that policymaking of this kind has worked with any regularity over a period of years.

Government policy in Britain and elsewhere remains largely, if not entirely, in the hands of the elected public officeholders, that is, of the parliamentary members and particularly their leaders. While the cohesion observed to be characteristic of parliamentary parties makes for a collective policy commitment, and so apparently for a responsibility often unachieved by American parties, the significance of this has now come to be questioned. A parliamentary party may appear responsible, and be so regarded by the electorate, but still have policies that are distinguishable only incrementally, if at all, from those of another party. No matter how cohesive, a party may be unable or unwilling to champion and carry out innovative policies emerging from a generalized program or to have a generalized program that differs sharply from that of the opposition. In this light, British parties in the 1950s and 1960s appeared to be hardly any more creative than their less cohesive counterparts in the United States or parties in other nations (King, 1969, p. 117). The fact that they remain successful vote-gathering mechanisms does not mean that they are effective in developing, enacting, and administering bold new policies. Such policies may come from other sources—civil servants, interest groups, scientific specialists, or even individual politicians—or they may not emerge at all.

It is an open question whether parties as such or just the parties now existing are incapable of major policy innovation. The first possibility derives from the belief that a party that wants to succeed electorally—to achieve majority or near majority status—must compromise by appealing to diverse interests and principles. The type of compromise may be the British, under which considerable diversity is submerged in the achievement of cohesion, or the American, under which the diversity is more openly exhibited within the legislative party. In either case the party blurs its collective image, perhaps more confusingly in Britain because there is a greater effort to claim a well-defined position. The American counterpart is the strictly presidential party presentation. At any rate, the broker party of one sort or another thus seems a product of electoral politics. The second possibility, while not denying altogether the brokerage pressure of electoral politics especially in a large and diverse nation, involves a greater emphasis on the particular limitations of the parties that currently dominate politics in Western democratic nations. As Lipset and Rokkan (1967) have demonstrated for Europe and Chambers (1967) for the United States, the existing parties derive from cleavages belonging to earlier eras. It is a short step to the view that the parties, while once focused around the issues that gave them life, cannot now mobilize to meet new sets of problems. They are restrained by their traditions, their organizational structures, and their residual electoral bases. The old parties adapt to some extent or presumably they would die, but their adaptation may be slow and unsatisfactory by the measure of urgency imposed by demands generated in a much more rapidly changing society. The projected effect is increased alienation from the political process (Burnham, 1965 and 1967).

Still another way of looking at the limitations of parties in contemporary society is to stress their association not just with the cleavages of the past but also with certain more general circumstances of an earlier time. This outlook is close to the first mentioned possibility that parties as such are ill-adapted to some of the present demands. The reference is to parties as we have conceived them during the last century or so and particularly during the high points of their organization and influence first in the United States and then in Western Europe. These modern parties seem to have developed in response to newly created mass electorates, heavily manual working class and often with little formal education. Mobilization by party seemed universal, whether through the American patronage machines or through the European socialist or labor organizations. It is true that some similar groups remain to be mobilized, especially among racial minorities and the very poor generally in the United States, but they do not constitute the bulk of the electorate or potential electorate. On the other side, in what can be called the new, postindustrial society, there is a large, growing, and ambitious class of highly educated, salaried professional, academic and, technical workers. For them party mobilization cannot have the attractions that it had for the industrial working class. Not only do these white-collar workers have a middle-class style of life ordinarily uncongenial to organization of the party type, but they do not provide even in a long-run sense anything like a majority base for a party that once seemed to derive from industrial workers. The new rising class, or newly enlarged class, might well be expected to pursue its political aims through more narrowly focused agencies, perhaps interest groups called professional associations or unions or specific candidate or issue organizations. Its use of parties, while intense, could well be sporadic or occasional. So far such use in the United States seems likelier than does the fulfillment of the proposal by Saloma and Sontag (1972) for much more durable party participation from a newly motivated, educated citizenry. Their hopes are associated with the Democratic party reforms of 1972 and especially with suggested membership organizations devoted to programs and policies.

Politics, it is plain, can be pursued by means other than parties. Those who now expect less of parties than was once customary will likely concentrate on learning more about the other means. This can be done without forsaking parties altogether and even without accepting much of the current denigration of parties. In a matter-of-fact way parties can well be regarded as useful although limited political agencies. Suppose that they are observed to do little more than provide labels for candidates, selected or self-selected in various nonparty as well as party procedures, and then influence voting behavior in general elections despite the absence of substantial organizational effort. Suppose also that the public officeholders elected under this labelling process are only influenced, not controlled, by their common party identification and so do not act cohesively as a governmental party or, if acting cohesively, do so without any programmatic policies developed meaningfully by other party participants. These suppositions, it is evident, describe most American parties of recent decades, and while emphasizing their limitations they plainly indicate that parties remain important factors in the political process. The party reformer who thinks that they are not important enough wants them to undertake additional activities or "functions," often assuming that for parties really to be fully or properly developed they should perform in these additional ways. So, it is argued, parties ought organizationally to monopolize candidate selection, perhaps even political recruitment more generally, and to innovate governmental policies drawn from broad programs evolved by membership organizations. This advocacy is a ready accompaniment, as suggested early in this chapter, of the approach to political parties as a separate subject of study rather than as elements in a political process that includes other means for influencing governmental action.

Many institutions and agencies as well as parties constitute politics in democratic societies. These other institutions and agencies surely bulk large even while parties have not withered away. In fact their activities would still seem of great importance during a period when parties, contrary to current expectations, might add somewhat to their activities and their influence. Interest groups of many kinds, issue-oriented mobilizations, specialized experts in and out of government service, mass-media campaigns, and individual candidate organizations all involve the pursuit of political objectives through nonparty channels. Politics is too large, diverse, and important to be left solely or mainly to parties.

REFERENCES

Abramson, Paul R. (1971). "Social class and political change in Western Europe: a cross-national longitudinal analysis." *Comparative Political Studies* 4:131–55.

Adamany, David (1969). *Financing Politics*. Madison: University of Wisconsin Press.

Adrian, Charles R. (1961). "Some general characteristics of nonpartisan elections." In Oliver P. Williams and Charles Press (eds.), *Democracy in Urban America*. Chicago: Rand McNally, pp. 251–63.

Alexander, Herbert E. (1966). *Financing the 1964 Election*. Princeton: Citizens' Research Foundation.

Alford, Robert A. (1963). *Party and Society*. Chicago: Rand McNally.

Almond, Gabriel, and James S. Coleman (1960). *The Politics of the Developing Nations*. Princeton: Princeton University Press.

American Political Science Association, "Toward a more responsible two-party system." *American Political Science Review* 44, Supplement.

Armstrong, John A. (1961). *The Politics of Totalitarianism*. New York: Random House.

Banfield, Edward C., and James Q. Wilson (1963). *City Politics*. Cambridge, Mass.: Harvard University Press.

Barnes, Samuel H. (1968). "Party democracy and the logic of collective action." In William J. Crotty (ed.), *Approaches to the Study of Party Organization*. Boston: Allyn and Bacon, pp. 105–38.

Beer, Samuel (1965). *British Politics in the Collectivist Age*. New York: Knopf.

Binkley, Wilfred E. (1943). *American Political Parties*. New York: Knopf.

Bryce, James (1891). *The American Commonwealth*. Chicago: Sergel.

Burnham, Walter Dean (1970). *Critical Elections and The Mainsprings of American Politics.* New York: Norton.

——————— (1967). "Party systems and the political process." In William N. Chambers and Walter Dean Burnham (eds.), *The American Party Systems.* New York: Oxford University Press.

——————— (1965). "The changing shape of the American political universe." *American Political Science Review* 59:7–28.

Burns, James M. (1963). *The Deadlock of Democracy.* Englewood Cliffs, N.J.: Prentice-Hall.

Butler, David, and Donald Stokes (1969). *Political Change in Britain.* New York: St. Martin's Press.

Campbell, Angus *et al.* (1960). *The American Voter.* New York: Wiley.

Campbell, Angus, and Henry Valen (1961). "Party identification in Norway and the United States." *Public Opinion Quarterly* 25:505–25.

Cassinelli, Charles W. (1962). "The totalitarian party." *Journal of Politics,* 24:111–41.

Chalmers, Douglas A. (1964). *The Social Democratic Party of Germany.* New Haven: Yale University Press.

Chambers, William N. (1967). "Party development and the American mainstream." In William N. Chambers and Walter Dean Burnham (eds.), New York: Oxford University Press, pp. 3–32.

——————— (1963). *Political Parties in a New Nation.* New York: Oxford University Press.

Charles, Joseph (1956). *The Origins of the American Party System.* Williamsburg: Institute of Early American History and Culture.

Converse, Philip E., and Georges Dupeux (1962). "Politicization of the electorate of France and the United States." *Public Opinion Quarterly* 26:1–23.

Crotty, William J. (1968). "The party organization and its activities." In William J. Crotty (ed.), *Approaches to the Study of Party Organization.* Boston: Allyn and Bacon, pp. 247–306.

Dahl, Robert A. (1966). *Political Oppositions in Western Democracies.* New Haven: Yale University Press.

Dawson, Richard E. (1967). "Social development, party competition, and policy." In William N. Chambers and Walter Dean Burnham (eds.), *The American Party Systems.* New York: Oxford University Press, pp. 203–37.

Duverger, Maurice (1954). *Political Parties.* Translated by Barbara and Robert North. New York: Wiley.

Dye, Thomas (1965). "State legislative politics." In Herbert Jacob and Kenneth Vines (eds.), *Politics in the American States.* Boston: Little, Brown.

Eckstein, Harry (1968). "Party systems." *International Encyclopedia of the Social Sciences.* New York: Macmillan, pp. 436–53.

——————— (1966). *Division and Cohesion in Democracy.* Princeton: Princeton University Press.

Eldersveld, Samuel J. (1964). *Political Parties: A Behavioral Analysis*. Chicago: Rand McNally.

Engelmann, Frederick C., and Mildred A. Schwartz (1967). *Political Parties and the Canadian Social Structure*. Scarborough: Prentice-Hall of Canada.

Epstein, Leon D. (1967). *Political Parties in Western Democracies*. New York: Praeger.

_____ (1958). *Politics in Wisconsin*. Madison: University of Wisconsin Press.

Eulau, Heinz (1957). "The ecological basis of party systems: the case of Ohio." *Midwest Journal of Political Science* 1:125–35.

Fainsod, Merle (1968). "The dynamics of one-party systems." In Oliver Garceau (ed.), *Political Research and Political Theory*. Cambridge, Mass.: Harvard University Press, pp. 221–46.

_____ (1953). *How Russia Is Ruled*. Cambridge, Mass.: Harvard University Press.

Ford, Henry Jones (1898). *The Rise and Growth of American Parties*. New York: Macmillan.

Gold, David, and John Schmidhauser (1960). "Urbanization and party competition: the case of Iowa." *Midwest Journal of Political Science* 4:62–75.

Goldwin, Robert A. (1964). *Political Parties U.S.A.* Chicago: Rand McNally.

Gosnell, Harold S. (1937). *Machine Politics: Chicago Model*. Chicago: University of Chicago Press.

Greenstein, Fred (1970). *The American Party System and the American People*. Englewood Cliffs, N.J.: Prentice-Hall.

Grodzins, Morton (1960). "American political parties and the American system." *Western Political Quarterly* 13:947–98.

Grumm, John A. (1958). "Theories of electoral systems." *Midwest Journal of Political Science* 2:357–76.

Heard, Alexander (1960). *The Costs of Democracy*. Chapel Hill: University of North Carolina Press.

Heidenheimer, Arnold J., ed. (1970). *Comparative Political Finance*. Lexington, Mass.: D. C. Heath.

Hennessy, Bernard (1968). "On the study of party organization." In William J. Crotty (ed.), *Approaches to the Study of Party Organization*. Boston: Allyn and Bacon, pp. 1–44.

Hofstadter, Richard (1969). *The Idea of a Party System*. Berkeley: University of California Press.

Holcombe, Arthur N. (1924). *The Political Parties of Today*. New York: Harper.

Jacob, Herbert, and Kenneth Vines (1965). *Politics in the American States*. Boston: Little, Brown.

Key, V. O., Jr. (1964). *Politics, Parties, and Pressure Groups*. New York: Crowell.

_____ (1956). *American State Politics*. New York: Knopf.

_____ (1950). *Southern Politics in State and Nation*. New York: Knopf.

King, Anthony (1969). "Political parties in Western democracies." *Polity* 1:112–41.

Kirchheimer, Otto (1966). "The transformation of the Western European party systems." In Joseph La Palombara and Myron Weiner (eds.), *Political Parties and Political Development*. Princeton: Princeton University Press.

Kirkpatrick, E. M. (1971). "Toward a more responsible two-party system: political science, policy science, or pseudo-science?" *American Political Science Review* 65:965–90.

Kornberg, Allan (1967). *Canadian Legislative Behavior*. New York: Holt, Rinehart and Winston.

La Palombara, Joseph, and Myron Weiner (1966). *Political Parties and Political Development*. Princeton: Princeton University Press.

Leiserson, Avery (1958). *Parties and Politics*. New York: Knopf.

Lijphart, Arend (1968). *The Politics of Accommodation*. Berkeley: University of California Press.

Linz, Juan J. (1970). "An authoritarian regime: Spain." In Erik Allardt and Stein Rokkan (eds.), *Mass Politics*. New York: Free Press, pp. 251–83.

——————— (1967). "The party system of Spain: past and future." In S. M. Lipset and Stein Rokkan (eds.), *Party Systems and Voter Alignments*. New York: Free Press, pp. 197–282.

Lipset, S. M., and Stein Rokkan (1967). *Party Systems and Voter Alignments*. New York: Free Press, pp. 1–64.

Lockard, Duane (1968). "State party systems and policy outputs." In Oliver Garceau (ed.), *Political Research and Political Theory*. Cambridge, Mass.: Harvard University Press, pp. 190–220.

——————— (1959). *New England State Politics*. Princeton: Princeton University Press.

Lowell, A. Lawrence (1901). "The influence of party upon legislation in England and America." *Annual Report of the American Historical Association,* pp. 321–542.

MacRae, Duncan, Jr. (1967). *Parliament Parties, and Society in France, 1946–1958*. New York: St. Martin's Press.

May, John D. (1969). "Democracy, party 'evolution,' Duverger." *Comparative Political Studies* 2:216–48.

McKenzie, Robert (1963). *British Political Parties*. New York: Praeger.

McPhee, William N., and Jack Ferguson (1962). "Political immunization." In William N. McPhee and William A. Glasser (eds.), *Public Opinion and Congressional Elections*. New York: Free Press.

McKenzie, Robert, and Allan Silver (1968). *Angels in Marble*. Chicago: University of Chicago Press.

Merelman, Richard M. (1970). "Electoral instability and the American party system." *Journal of Politics* 32:115–39.

Michels, Robert (1949; first published 1915). *Political Parties.* Translated by Eden and Cedar Paul. New York: Free Press.

Miller, Warren, and Donald E. Stokes (1963). "Constituency influence in Congress." *American Political Science Review* 57:45–56.

Neumann, Franz (1942). *Behemoth.* New York: Oxford University Press.

Neumann, Sigmund (1956). *Modern Political Parties.* Chicago: University of Chicago Press.

Nordlinger, Eric (1967). *The Working-Class Tories.* Berkeley: University of California Press.

Ostrogorski, M. (1902). *Democracy and the Organization of Political Parties.* London: Macmillan.

Ozbudin, Ergun (1970). *Party Cohesion in Western Democracies.* Beverly Hills: Sage.

Payne, James L. (1968). *Patterns of Conflict in Colombia.* New Haven: Yale University Press.

Peel, Roy V. (1935). *The Political Clubs of New York City.* New York: Putnam's.

Polsby, Nelson W., and Aaron Wildavsky (1971). *Presidential Elections.* New York: Scribner's.

Rae, Douglas W. (1967). *The Political Consequences of Electoral Laws.* New Haven: Yale University Press.

Ranney, Austin (1968). "The concept of 'party.' " In Oliver Garceau (ed.), *Political Research and Political Theory.* Cambridge, Mass.: Harvard University Press, pp. 143–62.

——————— (1962). *The Doctrine of Responsible Party Government.* Urbana: University of Illinois Press.

——————— (1965). *Pathways to Parliament.* Madison: University of Wisconsin Press.

Ranney, Austin, and Willimoore Kendall (1956). *Democracy and the American Party System.* New York: Harcourt, Brace.

Robinson, Edgar E. (1924). *The Evolution of American Political Parties.* New York: Harcourt, Brace.

Rose, Richard (1969). "The variability of party structures." *Political Studies* 17:413–45.

Rose, Richard, and Derek Urwin (1970). "Persistence and change in party systems." *Political Studies* 18:287–319.

——————— (1969). "Social cohesion, political parties and strains in regimes." *Comparative Political Studies* 2:7–67.

Saloma, John S., and F. H. Sontag (1972). *Parties: The Real Opportunity for Effective Citizen Politics.* New York: Knopf.

Sartori, Giovanni (1969). "From the sociology of politics to political sociology." In S. M. Lipset (ed.), *Politics and the Social Sciences.* New York: Oxford University Press, pp. 65–100.

Sartori, Giovanni (1970). "The typology of party systems—proposals for improvement." In Erik Allardt and Stein Rokkan (eds.), *Mass Politics*. New York: Free Press, pp. 322–52.

Scarrow, Howard A. (1964). "Nomination and local party organization in Canada." *Western Political Quarterly* 17:55–62.

Schattschneider, E. E. (1942). *Party Government*. New York: Rinehart.

Schlesinger, Joseph (1968). "Party units." *International Encyclopedia of the Social Sciences*. New York: Macmillan, pp. 428–36.

_____ (1965). "Political party organization." In James G. March (ed.), *Handbook of Organizations*. Chicago: Rand McNally, pp. 764–801.

Secher, H. Pierre (1958). "Coalition government: the case of the second Austrian republic." *American Political Science Review* 52:791–808.

Sindler, Allan P. (1956). *Huey Long's Louisiana*. Baltimore: Johns Hopkins.

_____ (1966). *Political Parties in the United States*. New York: St. Martin's Press.

Sorauf, Frank J. (1963). *Party and Representation*. New York: Atherton Press.

_____ (1964). *Political Parties in the American System*. Boston: Little, Brown.

_____ (1967). "Political parties and political analysis." In William N. Chambers and Walter Dean Burnham (eds.), *The American Party Systems*. New York: Oxford University Press, pp. 33–55.

Stokes, Donald E. (1967). "Parties and the nationalization of electoral forces." In William N. Chambers and Walter Dean Burnham (eds.), *The American Party Systems*. New York: Oxford University Press, pp. 182–202.

Sundquist, James L. (1973). *Dynamics of the Party System*. Washington, D.C.: The Brookings Institution.

Taylor, Michael, and V. H. Herman (1971). "Party systems and government stability." *American Political Science Review* 65:28–37.

Torgerson, Ulf (1970). "The trend toward political consensus: the case of Norway." In Erik Allardt and Stein Rokkan (eds.), *Mass Politics*. New York: Free Press, pp. 93–104.

Truman, David (1959). *The Congressional Party*. New York: Wiley.

Turner, Julius (1951). *Party and Constituency: Pressures on Congress*. Baltimore: Johns Hopkins Press.

_____ (1953). "Primary elections as the alternative to party competition in safe districts." *Journal of Politics* 15:197–210.

Valen, Henry, and Daniel Katz (1964). *Political Parties in Norway*. Oslo: Universitetsforlaget.

van den Bergh, George (1955). *Unity in Diversity*. London: Botsford.

Wahlke, John C. *et al.* (1962). *The Legislative System*. New York: Wiley.

Wallerstein, Immanuel (1966). "The decline of the party in single-party African states." In Joseph La Palombara and Myron Weiner (eds.), *Political Parties and Political Development*. Princeton: Princeton University Press, pp. 201–14.

Waltz, Kenneth N. (1967). *Foreign Policy and Democratic Politics*. Boston: Little Brown.

Wiatr, Jerzy J. (1970). "Political parties, interest representation and economic development in Poland." *American Political Science Review* 64:1239–45.

Williams, Philip M. (1964). *Crisis and Compromise*. London: Longmans, Green.

Wilson, James Q. (1962). *The Amateur Democrat*. Chicago: University of Chicago Press.

_____ (1974). *Political Organizations*. New York: Basic Books.

INDEX

Aberbach, Joel D., 103, 159
Abramson, Paul R., 245
Activists, 39–40, 42, 60–61
Adamany, David, 254
Adrian, Charles R., 232
Ahmed, Bashiruddin, 22, 58
Alford, Robert A., 3, 160, 244
Almond, Gabriel A., 3, 22, 32, 60, 160,
    177, 178, 179, 180, 199, 221, 233,
    236
American Political Science Association,
    237
Andersen, Kristi, 68
Anderson, Ronald, 90, 100, 102, 159
Armstrong, John A., 232
Attitudes
    formation, 82
    instability, 84
    salience, 88
    stability, 88, 104, 111
    structure, 83–89, 99, 101, 104, 105,
        107, 109
Axelrod, Robert, 147
Ayred, Richard E., 22

Bachrach, Peter, 5
Baer, Michael, 205, 206
Bailey, Stephen K. 217
Banfield, Edward C., 250

Baratz, Morton S., 4
Barbic, Ana, 13, 16
Barnes, Samuel H., 159, 256
Barton, Allen H., 158
Bauer, Raymond A., 163, 207
Beck, Paul A., 162
Beer, Samuel, 181, 195, 200, 208, 215,
    221, 256
Bendix, Reinhard, 3, 31
Benson, Lee, 160
Bentley, Arthur, 172, 174, 175, 208, 223
Berelson, Bernard, 3, 7, 160
Bernstein, Irving, 212
Bhatt, Anil, 22, 58
Bicker, William E., 159
Binkley, Wilfred E., 231
Block, William, 180, 215
Booms, Bernard H., 64
Bowen, William G., 22
Boyd, Richard W., 68, 128, 133, 135
Brady, Robert, 187
Braungart, Richard G., 197
Brody, Richard A., 26, 60, 68, 106, 126,
    160
Brown, Steven R., 86, 158
Brown, Thad A., 147, 162
Browne, William P., 198, 199, 200, 204
Bruner, Jerome S., 84
Bryce, James, 237

Buchanan, William, 163
Burnham, Walter Dean, 2, 138, 144, 145, 147, 148, 160, 162, 247, 269
Burns, James M., 237, 255
Butler, David, 27, 110, 160, 234, 245

Campaign activity, 10, 13, 18, 35, 50-52
Campbell, Angus, 27, 85, 90, 98, 99, 100, 112, 133, 148, 160, 162, 234, 248
Candidate selection, 257-260
  leadership recruitment, 257
Cassinelli, Charles W., 233
Chalmers, Douglas A., 268
Chambers, William N., 231, 246
Charles, Joseph, 231
Cherryholmes, Cleo H., 162
Clark, Peter B., 184
Class cleavage, 244
Clausen, P.E., 60
Cnudde, Charles F., 2, 32, 33
Cohen, Bernard, 183
Cole, G. D. H., 34
Coleman, James S., 7, 177, 178, 182, 233, 236
Communist party, 232-233
Conflict, involvement in, 8-9
  and voting, 9
Converse, Philip E., 27, 60, 68, 84, 85, 88, 90, 98, 99, 100, 133, 158, 160, 162, 248
Cooperative activity, 11-12
Crick, Bernard, 172
Crotty, William J., 253

Dahl, Robert A., 4, 27, 34, 70, 149, 222
Davis, Otto A., 113, 125, 160
Dawson, Richard E., 243
Decline-of-community model, 33-38
Democratic participation, 2, 4
Denney, William Michael, 143
de Sola Pool, Ithiel, 163, 207
Deutsch, Karl, 33
Dexter, Lewis A., 163, 205, 207
Downing, Randal, 181
Downs, Anthony, 95, 98, 160
Dudman, Richard, 197

Dupeux, Georges, 248
Duverger, Maurice, 237, 241, 249, 250
Dye, Thomas, 264

Eckstein, Harry, 3, 60, 181, 234, 265
Edinger, Lewis, 181, 214
Ehrmann, Henry, 181
Eldersveld, Samuel, 186, 252
Elections, 76, 157
  citizen control over, 2
  realignments of party strength, 137-144
Engelmann, Frederick C., 258, 265
Epstein, Leon D., 242, 250
Erskine, Hazel G., 79
Eulau, Heinz, 163, 243

Factions, 230
Factor analysis, 13, 15
Fainsod, Merle, 232, 240
Farkas, Susanne, 188
Fascist Italy, 232
Ferguson, Jack, 248
Ferguson, Leroy C., 163
Field, John O., 90, 100, 102, 159
Finer, Samuel E., 172, 176, 181, 208, 213, 214
Francis, Wayne, 207
Freedman, Anne, 203
Frohlich, Norman, 193
Froman, L. A., Jr., 162
Fry, Brian, 64
Functionalism, 236

Galbraith, John Kenneth, 192, 222
Garceau, Oliver, 203, 207
Gaudet, Hazel, 160
Glaser, William A., 148, 160
Goguel, Francois, 112, 160
Gold, David, 243
Gosnell, Harold, 112, 249
Greenstein, Fred I., 143, 243, 250
Greenstone, J. A
Greenstone, J. David, 171, 213, 217
Griffiths, Franklin, 204
Grossman, Joel, 181
Gurin, Gerald, 160

Hacker, Andrew, 209
Hadwiger, Don F., 215
Hagan, Charles B., 174
Halldorson, James R., 64
Heard, Alexander, 254
Hennessy, Bernard, 253
Herman, V. H., 240
Herring, E. Pendleton, 222
Hinich, Melvin J., 113, 125, 160
Hofferbert, Richard, 2
Hofstadter, Richard, 231, 237, 267
Holtzman, Abraham, 205, 208
Hyman, Herbert H., 143, 198

Ideology, 83–89, 91, 102, 107, 110
    ideologues, 85
Information
    acquisition of, 96
    costs, 96–97, 98, 111, 121
    levels of public, 79, 81, 82–83, 93,
        102, 156
Inkeles, Alex, 22, 32
Interest groups
    benefits derived by members, 184–
        185, 192
    catalytic groups, 195
    categoric group, 173
    as decision makers, 180–181
    definitions, 173–176
    elite interaction, 210–211
    entrepreneurial theory, 193
    expressive-benefit groups, 195
    formal association, 175
    growth within framework of law,
        198
    impact on society, 219–223
    inferential group, 173
    as input mechanisms, 177–179
    interaction with government, 206–
        209
    liberalism, 221–222
    lobbyists, 205–206, 209–213
    managerial groups, 186
    membership density, 199, 221
    mobilization, 216–218
    opposition, importance of, 218
    as organizations, 181–182

organizers, 194–195
origins and growth of, 189–201
pressure groups, 176
promotional groups, 195
representation, 213–216
role-based organizations, 188–189
role differentiation, 202–206
sectional groups, 176
strategies, 183, 200, 212
as system outputs, 179–180
Irwin, Galen, 13

Jennings, M. Kent, 143, 144, 162
Jensen, Richard, 148, 160
Jewell, Malcolm E., 205

Katz, Daniel, 248
Kelley, Stanley, Jr., 22
Kendall, Willimoore, 239
Kessel, John, 68, 159
Key, V. O., 68, 77, 112, 119, 121–124,
    133, 134, 137, 146, 158, 162, 183,
    187, 191, 197, 240, 242, 257
Kim, Jae-on, 6, 13, 17, 22, 40, 42, 49, 50
King, Anthony, 269
Kingdon, John W., 148
Kirchheimer, Otto, 268
Kirkpatrick, E. M., 237
Klingemann, Hans D., 102, 110, 159
Kolasa, Bernard D., 205
Kornberg, Allan, 265
Kramer, Gerald H., 135, 161
Krislov, Samuel, 211

Lane, Robert A., 5, 7, 27, 86, 87, 88, 89,
    94
LaPalombara, Joseph, 172, 216, 233
Lasswell, Harold D., 194
Latham, Earl, 172, 191
Lazarsfeld, Paul F., 3, 7, 112, 158, 160
Leader responsiveness, 60, 61, 63–68, 69
Lerner, Daniel, 33
Lijphart, Arend, 240
Lind, Alden E., 117
Lindblom, C. E., 222
Linz, Juan J., 158, 232, 245
Lippmann, Walter, 4, 93, 96

Lipset, Seymour Martin, 60, 148, 158, 160, 182, 194, 246, 269
Lipsky, Michael, 27
  typologies, 178, 182-189
Lobbyists, 205-206, 209-213
Lockard, Duane, 243
Lowell, A. Lawrence, 263
Lowi, Theodore, 221-222, 223
Luttbeg, Norman R., 158, 202

MacIver, Robert M., 175
MacRae, Duncan, Jr., 162, 262
Macridis, Roy C., 172, 196
Marshall, T. H., 3
Matthews, Donald R., 3, 162
May, John D., 250
McCloskey, Herbert, 1, 5, 84
McConnell, Grant, 180, 183, 208, 210
McCrone, Donald J., 2, 32, 33
McKenzie, Robert, 245, 251, 256, 268
McPhee, William N., 3, 7, 160, 248
Meldrum, James A., 162
Membership market, 196-197
Merelman, Richard N., 248
Merriam, Charles E., 112
Michels, Robert, 201, 238, 268
Michigan model of proximal orientations, 115-118
Milbrath, Lester W., 1, 5, 7, 27, 32-33, 46, 205, 206, 211
Mill, J. S., 4
Miller, Arthur H., 147, 162
Miller, Warren E., 60, 64, 85, 90, 94, 98, 99, 100, 113, 133, 147, 149, 150, 152, 153, 154, 157, 158, 160, 162, 248
Millett, John H., 213
Mobilization model, 33
Molleman, Henk, 13, 16

Nazi Germany, 232
Needler, Martin C., 2
Nettle, John Peter, 2
Neubauer, Dane, 33
Neumann, Franz, 232
Neumann, Sigmund, 237
Nie, Norman H., 6, 11, 13, 16, 17, 22, 32, 33, 34, 35, 39, 40, 41, 42, 49, 50, 58, 62, 64, 66, 68, 70, 76, 77, 91, 99, 101, 103, 104, 105, 107, 109, 118, 126, 149, 150, 151, 152, 153, 154, 155, 158, 159, 163
Niemi, Richard, 144, 162
Nordlinger, Eric, 245

Odegard, Peter H., 176, 209
Ogburn, W. F., 112, 160
Olsen, Marvin E., 32
Olson, Mancur, 7, 69, 182, 186, 189, 192, 195, 196
Opinion formation, 79-83
Oppenheimer, Joe A., 193
Ordeshook, Peter C., 68, 113, 125, 160
Ostrogorski, M., 238
Ozbudin, Ergun, 259, 265

Page, Benjamin I., 68, 106, 126
Palamountain, Joseph C., Jr., 211
Parkin, F., 211, 217
Participatory mechanisms, adequacy of, 4-5
Party affiliations, 49-50
Party support, social bases of, 53-55
Patterson, Samuel C., 205
Payne, James L., 252
Peak association, 187-188
Peak, G. Wayne, 197
Peel, Roy V., 249
Peltason, Jack W., 174
Pierce, John C., 90, 100, 102, 158, 159
Pierce, Roy, 27, 158, 159
Pitkin, Hanna Fenichel, 163
Pluralism, 172-173, 192
Policy domain, 184
Political activity, consequences of, 60-68
  rationality of, 68-70
Political beliefs, 56-59
Political campaigns, financing of, 254-255
Political inactives, 40, 61
Political orientations, 17-22
Political participation
  activists, 39-40, 42, 60-61

amount of, 23
black-white participation, 56–59
campaign activity, 10, 13, 18, 50–52
ceremonial, 2
citizen-initiated contacts, 10–11, 13
evidence from cross-national study, 15
frequency distributions in various
    countries, 24–25
importance of, 4
leader responsiveness, 63–68
nature of, 1–3
particularized contacting, 21–22, 69
partisan identification, strength of,
    17, 41
political beliefs, 56–59
and political parties, 49–53, 54–55
protests, 26–27
reasons for, 4
and socioeconomic level, 40–41
and socioeconomic status in cross-
    national perspective, 41–45, 62
study of, 5–6
unitary model of, 7, 28
and urbanization, 32–33
voting, 9–10, 13, 19–20, 53
Political parties, 49–53, 54–55
activists, 262
antisystem party, 240
authoritarian or totalitarian party,
    232
in Britain, 231, 233, 237, 238, 239
in Canada, 245
candidate-centered organizations, 254
candidate selection, 257–260
catchall parties, 251
caucuses, 249, 260
class-based voting in Britain, 245
cohesion, 263, 266
Communist party, 232–233
electoral system, 234
issue differentiation, 92, 99, 105, 111,
    118, 134
mass-membership party, 237, 249–
    250, 251, 263
multiparty competition, 234, 240
one-party domination, 242
organization, 248–256

parliamentary system, 264–265
party identification, 117, 125, 126,
    127, 129–130, 132, 134, 141, 142,
    145
patronage in America, 238, 250, 257
in Poland, 233
primary election, direct, 239, 242,
    258, 259
responsible-party school, 237
statutory party, 252–253
third parties, 241–242
trade unions, 251, 253
two-party competition, 234, 239–240
in the United States, 231–232, 237,
    239
working-class party, 244, 249, 260
Political protests, 26–27
Political socialization, 143
Politicization, process of, 30–38, 45–48
analysis of, 45, 47
decline-of-community model, 33–38
institutional constraints, 47
communal participation, 20–21, 53
and communication of preferences,
    60–63
community context and, 34–36
concentration of, 27–30
cooperative activity, 11–12
dimensions and modes of, 6–22
as educational device, 4
empirical structure of, 12–17
mobilization model, 33
and modes of activity, 48
and socioeconomic status, 46
Polsby, Nelson W., 163, 260
Pomper, Gerald M., 68, 91, 92, 98, 101,
    105, 107, 118, 119, 126, 159
Potter, Allen, 206
Powell, G. Bingham, 32, 33, 177, 178,
    179, 180
Pressure groups, 176
Prewitt, Kenneth, 32, 33
Price, Douglas, 145
Prothro, James W., 3, 162
Psychological involvement in politics, 17
Public opinion
    character of, variation in, 89–93

ideology, 83–89
nature of, 77–111
opinion formation, 79–83
psychology of, 78–89
representation of, 148–156
Putnam, Robert D., 221

Rabinowitz, George Burt, 161
Rae, Douglas W., 240
Raine, Alden S., 147, 162
Ranney, Austin, 60, 229, 239, 258, 259,
    261
Rationality, 115, 118–125, 153
    rational voting, 118, 121, 122
RePass, David E., 116, 119, 128, 129,
    132, 160
Rieselbach, Leroy N., 162
Riggs, Fred W., 188
Riker, William H., 68, 113, 160
Robinson, Edgar E., 231
Rogin, Michael, 201
Rokkan, Stein, 3, 31, 148, 160, 246,
    269
Rose, Arnold, 179
Rose, Douglas D., 158
Rose, Richard, 162, 208, 245, 266
Rosenthal, Howard, 148
Rossi, Peter, 158
Rusk, Jerrold G., 158, 161, 162

Salisbury, Robert H., 184, 189, 193,
    198, 199, 200, 202, 204
Saloma, John S., 270
Saloutos, Theodore, 194
Sarlvik, Bo, 159
Sartori, Giovanni, 235, 240, 248
Scarrow, Howard A., 258
Schattschneider, E., 180, 192, 222, 237,
    250
Schlesinger, Joseph, 234, 249
Schmidhauser, John, 243
Schwartz, Joel J., 117
Schwartz, Mildred A., 258, 265
Scoble, Harry M., 3, 186, 203, 217
Searing, Donald D., 117
Sears, David O., 158, 160
Secher, H. Pierre, 243

Self, Peter, 215
Seligman, Lester, 179
Sellers, Charles G., 162
Separation-of-powers formula, 243, 260,
    264, 265
Shabad, Goldie, 13, 16
Shanks, John Merrill, 161
Shapiro, Michael, 68, 160, 161, 162
Sharkansky, Ira, 2
Shively, Phillips W., 160
Shonfield, Andrew, 216
Siegfried, Andre, 112, 160
Sills, David, 176
Silver, Allan, 245
Silverman, Corinne, 207
Sindler, Allan P., 239
Skilling, H. Gordon, 204
Skolnick, Jerome, 27
Smith, Constance, 203
Smith, David, 172
Smith, M. Brewster, 84
Social Democratic party, 238
Sontag, F. H., 270
Sorauf, Frank J., 162, 236, 252
Stewart, J. D., 176, 213
Stokes, Donald, 27, 64, 85, 90, 94, 98
    99, 100, 110, 113, 133, 149, 150,
    152, 153, 154, 157, 158, 160, 162,
    234, 245, 247, 248
Storing, Herbert J., 215
Sundquist, James L., 138, 139, 141, 147,
    247

Taft, Philip, 180
Talbot, Nell S., 160
Talbot, Ross B., 215
Taylor, Michael, 240
Teune, Henry, 207
Thomassen, Jacques, 160
Thompson, Dennis F., 4, 5
Thorp, Bruce, 204
Tingsten, Herbert, 112, 160
Torgerson, Ulf, 268
Townsend, James R., 2
Trilling, Richard J., 162
Trow, Martin, 182
Truman, David B., 173, 174, 175, 185,

186, 187, 189, 190, 191, 193, 196, 197, 198, 208, 220, 264
Turner, J., 162
Turner, Julius, 242, 264

Urwin, Dereck, 162, 245

Valen, Henry, 248
van den Bergh, George, 241
Verba, Sidney, 1, 3, 6, 11, 13, 16, 17, 22, 26, 32, 34, 35, 39, 40, 41, 42, 49, 50, 58, 60, 62, 64, 66, 70, 76, 77, 149, 150, 151, 152, 153, 154, 155, 158, 160, 163, 179, 199, 220, 221
Vietnam, 60
Vose, Clement E., 188, 197, 199, 208
Voting, 9–10, 13, 15–16, 19–20, 66
    community context and, 35
    in India, 22
    initiative required for, 26
    in Yugoslavia, 16
Voting behavior
    defection, 134, 138–139, 144
    issue voting, 120, 121, 124, 128, 132
    nature of, 111–158
    rational voting, 120, 121
    voting choice, determinants of individual, 113–136

voting systems, macrocosmic change in, 136–148

Wagner, Richard E., 193
Wahlke, John C., 163, 264
Walker, Jack, 4, 70, 103, 159
Wallerstein, Immanuel, 233
Waltz, Kenneth N., 266
Watson, Richard, 181
Weiner, Myron, 1, 2, 233
Weisberg, Herbert F., 161, 162
White, Robert W., 84
Wiatr, Jerzy J., 233
Wildavsky, Aaron, 260
Wilson, James Q., 184, 249, 250, 252, 256
Winters, Richard, 64
Wittner, Lawrence S., 194
Wolfe, Arthur G., 158, 162
Wootton, Graham, 187
Wright, Charles R., 102, 198

Young, Oran R., 175, 193

Ziegler, Harmon, 174, 180, 197, 202, 205, 206, 207, 208